Edited by

Yohuru Williams and Jama Lazerow

Liberated Territory

UNTOLD LOCAL PERSPECTIVES

ON THE BLACK PANTHER PARTY

Duke University Press   Durham and London   2008

© 2008 Duke University Press

All rights reserved

Printed in the United States of America

on acid-free paper ∞

Designed by C. H. Westmoreland

Typeset in Warnock Light

by Keystone Typesetting, Inc.

Library of Congress Cataloging-in-

Publication Data appear on the last printed

page of this book.

For Samantha

CONTENTS

Yohuru Williams

INTRODUCTION

From Oakland to Omaha

HISTORICIZING THE PANTHERS

In late summer 1966, the *New York Times* reported on the activities of "an amalgamation of militant, youth oriented Negro groups" who were gearing up to demand the hiring of more black teachers, the elevation of blacks to positions of authority in the schools, and the addition of courses relevant to the black experience. One such group was the Black Panther Party, which had been founded in Harlem a scant six weeks before.[1] Of all the organizations, including the overtly black nationalist Yoruba Temple and Harlem People's Parliament and the militantly mainstream New York chapters of the Congress of Racial Equality and the Student Non-Violent Coordinating Committee (SNCC), none elicited more fear than the Panthers, whose statements took up nearly half of the brief article. Declining to confirm anything more than the existence of a Harlem branch of the party, an unidentified spokesman explained the group's agenda to Thomas Johnson, a reporter for the *New York Times.* "Harlem is the spiritual and historical home of the Black man in America," he proclaimed. It was "only natural that a Black Panther Party be established here."

Modeling themselves on the Lowndes County Freedom Organization (LCFO), which had been inspired by SNCC and which had recently organized an all-black political party with the black panther as its symbol, the Harlem Panthers nevertheless perceived their mission as distinctive.[2] In Lowndes County, Alabama, where black people constituted nearly 80 percent of the total population, the possibility of attaining black political power was a distinct reality. In other places, the Panthers posited, African Americans would need to harness political power through institution building and forging alliances with other parties and interest groups dedicated to improving conditions in communities with large numbers of black residents. Still, the political orientation of the party, coupled with its connection to Stokely Carmichael, the chairman of SNCC whose call for black power during the summer of 1966 had stoked fears about black separatism and by extension independent black organizing, significantly raised its profile among other militant groups operating in the city. Unsubstantiated rumors even linked Carmichael directly to the formation of the Harlem chapter.

In less than a year, however, the Harlem Panthers and dozens of other groups invoking the symbol of the black panther would be eclipsed by a West Coast incarnation of the LCFO—the Oakland Black Panther Party for Self-defense (BPP). Founded in October 1966 by two ex-college students, Huey P. Newton and Bobby Seale, while they were working in a government anti-poverty program, the Oakland BPP became the center of the Panther movement and later, through the sanctioning of chapters and branches, a national organization. The party focused on recruiting what Newton termed "the brothers off the block," ghetto youth disconnected from the civil rights movement and in need of political direction. But it also appealed to a wide variety of students, political organizers, activists, theorists, ex-soldiers, and scholars—female and male—who found much to celebrate in the group's politics and program. The headquarters in California sought organizational control over a rapidly expanding movement—especially over groups like the Harlem Panthers, which predated Oakland, or the many groups that sprang up without any direct connection to Oakland. It was a daunting task. Fiercely independent and typically oriented to local issues, local incarnations of the party exhibited, as it were, minds of their own. Still, despite continual national-local conflict, the BPP survived, indeed thrived, in the late 1960s and into the early 1970s.

Two important structural factors explain that success: the codification of the BPP's ideas and agenda into a ten-point platform and program and its focus on community service, most notably its newspaper and later its "survival programs" such as the Breakfast for School Children program. Neither had much to do with the Panthers' call for armed self-defense, a powerful recruitment tool in its own right, or their militant posturing.[3] At the same time, two events—both largely of their own making, both involving guns—explain how they catapulted to national stature, largely from the public's perception of them. The first was their armed march on the California Legislature on May 2, 1967 to protest a gun control bill aimed at their armed patrols of the police. As Jane Rhodes has observed, "The press beyond the San Francisco Bay Area knew little or nothing about the Panthers, leading them to search for categories to construct a media frame."[4] The media, in turn, focused on the guns, missing out on the larger political implications of the Panthers' momentous march, which was designed to draw attention to the dire circumstances of black people facing what they called an "occupying army" of police in the black community. Within a few weeks the guns would be gone, despite the media's persistent referencing of them. Then, that fall the Panthers' violent image was seemingly confirmed by a second incident when Huey Newton, one of the founders of the party, was involved in a late night shootout with Oakland police that left one patrolman dead, another injured, and Newton seriously wounded. Newton's murder trial the following summer made the twenty-six-year-old militant an international cause célèbre, allowing him a much larger platform from which to expound on the origins and goals of the party. Eldridge Cleaver, the Panthers' minister of information, immediately recognized an opportunity to generate national and international interest in the Newton case into an organizing opportunity, as well as to build political alliances. "Free Huey!" became the rallying cry for a generation of activists. Local black groups especially, including those that previously had not identified with the Oakland Panthers, latched onto them out of a sense of ideological affinity, or simply out of a desire to capitalize on the Panthers' notoriety.

In all these ways, despite its local origins in the Bay area, the Oakland BPP was tailor-made for export beyond the spatial confines of Oakland. The ten-point program provided would-be affiliates with a blueprint for achieving power in a local setting through what in contemporary terms might be best expressed as a "think globally, act locally" plan of action. Although most of it was couched as a wish list of sorts, the program was nonetheless critical as a uniform statement of the goals and aspirations of the women and men drawn to the Panther cause. Despite the differences over how the Panthers hoped to achieve those goals, their program answered in a succinct and provocative fashion the question "What does the Negro want?" at a time when fragmentation in the civil rights movement in the wake of landmark civil rights legislation led many to question what more could be done to help black people achieve political equality. In shifting the debate away from more abstract concepts such as absolute equality before the law and economic justice to more concrete questions such as corporate responsibility, governmental complicity, and the need for community action, the Panthers were uniquely situated—by way of their programmatic approach on the one hand and the spectacle of the gun on the other—to communicate that agenda to the world. While the omnibus point #10 of their 1966 platform expressed their desire for "land, bread, housing, education, clothing, justice and peace," Point #7 called on black people to "arm themselves for self-defense" against "POLICE BRUTALITY and MURDER."[5] The combination proved both lucrative and lethal, as would become clear shortly halfway across the country in Omaha, Nebraska.

The Terrible Summer of 1970

Just after 2:30 on the morning of August 17, 1970, in Omaha, Nebraska, police officers responded to reports of a screaming woman by surrounding a two-story house at 2867 Ohio Street in the heart of the city's predominantly black Near North Side. Despite a rash of bombings in the area, in their haste they ignored the suitcase wedged in the front door, suspecting it probably belonged to the woman. As three patrolmen made their way through the quiet, darkened structure, two others prepared to join them inside. One was Larry Minard, a twenty-nine-year-old father of five.[6]

Like the others, he paid little attention to the suitcase upon entering the building. However, after finding nothing suspicious in the house, he returned to the bag and either kicked it or tripped over it, triggering an explosion so powerful it knocked over a curious neighbor observing the police action from across the street. The results inside the house were far more devastating—in the words of one witness, it shattered the walls to "kindling." The blast sent one policeman hurling across the front lawn and another through the back door. Fortunately, most of the officers suffered only minor injuries—save for Minard, who died in an instant.

Within days during that late summer of 1970, yet another season of urban violence, police had attributed the bombing to the Black Panther Party, stoking fears that its calls for armed self-defense had given way to retaliatory violence against police. Indeed, the gruesome killing of the patrolman Larry Minard temporarily put the midwestern city at the epicenter of what seemed like a war. Ironically, given the heightened rhetoric of the moment, publicly at least, both sides claimed to be unwilling participants in that war. Still, both were keeping score. Less than a month before the Omaha incident, the Panthers accused police of orchestrating the slaying of Carl Hampton, a black militant and Panther associate in Houston. A few weeks later, Panthers and police clashed in the city of New Orleans after the Panthers allegedly attempted to murder two undercover police agents trying to infiltrate their headquarters. Significantly, in all three cities, the groups involved—the National Committee to Combat Fascism (NCCF) in Omaha and New Orleans, and the People's Party II in Houston—were not officially Black Panther organizations. No matter. The connections were there, alarming those who feared the rising tide of black revolution. "Both the Omaha dynamiting and the Houston shootout," observed the influential conservative columnists Rowland Evans and Robert Novak, "can be traced to local revolutionary organizations intimately connected with the Black Panthers."[7]

Since its days as a West Coast phenomenon, the party had, by 1970, blossomed into a national organization with perhaps thousands of members.[8] It also had a well-established reputation for violent run-ins with the law. The Panthers' early armed patrols of the police had predictably met with resistance; police responded by placing the party under surveillance and enlisting the aid of state lawmakers to destroy it. This campaign of harassment, coupled with the Panthers' denunciation of police as "pigs," made conditions ripe for conflict. Barely a year after the party's founding, the minister of defense, Huey Newton, stood accused of murdering an Oakland policeman. Convicted of manslaughter the following summer, Newton spent nearly three years in jail. By August 1970, when he was released (his conviction was later overturned on a technicality), Panthers and police were "caught in a spiral" detrimental to both. "In two years," observed the New York Times correspondent Martha Arnold, citing statistics from the Department of Justice, "11 Black Panthers have been shot dead and so have 10 policemen."[9]

In early October 1970, less than two months after Minard's death, Congress held hearings on a new bill authorizing the FBI to investigate the murder of policemen and firefighters. Decrying a "nationwide guerrilla conspiracy" to assassinate police officers, Senator Harrison A. Williams of New Jersey began by noting, "Since 1960 close to 600 police men have been murdered in this country; last year, there were a record number of 86 such murders."[10] Among those testifying were Captain Murdock J. Platner of the Omaha police and Deputy Police Commissioner Louis J. Sirgo of New Orleans, who, in separate statements, claimed to have evidence that the BPP regularly monitored police frequencies to hamper law enforcement agencies. Asked for his insight, California's chief deputy attorney general, Charles O'Brien, shared his fear that the ever "increasing thefts of heavy arms from military arsenals may one day result in terrorists being able to outgun police." Citing a "100 per cent increase" in California police deaths in 1970 alone, O'Brien fingered the Panthers, along with a radical faction of white revolutionaries, as leaders of a national conspiracy against police, which in his estimation had "undoubtedly contributed to more frequent police use of firearms and some of the tragedies which have resulted in police shooting innocent people."[11]

As early as fall 1968, conscious of the liabilities of its reputation, the party had tried to burnish its public image through a systematic effort at building community service projects. While many of its critics recognized the shift and applauded the Panthers for it, others, such as Evans and Novak, remained unconvinced. Omaha and Houston, they insisted, "help to dispel two widely held notions: first, the feeling by liberals that the Panthers, though unpleasant, are not really much to worry about; second, the comforting impression held by politicians that we have made it through most of the summer without racial trouble." Highlighting the local chapters and their auxiliary agencies, the columnists predicted more violence. "Unlike the centrally-directed Communist Party underground, black guerillas are decentralized and difficult to infiltrate. The hard fact is that police are losing the fight to control them. The terrible summer of 1970 may be followed by escalated black guerilla war year-round with frightful consequences that nobody today can dare guess."[12] Indeed, whatever good they claimed to be doing, repeated violent confrontations with police rendered Panthers across the nation more known for being criminal defendants than directors of social service programs. By the summer of 1971, some of their more high-profile court cases were still meandering through the system, often on appeal, including the New York 21, the New Haven 9, and the Milwaukee 3.

At the same time, police were sometimes criticized for increasing the visibility of and even sympathy for the Panthers. "The Panthers are troublemakers bent on disrupting the establishment," an editorial in the *Edwardsville* (Illinois) *Intelligencer* acknowledged. "However," the editors continued, "the evidence shows that much of their success, if that is what it can be called, is directly related to sympathy generated by police action against them."[13] In the *Syracuse Herald-Journal*, Louis Harris likewise observed, while "two of every three whites feel that the Black Panthers are a serious menace to the country," the group enjoyed significant support in the black community. To be sure, a Harris survey sponsored by *Time Magazine* found that only 25 percent of African Americans polled actually identified with the party philosophy, but, the pollster noted, "80 percent feel that shootings of the Panthers had made them feel that Blacks 'should stand together.' "[14]

Part of such popular support, though, derived from the way the Panthers had embedded themselves in the local community. That is, though the Panthers were a national organization, with a centralized, bureaucratic structure, and though they did opportunistically take advantage of local tensions, the oft-repeated police claim that Panther groups in their cities were run by "outside agitators" was hardly borne out by accounts of violence between Panthers and the police. While some high-profile and some lesser-known cases certainly fit the model—as in New Haven, Connecticut, in 1969 or in New Bedford, Massachusetts, in 1970—even in such instances, the party was composed of local people who were confronting local issues under the national banner of the Black Panther Party. The Panthers brought instant notoriety, *and* they had a ready-made program that was easily adaptable to the urban communities in which they thrived. Being relegated to the radical fringe by its critics while addressing the needs of its constituents arguably helped the group—in different ways for different lengths of time, depending on the locale—to *speak* for the community. In this sense, there is only very limited truth to Carl Oglesby's premature summation in the late 1960s of the Panthers' legacy that they "did not *organize* the ghetto, they only apostrophized it."[15]

Omaha The Background

Though every Panther story is unique when viewed from the local perspective, there is much about Omaha that elucidates the Panther experience generally. The party in Omaha was founded by local activists in 1968—its ties with Oakland initially less formal than in some other cities—though it was later disbanded by headquarters and reconstituted as a branch of the

NCCF. That group's community programs helped to establish it as a presence, but its focus on police brutality quickly brought conflict with the local police—and the FBI—who were well aware of the Panthers. Harassment began almost immediately, as did infiltration. Staffed by a diverse collection of persons, including displaced college students, community activists, organic intellectuals, and hardened street people, the Panther Party in Omaha fought back by stockpiling weapons and talking tough. Some moved from readiness and rhetoric to action.

Among these was a fifteen-year-old street kid named Duane Peak, who eventually would be charged with the Minard murder. In many ways, he was precisely the type of street soldier the Panthers hoped to recruit, the "brother off the block" whom Bobby Seale exalted in 1970 as the preferred subject of his and Huey Newton's organizing, the kind of "brother" who once politicized would make "revolutionaries who are way too much."[16] Born in Omaha, Peak lost his mother at an early age. Raised by his father and grandparents, he became a troubled youth who spent most of his time on the streets, where his constant run-ins with the law eventually forced his father to banish him from the home. By his early teens he was already exhibiting the type of antisocial behavior that the Panthers felt they could channel into positive revolutionary action. Did this include killing police officers? Despite his insistence that it was the Panthers who instructed him to plant the bomb, Peak changed his story so often it was difficult for prosecutors and police to keep up. More important, his tale seemed at odds with the positive work the organization had done in the community. Nevertheless, his gritty tale of survival on Omaha's mean streets in many ways mirrored the city's often violent frontier history.

Founded as a trading post in 1854, Omaha soon became a rough-and-tumble trading town where prospectors and traders met in search of fortune on the American frontier. Then, the Union Pacific helped to put it on the map; by 1892, that railroad history placed the town in the national spotlight after the reform-minded People's Party held its national convention there. Little reform came to the city itself, however. In the years between 1890 and the onset of the Great Depression, corruption was commonplace. The frontier tradition of gambling and prostitution, combined with a concomitant underground economy, produced numerous political scandals, many involving police.[17]

During the first half-century of the city's existence, its African American population remained relatively small. However, consistent with increased black migration to northern and western cities in the years around World War I, the city's black population exploded, doubling in size between 1910 and 1920, for example. Most blacks came to work in the city's meat-packing industry. Though blacks constituted only about 1 percent of the general population of the state as a whole, by the close of the decade they comprised nearly 5 percent of Omaha's population. Meanwhile, white residents resented the influx and responded with violence. Crucially, African Americans could expect scant protection from the police, who at times exhibited the same prejudice as did the local white populace.[18]

In 1919, for example, during the so-called red summer of race riots following World War I, locals accused city officials of inciting a riot that claimed three lives. Commenting on the violence in the *Crisis*, the organ of the NAACP, the editor observed, "For forty years Omaha was ruled by a political, criminal gang that was perhaps the most lawless of any city of its size in the civilized world. There had grown up during that period, a powerful group who lived on the proceeds of organized vice and crime. These included about three hundred and eighty-four (384) houses of prostitution, together with saloons, pool halls, organized bank robbers, organized highway robbers, and professional 'con' men and burglars."[19] And, despite public displays of contrition, Omaha would remain inhospitable to blacks. Malcolm X, né Malcolm Little, encountered the brutality firsthand. Born in Omaha in 1925, Malcolm was a baby when his family fled its borders in 1926 purportedly after receiving threats from the Ku Klux Klan.[20]

Perhaps partly because of this violence, the city's black population remained relatively small between 1940 and 1960, hovering around 6 percent of the total. The 1960s, however, witnessed another dramatic demographic surge: by 1965, fully 10 percent of the city was African American. In turn, Omaha's blacks faced problems typically associated with northern-style apartheid—poor education, unemployment, lack of recreational facilities for young people, police brutality, and especially run-down housing. Most of the new migrants concentrated on the city's Near North Side, which one contemporary described as "850 acres jammed with rat infested tenements wherein live all of Omaha's . . . Negroes." As late as 1966, Louis B. Olsen, a special assistant to the mayor, asserted that "less than 100 Negro families live in otherwise white neighborhoods." Conditions in the slums mirrored conditions in other cities: "The buildings," observed one source, "are old, dirty and dilapidated. Some still show scars of a tornado that hit the city in 1913."[21] Despite claims in 1960 of the president of Omaha's National Urban League (UL) that conditions for blacks could only be improved "through urban renewal," that year legislators, backed by Mayor James Dworak, announced their opposition to a proposed bill seeking federal funds to address Omaha's housing problems. Acknowledging areas of inadequacy, Dworak maintained that these problems could easily be addressed by strict enforcement of the current housing ordinance and through investment of private capital.[22]

Urban renewal advocates eventually won out over the next several years, but the proposed changes did little to alleviate housing problems in the African American community. Speaking candidly in 1966, Douglas Stewart, the executive director of the UL, credited Omaha with making some strides in employment and education, but in housing, he claimed, "It hasn't done a thing."[23] Nearly a third of the black families trapped in Omaha's Near North Side earned less than $5,000 a year, while new construction under urban renewal did little more than expand the ghetto's perimeters.[24] Newly constructed public housing projects failed to replace units destroyed by the expansion of the interstate and nearby Creighton University. Moreover, explained one resident, "The majority of the houses are owned by white people and they only come around to collect rent. You can't get them to fix anything."[25] Most important, perhaps, urban renewal concentrated these problems in a very small area where poverty and crime were allowed to flourish and where police and social services agencies acted more like agents of containment than conduits for peace and human decency.

Omaha 1966

By the summer of 1966, these conditions rendered the Near North Side a virtual powder keg. An incident of police harassment on July 3 provided just the spark to ignite the explosion. On that evening, a group of Near North Side youths tossed a firecracker and a bottle into a police cruiser answering a call about illegal fireworks. The heavy-handed response of the police catalyzed two days of rioting. Not unlike their counterparts in many communities experiencing riots that year, authorities in Nebraska, at least initially, publicly projected a degree of sympathy with the rioters. On July 4, while he was away at the National Governors' Conference, Nebraska's governor, Frank B. Morrison, described the Near North Side as "an environment unfit for human habitation."[26]

Black leaders likewise pointed to the deep-seated problems giving rise to violence, though they tended to broaden the discussion beyond the issue of inadequate housing, and they always emphasized the problem of police violence. Homer C. Floyd, the executive director of the city's Human Relations Board and a local civil rights activist, blamed overcrowded and substandard housing for a "very serious and explosive" situation, but also high unemployment, lack of recreational facilities, and especially excessive use of force by police. After meeting with Floyd and other black leaders in the riot's aftermath, Mayor A. V. Sorenson agreed that the violence was "an expression of discontent" and the manifestation of the desire of blacks "to be recognized and have all the nice things first-class citizens in America have."[27] After returning to the state on July 5 and touring the riot area, Governor Morrison, in the meantime, convened a meeting with four of those arrested. He then held a news conference proclaiming that *unemployment* had been the primary cause of the violence. Citing a 30 percent unemployment rate in Omaha's African American community (the State Employment Service claimed a rate between 8 and 10 percent), the governor pledged that an office of the state's Labor Department would be opened on the Near North Side to study the area's need for employment and job training.[28]

When Sorenson met with neighborhood youth, though, they complained that they hung out at the supermarket because there was nowhere else to go and, critically, that police used unnecessary force. In response, Sorenson announced plans for a commission to study ways of increasing opportunities for recreation in the riot-torn area. Two days later, on July 7, city and police officials, along with neighborhood church and social service agency representatives, announced the prospective opening of a canteen for teenagers in the area. In addition, Sorenson promised to "expand the number of housing units available to relieve pressure in the ghetto."[29]

Despite all of these expressions and efforts, Ernest Chambers, a man with deep ties to the community—a graduate of Creighton University, the owner of a barbershop, a longtime community activist, and the head of the Near North Side Police-Community Relations Council—blamed

Omaha police for the outbreak. More a student of Malcolm X than Martin Luther King, Chambers saw the system itself as inherently flawed and forcefully expressed his view that conditions would not change unless black people had the power to change them. In March, nearly five months before the riot, Chambers had presented a petition to Mayor Sorenson detailing the problems between police and the black community. Sorenson had agreed to meet with Chambers, although he later complained, "[Chambers] heaped a lot of abuse on me." Somewhat missing the point, Sorenson suggested that if blacks could somehow decide exactly what they wanted, then he would respond.[30] In an interview shortly after the July disturbances, Chambers complained, "The cause of the riots has not been removed yet." "As long as the cause remains"—that is, the police—"the incidents can be expected to continue."[31] Sorenson, however, was quick to defend his officers, noting, "Police are instructed to use restraint and they have exercised restraint in admirable fashion."

Within a month, Chambers's words proved prophetic as another round of racial violence hit Omaha. The catalyst, once again, was a police shooting, in this case of an unarmed teen. On the evening of Monday, July 25, a police officer, Floyd Matula, shot and killed a nineteen-year-old burglary suspect, Eugene Nesbitt, as he fled a car wreck after leading police on a high-speed chase through the Near North Side. That he had been shot in the back tended to obscure police claims that Nesbitt was a career criminal on bond for another burglary. Instead, angry residents demanded a full accounting of police actions.[32]

In the days following the Nesbitt shooting, media sources revealed organized campaigns *against police* in several cities, including Brooklyn, New York, and Cleveland, Ohio. In the last, a witness testified that a street gang called the Black Panthers had inspired the violence, nearly three months before the appearance of the Black Panther Party for Self-Defense in Oakland.[33] In Omaha, officials noted a discernible difference in rioting between that of July 4 and that of July 25. As Sorenson put it during a tour of burned and looted businesses on the Near North Side, "Anytime you've got Molotov cocktails ready, you have some planning."[34] Relying on the assessment of law enforcement personnel, authorities dropped the conciliatory policy they had adopted after the earlier outbreaks. Downplaying earlier concerns over police conduct in the Nesbitt shooting, on August 2 Governor Morrison announced that officials were "having no truck with advocates of violence." While acknowledging the need for an investigation, Mayor Sorenson warned, "We're not going to listen to a lot of grievances that have been chewed over and over again."[35] By the time the second riot had fizzled out, authorities had spent more than $70,000 for police overtime and the National Guard had arrested 150 people, while looters and arsonists were blamed for damaging 41 businesses. Predictably—in the view of Near North Siders such as Ernest Chambers—on August 19 Sorenson announced the full exoneration of Officer Matula in the Nesbitt killing.

Omaha in the Late 1960s
Spawning Ground for the Panthers

Over the next three years, Omaha teetered on the brink of violence as tensions engendered by the 1966 disturbances remained ever present. Black leaders were divided on precisely how to proceed. Thus, shortly after the riot on July 4, 1966, a small group of local black businessmen known as the Ad Hoc Responsible Citizens Committee criticized the city's black leadership for failing to articulate "a program for improving bad conditions wherever they are found."[36] The committee blamed internal discord within the black community for preventing leaders from fully addressing community needs. Mayor Sorenson, meanwhile, continued to focus on curtailing the expansion of poverty and continued unemployment. While jobs, housing, and education remained on his radar screen, however, the pressing question of police brutality—four more blacks would die in police encounters by 1969—did not.

Much to the chagrin of the local NAACP and UL, the Nation of Islam (NOI) took up the issue. Already widely branded in the press as a fanatical "reverse racist" organization akin to the Klan, the NOI found little sympathy in Omaha as a whole, and certainly not from police. Like the BPP later, the NOI had a ready-made program that emphasized, among other things, community development and self-help as means by which black people could help to regenerate their own community. And, like the BPP the NOI also emphasized the right of self-defense against police brutality. In the spring of 1967, Omaha police found out just how serious they were about it. In March of that year, a twenty-seven-year-old Muslim named Theopholis Lewis (a.k.a. Theopholis X) was arrested after an Omaha policeman was shot while attempting to prevent Lewis and other Muslims from selling their newspaper on a downtown street. During Lewis's hearing on April 3, a courthouse skirmish left yet another officer shot.[37]

The NAACP and the UL in the meantime were at their wits' end. The Muslim police shootings came amid a joint investigation by the organizations into the death of seventeen-year-old Richard Henry, whom police claimed hanged himself while in custody at the Douglas County Jail. On April 10, 1967, in a report to Robert Carter, the chief counsel of the NAACP, Lawrence W. M. McVoy II, a beleaguered NAACP board member who was also a member of the mayor's Human Relations team and his Police Relations Sub-Committee, warned that "the summer and its threats have returned."[38] In a follow-up letter to Gloster Current, the national director of branches, he confided, "We are in a big mess."[39]

Despite McVoy's concerns, the summer of 1967 came and went with only a few minor skirmishes. In October 1967, however, Ernie Chambers warned that the threat had not passed. Testifying before the National Advisory Commission on the Civil Disorders in Washington, D.C., and joined by other local leaders, including Father James Groppi of Milwaukee and Pari Thomas of New York, Chambers delivered an impassioned if ominous speech. Flanked by his colleagues, Chambers declared, "A policeman is an object of contempt. A policeman is a paid murderer. And you never find the policeman guilty of any crimes, no matter what violence he commits on a black person." "Black people," Chambers continued, "doing ordinary reasonable peaceful things in this country are attacked by police and the police are praised for it. And you talk about giving the police more money and more power." "You will appropriate all kinds of money to give to the National Guard [for] increased training in how to wipe us out," Chambers lectured the congressmen. "And yet it is [a] funny thing that in all the so-called riots, the police and National Guard kill far more people than the so-called rioters." "And as for the sniping," Chambers persisted, "don't you believe that. Why are no cops killed? They ought to be killed. I think the cops should be killed." "We are being forced by police misconduct to get together to fight the police," Chambers concluded. "We are going to fight your people like you fight us." "And don't say I am revealing too much," Chambers charged in a parting shot, "because if something happens to me, there are other people who come up. You might just want me in jail. But you get me off the scene, and I'll multiply."[40]

Six months later, in March 1968, the city erupted once again after attempts by demonstrators to disrupt a presidential campaign rally for George Wallace, the former governor of Alabama. Once a staunch segregationist, Wallace sought some redemption in advance of a run for the Democratic Party nomination. However, most African Americans remained skeptical. Chambers, who helped to organize the protest, later told reporters, "At Wallace's signal police were turned loose on those who demonstrated against his appearance." With no serious injuries in the initial fray, a fresh round of looting continued into the night, resulting in the fatal shooting of sixteen-year-old Howard Stevenson. The circumstances of that death would again cast suspicion on police. Sometime after midnight, police fired in the air to prevent a band of some sixty looters from entering a local pawnshop. The grateful owner engaged one of the officers to stay and protect his business. An hour later, the officer, James Abbott, called into headquarters to report a shooting, saying he had fired on an unarmed youth after spotting him climbing through a broken shop window. When the youth failed to respond to his verbal command to "hold it," Abbott said he fired his 12-gauge riot shotgun, killing him.[41]

As order returned to the city, and Near North Side residents paused to cleanse their sidewalks and their memories of the bloody stains of yet another African American youth fatally shot by police, an internal investigation cleared Abbott of any criminal wrongdoing. Despite pledges by city officials to confront the issue of police-community relations, encounters like the ones detailed by Chambers continued to plague the Near North Side. The climax came on June 24, 1969, after police received a call about an attempted burglary at the federal housing project. During the course of that investigation, Officer James Loder chased a suspect he claimed to have seen jump from the window of an apartment. A military veteran with less than three years of experience on the police force, Loder perhaps was relying more on rookie instincts than police training when he drew his service revolver in the course of the pursuit. Witnesses later reported that he "fired for no apparent reason." In any event, despite firing from a distance police determined to be 139 feet away, the bullet struck the suspect, fourteen-year-old Vivian Strong, in the back of the head, killing her instantly.[42]

The shooting made national headlines when it was discovered that Loder was the adopted son of the actress Hedy Lamarr. This angle of the story inevitably overshadowed the victim in national coverage of the incident, but on the streets of Omaha the death of Vivian Strong ushered in yet another round of urban unrest, touching off three more days of rioting. Unlike earlier outbreaks, police later claimed, many of the acts of violence in 1969, including sniping incidents, a firebombing, and break-ins, were more deliberate. Officials postulated that "militants from other cities" had come to Omaha to participate in the violence.[43]

The Panthers Come to Omaha

For many, the likely suspects of such offensive actions were the Black Panthers. By the summer of 1969, at least for police, they had eclipsed the NOI and Ernie Chambers as the preeminent threat to Omaha's peace and security. Moreover, from its inception, the Omaha Panthers had maintained close working relations with Panthers in Des Moines, Iowa, and Kansas City, and Missouri. And, local police insisted, during the disturbances after Vivian Strong's death, Omaha's sister chapters and branches networked together to coordinate the sniping attacks and other acts of terror designed to prevent law enforcement officers from reestablishing order.[44]

The official inquiry into the Strong shooting commenced with promises of a full investigation by civic authorities; in short order, the episode ended as had many other purported acts of police brutality in Omaha. Officer Loder was arrested, charged with manslaughter, and acquitted. This time, though, prominent among the many organizations protesting the verdict was the Omaha Black Panther Party. Indeed, it was in the cauldron of the 1969 riot and its aftermath that the Omaha group came into its own, though it had been born much earlier.

In their efforts to uncover the history of the Omaha BPP, police surmised that it first came to Nebraska sometime in July 1968 after Eddie Bolden, a poverty worker in Omaha, traveled to San Francisco and met with the BPP to inquire about starting a branch. Like many other emissaries from various parts of the country, certainly at that particularly flush moment in the Panthers' national history, Bolden received a favorable welcome in Oakland. Upon his return, he claimed authorization to establish an affiliate. Setting up shop at 3120 North 24th Street on the Near North Side, he apparently garnered a paltry membership. Police estimated that "approximately 10 people actually joined and there were about 20 more closely associated with them."[45] But the popular reception was another matter. Shortly after Bolden's return, for example, Eldridge Cleaver, the Panthers' minister of information, came to town to speak, and nearly four hundred people turned out in the city park to hear him. Under investigation himself for allegedly participating in sniping attacks on Oakland police, Cleaver boldly proclaimed, "We are going to fight and we will decimate this country," "we are going to move against this system in harmony with Mao Tse-tung, with Ho Chi Minh, with Fidel Castro. . . ."[46]

Cleaver brought several Panthers with him from California, among them Wilfred Holliday, who stayed. According to police closely monitoring the nascent group, Holliday first introduced calls for violence against police. In September 1968, police discovered a bomb that had failed to explode outside City Hall. Although they had no evidence linking the Panthers with the attempted crime, police claimed that Bolden and Holliday had been observed purchasing batteries "similar to the ones used in the bomb."[47] Meanwhile, two early recruits, David Rice and Edward Poindexter, would become key group leaders, attempting to replicate the efforts of the Panthers elsewhere. They established community political education classes and a community newsletter, as well as armed patrols of the police. As Rice later recalled, "We . . . set about to make ourselves more visible in the African community, participating with other organizations in community meetings; holding frequent rallies; starting a newsletter (*Freedom by Any Means Necessary*); doing cop patrols, in which we would document police behavior, sometimes show up at scenes of cop harassment of our people and have our guns in plain view, etc.; opening up our Vivian Strong Liberation School for Children; and otherwise doing what we could to serve the African community."[48]

As in other communities where the Panthers became a force, authorities experimented with various ways of undermining them. Following the pattern already established during the 1966 riot, Omaha officials held out an olive branch by employing Panther leaders in local social service and antipoverty agencies. In February 1969, David Rice, the Panthers' deputy minister of information, was hired by the Greater Omaha Community Action Agency as a community organizer and service worker. The *Omaha World Herald* identified him as "a civil rights activist who has written for underground and neighborhood newspapers."[49] It further noted that "his articles have been critical of Omaha police schools and city officials." In the meantime, Eddie Bolden, the Panthers' defense captain, became a teacher's aide for the federally funded Opportunities Industrialization Center (OIC). The hires did not sit well with Congressman William Scherle of Iowa, who complained during congressional hearings on the BPP, "I think the thing that concerns me so much is the great association of militancy with our poverty agencies."[50] At the same time, this association provided the government with a means of incorporating—the language of the day was "co-opting"—black militants such as Rice and Bolden into "the system," precisely what the Panthers opposed. While presumably giving them a place at the table, their appointments made them accountable for their actions and also challenged their street credibility with other militants.[51] If Newton and Seale, both of whom were working at an anti-poverty agency in North Oakland when they founded the party in 1966, had used U.S. government space, equipment, and funds to hatch a scheme to upend that very government, by 1969 in Omaha the tables had been turned.[52]

Critics like Scherle may not have liked it, but having Panthers on the government payroll provided law enforcement agencies with a convenient mechanism for creating dissension within, a principal goal of a national campaign to destroy the BPP from late 1968. Understanding that the Omaha Panthers devoted a healthy portion of their salaries to party work, authorities knew that terminating them from the government payroll or getting comrades to question their commitment in working for the state presented equally tempting opportunities for those seeking to contain, even roll back, the Panther threat. In Omaha, the official campaign of harassment stretched from the local police to the halls of Congress, where Congressman Scherle brought his full political weight to bear in hopes of exposing the Panthers as the criminal frauds he imagined them to be. He promptly launched a letter-writing campaign to have militants working in anti-poverty agencies fired. He was supported by the U.S. attorney for the District of Nebraska, who wrote to express his own concerns about militants employed by programs funded with federal dollars. Referring to David Rice as a "bum" who "sneers at the Constitution and its provisions," the U.S. attorney complained to the congressman that "the most tragic thing is, this man is an employee of the Greater Omaha Community Action group financed by O.E.O. [Office of Economic Opportunity] money." "It causes me to lose sleep," he confided, "to think that I am paying a portion of the salary of this American rat." During a congressional investigation into the Des Moines, Kansas City, and Omaha chapters, Scherle freely admitted that his office "sent a letter to the OIC regarding" the employment of another Panther in a federally funded poverty program. "Once again," he claimed, "there was nothing done about that." Meanwhile, local police were hampered in their investigation. Informants who reported to the police on BPP activities regularly related tales of Panther ploys to foil police but rarely provided any evidence. Although nationally the Panthers were accused of using strong-arm tactics to supply their breakfast for children program, in Omaha, despite allusions to intimidation, Murdock Planter, the head of police intelligence, was forced to admit, "I have no proof that it [support for their program] was anything other than voluntary."[53]

As elsewhere, however, the absence of such evidence did not stop law enforcement from continuing its efforts.[54] An anonymous letter in the spring of 1969 resulted in the expulsion of Rice from the party. Roosevelt ("June Bug") Hilliard, the Panthers' national deputy chief of staff, later claimed that the purge—part of a national ongoing effort—resulted from Rice's "reluctance to follow the party line" and, apparently despite the experience of founders Newton and Seale, for "accepting employment in Government-funded programs that 'misled' black people furthering their oppression."[55] Later, in August of 1969, the rest of the Omaha group joined Rice in banishment from the membership rolls of the BPP.

Within a few days of being officially disbanded, however, an NCCF branch was established, with Edward Poindexter as its leader. Born in Omaha in 1944, he graduated from Creighton Preparatory School and took courses at Creighton University. He wrote for the local underground paper, *Buffalo Chip*, where he regularly traded ideas with other local militants before joining the Panthers. Under Poindexter, the NCCF continued its community programs and remained affiliated with the BPP national office. During the summer of 1969, the group had made a concerted effort to attract more young people by founding the Black Association for Nationalism through Unity (BANTU). The initiative, spearheaded by Robert Griffo, BANTU's minister of student affairs, raised the ire of school officials and police who claimed that the Panthers were using it as a platform to indoctrinate children. Undaunted, in December Poindexter announced a coalition with the Missouri BPP. At this point, police estimated the Omaha outfit to be about twenty strong, with a little more than twenty more supporters.[56] Mostly remnants of the disbanded Omaha chapter, the majority were everything but Panthers in name and continued the party's work. Congress noted, "The NCCF in Omaha . . . illustrates how one such committee operated. The committee functioned in a city where there was no Black Panther Party chapter and implemented the same 'community' projects expected of the chapter's propaganda in behalf of community control of police forces; free breakfasts for school children; and a liberation school."[57]

Operations with the NCCF in Omaha ran smoothly throughout late 1969 and into the first months of the following year, but by the early spring of 1970 problems again plagued the local organization. First, a former Air Force sergeant was arrested on charges that he tried to sell a small cache of stolen weapons to the NCCF. According to police, the "Panthers" were never able to secure enough money to finalize the purchase, and in May the sergeant was arrested. Indeed, it is not entirely clear just what the nature of the Omaha group was when Officer Larry Minard of the Omaha police was murdered that August. In the summer of 1968, Omaha was an officially recognized chapter of the BPP. When the party provided an official list of all recognized chapters and branches in May 1970, Omaha was on the list as an NCCF.[58] But less than a month before the fatal explosion of August 17 that killed Minard, a notice in the July 25 issue of *The Black Panther* announced, "The National Committee to Combat Fascism in Omaha, Nebraska is no longer functioning as an organizing bureau of the Black Panther Party, or from herefore connected with the Black Panther Party in any way."[59]

Omaha's second expulsion was part of a national round of purges initiated by the party nearly two years earlier to rid it of spies and *agents provocateurs*. Increasingly after late 1968, the party found itself deluged by individuals whose behavior ran counter to professed party aims. Although designed to bring the organization under tighter control, the BPP purges had two unintended consequences. First, they created a roving population of Panthers in search of legitimate chapters or branches to join, which heightened confusion within the organization. Second, they increased the number of Panther "wannabe" outfits by stripping them of their ties to the national office in Oakland, California. This was precisely the case in Omaha, where the NCCF continued to operate despite news of its purge. Having investigated the growth of and support for the BPP, Congress later acknowledged, "Instances were discovered in which would-be Panthers followed the example of the Omaha National Committee to Combat Fascism and continued to operate in spite of withdrawal of recognition by the national organization, or did not even seek national recognition in the first place."[60] In turn, police and the FBI took advantage of these developments for counterintelligence initiatives, some of which ended in violence, including the deaths of police officers. The federal government would claim that during 1970 "six policemen lost their lives as a result of acts attributed to self-styled Panthers in Sacramento, Omaha, Chicago, Detroit, Toledo, and Baltimore."[61]

The Minard Murder and the Omaha Panthers

As noted, shortly after the Minard murder, police apprehended Duane Peak in connection with the crime. Initially, Peak accepted full responsibility. He not only admitted planting the explosives and making the telephone call but also offered a motive, claiming he had set the trap to frighten the officers in hopes they would "treat black people better." After several meetings with police, however, he changed his story, telling investigators that the plot was the brainchild of leaders in the local NCCF, which he said he joined in November 1969. The teen said David Rice instructed him to plant the booby trap. In securing a warrant to search Rice's home, Omaha police identified him as a known member of the NCCF, which, they observed, "advocates the violent killing of Police Officers." When the search turned up explosives, police arrested Rice and five other NCCF members, including Ed Poindexter.[62]

In Omaha at least, authorities assumed the guesswork was over, and, with the two main Panther leaders incarcerated, they joined officials from scores of other cities in calling for federal help in dealing with the Panther menace and testified when Congress opened an investigation of the party. For the explosion that killed Larry Minard was one of three on the same day in three different cities—Omaha, Columbus, and Minneapolis—two of which, the Minnesota and Nebraska bombings, had law enforcement operations as their targets.[63] However, as details in the Minard case emerged and cast police in a dubious light, cries arose of an alleged frame-up of local Panthers.

The fact that the two main suspects, Rice and Poindexter, had solid alibis for their whereabouts on the night of the bombing was only the tip of the iceberg in what some considered a mountain of evidence exonerating them. That two men stood to be convicted on the testimony of fifteen-year-old Duane Peak, who was offered a plea deal of second-degree murder after fingering the NCCF, did not sit well with others. One of these was Frank Morrison, the former governor of Nebraska who agreed to defend Rice.

At trial, Morrison painted Peak, who had since turned sixteen, as a juvenile delinquent and a liar. But he reserved his greatest indignation for the state of Nebraska. "For the first time in my life," he told the jury, "I have seen the state try to convict basically on the testimony of one witness and that witness is an admitted perjurer." In a bit of courtroom theatrics, the former governor produced a large model of the scales of justice. Dropping weights on each side as he methodically went over the state's case, the scales eventually tipped in favor of an acquittal. Morrison's defense was not all flash-and-show, however. In his summation, he placed the killing of Officer Minard in the broader context of race relations in Omaha. Conjuring up the still fresh memory of the 1969 riot, Morrison pleaded with the jury to free his clients. "Vivian Strong and Larry Minard didn't die in vain," he told them, and then, his rhetoric soaring, he added, "this great city under God can have a new birth of freedom." Special Prosecutor Arthur O'Leary was having none of it. In his closing remarks, he asked the jury to consider the violent rhetoric of the Black Panther Party. Referring to Peak as merely "an errand boy," O'Leary wondered aloud, "Where did Peak learn to hate?" "His teachers of hate," he insisted, "were [Panthers] Rice and Poindexter." Rejecting Morrison's attempt to link the bombing to police brutality and the 1969 riot, O'Leary reminded the jury that on the night he was murdered, Larry Minard "was hardly in a position of brutalizing a member of a minority race." "He was only answering a distress call."[64] Once again—as in Detroit, Michigan, and Birmingham, Alabama—despite the complex history of the Omaha Panthers, the issue had come down to this: there was a war going on between police and Panthers, and sides had to be taken. There was, seemingly, no middle ground.

The jury sided with the prosecution, and Poindexter and Rice were sentenced to life. In 1976, their last, best hopes for an appeal were dashed when the U.S. Supreme Court, on its final day of action before adjourning for the summer, ruled that criminal defendants had no constitutional right to appeal their state court convictions to federal tribunals on the grounds that police illegally seized evidence used against them.[65] Years later, the discovery of documents indicating that the Omaha BPP was under surveillance by the Bureau of Alcohol, Tobacco and Firearms and the FBI led some to question whether Poindexter and Rice might have been victims of a government frame-up. Among other things, those documents revealed that police had suppressed audio evidence of possible aid to the defense— that is, the recording of the fatal 911 call that had lured the Omaha police to the scene of the bombing. Although officials claimed that the tape containing the call had been accidentally destroyed, an FBI memo written during trial noted, "Assistant COP GLENN GATES, Omaha PD, advised that he feels that any use of tapes of this call might be prejudicial to the police murder trial against two accomplices of PEAK and, therefore, has advised that he wishes no use of this tape until after the murder trials of PEAK and the two accomplices has [sic] been completed."[66]

The Panther Story as Local History

Despite new scholarship, the image of the Black Panther Party remains frozen in a particular historical moment, ever memorialized by the portrait of Huey Newton with shotgun and spear defiantly posed in an African wicker chair. This interpretive slant, if it can be called that, reached its fullest expression in journalistic accounts of the party, particularly in Hugh Pearson's enormously influential 1994 screed, *Shadow of the Panther*. But, the perspective is also alive and well in the historical profession itself, permeating much scholarship on the late 1960s when black militants, chiefly led by the Panthers, traded bullets with police in a kind of turf war for the control of the nation's inner-city streets. The roots of this interpretation can be traced to the violent rhetoric of the Panthers against police brutality, and to the reaction of police to that rhetoric, but historians cannot leave it at that.

Duane Peak is a case in point. Like more famous actors in the Panther story, he offers an interesting entry into this still confusing historical thicket. Was he a government informant or *agent provocateur?* Was he manipulated and if so by whom? What was the extent of federal surveillance on the Panthers in Omaha? As the diverse local histories in this volume demonstrate, the Panther story is far more complex than even the answers to such questions can provide. Our authors seek to answer broader and deeper questions about the Panther moment in historical context. The essays we present here offer an opportunity—for the first time, really—for professional historians to go beyond the rhetoric, the confrontations, and the subsequent trials and into the history of who the Panthers were, what they believed, what they did, how they changed over time, what effect they had on their historical moment—and to do so without ignoring the more sensational aspects of the battles that were "good copy" for them and that have passed into legend since. Merely scratching the surface of Omaha—long forgotten in the lore of the Oakland, Chicago, and New York Panthers—demonstrates how much we have to learn.

The Omaha story shares certain characteristics with the Oakland story, to be sure. At the same time, the Omaha Black Panthers, in being far from Oakland, illustrate just how difficult this process of uncovering can be. Jama Lazerow's study of New Bedford in the Northeast illustrates the significance of a group virtually unknown in Panther scholarship, the Cape Verdeans, while raising perplexing issues about local, regional, and national relationships among different Panther formations. Robert Widell's foray into the Deep South, in storied Birmingham, Alabama, complicates the issue of just who the Panthers were when viewed as a *movement*. In the Midwest, using the tools of both social and intellectual history, Ahmad A. Rahman takes us inside the Detroit Panther Party, revealing previously unknown aspects of the Panther underground and aboveground, and the relationship between the two. Finally, in Milwaukee, I seek to show that even where the story begins with police-Panther violence, the history of the party at the local level is far more complex than it appears at first blush. Then, in a multidimensional epilogue, Devin Fergus's meditation on the meaning of the Panthers' turn to constitutionalism in the 1970s, coupled with his use of Winston-Salem, North Carolina, as a local case, allows us to see the Panthers on a larger stage and from new historiographical perspectives.

Although it laid claim to constituting a national leadership with national spokespersons who charted its course, the Black Panther Party in fact began as a local organization and functioned often as a local organization. Significantly, Congress, in investigating the Minard murder, thought it best not to consider the party as a whole but as the whole in its parts—namely, the individual chapters and branches that comprised it. Similarly, in a 1972 commentary on the party, reporters Austin Scott and Bob

Greene recognized that "contrary to their popular image Panther chapters have always differed widely from each other, each taking its tone from its own leaders."[67] In scholarship, as in popular imagery, the typical order of understanding the Panthers inverts reality: to understand the party's internal dynamics, we need to look closely at how it functioned at the local level.[68]

As the essays in this volume demonstrate, the conflict between the Panthers and police may have been a major Panther story, but it can no longer pass for Panther history. Mayor Sorenson of Omaha liked to say, quoting what he called his little brown book—"A Way of Life by Sir William Olser"—"Our main business is not to see what lies dimly at a distance, but to do what lies clearly at hand." What clearly lies at hand in the case of the Black Panther Party is a *historical* examination beyond Oakland, California. For to continue to focus on Oakland is to miss the real significance and importance of the party—and, ironically, its national appeal. In every city where the Panthers established themselves there had been a domestic disturbance and widespread complaints about police corruption and police brutality. But there was also the quadruple denial of adequate housing, employment, education, and youth recreation. Moreover, urban renewal, democratic politics, federal anti-poverty initiatives, and, of course, the spark for many of those initiatives—the so-called riots of the age—increased the Panther appeal among those tiring of the slow pace of the civil rights struggle.

In investigating this multidimensional appeal, in all its local diversity, we provide here neither a comprehensive history of the party nor one that imposes consistent themes throughout. Rather, we seek a wider lens through which to view it—that is, a template for future research among professional historians. For this reason, before the detailed local histories that compose the essence of the book, we offer a historiographical survey— standard practice among historians but entirely unknown in Panther studies. With local history as our anchor, we hope to help birth a scholarship that, at long last, moves the Black Panther Party from story to history.

Notes

1 For the story of the Harlem Panthers told here, see "3 Harlem Schools Facing Boycotts," *New York Times*, August 26, 1966, 17; "Black Panthers Picket a School," *New York Times*, September 13, 1966, 38.

2 On the LCFO, see Clayborne Carson, *In Struggle: SNCC and the Black Awakening of the 1960s* (Cambridge, Mass.: Harvard University Press, 1981); James Forman, *The Making of Black Revolutionaries* (New York: Macmillan, 1972).

3 On the Panthers and armed self-defense generally in this era, see Peniel E. Joseph, *Waiting 'Til the Midnight Hour: A Narrative History of Black Power in America* (New York: Henry Holt, 2006); Curtis J. Austin, *Up Against the Wall: Violence in the Making and Unmaking of the Black Panther Party* (Fayetteville: University of Arkansas Press, 2006); Timothy B. Tyson, *Radio Free Dixie: Robert F. Williams and the Roots of Black Power* (Chapel Hill: University of North Carolina Press, 1999); Christopher B. Strain, *Pure Fire: Self-Defense as Activism in the Civil Rights Era* (Athens: University of Georgia Press, 2005).

4 Jane Rhodes, "Fanning the Flames of Racial Discord: The National Press and the Black Panther Party," *The Harvard International Journal of Press Politics* 4, no. 4 (1999): 95–118.

5 *The Black Panther*, November 23, 1967, 3; see, too, revised program printed in the *Black Panther Intercommunal News Service*, May 13, 1972, p. B of the supplement to the newspaper.

6 Details from testimony of Captain Murdock J. Planter, United States House of Representatives, Committee on Internal Security (CIS), National Office Operations and Investigation of Activities in Des Moines, Iowa, and Omaha, Nebraska, 91st Congress, 2nd sess. (Washington, D.C.: U.S. Government Printing Office, 1971), 4881–4890, part 4; "Apparent Dynamite Trap Kills Omaha Policeman," *Chronicle Telegram* (Elyria, Ohio), August 17, 1970, 3; "Blasts Rip Buildings in Three U.S. Cities," *Indiana Evening Gazette*, August 17, 1970, 1, 8; "Minard Trial Security Precautions Are Strict," *Lincoln Star*, April 2, 1971, 1; "3 Policemen Describe Night Patrolman Killed," *Lincoln Star*, April 3, 1971, 3; Diane Myers, "Summary of the Mondo We Langa and ED Poindexter Case," http://www.n2pp.info/case1.htm; "Youth Arrested in Omaha in Slaying of a Policeman," *New York Times*, August 29, 1970, 12; "15 Blacks in Omaha Charged in Slaying," *New York Times*, August 25, 1970, 28; "2 Charged in Omaha Blast," *New York Times*, September 2, 1970, 28.

7 "Guerilla War Is Worsening," *Stevens Point Daily Journal* (Wisc.), August 28 1970, 4.

8 Numbers are the bugbear of Panther history for a variety of reasons, most notably because the Panther story is really a local story—a central premise of this volume—and thus national figures are impossible to determine without careful local studies.

9 Martha Arnold, "Panthers, Police Caught in a Spiral," *Edwardsville* (Ill.) *Intelligencer*, November 10, 1970.

10 "Assassin Conspiracy Feared," *Lima* (Ohio) *News*, October 7, 1970, A-8.

11 Ibid.

12 "Guerilla War Is Worsening."

13 "Vigil—Not Harassment," *Edwardsville Intelligencer*, November 10, 1970, 4.

14 "Black Panthers," *Syracuse Herald-Journal*, May 11, 1970, 15.

15 Carl Oglesby, "Notes on a Decade Ready for the Dustbin," *Liberation*, August/September 1969, in *The Movement Toward a New America: The Beginning of a Long Revolution*, comp. Mitchell Cohen (New York: Knopf, 1970), quotation, 743.

16 Bobby Seale, *Seize the Time: The Story of the Black Panther Party and Huey P. Newton* (New York: Vintage, 1970), 16, 33–34.

17 David L. Bristow, *A Dirty, Wicked Town: Tales of 19th Century Omaha* (Caldwell, Idaho: Claxton, 2000); Alfred Sorenson, *History of Omaha: From the Pioneer Days to the Present Time* (Omaha: Gibson, Miller and Richardson, 1889); Robert G. Athearn, *Union Pacific Country* (Chicago: Rand McNally, 1971).

18 Norma Jean Deeb, "An Analysis of the Implemented Desegregation Plan of the Elementary Schools of Omaha, Nebraska" (Ph.D. diss., University of Nebraska, Lincoln, 1988); Richard Melvin Breaux, "'We Must Fight Race Prejudice Even More Vigorously in the North': Black Higher Education in America's Heartland, 1900–1940" (Ph.D. diss., University of Iowa, 2003); James Watt Hewitt, "Slipping Backward: The Nebraska Supreme Court, 1938–1995" (Ph.D. diss., University of Nebraska, Lincoln, 1988); Jeffrey Don Ostler, "The Fate of Populism: Agrarian Radicalism and State Politics in Kansas, Nebraska, and Iowa, 1880–1892" (Ph.D. diss., University of Iowa, 1990); James Byron Potts, "Nebraska Territory, 1854–1967: A Study of Frontier Politics" (Ph.D. diss., University of Nebraska, Lincoln, 1973).

19 "The Real Cause of Race Riots," *Crisis* 19 (December 1919): 56. On the Omaha race riot, see Clayton D. Laurie, "The U.S. Army and the Omaha Race Riot of 1919," *Nebraska History* 72, no. 3 (1991): 135–43; Clare V. McKanna Jr., "Black Enclaves of Violence: Race and Homicide in Great Plains Cities, 1890–1920," *Great Plains Quarterly* 23, no. 3 (2003): 147–60.

20 Malcolm X and Alex Haley, *The Autobiography of Malcolm X* (New York: Grove, 1965); Peter Goldman, *The Death and Life of Malcolm X* (Urbana: University of Illinois Press, 1979); George Breitman, ed., *By Any Means Necessary: Speeches, Interviews, and a Letter by Malcolm X* (New York: Pathfinder, 1970).

21 "Omaha Pressing Better Conditions to Ease Plight of Negro Citizens," *Fond du Lac Commonwealth Reporter*, August 16, 1966, 15.

22 "Dworak Assails Urban Plan"; "3 Urban Renewal Measures Are Held," *Lincoln Evening Journal and Nebraska State Journal*, May 12, 1961, 3. On the early history of the Urban League in Omaha, see Dennis N. Mihelich, "World War II and the Transformation of the Omaha Urban League," *Nebraska History* 60, no. 3 (1979): 401–23.

23 Douglas Stewart quoted in "Edgy Calm Follows Rainfall in Violence-Plagued Omaha," *Union Bulletin* (Walla Walla, Wash.), July 7, 1966, 13.

24 "Omaha Pressing Better Conditions to Ease Plight of Negro Citizens," *Fond du Lac* (Wisc.) *Commonwealth Reporter*, August 16, 1966.

25 "Rain Helps End Riots in Omaha," *Port Arthur* (Tex.) *News*, July 8, 1966, 11.

26 "Civil Rights: Omaha Disorders," *Facts on File World News Digest*, August 17, 1966, *FACTS.com*, Facts on File News Services, Delaware State University, Dover, March 14, 2005, http://www.2facts.com; "Officials Seek to Fulfill Promises after Rioting," *Lincoln Star*, July 8, 1966, 3.

27 "Civil Rights: Omaha Disorders," *Facts on File World News Digest*, August 17, 1966, *FACTS.com*, Facts on File News Services, Delaware State University, Dover, March 14, 2005, f://www.2facts.com; "Officials Seek to Fulfill Promises after Rioting," *Lincoln Star*, July 8, 1966, 3.

28 "Civil Rights: Omaha Disorders," *Facts on File World News Digest*, August 17, 1966, *FACTS.com*, Facts on File News Services, Delaware State University, Dover, March 14, 2005, http://www.2facts.com; "Officials Seek to Fulfill Promises after Rioting," *Lincoln Star*, July 8, 1966, 3.

29 "Civil Rights: Omaha Disorders," *Facts on File World News Digest*, August 17, 1966, *FACTS.com*, Facts on File News Services, Delaware State University, Dover, March 14, 2005, http://www.2facts.com; "Officials Seek to Fulfill Promises after Rioting," *Lincoln Star*, July 8, 1966, 3.

30 Lawrence H. Larsen and Barbara J. Cottrell, *The Gate City: A History of Omaha* (Boulder, Colo.: Pruett, 1982), 272–74.

31 "Omaha Pressing Better Conditions to Ease Plight of Negro Citizens," *Fond du Lac* (Wisc.) *Commonwealth Reporter*, August 16, 1966, 15; "Why Were Omaha Negroes Rioters?" *Post Crescent* (Appleton, Wisc.), August 16, 1966, B12.

32 "Omahan 19, Shot and Killed by Officer Following Chase," *Lincoln Star*, July 26, 1966, n.p.; "Matula Acted Properly Shooting Report Shows," *Lincoln Star*, August 19, 1966, 3.

33 "Gang Planned Terror," *Lincoln Star*, July 28, 1966, 1.

34 "Omaha Mayor Vows 'We're Not Tolerating Any More of This,'" *Daily Tribune* (Great Bend, Kans.), August 2, 1966, 10.

35 "Policy Change Revealed in Negro Trouble Probe," *Lincoln Star*, August 3, 1966, 2.

36 "Negro Group Critical of Omaha Meets," *Lincoln Star*, July 21; 1966, 50.

37 "2 Muslims Sentenced to Prison," *Lincoln Evening Journal and Nebraska State Journal*, November 15, 1967, 24.

38 Lawrence McVoy to Robert Carter, April 10, 1967, NAACP Papers, Group IV, Box C, Folder 20: Omaha, 1966–1969, MS Division, Library of Congress, Washington, D.C.

39 Lawrence McVoy to Gloster Current, April 12, 1967, NAACP Papers, Group

IV, Box C, Folder 20: Omaha 1966–1969, MS Division, Library of Congress, Washington, D.C., April 12, 1967.

40 Quoted in Drew Pearson's editorial, "Merry Go Round," *Daily Tribune* (Great Bend, Kans.), October 24, 1967, 4.

41 "Wallace Visit Spurs Disorder in Omaha," *Post Crescent* (Appleton, Wisc.), March 5, 1968, 5; "Riot Police Reinforced in Omaha," *Post Standard* (Syracuse, N.Y.), March 6, 1968, 3; "Omaha Quiet, Police Beef Up Patrols," *Stevens Point Daily Journal* (Wisc.), March 6, 1968, 13.

42 "Hedy's Son in Center of Omaha Furor," *Bucks County* (Pa.) *Courier Times*, June 26, 1969, 1; "Violence Hits Kokomo; Other Cities Cool It," *Van Wert* (Ohio) *Times Bulletin*, June 28, 1969, 1; "More Racial Violence in Omaha, Neb.," *Valley Independent* (Pa.), June 26, 1969, 17.

43 "Hedy's Son in Center of Omaha Furor," *Bucks County* (Pa.) *Courier Times*, June 26, 1969, 1; "Violence Hits Kokomo; Other Cities Cool It," *Van Wert* (Ohio) *Times Bulletin*, June 28, 1969, 1; "More Racial Violence in Omaha, Neb.," *Valley Independent* (Pa.), June 26, 1969, 17.

44 Planter testimony, CIS, "National Office Operations," 4882.

45 Ibid., 4881.

46 Quoted in "Strategy Planned at Panther Pow Wow," *Lima* (Ohio) *News*, December 28, 1969, B10; also, "Panthers Map New Strategy," *Port Arthur* (Tex.) *News*, December 31, 1969, 4.

47 Planter testimony, CIS, "National Office Operations," 4882.

48 Quoted at http://www.n2pp.info/buffalochip.htm. Accessed January 1, 2008.

49 Planter testimony, CIS, "National Office Operations," 4896.

50 Ibid., 4887.

51 Joan Roelof describes how foundations use their resources to further political agendas, explaining how "philanthropy suggests yet another explanation for the decline of the 1960s' and 1970s' protest movements." "Radical activism," she continues, "often was transformed by grants and technical assistance from liberal foundations into fragmented and local organizations subject to elite control." Joan Roelof, *Foundations and Public Policy: The Mask of Pluralism* (Albany: State University of New York Press, 2003).

52 "Using the Poverty Program," in Seale, *Seize the Time*, 35–44.

53 Planter testimony, CIS, "National Office Operations," 4885. For similar findings by the FBI in New Bedford, see Jama Lazerow's essay in this volume, "The Black Panthers at the Water's Edge: Oakland, Boston, and the New Bedford 'Riots' of 1970."

54 Indeed, support for the program was precisely what J. Edgar Hoover, the director of the FBI, worried about.

55 United States House of Representatives, CIS, *Gun-Barrel Politics: The*

Black Panther Party, 1966–1971, 92nd Congress, 1st sess. (Washington, D.C.: U.S. Government Printing Office, 1971), 77.

56 Planter testimony, CIS, "National Office Operations," 4881.

57 CIS, "Gun-Barrel Politics," 59.

58 "A Black Panther Party List of All Recognized Chapters, Branches and N.C.C.F.'s," *The Black Panther*, May 9, 1970.

59 *The Black Panther*, July 25, 1970; also quoted in CIS, "Gun-Barrel Politics," 89.

60 CIS, "Gun-Barrel Politics," 78.

61 Congressional statistics based on statements by Director Hoover of the FBI to a House subcommittee on November 19, 1970, quoted in ibid., 111.

62 Excerpts of Peak's confession, in *State v. Rice*, 188 Neb. 728, 199 N.W.2d 480 (1972).

63 The Minnesota bombing targeted the Minneapolis federal building, resulting in one injury and approximately $500,000 in damages. Arrested before he could carry out his plans, a former Air Force officer was indicted in the Columbus plot. He later told authorities that the bombings were intended as diversions to allow him to commit robberies. "Blasts Rip Buildings in Three U.S. Cities," *Indiana Evening Gazette*, August 17, 1970, 1, 8; "AF Officer Is Charged in Ohio Store Bombings," *Chronicle Telegram* (Elyria, Ohio), August 17, 1970, 3.

64 "Black Militants' Fate in Hands of the Jury," *Lincoln Star*, April 15, 1971, 3.

65 "High Court Curbs Right to Appeal," *Middletown* (N.Y.) *Times Herald Record*, July 7, 1976, n.p.

66 To DIR., FBI (157–8415) 10/13/70 from SAC, OMAHA (157–8871) (P) Dwayne Christopher Peak et al., Re: Bulletin to Omaha dated 9/17/70 entitled "UNSUB; Bomb Explosion 2867 Ohio Street, Omaha, Nebraska, 8/17/70, RU." In 2005 a copy of the missing tape was finally located and submitted as evidence for a new trial for the convicted Panthers. A voice expert determined that the voice on the tape was not that of Duane Peak, bolstering their claim that they had been victims of a cover-up. Efforts at winning a new trial continue. Joe Allen, "Black Power, Racism and COINTELPRO in the Heartland Justice for the Omaha Two," *Counterpunch*, January 9, 2007, 1.

67 "Have the Black Panthers Really Changed at All?" *Indiana Evening Gazette*, March 7, 1972, 17.

68 At the same time, chapter 2 through 5, which chart the genesis, nature, and development of the Panthers in four locales, hardly represent full-scale, urban history treatments such as one can find in Robert O. Self, *American Babylon: Race and the Struggle for Postwar Oakland* (Princeton, N.J.: Princeton University Press, 2003); and Matthew J. Countryman, *Up South: Civil Rights and Black Power in Philadelphia* (Philadelphia: University of Pennsylvania Press, 2005). Space constraints prevent such analysis. More important, though, while we obviously feel that the appeal of the BPP cannot be understood outside the context of community circumstances and hope that urban historians will be able to draw on the essays here as a starting point for deeper research and analysis of the party, we offer these local studies primarily as examples of careful and sustained attention to Panther dynamics in specific places to identify the enormously complex realities of the Panther moment.

1

Bringing the Black Panther Party Back In

A SURVEY

It is by now a truism that historical scholarship—not least, about America—has been "remade" since the 1960s.[1] If complaints persist about over-specialization, there is little dispute that the historian's lens has widened vastly over the last generation to take in a great diversity of people, subjects, sources, methods, concepts, and perspectives.[2] Though not the first such historiographical attempt, this "new history" has fashioned itself as a "history from the bottom up," privileging the experiences of "ordinary people" who sometimes did extraordinary things as individuals and in social movements.[3] Women, people of color, working people generally—and, perhaps more important, the concepts of gender, race, and class—have been at the literature's core, in increasingly complex arrangements.[4] Virtually untouched in this "remaking" is the armed revolutionary organization, the Black Panther Party (BPP), which existed from 1966 to 1982.[5]

When viewed especially in its late 1960s and early 1970s incarnation, the BPP was not simply an organization, but a *movement*—in the range of people the Panthers attracted and absorbed, in the individuals and even entire groups who identified with the Panther style and ideology, and in the way entire communities became swept up in Panther causes and programs. The Panthers established chapters or branches in most major American cities and several abroad, with numbers of members and supporters running into the thousands. Critically, they also provided an organizational model for Latinos, Asians, poor whites, and even the elderly, gaining the sobriquet by the climax of the 1960s as the "vanguard of the revolution."[6] By early 1970, some polls showed them with the support of nearly two-thirds of the African American community in major urban centers.[7] All this hardly escaped the FBI, whose director, J. Edgar Hoover, repeatedly referred to the Panthers after 1968 as "the greatest threat to the internal security of the country"; it followed, therefore, that the Panthers bore the brunt of FBI counterintelligence operations directed at African Americans in this period (233 of 295).[8] Whether one views their igno-minious decline in the 1970s as a product of such state repression, internal dissolution, or some combination thereof, for a time at least the Panthers had more support among black Americans than any other avowedly revolutionary (and black-led) organization in American history. All told, in numbers, reach, ideology, program, and social and political impact, they represented a moment of world-historic importance.

In their heyday, the Panthers attracted the attention of the Left and the Right, black and white, young and old, male and female, community activist and government official—in the florid language of Richardson Preyer, the chairman of the House Committee on Internal Security (formerly the House Committee on Un-American Activities or HUAC), they "fascinated the left, inflamed the police, terrified much of America."[9] But, none were more taken with the Panthers than the media. They were "good copy . . . and there is no lack of 'news' about them," wrote the journalist Robert Scheer in October 1968, warning presciently, however, that "for all this exposure, the Panthers are treated as nothing more than a bizarre happening in violence." According to Scheer, that treatment was intentional, as "the television networks offer up their version of the Panther movement in order to convince us that it is simply an exercise in mindless freak theater—entertaining, provocative, insignificant—and that the Panthers' confrontation with society is a momentary spectacle, isolated from history." But, "the Panthers do have a history," he insisted, recommending to readers of the radical magazine *Ramparts* some excerpts from what became a classic of the Panther memoir genre, *Seize the Time* by Bobby Seale, the co-founder and chairman of the party.[10] Yet, more than forty years later, that history is just beginning to be written by professional historians.

At first blush, this historiographical lacuna is surprising. After all, the 1960s have become a veritable cottage industry, not just in the form of memoirs, film, music, art, and literature, but in the social sciences and, increasingly, historical studies.[11] Meanwhile, African American history is among the most vibrant subfields in American history generally, with work on the civil rights era (1930s–1970s) especially rich and finely textured.[12] Yet, while the League of Revolutionary Black Workers, a short-lived Detroit-based black power organization of the late 1960s, receives lavish and detailed treatment in the *Encyclopedia of the American Left*, the BPP entry is cursory and one-dimensional.[13] More recently, in Robin D. G. Kelley's provocative and deservedly praised *Freedom Dreams*, chapter 3, which deals with the 1960s and 1970s, focuses not on the Panthers but on the much smaller and geographically circumscribed Revolutionary Action Movement (RAM).[14] And so it goes, in surveys, monographs, and journal literature.

Texts without Context The Marginalization of the Panthers

Unsurprisingly, then, college textbooks—typically revised every few years to reflect the latest scholarship—are generally unenlightening, often misleading, sometimes plain wrong on the subject of the BPP, regardless of focus. *The National Experience*, a venerable and still popular traditional text, at the crucial moment of 1993 (see below), contains no description of the Black Panther Party at all. However, the authors use "In Defense of Self Defense," a famous essay by Huey Newton, one of the founders of the Black Panthers, as an inset primary document next to an excerpt from Martin Luther King's book, *Where Do We Go from Here?* The headings read, "The Case for Violence," and "The Case against Violence," respectively.[15] That is, the Panthers are equated with violence. Thus, one of the most widely used of all texts, *The American Promise*, which claims to offer "*both* the structure of a political narrative *and* the insights gained from examining social and cultural experience," offers only this about the Panthers, in the context of black power advocates insisting that "Black people should and must fight back": "After police killed an unarmed teenager in San Francisco in 1966, Huey Newton and Bobby Seale organized the Black Panther Party for Self-Defense in 1966 and armed its members for self-defense against police brutality."[16]

In the "political history" text, *The American Nation*, by Columbia University's John Garraty, the paragraph in which the Panthers appear is in his discussion of the "new racial turmoil" of the 1960s. Here, "extremists formed the Black Panther party and collected weapons to resist police. 'Shoot, don't loot,' the radical H. Rap Brown advised all who would listen" —the latter sentence being somewhat of a non sequitur, as Brown was never of any institutional significance to the Panthers, with only a titular position in the organization for a few months in 1968. Readers are informed as well that the Panthers demanded compensation for past injustices, and that they ran for president their minister of information, Eldridge Cleaver, identified as "a convict on parole" who was nevertheless "an articulate and intelligent man" who had written the much-praised book *Soul on Ice*.[17]

Nation of Nations, a "narrative" text, devotes *its* paragraph-and-a-half on the Panthers to, once again, militancy and violence, this time seeming to confuse two incidents from the party's early history, running together two of Newton's infamous run-ins with the police. The apparent conflation, which an average student would almost certainly assume, allows the authors to concisely note Newton's celebrated three years in jail for manslaughter of a police officer in October 1967 and his legendary and colorful challenge to a San Francisco cop eight months earlier, "O.K., you big fat racist pig, draw your gun." Even at its height, though, "the group never counted more than 2000 members nationwide," and "most African Americans remained committed to the goals that defined the civil rights movement: nonviolence, not armed confrontation; integration, not segregation."[18] Unintentionally—and quite unfortunately, given the Panthers' consistent opposition to ghetto "rioting"—the marginal text clue next to the paragraph introducing the BPP ("Black Panthers") sits above a picture of a National Guardsman with the flames of the Watts riot of 1965 in the background. Just below the picture is the subheading, "Violence in the Streets." Following similar themes, another "narrative" text, George Tindall's *America*, describes the Panthers as "a self-professed group of urban revolutionaries" who "terrified the public, but eventually fragmented in spasms of violence."[19]

Created Equal, a text stressing as two of its four major themes "diversity" and "class and systems of power," dispatches the Panthers in two sentences deep in a paragraph about violence during the "shift from civil rights to black power." Here, the BPP formed in response to police brutality, engaged in several shootouts, and was "eventually decimated by an FBI campaign against them."[20] *Liberty, Equality, and Power: A History of the American People* is a text that is supposed to do just about everything: "[capture] the drama and excitement of America's past," "[integrate] social and cultural history into a political story," and "[synthesize] the finest older historical scholarship with the best of the new to create a narrative that is balanced, lively, and accessible." Here, the Panthers receive a sentence-

and-a-half in a section co-authored by an expert in twentieth-century foreign affairs and a specialist in American legal history. The BPP is teamed with SNCC's Stokely Carmichael, for a time the prime minister of the party, as opponents of "gradualism and nonviolent methods"; the example offered is a "Black Panther manifesto [which] . . . called for community 'self-defense' groups as protection against police harassment, the release from jail of all African American prisoners . . . , and guaranteed employment for all citizens."[21] The last phrase, of course, would come as something of a surprise to an avid reader of American history texts, given that the Panthers have appeared thus far merely as a *military* phenomenon. At the very end of the one sentence the group receives in *American People: Creating a Nation and a Society*, yet another text that claims to balance political and social history, there is this suggestion of a more nuanced view: "The Black Panthers, radical activists who organized first in Oakland, California, and then in other cities, formed a militant organization that vowed to eradicate not only racial discrimination but capitalism as well."[22] Indeed, the social history-oriented *Who Built America?* notes in its half-paragraph on the Panthers that they saw themselves as "the vanguard of the socialist revolution they forecast for the United States." The text adds that "by 1969 [the Panthers'] inflammatory rhetoric . . . drew heavy media attention, and it [the authors leave unclear whether "it" refers to the Panthers' inflammatory rhetoric or to the media attention] provoked several shootouts with the police and the FBI, who now targeted the Panthers as dangerous revolutionaries."[23] Meanwhile, *Out of Many: A History of the American People*, which professes uniqueness in its community focus, points out that while armed self-defense was the Panthers' strategy, "in several communities, [they] also ran breakfast programs for schoolchildren, established medical clinics, and conducted educational classes."[24]

A People and a Nation, whose goal is to "fully" integrate social history into "the traditional fabric of party politics, congressional legislation, wars, economic patterns, and local and state government," does seek to combine many of these themes into one short paragraph. Here, the BPP was a blend of "black separatism and revolutionary communism," seeking to destroy both capitalism and "the military arm of [their] oppressors" (the police), with members carrying guns and talking about "killing 'pigs,'" though also establishing community programs.[25] But other texts are similarly "nuanced" in sometimes profoundly misleading ways. For example, *America's*

History notes that as the Panthers became national their initial "militant self-defense" posture was supplemented with "community organizing projects, including interracial efforts." Incongruously, the authors then add, "but [the Panthers'] affinity for Third World revolutionary movements and armed struggle became their most publicized attribute"—as if the latter and the former were incompatible.[26]

Students, even some college professors, are not in the habit of reading lots of textbooks. If they read all those reviewed here, however, they would emerge with a composite, sometimes confusing picture of an extreme and apparently quite small group that advocated armed "self-defense" and black nationalism (and, perhaps, socialism and racial separatism); developed a range of community programs for reasons that are not entirely clear; and drew significant enough media and government attention to lead ultimately to repressive state violence, at least partly brought on by their own actions. Always, the Panthers are discussed as part of the black power movement and associated in the public imagination with militancy and violence, especially the urban "riots" of the late 1960s.[27] Their placement in the American story, therefore, conveniently puts the Panthers always at the margins.[28]

Sources Surveys of the 1960s

It is difficult to ascertain just what or whom textbook writers are relying on to write a few sentences about the Black Panther Party. Of the texts reviewed here, only one makes direct reference in its bibliography to materials on the Panthers per se.[29] There are several overviews that use the same sources, however. Perhaps the most ubiquitous is Allen Matusow's now classic work, *The Unraveling of America*, a volume on the 1960s in the New American Nation Series.[30] In a generally unflattering portrait—damning leading Panthers with faint praise about their "audacity" and "talk," and condemning them for engaging in a "revolutionary charade"—Matusow dispenses with their historical significance by making them a product of white guilt: "a handful of blacks with a mimeograph machine" who "existed mainly in the demented minds of white leftists."[31]

Another apparent source is Todd Gitlin's memoir/history, *The Sixties: Years of Hope, Days of Rage*, in which the Panthers belong to the latter moment the activist-turned-academic calls "the Late Sixties" in a final section titled "Forcing the Revolution."[32] Cast as a godsend for "the white Left"—along with the author, the book's focus—the Panthers appear in league with those whose only common ground is their association with violence: "Lyndon Johnson and Richard J. Daley and James Earl Ray, Ronald Reagan and J. Edgar Hoover and Sirhan Sirhan, 'Eve of Destruction' and *Bonnie and Clyde*, Green Berets and Black Panthers and the N.Y.P.D. . . ."[33] Thus, in his only sustained treatment of the BPP, under the label of "The Bogey of Race," Gitlin notes, "They called themselves a party, but the Panthers were closer to an outlaw political gang. . . ."[34] Mostly, the narrative mocks both the Panthers and their white supporters: "in the person of the Panthers . . . the anarchist impulse could be fused with the Third World mystique, the aura of violence, and the thrust for revolutionary efficiency"; " 'PE' [political education] as the Panthers understood it was a close reading of Mao's *On Liberalism* and other such samples of philosophical baby talk"; "ghettoites and Ph.D.'s in Leninist study groups and 'free universities' were huddling under two wings of the same zeitgeist."[35] In both Matusow and Gitlin, the Panthers constitute Exhibit A in the case for the decline of the hopes of the early 1960s into the nihilism of despair that putatively characterized the late 1960s, what some have called the "declension model" of the era's descent from the "good sixties" to the "bad sixties."[36]

Of the more broad-based 1960s surveys listed in the textbook bibliographies, none appears more frequently than *The Age of Great Dreams* by perhaps the era's leading historian, David Farber.[37] His several pages on the Panthers begin with the categorical statement that "above all, the Panthers believed that the black community needed to arm," followed by discussions of their paramilitary dress and violent rhetoric ("offing the pigs"), which Farber sees as an example of the group as "superb self-promoters," and shootouts with police.[38] Acknowledging that "a few committed Panthers, many of them women, set up free breakfast programs, medical clinics, and other community-based programs in several cities," and noting that some Panthers eventually went into traditional electoral politics, he stresses that "many Panthers simply became caught in their own rhetoric of violence."[39] The latter was then seized upon by police and the FBI.

Another popular overview, David Burner's *Making Peace with the 60s*, similarly emphasizes the association of the Panthers with violence, only even more so than does Farber. Burner cites their use of Mao's ditty regarding political power and the gun, as well as Newton's "life of crime and violence" before organizing "brothers off the block" (because he "disdained young blacks who held regular jobs"), and his years after release from prison as a cocaine addict and murderer. Cleaver, after having served nine years in prison, became a Panther leader who "beat and pistol-whipped dissenters within the Panther ranks." Rap Brown, as minister of justice, asked a crowd, "How many white folks did you kill today?"[40] As for community programs, "In Oakland and other cities the breakfast program for children, often used in justification of the Panthers, was increasingly based on extortion. Convenience stores that did not contribute food were in some instances firebombed. The Panthers almost from the beginning also ran a protection racket in Oakland, whereby crime was allowed to flourish."[41] Burner acknowledges, in a tag line, that "one breakfast program in New Haven, Connecticut, does seem to have operated without criminality." Even that small concession does not appear in Maurice Isserman's and Michael Kazin's *America Divided*, the most recent 1960s survey used frequently in college courses. The Panthers receive mention, briefly, three times in this most substantial of all such books: first as romantic third worldists, then as secular millennialists, and, finally, as coked-up gangsters.[42]

If these are the principal sources for textbooks, what sources do *they* rely on? In the absence of any real historical scholarship on the subject, Matusow and Gitlin relied on primary sources from the late 1960s and early 1970s: journalists' accounts, early memoirs, and Panther speeches and manifestos.[43] Farber's bibliographic essay gives no hint of sources for his portrait of the Panthers, nor does Burner's. The latter, however, does mention two in the text itself: the journalist Hugh Pearson, using Pearson's relentlessly hostile biography of Huey Newton, *The Shadow of the Panther*, published in 1994; and Peter Collier and David Horowitz, apparently using their "second thoughts" anti-Left memoir, *Destructive Generation*, published in the late 1980s.[44] Though the latter had no source notes, and the former employed the journalist's form of including sources for direct quotations and salient claims only, their approach is close enough to suggest a reliance of Pearson on Collier and Horowitz, and both on earlier exposés by the journalist Kate Coleman and her colleague Paul Avery.[45] Together, the picture they paint is not simply of the BPP's descent into criminality and violence; they trace both to the founders' lives before the party's establishment. Pearson further diminishes the entire Panther story by proclaiming it little more than a media creation. Indeed, on the penultimate page of his book, he proclaims, "One of the things that struck me as I wrote was how disappointed, even angry, I often became at our society and myself, for paying so much attention to an organization that, arguably, in so many ways amounted to little more than a temporary media phenomenon."[46]

Significantly, Isserman and Kazin use only Pearson as a source.[47] Meanwhile, others—journalists and historians of many stripes, in prominent book reviews and influential surveys—have taken the perspective to its logical extreme. The liberal historian David Oshinsky declares that the Panthers were "founded . . . by an Oakland street felon" and were led by men with "impressive rap sheets," who "kept dealing and killing and shaking down the streets," while the New Left applauded from the sidelines.[48] The *New York Times* editorialist Brent Staples identifies the Panthers as "a former California street gang that informants [unnamed] have told us was routinely involved in murder and the protection racket."[49] Most recently, a prominent historian of postwar America, William O'Neill, calls them "a radical paramilitary group that . . . evolved out of a street gang," "more a criminal gang than a political organization."[50]

The precise fit of this scholarly perspective to the popular is dramatically revealed by a story Mario Van Peebles tells about his attempt to shop the script for the movie that eventually became *Panther* in 1995. According to Van Peebles, he and his father, Melvin, encountered one studio executive early on who claimed to be in love with their idea of making a mainstream film about the BPP, but wondered if it were not possible to make one of the lead Panthers *white* so the target audience could "identify." When Van Peebles explained that there *were* no white Panthers as such, he quotes the executive as saying they could create a "[Berkeley] student [who] could teach the Panthers to stand up for themselves, to believe in themselves. He could turn them on to all that revolutionary literature they read, and because he's white, he's forced to stay in the background to politically guide them." Deciding to see just how far this line of discussion might go, Van Peebles then suggested to the producer, helpfully, "So, the white character is sort of a coach and the Panthers would be like a black militant basketball team battling the forces of oppression?" To which, according to Van Peebles, the executive enthusiastically responded, "Exactly!" He explained, "Regardless of what the historical truth was, you're talking about the most feared black militant group in American history, period. Most suburban white people thought the Panthers wanted to take what *we* had. Thought they hated us. There is simply no way to do this film about a group of armed, supposedly antiwhite revolutionaries without the film itself being perceived as antiwhite unless there's a white star on that poster. . . ."[51]

Regardless of what the historical truth was: therein lies the rub about the history of the Black Panther Party. Whether as a foil for the nonviolent civil rights movement, as an exemplar of the so-called declension model of the 1960s, as the mere children of Malcolm X, as most colorful of the new black power groups—or as simply the far end of the radical fringe—the Panthers are easily celebrated, condemned, or dismissed but rarely investigated in depth. Literature of a historical nature—that is, material or analysis of past events—is not the same as historical literature, which has its own canons, standards, ethics. The latter is missing from the bookshelves. It is our view that the former, however valuable, can only be a prologue to the task that the latter demands: a real historiography of the Black Panther Party, a historiography built from the ground up.

That is, a recognizable Panther historiography must de-center the story, just as civil rights studies has.[52] It is not simply a matter of the party differing over time and space, with its real or imagined usefulness or menace in a particular locale owing to both its national reputation and its emphasis on local issues. Rather, certainly after the organization became truly national in 1968, the Panthers were not involved in national membership drives, like those of, say, the National Association for the Advancement of Colored People (NAACP); more often than not, local chapters or branches were constituted by local people looking to validate their existence—and sometimes to take their work to a higher political level. Moreover, when national (or even regionally dominant) Panthers entered the picture, there was tension, not only with local authorities, but typically with local activists themselves, including those who sought to become Panthers. In short, the history of the Panthers in their "movement" heyday was much more than the local confirmation of a national story—the whole was more than just Oakland; more than just Huey, Bobby, and Eldridge; more than the sum of its parts.

A historian's history of the BPP will thus be far more complex than any of the "history" thus far would suggest. Remarkably, despite the changes in approach and authorship in four broad, sometimes overlapping periods over the long generation since the Panthers emerged—from the party's origins until 1977, 1978–87, 1987–96, and 1997 to the present—the tale has almost always oscillated between celebration and condemnation, typically focusing on the famous and the fallen. Only recently, in the fourth, still developing period have some historians begun to move away from those poles and away from the subject matter that makes those poles so attractive.

Early Attempts to Make Sense of the Panthers as the "Greatest Threat" 1968–77

During their early years, when the Panthers were under attack in the media and by various state agencies, three kinds of writing—dueling journalistic accounts, personal reminiscences and renegade revelations, and federal government reports—constituted a war of words that matched the war of deeds going on in the streets. The war of words constituted a kind of propaganda battle—after all, in the Panther "moment" of the great upsurge of the 1960s, not only lives but also the life of the movement were at stake. However, Hoover set the tone with his declaration that the Panthers were "the greatest threat to the internal security of the United States," and much that was written in this period was written in the shadow of that statement.

In fact, almost from the moment of their inception in late 1966 as an armed revolutionary group patrolling police in Oakland, and certainly after their sensational appearance in the California State Capitol Building the following May—en masse, carrying weapons—journalists in the print and electronic media cast the Panthers as a shocking development in the black freedom struggle, encapsulated in the street argot "niggers with guns." By May 1969, in one of the first overall accounts of the party, a pamphlet of the Church League of America warned ominously that "during the past two years, in the great industrial cities of the United States, members of the Black Panther Party have been linked by police with crimes that range from murder and a conspiracy to bomb buildings through armed robbery and arson to the stock-piling of automatic weapons and the possession of narcotics."[53] Interpreting the Panther Program's first point—"we want power to determine the destiny of our black community"—as a call for a socialist state, the league warned that "the Black Panthers and their many militant, radical supporters must be stopped before they can do serious harm to our society."[54] By the following year, having garnered a measure of white *liberal* support, in great part because of what appeared to be a concerted campaign of police repression, ridicule was the more common reportorial device. The most notable example of the latter was Tom Wolfe's *Radical Chic* of 1970, which, among other things, exposed the long fascination of the Panthers with the entertainment world, and vice versa.[55]

At the other end of the journalistic spectrum were the Panthers' champions, most prominently those associated with *Ramparts*, the radical magazine published in San Francisco. *Ramparts* hired Cleaver after he was paroled in December 1966; while there in 1967, he became a Panther—in part, he later claimed, because of a confrontation he witnessed between police and Newton in front of the office of *Ramparts* that February—and, as the Panthers' minister of information and the editor of the group's newspaper, he would finish writing his instantly acclaimed collection of prison essays and letters, *Soul on Ice*, a Ramparts book.[56] It was no coincidence, then, that another Ramparts book, Gene Marine's *The Black Panthers* of 1969, was the first full-scale attempt to tell the Panther story, in this case by a white reporter writing for whites at the suggestion of *Ramparts*.[57] Although claiming, more than once, to be "afraid of the Black Panther Party"—writing, "deep in my white possibly racist, probably unrevolutionary heart"—Marine was clearly sympathetic to his subjects, and he said so.[58] Although the introduction notes that the Panthers "exist now [June 1969] in every major city in America and in quite a few smaller ones," the book nevertheless told an Oakland-centered story, mentioning places outside California only in the final pages of the volume, and then only in snippets. Still, *The Black Panthers* was filled with insight into the complexities of the personalities and politics involved, raising as many questions as it provided answers, even if it poses difficulties for the historian in its telling of stories without attribution or source citation. Most insightful of all, perhaps, was Marine's comment that, by the end of 1968, "the story of the Black Panther Party fragments. From here on, there is no Panther story; there are only Panther stories, most of them local, and no one can keep up with them all."[59] It would take more than a generation for scholars to take up that implicit challenge.[60]

From whatever perspective, writers told the Panther story as one story, typically emanating from Oakland, typically centering on leading figures—Cleaver, Seale, and especially Newton. Thus, the first history/memoir of the party to emanate from the party itself, advertised in the pages of *The*

Black Panther as "The Biography of Huey P. Newton," and well over a year in gestation, was Seale's now classic work, *Seize the Time*. Here, Seale set down, on tape and then with the editorial assistance of Art Goldberg of *Ramparts*, some of his own history, but mainly the origins and development of the BPP from his first meeting with Newton in 1962 until the early days of 1970 when the manuscript cuts off.[61] Written in the heat of battle from jail, with Newton also imprisoned and Cleaver in exile, Seale claimed to set forth the nature of the Panther movement and ideology—"what it really does, the kind of people who are in it, their everyday lives, the things that have happened"—as "the true story of the Black Panther Party."[62] Covering an enormous amount of ground, from the everyday to the era's celebrated trials, the book is a treasure trove of information, but, like any other *primary* source, it ought not be confused with the work that historians do.[63] Far more problematic is Chuck Moore's *I Was a Black Panther*, an "as told to" book published the same year with an author's note indicating that what the narrator, "Willie Stone," related were the true experiences of a boy who joined the Black Panthers, though names and places had been changed, with the events "largely as they are told here." Riddled with errors, the book appears to be more fiction than anything else, more a children's book (told from a young black teen's point of view) than a genuine history or autobiography. And, though told from the perspective of an alleged rank-and-file Panther, the book mostly highlights leaders, such as Carmichael, Brown, Cleaver, and Newton.[64]

A very different, though no less politically charged, autobiographical account from this period is *Look for Me in the Whirlwind: The Collective Autobiography of the New York 21*.[65] In the book, recorded while they were still on trial for conspiracy to commit murder, arson, and numerous acts of sabotage, and published just months after their acquittal in May 1971, sixteen of the defendants provided a wealth of information, mostly about the background to their joining the party; only the volume's last quarter concerns their lives as Panthers. Here, though—finally—was a series of personal stories outside the Oakland orbit. Typical of the genre, however, dating was vague, sometimes inaccurate; stories contradicted each other; some stories seemed self-serving or merely unreflective; and the reader had no access to the questions asked, or to the questioner.[66] Most important, perhaps, these strung-together oral histories were constructed amid one of the most tumultuous periods of BPP history, when these Panthers were expelled from the party just prior to a bloody split between Huey Newton and Eldridge Cleaver, with New York mostly siding with the Cleaver faction.[67]

The other significant Panther history/memoir of the era—arguably, the most important—was Huey Newton's *Revolutionary Suicide*, published in 1973. An entirely different enterprise than the collection of speeches and writings he had published the year before, *To Die for the People*, here was Newton, for the first time, telling his own story and the story of the party he had founded.[68] It was, as the *New York Times*'s Christopher Lehmann-Haupt put it, "an ultimate revelation, a collapse of last barriers, a closing of the circle."[69] Written, apparently, with a great deal of help from his future dissertation advisor, J. Herman Blake, it was, by far, the most coherent, logically consistent, and moving of the early autobiographies.[70] Nevertheless, the moment of its composition is critical to determining its usefulness. Written in the aftermath of the split, which, in turn, brought a marked turn away from militant rhetoric and a reevaluation of key tenets of party ideology, the book emerged in the shadow of a consolidation of Panther forces to Oakland from the hinterland, in part for local electoral campaigns.[71] The work, then, was as much a political tract as a reliable source for Newton's life or the life of the party.

Meanwhile, some who left the party sought to expose its "true" nature and history. The first effort began the very month Seale undertook what became *Seize the Time*. In October 1968, Earl Anthony, an organizer of the Los Angeles chapter but by then increasingly out of favor with party leadership, signed with Dial Press to write a history, because "the story of the Party needed to be told."[72] For that privately rendered decision, as well as his divergent views from the party hierarchy on the subject of black nationalism—he claimed to be deeply upset by communist influence on the party—he was expelled in March 1969 just before completing the manuscript.[73] He titled the book, *Picking Up the Gun: A Report on the Black Panthers*. Tainted by his long-simmering disillusionment from the party, by his own later account the book had one other demerit not known publicly until he wrote a second one, published in 1990: from the moment of his involvement with the Black Panther Party, Earl Anthony was working for the FBI.[74]

Whether or not members of the House Committee on Internal Security knew about Anthony's ties, they made copious use of his book, along with

ent repression and several on-
his purpose was at least initially
ion. Indeed, by 1980, Michael
o the founder of the Panthers)
al history of the party in retro-
uspense novel," with a "cast of
Black Militancy," the book, for
ts, tried to make some sense of
, Newton's was the first popular
ad begun as a local organization
nfortunately, because of its at-
he final demise of the Panthers
nd Liberation School in 1982—
cause he failed to immerse him-
.[93] Too, the volume, titled, *Bitter
er Party*, continued to center the
the grassroots. Most significant,
ted the heart of Newton's story,
by way of violent confrontations
ook far more balanced than past
sis . . . the Panthers were more
uch but guilty of precious little."[94]
ided the search for legacy in its
d good ideas and great potential,
gressive campaign of harassment
ctive dovetailed with more rigor-
government repression of the civil
ow's *The FBI and Martin Luther
 now well established—a national
his honor—the repression legacy
if it were the only story. Moreover,
ion of what the Panthers had been
was out to destroy them—it invited
arly days, which was still heard in
 Chamberlin put it in May 1970:
 create reflex situations that may
ir behavior."[95] That interpretation

the testimony of other ex-Panthers, in a series of reports in 1970 and 1971. Significantly, their investigation began in October 1969, a month after the appearance of Marine's sympathetic *The Black Panthers*; their hearings began the month Seale finished *Seize the Time.* In the foreword to the most frequently cited of these reports, *Gun-Barrel Politics*, Chairman Richard Ichord of Missouri emphasized that the primary interests of his committee were the Panthers' use of "force, violence, terrorism, or other unlawful means" and the extent to which they were "controlled, directed, or assisted by those who seek to overthrow . . . [the] government of the United States," especially "foreign communist powers, their agents or nationals."[75] At publication, Richard Preyer of North Carolina wrote in his summation that the "Black Panther Party, as a national organization, is near disintegration," but that was hardly the committee's view at the outset of its investigation. Indeed, he wrote, "It is hard to believe that only a little over a year ago the Panthers, despite their small number, ranked as the most celebrated ghetto militants." Most important, Preyer exposed just how "political" the committee's report was. It sought, for example, to present the party in a "spirit of fairness and balance" when, "without departing from the facts," it could have conveyed a "stronger sense of outrage," he reminded readers. But that might revive "a flagging Panther Party" by allowing the group to charge "'oppression,'" which members "wear . . . like a badge."[76] In addition, Preyer claimed, "If it is correct that the Black Panther Party is presently suffering from a terminal illness, then this report may be of historical interest." He nevertheless believed that the committee report offered "some 'lessons learned' which apply to all such paramilitary groups based on hate," such as the necessity to curb "violent ranting," even if "it is . . . plain that the Panthers are totally incapable of overthrowing our Government by violence."[77] Still, "short of revolution," they might provoke a choice in "our society" between tyranny and anarchy, noting that "society will choose tyranny." And, finally, Preyer asked, "How has such an organization been able to flourish in our society," and then advanced one reason: "they were glamorized by the press."[78] Here, in summary form was the paradox of the detractors' history of the party for a generation: prone to violence and dangerous even if only because they might provoke government tyranny in response, the Panthers were, more than anything, a media creation.

The House Committee also produced reports on the Panther newspaper and studies of Panthers in Seattle, Kansas City, Des Moines, Omaha, India-

napolis, Detroit, and Philadelphia. But, as with *Gun-Barrel Poli[*
work was done quickly, taking the testimony of disaffected ex-m[
and investigators, while relying heavily on Anthony's *Picking Up th[*
Meanwhile, G. Louis Heath published two large collections of p[
sources; the long introduction to one, *Off the Pigs!*, drew, in turn, or[
government reports.[79] Still, the Watergate political scandal produc[
vestigations into government efforts to destroy 1960s activists—n[
the Church Committee (1975–76)—which laid the ground for a new[
in the war of words marking the Panther "moment" of 1968–71.[
Church report introduced a new word into the American vocabulary[
its Book III, "COINTELPRO: The FBI's Action Program against Ame[
Citizens." Though parts of this FBI counterintelligence program c[
from the mid-1950s had been known to activists as early as 1971, Bo[
provided the grist for a cottage industry of Panther books that mig[
called "repression studies,"[81] for the prime victim of COINTELPRO, a[
height of its sophistication, was the Black Panther Party.[82]

Repression, Dissolution, and Resurrection 1978–87

Athan Theoharis's 1978 volume, *Spying on Americans*—though not ab[
the Panthers per se—inaugurated more than a decade of repression st[
ies. Ironically, while sympathetic to the BPP, this scholarship offered [
little about the group.[83] Indeed, like the very different exposés of Pant[
criminality by journalists such as Kate Coleman and Peter Avery d[
ing the same period, the repression approach made objects, rather th[
agents, of perhaps the most dynamic group the 1960s produced.[84] O[
entry in the genre was a doctoral dissertation, posthumously reprinted[
book form, by none other than Huey Newton himself.[85] Notably abse[
from that study were the tales of Panther accomplishments that had pun[
tuated the pages of *Revolutionary Suicide*, now replaced by a rich, if [
times poorly documented, catalog of crimes against the party committe[
in the name of national security. Moreover, Newton's focus was on th[
leadership located in Oakland.

Meanwhile, a trickle of scholarly studies began to emerge, even befor[
the Panthers' final demise in the early 1980s, but again centered on the Ba[
Area—and not by historians.[86] It showed. Take, for example, Helen Stew[
art's 1980 doctoral dissertation in sociology at Brandeis University. At on[

the continuing investigations into governm[
going lawsuits by the Panthers themselves, l[
lost in the larger public interest in repress[
Newton (a freelance writer of no relation t[
published the first real attempt at a nation[
spect.[91] Though advertised as a kind of "s[
characters [who] read like a Who's Who of[
the first time outside government docume[
the story from a local perspective.[92] Indeed[
history to acknowledge that the Panthers h[
and later returned to their local roots. U[
tempt at breadth at such an early date—t[
came only with the closing of their Oakla[
Newton made numerous errors, surely be[
self in the communities he was describing[
Grain: Huey Newton and the Black Panth[
party story on the leadership rather than [
though, government repression constitu[
with the various chapters' histories told [
with police. Thus, the conclusion to a b[
journalistic accounts: "In the final analy[
sinned against than sinners, accused of m[

In one sense, this repression model a[
implicit notion that the Panthers had ha[
which had been arrested by an overly ag[
by law enforcement officials. The perspe[
ous historical studies then emerging on [
rights movement, such as David Garr[
King, Jr. But, whereas King's legacy was[
holiday would soon be instituted in [
tended to dominate the Panther story as [
while the repression legacy was vindica[
saying all along—that law enforcement [
the rejoinder offered from the group's [
some quarters. As the columnist John[
"Naturally, if you inspire fear, you wil[
burst the bounds of dispassionately fa[

allowed for the BPP as a political entity *and* a street gang that elicited violent government response to its militant posturing—precisely what unsympathetic journalists, renegades, and government investigators had been claiming since the late 1960s. Michael Newton perceptively observed in 1980, "For the Black Panther Party, success and achievement were always ephemeral concepts, embodied in the hearts and minds of people rather than written in the records of things and deeds." Thus, in his formulation, "The Panthers demonstrated that blacks could stand against the establishment on their own terms—albeit at the risk of death—and that demonstration marked a new stage of evolution in the black liberation movement. Black Panthers seized the time and, for the brief, tumultuous moment it was theirs, they wrung it dry."[96] That, of course, was a weak legacy at best, actually reinforcing the notion that the Panthers were mere loudmouths. Thus, like Marcus Garvey and Malcolm X before them, their real value was in their martyrdom, actual or imagined, rather than in the movements they spawned.

Significantly, it would take an ex-Panther championing the rank-and-file experience to elevate the discussion to a new level—to, in a sense, resurrect the Panther experience. JoNina Abron, the last editor of *The Black Panther*, who later earned a doctorate in English, published a short article in *The Black Scholar* in 1986 that resuscitated, in scholarly form, the community service emphasis deployed by Huey Newton in his autobiography. With considerably greater skill than Newton had mustered early in the previous decade, though, she anticipated the question raised in the most well-read of the repression studies. In 1989, Kenneth O'Reilly's book *"Racial Matters": The FBI's Secret File on Black America, 1960–1972* suggested by implication the obvious: If everyone was being spied on, what precisely was the legacy of any one group, such as the Panthers? Abron's prescient answer represented a new attempt to document the BPP's contributions in three key areas where ordinary Panthers had played key roles: its survival programs, its ideological development, and its forays into electoral politics. In doing so, she was among the first in the scholarly community to discuss what the Panthers had accomplished outside the realm of their defense posturing and violent confrontations with police, even beyond their contributions to the elevation of "Black Pride." Most important, she called for future work that would acknowledge the party's dynamic nature.[97] In doing so, Abron set the stage for a new era of writing about the Panthers.

The new era dawned with the publication in 1987 of a strikingly honest and moving autobiography by the New York Panther Assata Shakur (née JoAnne Chesimard). Though her life in the party, beginning in September 1970, occupies only one chapter, the book was foundational in its scope and analysis: here was an ex-Panther, a female, a critic whose focus was not Oakland.[98] In exile after her escape from prison in 1979 where she was serving a life sentence for the murder of a New Jersey state trooper earlier in the decade, Assata published her autobiography during a new Gilded Age in which issues of economic inequality, poor housing conditions, and police brutality faded from the public spotlight, while white vigilantism against urban blacks dominated headlines and found a regular audience among moviegoers.[99] At the same time, 1987 also witnessed Michael McGee, a Milwaukee councilman and former Black Panther, generate national headlines after he seemed to threaten violence to force area business leaders to create more jobs for the city's African Americans.[100] The following year, the rap group Public Enemy, which was based in New York, inaugurated hip-hop's penchant for 1960s-style radicalism in one of its early singles, "Rebel without a Pause." Over a James Brown sample, Chuck D boomed,

> Hard—my calling card
> Recorded and ordered—supporter of Chesimard
> Loud and proud kickin' live next poet supreme
> Loop a troop, bazooka, the scheme
> Flavor—a rebel in his own mind
> Supporter of my rhyme
> Designed to scatter a line of suckers who claim I do crime.[101]

A new generation who knew little about the Panthers but their reputation for militancy and violence would provide a ready readership for a spate of books about the now defunct organization.

Perhaps most important in the creation of that literature was the shooting death of Huey Newton by a small-time drug dealer on the streets of West Oakland in 1989. The cult of the party's founder had been a large part of its propaganda machine virtually from the beginning. Nothing so personified the group—arguably the era itself—than the famous poster of

Newton in an African wicker chair on a leopard skin rug, flanked by metal shields, holding a spear in one hand and a rifle in the other.[102] Though in his 1973 autobiography he tried to suggest that the party was larger than the man, his behavior in its aftermath suggests he had a chilling effect on both voices of dissent in the party and on the construction of its history.[103] Thus, for example, rumors and published reports suggest that Seale was violently expelled from the party—allegedly over a proposed movie deal about the Panthers—but *A Lonely Rage* avoids the specifics of his 1974 exodus altogether, choosing instead to speak in general terms of the pressures associated with leadership and suddenly feeling a middle-of-the-night urge to escape it all.[104] Moreover, in interviews for Henry Hampton's *Eyes on the Prize* in the late 1980s, Seale remained deferential to Newton, crediting him with most of the party's accomplishments.[105] Newton's demise, however—because the threat of reprisal was removed, because criticism of the party was no longer disloyalty to a legacy so identified with him, or simply because of the opportunity to capitalize on renewed interest—produced a spate of new writing on the Panthers.[106] During the last moments of his life, in classic Newton fashion, he allegedly declared, "You can kill my body, but you can't kill my soul. My soul will live for ever." But, out of his passing came, finally, some reflection on the good and the bad of the Panther "moment."[107]

Much of that reflection continued to focus on the bad. Even if, as one activist recalled, "belonging to the NAACP during the 1930s was like being a Black Panther in the 1960s," the image of Black Panthers as violent thugs remained a constant in the popular imagination, thanks to a journalistic tradition focusing especially on Newton's involvement in criminal activities from the drug trade to murder.[108] The new wave of Panther autobiographies ushered in by *Assata*—five in less than a decade—shed some light on these allegations.[109] More important, though, these books expanded the discussion of the party to areas not previously examined, especially the role of women and the rank and file. Wittingly or not, Assata had set in motion a readiness to make claims in her own right for those—her comrades and herself—who had labored under the banner of the Panther and not in the shadow of its leader. Assata's book, and especially Newton's murder, thus cleared the way for a fresh analysis. From 1968, the focus had been on Newton, on the national leadership, on Oakland, while developments were often more reflective of local conditions throughout the country.

Published in 1990, Earl Anthony's book *Spitting in the Wind* was the first of the post-Newton autobiographies. Unremarkable save for the admission to having lied in the first book, *Spitting in the Wind* was nonetheless important because it provided a view of the party's daily operation, classifications of its members, commentary on its social programs, and analysis of its troubled relationship with law enforcement from a person on the FBI payroll. The same year, Kim Kit Holder, a former New York Panther, completed a doctoral dissertation that provided a framework and sources for teachers wishing to teach the Panther movement. Clearly a response to growing interest in the party, the thesis also addressed some of the myths and fallacies about it. It included personal experiences from the New York story based on Holder's own involvement as well as interviews he did with ex-Panthers in 1988 and 1989.[110] Most notably, perhaps, writing in the immediate aftermath of Newton's death, Holder concluded, "The ideas of the B.P.P. . . . did not die with Huey on that Oakland street, since the ideas of the Party were never the sole possession of Newton."[111]

In many ways, Holder's was a dramatic leap forward, telling the story of the Panthers through the diverse experience of black women and men throughout the country.[112] De-centering the Oakland base and the south-to-west migration phenomenon of the standard tale, he offered a glimpse into the party's national appeal at the local level. Others followed. Frances Carter, who constituted a substantive portion of David Hilliard's 1993 book *This Side of Glory*, was from Connecticut, while Elaine Brown, though rising to the very pinnacle of the party during the mid-1970s, was from Philadelphia.[113] The most celebrated and influential of the Panther books, Brown's 1992 *A Taste of Power* complicated the male-centered narrative generally employed to tell its story. In its Oakland-centered account of party dynamics and in its focus on state repression as the main force upending what Brown claimed was the Panthers' most revolutionary dimension—its subversion of conventional sexual politics—her story is traditional. In its exploration of the BPP attempt, at least in her view, at upending traditional notions of gender, it was the most ambitious of Panther memoirs yet. At the same time, Brown's (and Hilliard's) brutal honesty about drug use, internal violence, sexual abuse, and other excesses, along with Anthony's revelations and, to a lesser extent, Holder's, invited criticism of Panther "pathology" that had been a staple of journalistic and government accounts from the very beginning.[114]

Brown and Hilliard especially, given their prominence in the party, opened the door to attacks from new, perhaps unlikely sources. In an explosive op-ed piece in the *New York Times*, for example, Alice Walker pounced on the Panthers' alleged sexism, even suggesting that the machismo of Panther men masked their homoerotic fantasies.[115] More generally, continuing criticism echoed the then thirty-year-old Moynihan Report, which had, in the aftermath of the devastating Watts rebellion, famously flagged the increasing number of out-of-wedlock births as a key to a social pathology in black "family structure" and, thus, the problem blocking successful integration of the African American community into American society.[116] From one perspective, the Black Panthers' social program represented a direct internal response to the problems of crime, drugs, single parenting, and poverty facing African Americans, poor whites, and other minorities in the inner cities. There was, therefore, more than a touch of irony in many party accounts that harped on the issues of violence, sex, and drugs in an attempt to underscore the "pathology" of its leaders, most notably that of Huey Newton. Moreover, if anyone understood the cycle of poverty, it was people such as Brown and Hilliard, who grew up under the conditions described if not fully appreciated by Moynihan.[117] Yet, the now generation-old critique received its fullest expression in Hugh Pearson's *The Shadow of the Panther*, published in 1994. The first journalistic account of the party in more than a dozen years, it was short on scholarship and long on interpretation.[118] Employing few oral interviews, exhibiting little sense of the historical context from which the Panthers emerged, and returning to the Newton-centered model (the book's subtitle is *Huey Newton and the Price of Black Power in America*), Pearson depicted the Panthers as an "on-going criminal enterprise" from the beginning of its existence whose significance was essentially a creation of the media.[119]

Ultimately, the reception Pearson's book received from mainstream historians would be almost uniformly uncritical.[120] To be sure, in a review immediately after publication, the historian Michael Kazin criticized several features of *The Shadow of the Panther*, not least its questionable use of sources. As Kazin observed, "Pearson's presentation lacks the empirical rigor a subject this controversial deserves. Too often he cites but one interview as evidence for a key fact; on occasion . . . he gives no source at all. . . . And, among numerous citations in the book to memoirs by David

Horowitz and Elaine Brown, I could locate only one corresponding page that is given." "Such sloppiness," Kazin charged, "smacks of a rush to publication; it tarnishes what is a serious attempt to grapple with a painful episode of our recent past."[121] And yet, as noted above, in Kazin's own survey of the era published six years later and touted as "the most comprehensive" of all the 1960s surveys, the principal source for the authors' few, negative comments about the Panthers is none other than Pearson himself. Less perplexing is David Burner's 1996 overview, *Making Peace with the 60s*, which describes Pearson's account as "written by a black journalist"—apparently, thus granting it authority—and then relies almost exclusively on Pearson to portray the Panthers as a violence-prone criminal clique.[122]

Meanwhile, key Panther texts from the party's heyday were reprinted.[123] Elsewhere, two political scientists depicted the Panthers as the black incarnation on the far left of the storied white supremacist Klan.[124] At the other end of the scholarly spectrum, the Panthers continued to be seen in an older formulation, as in James Davis's *Spying on America*, a rudimentary account of government repression adding nothing new to the story of the "violence prone Panthers," as the author identified them. Still, by 1994, the renewed interest in the party had resurrected talk of a feature film—the very issue that had allegedly led to Seale's expulsion back in 1974. Envisioning the same success Spike Lee's *Malcolm X* enjoyed in 1992, Gramercy Pictures released *Panther* in 1995. Claiming a desire to "inform a new generation about a group of black activists who made a difference in the 1960s," Melvin Van Peebles and his son, Mario, produced a fictionalized version of the Panther story, which Bobby Seale would refer to as "bootleg fiction." In negotiations with Warner Brothers about a movie of his own, Seale declared, "The true story has not been told."[125]

The film may have inspired a host of new biographies and autobiographies with a similar bent, by definition problematic for historians. William Lee Brent's *Long Time Gone* of 1996, for example, noted on the book jacket that "interest in the Black Panther Party has grown in recent years" with the movie *Panther* including "a scene that was in part based (in a widely fictive version) on the gas station stickup" that prompted Brent to leave the country. In fine print above the copyright information is an author's note, which reads, "While this is a work of nonfiction, some names have been changed."[126] The Panthers were not the first to employ this technique, of course; journalists had been doing it for a generation. Whether such liberties in "storytelling" sought to mitigate criminal responsibility, to self-aggrandize, to augment the strength or weakness of the party, or simply to sell books, ironically they paralleled disturbing developments in historical studies, as historians too were increasingly making up dialogue and embellishing their accounts by the 1990s.[127]

The Promise and Problems of a New History
of the Black Panther Party The Late 1990s to the Present

Only in the late 1990s did a new generation of historians, using the methods of their craft, turn their attention, finally, to the Black Panther Party.[128] By 1998, a large, path-breaking anthology called *The Black Panther Party [Reconsidered]* appeared, with the most intriguing essays written by historians—Tracey Matthews on gender and Nik Pal Singh on the black radical tradition—though ex-Panthers and scholars outside the field dominate the book.[129] At about the same time, however, a rash of doctoral dissertations with history department pedigrees were completed, marking a new departure.[130]

The "class of '98"—whose work bore published fruit as early as 1999—paved the way for more doctoral work.[131] This new scholarship produced new insights. Already in 1997, Jennifer Bradford Smith and Yohuru Williams had chronicled the BPP's impact on the worldwide freedom struggle, while Jeffrey Ogbar complicated the party's image in a comparison with the Nation of Islam, using previously untapped resources.[132] The following year, these studies were augmented by dissertations on a host of issues, including the role of violence and gender relations, the party's relationship with the larger black power movement, and perhaps most important its local influence.[133] By the opening years of the new century, historians plumbed BPP educational innovations, echoing in a far more sophisticated manner Holder's earlier work.[134] Others turned to close examinations of politics, offering innovative perspectives not seen before in Panther studies.[135] Still others, such as Matthew Countryman on Philadelphia and Rhonda Williams on Baltimore, though not focusing on the Panthers per se, provided models of deeper research and richer analysis that Panther studies require.[136] At the same time, the repression model received attention in Rose Thevenin's "The Single Greatest Threat," while the question of violence in the party's rise and fall nationally received sustained treatment in Curtis Austin's *Up Against the Wall: Violence in the Making and Unmaking of the Black Panther Party.*[137] And, if the most promising new work attended to the local community, Chicago, Atlanta, and even New Haven, Connecticut, now came under scrutiny. Still, only a handful of communities outside of California had received any published attention.[138] And, in popular music, Huey Newton remained the standard frame of reference; in popular history, the national story and murder mysteries remained standard fare; in the popular imagination, photographs—and now art—remained a standard way of accessing the Panther legacy.[139]

Indeed, despite the recent literature's promise, there continue to be problems in the new Panther history. At one side are continued attempts to tell the national story without sufficient immersion in the local context, a research decision that can lead to an over-reliance on government reports that constituted much Panther history in the first phase of writing about the organization. Thus, a recent doctoral dissertation on party ideology actually adopts the *argument* of *Gun-Barrel Politics*, as well as its data and sources.[140] Moreover, the fascination with the Oakland story continues.[141] At the other side are attempts to tell the local story without a careful and critical use of oral sources. A recent study of "performative violence" in the 1960s, for example, contains a chapter on the Detroit Panthers, a group almost entirely lost to historians.[142] Here, the historian reveals that, after months of searching for ex-Panthers to interview, he could find only one person who would talk to him, the lone respondent to an advertisement the author placed in a local black newspaper. That source, identified by a pseudonym in the text, agreed to be interviewed if he remained anonymous—not only to the readers, but to the author as well.[143]

Meanwhile, the Panther memoir-histories roll off the presses. Among the most recent are those by Afeni Shakur, a veteran of the New York 21 now more well-known for her late son, Tupac, than for her days as a Panther; by the relatively unknown North Carolina Panther Evan D. Hopkins; and by perhaps the most famous living ex-Panther, Mumia Abu-Jamal, who is in jail for killing a Philadelphia policeman nearly a quarter century ago.[144] Each in its own way reveals the pitfalls awaiting professional historians who seek to make sense of the Panther "moment." As the philosopher Paul Ricoeur cautions us, "Testimony constitutes the fundamental transitional structure between memory and history"—the three ought never to be confused.[145]

The Shakur book offers little about her biographical arc into the BPP that cannot be gleaned from the stories she told in *Look for Me in the Whirlwind* more than a generation ago. It does suggest that the Panthers' long, tortuous relationship with the media, especially entertainment media, continues as both a part of party history and as a potential obstacle to historical scholarship about it. The same year that the Van Peebles released *Panther*, the television actress Jasmine Guy met Afeni Shakur at a New York City courthouse where Tupac was being tried in a sexual assault case. Guy had been writing a screenplay whose protagonist was a composite of Shakur and the most famous female black revolutionary of the day, Angela Davis, and was hoping for a few insights.[146] The result, a decade later, is a book in which Guy, who is as much the story as is her subject, repeatedly ignores what might be of interest to historians: Shakur's own apparent confusion about what attracted her to the Panthers, their community programs or their defiant posture; her insistence that it was not COIN-TELPRO but the Panthers themselves that did them in; her inconsistent reporting on Panther gender relations; her admission to having shot at a man in a tollbooth during an armed robbery, apparently before her arrest in the Panther 21 case; her lack of attention to the split between Newton and Cleaver and the critical role that the New York chapter played in that momentous event in the party's history.[147] What Guy does not ignore— indeed, repeatedly comes back to throughout the book—is what a terrific movie Afeni Shakur's life would make.[148]

Afeni Shakur was born in North Carolina and became a Panther in New York during its expansive phase, gaining national attention because of her charisma, which surfaced during her court case. Evans D. Hopkins was born in Virginia and became a Panther in North Carolina as a high school student during its contracting phase in the fall of 1971. Though he spent time in Oakland as well, he never achieved fame as a Panther; moreover, the most interesting details about the party come in the first part of his memoir, which tells the local story in precisely the kind of detail of use to the historian: precise numbers involved, membership classification and the process of becoming a member, the look and feel of individual members, the nature and evolution and party activities and ideology. Unfortunately, there is a disclaimer reminding us of the pitfalls of Panther storytelling.

A "Note to the Reader" following the copyright page reads, "This book is a memoir of my experiences. The names of some persons have been changed, *as have certain physical characteristics and other descriptive details*" (emphasis added).

Among the most significant of the recent crop of memoir-histories is Mumia's *We Want Freedom*, which seeks to tell both a personal story and a history of the party generally.[149] Unfortunately, though remarkable given the conditions under which it was written, the book does not deliver on either score. First, his own direct testimony comprises barely a quarter of the volume, and the Philadelphia story—he joined there in mid-1968—even less. Moreover, much of the latter was covered in an early interview with the local captain, Reggie Schell, which can be found in Dick Cluster's *They Should Have Served That Cup of Coffee*, published in 1979. More important, while broad in sweep and often movingly written, the book offers a patina of history, overtly political in its celebration of much of the Panther story, employing (often excessively quoting from) mostly old and one-sided secondary sources, accepting uncritically primary sources (from Seale and Cleaver to the ex-Panther women he interviewed), often omitting the specific historical context, and sometimes paying too little attention to chronology, occasionally to the point of being discursive.[150] Though making judgments about both personalities and policies, the volume tells far more than it analyzes.

Kathleen Cleaver, a former member of the Panther Central Committee, raises the problem of "recreating Black Panther history" in her introduction to Mumia's book, even referring to "what has been passed on as 'history.'"[151] The warning seems aimed, at least in part, at those "young scholars [who] more and more are devoting attention to specific aspects of the Black Panther Party."[152] For her, this is "not a simple task" because of COINTELPRO tampering with documents of the era. Her prime example is Anthony's *Picking Up the Gun*.[153] As it happens, when Mumia discusses the BPP's struggles with other black liberation groups in its early years, one of his key sources is none other than that book.[154] But, more pertinent for our purposes is that it seems not to have occurred to either Cleaver or Mumia—at least, they do not acknowledge it—that, for the historian, one of the reasons writing Panther history is "not a simple task" is the problematic nature of Panther sources themselves, whether at the time or today.

Indeed, if ex-Panther voices, along with others who have stories to tell, are inevitable in telling the Panther story, they cannot tell it by themselves. Surely Allessandro Portelli is correct that "the unique and precious element which oral sources force upon the historian and which no other sources possess in equal measure is the speaker's subjectivity."[155] Historians of the Black Panther Party, then, must be as critical in their use of interviews as they are about written documents. In tandem, used for neither celebration nor condemnation, those sources might finally open to us some *historical* understanding of how those involved experienced that moment of American radicalism and revolution, and even more certainly how that moment was experienced in all its variety at the level where it mattered most—in the local community. That would mark a historiographical breakthrough about not only the Black Panthers, but the era they helped define.

Notes

1 Eric Foner, ed. (for the American Historical Association), *The New American History* (Philadelphia: Temple University Press, 1990), vii.

2 An early synthetic treatment is "The Practice of American History: A Special Issue," *Journal of American History* 81, no. 3 (December 1994).

3 For an important corrective to the notion that the generation of the 1960s and their students created something brand new, see Ellen Fitzpatrick, *History's Memory: Writing America's Past, 1880–1980* (Cambridge, Mass.: Harvard University Press, 2002).

4 An excellent example is the recent sponsorship (October 2004) by the Newberry Library Seminar in Labor History, in conjunction with the Labor and Working Class History Association, of the paper "Prostitution Blues: Black Women's Sex Work as a Musical Theme, 1920–1940."

5 We do not attempt an exhaustive literature review here; rather, we seek to conceptualize how the Panthers have been treated over time in order to find a way forward.

6 We are deliberately vague regarding numbers precisely because much of what we know comes from journalistic accounts with a national focus, relying on government officials and Panthers with reason to inflate or deflate. Alternatively, Panther memoirs are imprecise about involvement, on what specific basis, at particular moments in time—typical historians' concerns. Because of the complex local context where Panthers—or Panther-like groups—appeared, only in-depth community studies can clarify questions about participation in the Panther movement. For one attempt by a sociologist to count chapters, branches, and members, see Charles A. Pinderhughes, "Periodizing the Black Panther Party" (paper delivered at the Black Panther Party in Historical Perspective conference, Wheelock College, Boston, June 11–13, 2003, possession of the authors). On the Panthers as a "vanguard," see, e.g., *The Guardian*, April 19, 1969, reprinted in Philip S. Foner, ed., *The Black Panthers Speak* (1970; repr., New York: Da Capo, 1995), 225–29; U.S. House of Representatives, Committee on Internal Security (CIS), *Gun-Barrel Politics: The Black Panther Party, 1966–1971*, 92nd Congress, 1st sess. (Washington, D.C.: U.S. Government Printing Office, 1971), 94; Julian E. Williams, *The Black Panthers Are Not Black . . . They Are Red!* (Tulsa: Christian Crusade, 1970), 21; Special Agent in Charge, Chicago FBI, Re GG Letter, May 21, 1969, in "Black, White, SDS, Mobe and Peace," Roz Payne Archives, Burlington, Vt.

7 Foner, *The Black Panthers Speak*, xii–xxiv.

8 Hoover's statement quoted in Kenneth O'Reilly, *"Racial Matters": The FBI's Secret File on Black America, 1960–1972* (New York: Free Press, 1989), 290; Ward Churchill, "'To Disrupt, Discredit and Destroy': The FBI's Secret War Against the Black Panther Party," in *Liberation, Imagination, and the Black Panther Party: A New Look at the Panthers and Their Legacy*, ed. Kathleen Cleaver and George Katsiaficas, 182–83 (New York: Routledge, 2001).

9 CIS, *Gun-Barrel Politics*, 143.

10 "Editor's Note" to "The Biography of Huey P. Newton," reprinted in Mitchell Goodman, comp., *The Movement Toward a New America: The Beginnings of a Long Revolution (A Collage), a What?* (New York: Alfred A. Knopf, 1970), 202. Seale's book was eventually published under the title *Seize the Time: The Story of the Black Panther Party and Huey P. Newton*, ed. Art Goldberg (New York: Vintage, 1970). Two years later, activist Julian Bond made a similar case in his preface to the first collection of published Panther writings and speeches: "So much has been written and spoken about the Black Panthers in the press and over the radio and TV that one might suppose that most people know what the organization really stands for and seeks to achieve. But this is far from the case. Only rarely does the press report what the Panthers are actually saying and doing. . . . The result is most people have obtained their impression of the Panthers from statements issued by those who wish to see them eliminated as a factor in American life" (Foner, *The Black Panthers Speak*, xix).

11 After more than a decade of scholarly overviews, Maurice Isserman and Michael Kazin, *America Divided: The Civil War of the 1960s* (New York: Oxford University Press, 2000) represented a historiographical watershed. The maturing of the monographic literature was signaled two years earlier by Doug Rossinow's *The Politics of Authenticity: Liberalism, Christianity, and the New Left in America* (New York: Columbia University Press, 1998); a foreshadowing of a new day for

the history of the 1960s came several years earlier with David Farber's collection, *The Sixties: From Memory to History* (Chapel Hill: University of North Carolina Press, 1994). For a meditation on the state of the field, ca. 2000, see Jama Lazerow, "1960–1974," in *A Companion to 20th Century America*, ed. Stephen J. Whitfield, 87–101 (Malden, Mass.: Blackwell, 2004). An earlier, more popular rendering is Rick Perlstein, "Who Owns the Sixties? The Opening of a Scholarly Generation Gap," *Linguafranca* 6 (1996): 30–37. More evidence of the coming of age of 1960s historiography is the appearance, in 2004, of H-1960s@H-NET.MSU.EDU. For the most recent overview, which is broader than its title would suggest, see M. J. Heale, "The Sixties as History: A Review of the Political Historiography," *Reviews in American History* 33, no. 1 (March 2005): 133–52. An excellent meditation on the 1960s from a broadened New Left perspective, including commentary on the Panthers, is Van Gosse, "A Movement of Movements: The Definition and Periodization of the New Left," in *A Companion to Post-1945 America*, ed. Jean-Christophe Agnew and Roy Rosenzweig, 277–302 (Panthers on 284–86, especially 286) (Malden: Blackwell, 2002). For a less sophisticated audience, see Van Gosse, introduction to his *The Movements of the New Left, 1950–1975: A History with Documents*, Bedford Series in History and Culture (Boston: Bedford/St. Martin's, 2005), 1–38 (Panthers on 19).

12 Here, we employ the expansive temporal definition of the civil rights era increasingly popular among historians, e.g., Nik Singh, *Black Is a Country: Race and the Unfinished Struggle for Democracy* (Cambridge, Mass.: Harvard University Press, 2004). See, too, Jacquelyn Dowd Hall, "The Long Civil Rights Movement and the Political Uses of the Past," revised version of her presidential address to the Organization of American Historians, Boston, March 27, 2004, in *Journal of American History* 91, no. 4 (March 2005): 1233–63. For abundant evidence of the volume and maturity of African American historiography, see Evelyn Brooks Higginbotham, ed., *The Harvard Guide to African-American History* (Cambridge, Mass.: Harvard University Press, 2001). Only the "International Relations" and "Politics" sections regularly rival "African-American" in the "Recent Scholarship" lists at the back of every *Journal of American History*.

13 Mari Jo Buhle et al., eds., *Encyclopedia of the American Left* (Urbana: University of Illinois Press, 1992), 415–19 (League); 96–98 (BPP).

14 Robin D. G. Kelley, *Freedom Dreams: The Black Radical Imagination* (Boston: Beacon, 2002), chap. 3 ("'Roaring from the East': Third World Dreaming"), 60–109.

15 John Blum et al., *The National Experience: A History of the United States*, 8th ed. (New York: Harcourt Brace, 1993), 854–55, as of this writing the latest edition of this text.

16 James Roark et al., *The American Promise: A History of the United States*, 36th ed. (Boston: Bedford/St. Martin's, 2005), xxxi, 1040. For a list of the "most used textbooks in U.S. survey courses, ranked by course adoptions, spring 2004," see table 2 in Daniel J. Cohen, "By the Book: Assessing the Place of Textbooks in U.S. Survey Courses," *Journal of American History* 91, no. 4 (March 2005): 1410.

17 John Garraty, *The American Nation: A History of the United States*, 9th ed. (New York: Longman, 1998), 834. The language is unchanged in the 11th edition, updated in 2005 by Mark C. Carnes and John Garraty (827). Actually, it was the white liberals and radicals in the Peace and Freedom Party who ran Cleaver for president. For background, see Joel Wilson, "Invisible Cages: Racialized Politics and the Panther-Peace and Freedom Alliance," in *In Search of the Black Panther Party: New Perspectives on a Revolutionary Movement*, ed. Jama Lazerow and Yohuru Williams, 191–222 (Durham, N.C.: Duke University Press, 2006). Brown was made minister of justice of the party at the outset of a short-lived "alliance" with the Student Non-Violent Coordinating Committee (SNCC)—Cleaver called it a "merger," to the immediate chagrin of many SNCC leaders, who thought of it as a "coalition"—in February 1968. By midsummer of that year, relations had so deteriorated that all official links were severed. The Panthers are yoked to Brown, in a fashion, in another text, which depicts the Panthers only in their call for "picking up the gun." "H. Rap Brown," *America: Past and Present* proclaims, "told an African American crowd in Cambridge, Maryland, to 'get your guns' and 'burn this town down'; Huey Newton, one of the founders of the militant Black Panther party, proclaimed, 'We make the statement, quoting Chairman Mao, that Political Power comes through the Barrel of a Gun.'" The picture accompanying this page of the text is a poster for the Woodstock music festival of 1969 ("3 Days of Peace and Music"). See Robert A. Divine, *America: Past and Present*, 7th ed. (New York: Pearson, 2005), 883. For another text that empha- sizes only the Panthers' romance with violence, again associating them with Brown, see William J. Rorabaugh et al., *America's Promise: A Concise History of the United States* (Latham, Md.: Rowman and Littlefield, 2004), 2:611. Here, "[Stokely] Carmichael's successor in SNCC, H. Rap Brown, used even more in- flammatory language [than Carmichael's] by declaring, 'Don't be trying to love that honky [white man] to death. Shoot him to death.'" "In Oakland, California," continues the next and final paragraph of this section, called "Militants Speak Out, 1963–1966," "Huey Newton and Bobby Seale organized the Black Panther Party in 1967 [*sic*] to urge blacks to undertake 'armed self-defense.' They quoted the Chinese communist leader Mao Zedong's statement that 'political power comes through the barrel of a gun.'"

18 James West Davidson et al., *Nation of Nations: A Narrative History of the American Republic*, 5th ed. (Boston: McGraw-Hill, 2005), 990. The figure of 2,000 likely comes from CIS, *Gun-Barrel Politics*, 69 and n. 1, which described "an organization of from 1,500 to 2,000 members," the latter estimate from a book by ex-Panther Earl Anthony, the former from the testimony of the committee's chief investigator, Robert Horner. Anthony's figure is from his *Picking Up the Gun: A Report on the Black Panthers* (New York: Dial, 1970), viii, heavily used in CIS, *Gun-Barrel Politics.* In his *Spitting in the Wind: The True Story Behind the Violent Legacy of the Black Panther Party* (Malibu: Roundtable, 1990), Anthony revealed that he had been an FBI informant inside the party. As for the civil rights movement, recent scholarship has dramatically altered the dichotomous view offered by Davidson. See, e.g., Jeanne Theoharis's introduction to *Freedom North: Black Freedom Struggles Outside the South, 1940–1980,* ed. Jeanne Theoharis and Komozi Woodard, with Matthew Countryman, 1–15 (New York: Palgrave Macmillan, 2003). For a current text rendition of the Panthers as "entirely outside the mainstream civil rights movement," see Alan Brinkley, *American History: A Survey,* 11th ed. (Boston: McGraw-Hill, 2003), 840.

19 George Brown Tindall and David E. Shi, *America: A Narrative History,* 6th ed. (New York: Norton, 2005), 1368. An earlier (brief) version (1998) used more redolent language: "[The Panthers] terrified the public by wearing bandeleros and carrying rifles." There, the authors also incorrectly associated the BPP with "the separatist demands of Marcus Garvey"; in fact, the Panthers not only opposed separatism but were frequently at odds with other radical black organizations precisely because they consistently called for coalition with like-minded whites. But the same kind of false linkage of the Panthers to the separatism of the black power movement can be found in Pauline Maier et al., *Inventing America: A History of the United States* (New York: Norton, 2003), 2:961. David Goldfield et al., *The American Journey: A History of the United States* (Upper Saddle River, N.J.: Prentice Hall, 2001), 922, discusses the Panthers under the subheading "Minority Separatism," following a section on Malcolm X, a black Muslim who "emphasized the African cultural heritage and economic self-help and proclaimed himself an extremist for black rights." The Panther section begins, "The Black Panthers pursued similar goals." Seen as having had a political program, contra the Watts rioters, the Panthers were "shaken" by Newton's 1967 jailing, Cleaver's 1968 exile, and Fred Hampton's 1969 death in "an unjustified police raid." They "imploded when they attracted thugs and shakedown artists as well as visionaries," even though they did survive, if in radically reduced numbers, through the 1970s and into the early 1980s.

20 Jacqueline Jones et al., *Created Equal: A Social History of the United States* (New York: Longman, 2003), 884.

21 John M. Murrin et al., *Liberty, Equality, Power: A History of the American People* (Fort Worth, Tex.: Harcourt Brace, 1999), 1009.

22 Gary B. Nash et al., *The American People: Creating a Nation and a Society,* 6th ed. (New York: Longman, 2004), 981. Here, H. Rap Brown as an exhorter of violence *follows* the Panthers. Finishing a paragraph that begins with

"Black Power led to demands for more drastic action," the authors write, "H. Rap Brown . . . became known for his statement that 'violence is as American as cherry pie.'"

23 America Social History Project, *Who Built America? Working People and the Nation's Economy, Politics, Culture, and Society*, 2nd ed. (New York: Worth, 2000), 2:630.

24 John Mack Faragher et al., *Out of Many: A History of the American People*, 3rd ed. (Upper Saddle River, N.J.: Prentice Hall, 2000), 897.

25 Mary Beth Norton et al., *A People and a Nation: A History of the United States*, 7th ed. (Boston: Houghton Mifflin, 2005), 848. An earlier version referred to the Panthers' "black nationalism," as opposed to their "black separatism" (5th ed., 938); the latter characterization is simply contrary to fact. The idea that the Panthers "blended" ideologies is not common in the texts; more typical is Faragher, *Out of Many*, which sees the Panthers as the "boldest expression of a new Black Power movement" that "derived from a century-long tradition of black nationalism" (895, 897). Maier, in *Inventing America*, does note that the Panthers "preached black nationalism and socialism and set up educational and breakfast programs," but then quickly adds, "its members also illegally armed themselves and patrolled the streets to monitor the police" (961). Aside from the reversal of Faragher's emphasis on guns versus butter, *Inventing America* is doubly misleading here: most Panther guns were legally obtained and carried, and their patrols were generally only in Oakland in the first months of the organization's existence.

26 James A. Henretta et al., *America's History*, 5th ed. (Boston: Bedford/St. Martin's, 2004), 861.

27 Significantly, Foner, whose work has been deeply influenced by Marxism and other radical traditions, does not even mention the Black Panthers in his masterful synthesis of American history, *The Story of American Freedom* (New York: Norton, 1998). He does, however, have a paragraph on them in his new text, *Give Me Liberty! An American History* (New York: Norton, 2005), 2:997–98. Following the standard form (under the heading "The Changing Black Movement"), subheadings include "The Ghetto Uprisings," "Malcolm X," and finally "The Rise of Black Power," where the Panthers appear. "Notorious for advocating armed self defense in response to police brutality," they "alarmed whites by wearing military garb, although they also ran health clinics, schools, and children's breakfast programs. But internal disputes and a campaign against the Black Panthers by police and the FBI, which left several leaders dead in shootouts, destroyed the organization" (998).

28 To be sure, the Panthers enjoy expanded, sometimes nuanced treatment in texts dedicated specifically to the African American experience or to those designed for courses in black and Africana studies, though even here the narrative is problematic. In passages from substantial paragraphs to several pages, these volumes do offer novice readers some sense of the party's complex origins and nature, the larger context in which it emerged, its combination of armed self-defense and community programs, and the arc of its development from the mid-to-late 1960s to the late 1970s. Moreover, some of these texts draw on not only recent anthologies but some recent local histories. Still, the authors disagree about how to situate the Panthers (as a black power group or not, for example). More important, a surprisingly discursive narrative style can easily mislead (precisely when the Panthers became a Marxist-Leninist organization, for example). Finally, errors of commission and omission mar even these texts (who led the Sacramento action in 1967, the source and nature of the Panthers' sometimes violent struggles with other organizations, for example). See Robin Kelley and Joe William Trotter, *The African-American Experience* (Boston: Houghton Mifflin, 2001); Vincent Harding, Robin D. G. Kelley, and Earl Lewis, "We Changed the World, 1945–1970," in *To Make the World Anew: A History of African-Americans* (New York: Oxford, 2000); Clay Carson, Emma J. Lapansky-Werner, and Gary B. Nash, *African-American Lives: The Struggle for Freedom* (New York: Pearson Education, 2005); Nell Erwin Painter, *Creating Americans: African-American History and Its Meanings, 1619 to the Present* (New York: Oxford, 2006); John Hope Franklin and Alfred A. Moss Jr., *From Slavery to Freedom: A History of African Americans*, 8th ed. (1947; repr., Boston: McGraw-Hill, 2000); Maulana Karenga, *Introduction to Black Studies* (Los Angeles: University of Sankore Press, 2002).

29 Faragher's *Out of Many* lists the autobiographies of Elaine Brown (*A Taste of Power: A Black Woman's Story* [New York: Doubleday, 1992]), which is most revealing on the Panthers of the 1970s, and of David Hilliard (with Lewis Cole, *This Side of Glory: The Autobiography of David Hilliard and the Story of the Black Panther Party* [Boston: Little, Brown, 1993]), which contains a wealth of information—sometimes undigested—on the larger story. A couple of the texts list Eldridge Cleaver's *Soul on Ice*, which, though published when Cleaver was a Panther, was written before he joined and deals with other issues. The others list only general histories of the 1960s or race struggles (discussed in this section) that do touch on the Panthers and may have contributed to the authors' perspectives. Finally, we cannot rule out the possibility—especially given the striking similarity in approach and language of some of these passages—that some text authors are simply lifting their view of the Panthers from other texts.

30 Allen Matusow, *The Unraveling of America: A History of Liberalism in the 1960s* (New York: Harper and Row, 1984). Though now over twenty years old—a long time in current historiographical terms—*The Unraveling of America* is a standard reference for scholars working in the field. See, for example, Kevin Boyle's review of Isserman and Kazin, *America Divided*, in *Reviews in American History* 29 (June 2001): 304–9, in which he names Matusow's book among the top three of the best overviews of the 1960s (309n3).

31 Matusow, *The Unraveling of America*, 367, 368, 371, 373.

32 Todd Gitlin, *The Sixties: Years of Hope, Days of Rage* (Toronto: Bantam, 1987), 242, 285–438.

33 Ibid., 348, 318.

34 Ibid., 349.

35 Ibid., 350, 351.

36 Wini Breines, "Who's New Left?" *Journal of American History* 75 (1988): 528–45.

37 David Farber, *The Age of Great Dreams: America in the 1960s* (New York: Hill and Wang, 1994). In addition to his essay collection, *The Sixties*, Farber is, with Beth Bailey, the editor of *The Columbia Guide to America in the 1960s* (New York: Columbia University Press, 2001).

38 Farber, *The Age of Great Dreams*, 206–8.

39 Ibid., 208.

40 David Burner, *Making Peace with the 60s* (Princeton, N.J.: Princeton University Press, 1996), 69–71. In addition to his perspective, there is the problem of Burner's rendition of the facts. Among the slight errors, for example, is the incorrect assertion that Newton was released from jail in 1969 (August 1970), that Cleaver was in jail for rape (assault), and that the alleged beating of Panther dissenters in 1967 was to enforce agreement on a future Free Huey movement (disagreements with SNCC in the summer of 1968, after the Free Huey movement had begun, were about bringing the case of Panther repression before the United Nations). Later (72), Burner incorrectly associates the Panthers with the Republic of New Afrika, and the latter's goal of establishing a separate black state in the South, something the Panthers explicitly and publicly opposed. Meanwhile, in this regard, the use of the Brown quotation is somewhat confounding in light of Burner's statement on the previous page (69) that "the Panthers generally welcomed white radicals as allies and held a vision of world revolution among all peoples." Finally, Newton is incorrectly identified as an ex–Black Muslim (142).

41 Ibid., 71.

42 Isserman and Kazin, *America Divided*, 177–78, 247, 275. The millennialist notion was likely taken from Hugh Pearson, *The Shadow of the Panther: Huey Newton and the Price of Black Power in America* (Reading, Mass.: Addison-Wesley, 1994), 153.

43 The one serious historical monograph used by Matusow, though viewing the Panthers from the outside in, is Clayborne Carson, *In Struggle: SNCC and the Black Awakening of the 1960s* (Cambridge, Mass.: Harvard University Press, 1981).

44 Pearson, *The Shadow of the Panther*; Peter Collier and David Horowitz, *Destructive Generation: Second Thoughts about the '60s* (Los Angeles: Second Thoughts Books, 1989), esp. chap. 4 ("Baddest: The Life and Times of Huey P.

Newton"). Also, see Horowitz's ostensible review of Elaine Brown's autobiography, "Black Murder Inc.," *Heterodoxy* (March 1993), 1, 11–15.

45 Kate Coleman and Paul Avery, "The Party's Over," *New Times*, July 10, 1978, 23–47; Coleman, "Souled Out," *New West*, May 19, 1980, 17–27. Horowitz makes the claim that he was the source for Coleman's original exposé in "Op-ed: Reply to Paul Berman," *FrontPageMagazine.com*, January 8, 1998.

46 Pearson, *The Shadow of the Panther*, 347.

47 And, earlier, Isserman said about *Destructive Generation*: "On the whole the book tries too hard to be the *Witness* of the 1980s, but it has some insights to offer on such topics as the Weather Underground and the Black Panthers." "*Review Article*: The Not-So-Dark and Bloody Ground; New Works on the 1960s," *American Historical Review* 94 (October 1989): 991n2. Another key overview that makes liberal use of Pearson, as well as of the earlier work by Matusow, is James T. Patterson's prize-winning entry in the Oxford History of the United States, *Grand Expectations: The United States, 1945–1974* (New York: Oxford University Press, 1996). Here, Patterson *begins* his discussion of the Panthers with their community programs, leaping deep into their history—in order to dispense with them: "[The Panthers] set up free health clinics, ran educational programs, and offered free breakfasts for schoolchildren. The emphasis, however, was military" (650). And so, "the Panthers were not so much a political group as they were angry young men attracted to Third World revolutionary ideology, paramilitary activities, and in some cases violence" (660). Oddly, Patterson claims that the Panthers "had virtually broken up" (660) by 1969 (two years before they underwent a damaging schism and three before they called their minions back to Oakland) and that by 1968 (661) they had some five thousand members (a substantial inflation from the standard estimate of two thousand at their peak).

48 Review of David Horowitz, *Radical Son: A General Odyssey*, in *The New Leader*, December 16, 1996, 5–7.

49 Review of Isserman and Kazin, *America Divided*, in *New York Times Sunday Book Review*, January 16, 2000, 10.

50 William O'Neill, *The New Left: A History*, American History Series (Wheeling, W.Va.: Harlan Davidson, 2001), 34n40.

51 Mario Van Peebles, Ula Taylor, and J. Tarika Lewis, *Panther: A Pictorial History of the Black Panthers and the Story Behind the Film* (New York: New Market Press, 1995), 136.

52 The civil rights literature is voluminous. For a recent overview, see Steven J. Lawson's updated version of his 1991 essay, "Freedom Ten, Freedom Now: The Historiography of the Civil Rights Movement," in his *Civil Rights Crossroads: Nation, Community, and the Black Freedom Struggle* (Lexington: University Press of Kentucky, 2003), 3–28. As Patrick Jones puts it in his review of a new book on

the civil rights movement in Cambridge, Maryland, the current watchwords are "complexity" and "multiple and often contradictory currents," quoting the author as calling for a civil rights history that is seen as "a varied phenomenon, replete with insolvable paradoxes and contradictions." Review of Peter B. Levy, *Civil War on Race Street: The Civil Rights Movement in Cambridge, Maryland* (Gainesville: University Press of Florida, 2003), in H-1960s@H-NET.MSU.EDU (July 2004).

53 National Laymen's Council of the Church League of America, comp., *The Black Panthers in Action* (Wheaton, Ill.: The Church League of America, 1969), 5.

54 Ibid., 31.

55 Tom Wolfe, *Radical Chic and Mau-Mauing the Flak Catchers* (New York: Bantam, 1970). Another in the same genre—not simply in characterization, but in fictionalizing—is Gail Sheehy's dismissive book on the New Haven murder trial of Bobby Seale, Erika Huggins, and seven others, *Panthermania: The Clash of Black Against Black in One American City* (New York: Harper and Row, 1971). For a more sympathetic view that depicted the Panthers in one location (New York City) as an expression of local needs and issues rather than as some alien life form injected from without, see Murray Kempton's story of the Panther 21 case, *Briar Patch: The People of the State of New York Against Lumumba Shakur et al.* (New York: Dell, 1973). The media's role is analyzed in Michael E. Staub, "Black Panthers, New Journalism, and the Rewriting of the Sixties," *representations* 57 (winter 1997): 52–72; and, more comprehensively, in Edward P. Morgan, "Media Culture and the Public Memory of the Black Panther Party," in Lazerow and Williams, *In Search of the Black Panther Party*, 324–73. Jane Rhodes's *Framing the Black Panthers: The Spectacular Rise of a Black Power Icon* (New York: New Press, 2007) arrived too late for inclusion in this essay.

56 Eldridge Cleaver, *Soul On Ice* (New York: McGraw-Hill, A Ramparts Book, 1968). The first person Cleaver thanked in his short acknowledgments to the book was Edward M. Keating, the founder and publisher of *Ramparts* (vii). The manuscript was completed in the spring of 1967, as is clear from the date of its first introduction by Maxwell Geismar in June 1967 (xv). Cleaver explained how he "fell in love with the Black Panther Party immediately upon [his] first encounter with it" in "The Courage to Kill: Meeting the Panthers" (June 15, 1968) in his *Post-Prison Writings and Speeches*, ed. with an appraisal by Robert Scheer (New York: Random House, 1967, 1968, 1969), 23–39 (quotation, 23). The latter was also a Ramparts Book. Newton told his own story about trying (at first unsuccessfully) to recruit Cleaver to the Panthers in *Revolutionary Suicide*, with the assistance of J. Herman Blake (1973; repr., New York: Writers and Readers, 1995), 128–33. Meanwhile, three thousand miles away in New York City, Shaba Om, one of the Panther 21, claimed to have first *seen* the Panthers when he spied them on the cover of *Ramparts* magazine at a newsstand in Midtown. See Kuwasi

Balagoon et al., *Look for Me in the Whirlwind: The Collective Autobiography of the New York 21* (New York: Vintage, 1971), 285. One of the lower-level editors at *Ramparts* in these early days was one of the party's key detractors in later years, David Horowitz.

57 Gene Marine, *The Black Panthers: Eldridge Cleaver, Huey Newton, Bobby Seale; A Compelling Study of the Angry Young Revolutionaries Who Have Shaken a Black Fist at White America* (New York: Signet, 1969). Examples of Marine's self-identification and his target audience are in his introductory and concluding chapters (esp. 9, 214). He thanks *Ramparts* for "thinking up the idea" (10–11).

58 Ibid., 11. See his other claims to have been frightened by the Panthers (212, 224). His last sentence, "I hope you are, too," as well as his frequent direct address to the reader, suggest that at least part of his intent was to call for an end to police brutality and white racism. He claims to have "done [his] best to *report* on the origins and development of the Black Panther Party and on its expressed and implied philosophies," while being sympathetic to them (10, 11). Another journalistic account, Don A. Schanche's *The Panther Paradox: A Liberal's Dilemma* (New York: David A. McKay, 1970), bears a patina of resemblance to Marine's in its call for an end to "police misbehavior" and "the germs of the disease of racism" among whites, but the book's tone is entirely different, while offering little that is new about the nature and shape of the party at the time. Comparing the Panthers to Hitler's Brown Shirts (ix), writing of "the madness and suicidal rage of the poorly educated, well-indoctrinated kids of the party" (229), of "naïve, malleable ghetto kids" (ix), he saved the better part of his fire not for "the conditions that made such ripe subjects for their indoctrination in total despair" (229), but for Eldridge Cleaver. Claiming to have once admired him, only to be disappointed by his voluntary exile "to avoid facing peaceful judicial procedures" and his deportment once ensconced in Algiers, Schanche realizes in the end that rather than Panther "sloganeering" being "an immature cry for attention," it was rather the prelude to "suicidal acts of doomed revolutionaries" (225). His description of Panther militarism drips with the condescension he maintained throughout (76–79).

59 Marine, *The Black Panthers*, 194.

60 For other early journalistic accounts, told from the top, generally uncritical, and often as much about the authors as the subject matter, see Edward Keating, *Free Huey: The True Story of the Trial of Huey P. Newton for Murder* (New York: Dell, 1970); Gilbert Moore, *A Special Rage* (New York: Harper and Row, 1971); Reginald Major, *A Panther Is a Black Cat* (New York: William Morrow, 1971); Donald Freed, *Agony in New Haven: The Trial of Bobby Seale, Ericka Huggins and the Black Panther Party* (New York: Simon and Schuster, 1973).

61 The original introduction, written by Cleaver in late October 1968, never made it into the book. See Cleaver, "Introduction to the Biography of Huey P.

Newton," in his *Post-Prison Writings and Speeches*, 40–42. Here, Cleaver notes that he and Scheer "took Bobby Seale down to Carmel, California, and we secluded ourselves in a little cabin, and placed a tape recorder in front of Bobby, and put a microphone in his hands, and asked him to talk about Huey P. Newton" (42). In the final version, Seale wrote the foreword from the San Francisco County Jail in 1969–70.

62 Seale, *Seize the Time*, ix, x.

63 Scholars have no trouble recognizing the problematic nature of autobiography regarding other leading personalities of the 1960s. See, for example, the commentary on Muhammad Ali's *The Greatest: My Own Story*, with Richard Durham (New York: Random House, 1975) in Mike Marqusee's *Redemption Song: Muhammad Ali and the Spirit of the Sixties* (London: Verso, 1999), 284–85. Nor do scholars fail regularly to note, in their use of the most prominent of all autobiographies of this age, *The Autobiography of Malcolm X* (New York: Grove Press, 1965), that the contents are what Malcolm told Alex Haley.

64 Chuck Moore, *I Was a Black Panther* (Garden City, N.Y.: Doubleday, 1970).

65 Balagoon, *Look for Me in the Whirlwind*.

66 Ibid. For example, Afeni Shakur claimed to have seen Bobby Seale in Harlem in early 1967 (287); Katara (142–43) and Lumumba Shakur (148–49) contradicted each other on the relation between gangs and police in 1950s New York; the veracity of Bob Collier's description of organizing in the Lower East Side before he joined the Panthers is impossible to assess (255–56). No matter. Haywood Burns, of the National Conference of Black Lawyers, who wrote the introduction, claimed, "The authors' faithful recording, without turning up the volume or throwing in adjectives, *makes the case for them*" (x) (emphasis added).

67 Burns alluded to the problems at the end of his introduction to the book, claiming that joining the party was not the culmination of the authors' growth in consciousness and move to activism but "just part of an ongoing process" and that "internal dissension within the Black Panther Party is of no consequence to this process; with or without the Party, the process will go on" (ibid., xiv). From their indictment in April 1969, they were known as the Panther 21; by the time of the writing and publication of the book, they had become known as the *New York 21* (hence the subtitle). They were expelled from the party shortly after the publication of their "Open Letter to Weatherman Underground from Panther 21" (*East Village Other*, January 19, 1971), which contained thinly veiled criticism of Oakland's flagging militancy. For evidence that the Cleaver-Newton tension long antedated 1971, see Hilliard and Cole, *This Side of Glory*. Ray Locke, in his 1991 epilogue to Michael Newton's *Bitter Grain: Huey Newton and the Black Panther Party* (1980; repr., Los Angeles: Holloway House, 1991), notes that Earl Anthony (*Spitting in the Wind*) "infers . . . that there was an ongoing struggle for

Panther leadership, mostly between Newton and Cleaver, right from the beginning" (230). Mumia Abu-Jamal (né Wesley Clark), in his recent autobiography/history, notes "There was, in fact, more than one split; there were several." Mumia Abu-Jamal, *We Want Freedom: A Life in the Black Panther Party* (Cambridge, Mass.: South End, 2004), 229.

68 H. Newton, *To Die for the People: The Writings of Huey P. Newton* (New York: Vintage, 1972). In addition to Cleaver's *Post-Prison Writings and Speeches*, the other key documentary collection of this early period is Foner's *The Black Panthers Speak.*

69 Christopher Lehmann-Haupt, "Panther's Ultimate Revolution Outraged, Frustrating, Boring," reprinted in the *Edwardsville* (Ill.) *Intelligencer*, April 24, 1973, 9.

70 Lehmann-Haupt wrote, "While the narrative voice is personal, it isn't personal enough to convince us that this is really Huey Newton speaking" (ibid.). For Blake's recent claim that he wrote not only *Revolutionary Suicide* but much of *To Die for the People*, see Roz Payne, "WACing Off: Gossip, Sex, Race, and Politics in the World of FBI Special Case Agent William A. Cohendet," in Lazerow and Williams, *In Search of the Black Panther Party*, 180n22.

71 "On the Defection of Eldridge Cleaver from the Black Panther Party and the Defection of the Black Panther Party from the Black Community: April 17, 1971"; "On the Relevance of the Church: May 19, 1971"; "Black Capitalism Re-analyzed I: June 5, 1971"; and "Black Capitalism Re-analyzed II: August 9, 1971"; all in Newton, *To Die for the People.*

72 Anthony, *Picking Up the Gun*, 155–56.

73 Ibid., viii, 159.

74 Anthony, *Spitting in the Wind.*

75 CIS, *Gun-Barrel Politics*, vii. Completed April 12, 1971, the report was ordered to be printed by the whole House, August 18, 1971.

76 Ibid., 143.

77 Ibid., 144.

78 Ibid., 145.

79 G. Louis Heath, *Off the Pigs!: The History and Literature of the Black Panther Party* (Metuchen, N.J.: Scarecrow, 1976); Heath, *The Black Panther Leaders Speak: Huey P. Newton, Bobby Seale, Eldridge Cleaver and Company Speak Out Through the Black Panther Party Official Newspaper* (Metuchen, N.J.: Scarecrow, 1976).

80 U.S. Senate, *Supplementary Detailed Staff Reports of Intelligence Activities and the Rights of Americans, Book III: Final Reports of the Select Committee to Study Governmental Operations with Respect to Intelligence Activities*, 94th Congress, 2nd sess. (Washington, D.C.: U.S. Government Printing Office, 1976).

81 "The Black Panther Party . . . was not included in the first two lists of primary ["Black Nationalist-Hate Groups"] targets (August 1967 and March 1968) because it had not attained national importance. By November 1968, apparently the BPP had become sufficiently active to be considered a primary target" (ibid., 22).

82 Significantly, one of the few scholarly essays on the party in the early period was a content analysis of the Panthers' de-emphasis of militant rhetoric in the face of government repression. See John A. Courtright (speech and dramatic arts), "Rhetoric of the Gun: An Analysis of the Rhetorical Modifications of the Black Panther Party," *Journal of Black Studies* 4, no. 3 (March 1974): 249–67. At the same time, a new literature developed about Panthers and political prisoners, especially Field Marshall George Jackson. See Eric Mann's celebratory *Comrade George* (New York: Hovey Street, 1972); and the more critical Gregory Armstrong, *The Dragon Has Come* (New York: Harper and Row, 1974). See also, Jo Durden-Smith, *Who Killed George Jackson?* (New York: Alfred A. Knopf, 1976); and Dan Hammer and Isaac Cronin, eds., *Bad: The Autobiography of James Carr* (New York: Carroll and Graf, 1975). Two decades later, the writing about Jackson had turned much more critical. See, e.g., Eric Cummins, "The Construction of George Jackson," in his *The Rise and Fall of California's Radical Prison Movement* (Stanford, Calif.: Stanford University Press, 1994), 151–86; Paul Liberatore, *The Road to Hell: The True Story of George Jackson, Stephen Bingham, and the San Quentin Massacre* (New York: Atlantic Monthly, 1996). Jackson's own works are *Soledad Brother: The Prison Letters of George Jackson* (New York: Bantam, 1970); *Blood in My Eye* (New York: Random House, 1972).

83 E.g., Frank J. Donner, *The Age of Surveillance: The Aims and Methods of America's Political Intelligence System* (New York: Vintage, 1978); Ward Churchill and Jim Vander Wall, *Agents of Repression: The FBI's Secret Wars against the Black Panther Party and the American Indian Movement* (Cambridge, Mass.: South End, 1988); Churchill and Vander Wall, *The COINTELPRO Papers: Documents from the FBI's Secret Wars Against Dissent in the United States* (Cambridge, Mass.: South End, 1990). Foreshadowing this literature was an explosive though not entirely reliable exposé by Louis Tackwood, an alleged informant for the Los Angeles Police Department. See Citizens Research and Investigation Committee and Louis Tackwood, *The Glass House Tapes* (New York: Avon, 1973); also, Nelson Blackstock, *COINTELPRO: The FBI's Secret War on Political Freedom* (New York: Pathfinder, 1975).

84 E.g., Coleman and Avery, "The Party's Over."

85 Huey Newton, "War Against the Panthers: A Study of Repression in America" (Ph.D. diss., University of California, Santa Cruz, 1980), published under the same title by Harlem River Press in 1996, seven years after Newton's death.

86 Carolyn R. Calloway (communications), "Group Cohesiveness in the Black Panther Party," *Journal of Black Studies* 8, no. 1 (September 1977): 55–73, detailed the internal and external sources of party strength, using some issues of the party newspaper but mainly the standard sources of the first period—Anthony, Cleaver, Major, Marine, Newton, and Seale—as well as theoretical work in social psychology. The sociologist Jimi Mori's "The Ideological Development of the Black Panther Party," *Cornell Journal of Social Relations* 12, no. 2 (fall 1977): 137–55, again relying on theory and the foundational works mentioned above, remains one of the most insightful analyses of party ideology despite its focus on the national story and the absence of attention to any but national leaders.

87 Helen Stewart, "Buffering: The Leadership Style of Huey P. Newton, Co-Founder of the Black Panther Party" (Ph.D. diss., Brandeis University, 1980), 2.

88 For the story of Newton's mother insisting on $5,000 for her cooperation in a journalist's early book on the Panthers, see Schanche, *The Panther Paradox*, 146–47.

89 S. J. Guffev, "Bobby Seale Now Living in Denver," *Gettysburg Times*, July 15, 1982, 7.

90 The same year, from a different political perspective and compromised by speculation about the deal he had made to return to the United States, Eldridge Cleaver published his post-exile autobiography, *Soul on Fire* (Waco: Word, 1978). Tracing his evolution from criminal to revolutionary to conservative born-again Christian, and providing some new details about his beliefs and actions at different moments in time, the book revealed little about the internal workings of the party itself.

91 M. Newton, *Bitter Grain.*

92 Ibid. Quotations are from the back of the 1991 edition.

93 His one-page summary of the Massachusetts story, for example, contains some eight errors (156). For more on that story, see Jama Lazerow's essay "The Black Panthers at the Water's Edge: Oakland, Boston, and the New Bedford 'Riots' of 1970" in this volume.

94 M. Newton, *Bitter Grain*, quotation, 216.

95 John Chamberlin, "Chaplin's View Queer," *Coshocton* (Ohio) *Tribune*, May 6, 1970. "The Panthers do good things. They feed children. Eldridge Cleaver writes eloquent books, and some of his essays may live as literature. However, if the Panthers are going to threaten to cut off Senator McClellan's head, or kill Richard Nixon, they are going to create fear. And they will have difficulty obtaining a fair hearing from people they have scared half to death."

96 M. Newton, *Bitter Grain*, 217.

97 JoNina Abron, "The Legacy of the Black Panther Party," *The Black Scholar* 17, no. 6 (November/December 1986): 33–36.

98 Assata Shakur, *Assata: An Autobiography* (London: Zed, 1987), chap. 15.

99 On the silver screen in 1987 was the fourth installment of the legendary *Death Wish* series, which first appeared in 1974. Chronicling the life of a mild-mannered white architect, Paul Kersey, who embarks on a career as a vigilante after his wife and daughter are brutally murdered, the audience witnesses his continuing revenge against mostly minority victims (criminals). In its 1987 incarnation, subtitled *The Crackdown*, Kersey wages war on Los Angeles gang members after they threaten him and his neighbors. A sobering reminder of art imitating life and life art, nearly four years before on the afternoon of December 22, 1984, a New York subway passenger named Bernard Goetz gunned down four black teenagers with long criminal records aboard a downtown train after he claimed they tried to rob him. Though the only weapon recovered from the boys was a screwdriver, and Goetz fired an additional shot into one while he lay bleeding, the "subway vigilante" would be hailed throughout New York and the nation for his courageous act of self-defense. George Fletcher, *Bernard Goetz: A Crime of Self Defense* (Chicago: University of Chicago Press, 1990).

100 See Yohuru Williams's essay " 'Give Them a Cause to Die For': The Black Panther Party in Milwaukee, 1969–77" in this volume.

101 Public Enemy, "Rebel without a Pause," Def Jam Records, 1988.

102 Cleaver staged the photo, which was taken at the home of his lawyer, Beverly Axlerod. In *Revolutionary Suicide*, Newton would claim to have always hated the poster, though the book, as noted above, was his opportunity to distance himself from Cleaver's embrace of insurrectionary violence.

103 Though often thinly sourced, Hugh Pearson's *The Shadow of the Panther*, 251ff., contains enough material on Newton's behavior after his release from prison in August 1970 to verify his continued dominance over the party.

104 The most graphic description of the expulsion, based largely on sources provided by David Horowitz, and which Seale vehemently denies, can be found in ibid., 264.

105 "Power (1967–68)," *Eyes on the Prize II: American at the Racial Crossroads, 1965–1985*, video recording (WGBH, Boston; produced by Blackside, Inc. and the Corporation for Public Broadcasting, ca. 1989).

106 The most important memoirist of this period, Elaine Brown, it should be noted, claimed, "The writing [of my book] required eight years of my life to complete." Brown, *A Taste of Power*, lx.

107 Pearson, *The Shadow of the Panther*, 315.

108 Quoted in William H. Chafe, *Civilities and Civil Rights: Greensboro, North Carolina, and the Black Struggle for Freedom* (Oxford: Oxford University Press, 1981), 23.

109 Anthony, *Spitting in the Wind*; Brown, *A Taste of Power*; Hilliard and Cole, *This Side of Glory*; William Lee Brent, *Long Time Gone* (New York: Times, 1996).

110 Kit Kim Holder, "The History of the Black Panther Party 1966–1972: A Curriculum Tool for Afrikan-American Studies" (Ph.D. diss., University of Massachusetts, 1990). "Part of the anti-Newton actions of 1971," Holder claimed to have interviewed Newton himself, on July 16, 1989, just weeks before his death, stating, "Much of what he said concerning the Party contradicted the information I had previously gathered" (343). There is no summary of what Newton said.

111 Ibid., 346.

112 Less significant was David R. Cillay's narrowly conceived master's thesis (English), "The Formative Years of the Black Panther Party for Self-Defense" (University of Portland, 1989), which ends with the Sacramento action of May 2, 1967. More useful in its attempt to move beyond the Bay Area, despite its uncritical use of FBI materials, is Benjamin Friedman's "Fighting Back: The North Carolina Chapter of the Black Panther Party" (master's thesis, George Washington University, 1994).

113 At the same time, the latter two writers experienced the Panther "moment" from central headquarters. Meanwhile, journalists and others continued to focus on that space and the people who occupied it. See, e.g., Kathleen Rout, *Eldridge Cleaver* (Boston: Twayne, 1991) and, of course, the far more influential Pearson, *The Shadow of the Panther*, whose protagonist is Huey Newton.

114 Too, Brown's obsessive attention to her own sexual exploits—her description of how she allegedly ended up in bed with Eldridge Cleaver (*A Taste of Power*, 129–30), for example—render the book, at times, a kind of romance novel.

115 "They Ran on Empty," *New York Times*, May 5, 1993, A23, and Brown's trenchant response, "Attack Racism, Not Black Men," ibid. For a perspective that seems to follow Walker, see Wini Breines, "Sixties Stories' Silences: White Feminism, Black Feminism, Black Power," *NWSA Journal* 8, no. 3 (fall 1996): 101–21.

116 *The Negro Family: The Case for National Action* (Washington, D.C.: Office of Policy Planning and Research, U.S. Department of Labor, 1965).

117 For the type of deep research and analysis we suggest here, see Rhonda Williams, *The Politics of Public Housing* (Oxford: Oxford University Press, 2004), which shows how the stereotyping of black women, especially mothers, driven by political agendas of the Left and Right, has obscured these women's contributions to grassroots political organizing, preventing an assessment of the successes and failures of government anti-poverty policy and programs.

118 For oddities in dating, especially regarding the nature of the civil rights movement, faulty history of the Panthers and other groups, and lack of historical context (or the misconstruing of it), see Pearson, *The Shadow of the Panther*, 22, 88, 103, 111, 137, 144, 151, 178; for reaching beyond sources, unquestioning acceptance of some sources, or simply having none at all, see 25–26, 198, 200, 221, 224, 237, 257; for general contempt for political radicals of the period in general and the Panthers in particular, see 68, 106, 152, 167; for personal investment in denigrating the Panthers, see 96, 99, 335, 338, and his acknowledgments.

119 Of many examples interpreting Newton's politics as a "rationale" for his criminality and for his criminal nature generally, see ibid., 69, 95, 112, 116, 117,

129. At the book's end, Pearson wonders "if the media intentionally placed so much emphasis in the late 1960s and early 1970s on African American leaders with criminal mind-sets, encouraging the notion that 'true blacks' are those most alienated from American society" (ibid., 338); also, 340.

120 See copious examples in monographs, surveys, and texts, above.

121 Michael Kazin, "Cat on a Hot Tin Roof," *Washington Post*, July 10, 1994, 5.

122 Burner, *Making Peace with the 60s*, esp. 69–72, quotation, 71, where Burner uses Pearson to indict Newton for two murders, adding, without evidence or explanation, that the Panther leader "was guilty . . . almost certainly [of] many more" (71). For the most recent endorsement of Pearson by a mainstream historian, see David Garrow, "Picking Up the Books: The New Historiography of the Black Panther Party," *Reviews in American History* 35 (December 2007): 669n32.

123 Notably, Seale's *Seize the Time*, Newton's *Revolutionary Suicide*, and Foner's *The Black Panthers Speak*.

124 E.g., John George and Laird Wilcox, *Nazis, Communists, Klansmen, and Others on the Fringe: Political Extremism in America* (Buffalo, N.Y.: Prometheus, 1992), 132–41.

125 Margaret LeBrun, "Fighting for Respect," *Syracuse Herald Journal*, May 4, 1995, 6–8.

126 For a biography published the same year that touches on the Panther movement in prisons, see Lori Andrews, *Black Power, White Blood: The Life and Times of Johnny Spain* (New York: Pantheon, 1996).

127 For salient examples in American history, see John Demos, *The Unredeemed Captive: A Family Story from Early America* (New York: Alfred A. Knopf, 1994); Stephen B. Oates, *The Approaching Fury: Voices of the Storm, 1820–1861* (New York: HarperCollins, 1997); Tera W. Hunter, *To 'Joy My Freedom: Southern Black Women's Lives and Labors after the Civil War* (Cambridge, Mass.: Harvard University Press, 1997).

128 Though, as Van Gosse reminds us about the related "historiography of Black Power," despite the "notable" "flood of memoirs, essay collections, Hollywood films, and other evocations of Malcolm X and the Black Panther Party . . . we are still at the beginning." "A Movement of Movements: The Definition and Periodization of the New Left," in *A Companion to Post-1945 America*, ed. Jean-Christophe Agnew and Roy Rosenzweig, 286 (Malden, Mass.: Blackwell, 2002).

129 Charles E. Jones, ed., *The Black Panther Party [Reconsidered]* (Baltimore: Black Classic Press, 1998). Of the collection's nineteen contributors, only three were historians. A second important anthology appeared in 2001 (Cleaver and Katsiaficas, *Liberation, Imagination, and the Black Panther Party*), though in that case, none of the nineteen authors was a historian.

130 Jeffrey Ogbar, "From the Bottom Up: Popular Black Reactions to the Nation of Islam and the Black Panther Party, 1955–1975" (Ph.D. diss., Indiana

University, 1997); Jennifer Bradford Smith, "An International History of the Black Panther Party" (Ph.D. diss., State University of New York, Buffalo, 1997); Yohuru Williams, "No Haven: Civil Rights, Black Power, and Black Panthers in New Haven, Connecticut, 1956–1971" (Ph.D. diss., Howard University, 1998); Curtis Jerome Austin, "The Role of Violence in the Creation, Sustenance, and Destruction of the Black Panther Party, 1966–1972" (Ph.D. diss., Mississippi State University, 1998); Robert Owen Self, "Shifting Ground in Metropolitan America: Class, Race, and Power in Oakland and the East Bay, 1945–1977" (Ph.D. diss., University of Washington, 1998); Jon Frank Rice, "Black Revolutionaries on Chicago's West Side: A History of the Illinois Black Panther Party" (Ph.D. diss., Northern Illinois University, 1998); Tracye Ann Matthews, "'No One Ever Asks What a Man's Place in the Revolution Is': Gender and Sexual Politics in the Black Panther Party, 1966–1971" (Ph.D. diss., University of Michigan, 1998); Monica Marie White, "Panther Stories: A Gendered Analysis of the Autobiographies of Former Black Panther Members" (Ph.D. diss., West Michigan University, 1998); Winston A. Grady-Willis, "A Changing Tide: Black Politics and Activism in Atlanta, Georgia, 1960–1977" (Ph.D. diss., Emory University, 1998); Daniel Edward Crowe, "The Origins of the Black Revolution: The Transformation of San Francisco Bay Area Black Communities, 1945–1969" (Ph.D. diss., University of Kentucky, 1998) (Crowe's master's thesis [University of Kentucky, 1995] was entitled, "'All Power to the People': A History of the Black Panther Party, 1966–1975"). Clearly, these theses, in gestation in the mid-1990s, were at least partly a response to the spate of memoirs and books of the post-Newton era.

131 Garland published Smith's dissertation under the same title in 1999; a revised version of Yohuru Williams's appeared as *Black Politics/White Power: Civil Rights, Black Power, and the Black Panthers in New Haven* (St. James, N.Y.: Brandywine, 2000); Self's as *American Babylon*. Ogbar published a wider ranging, *Black Power: Radical Politics and African American Identity* (Baltimore: Johns Hopkins University Press) in 2004. On doctoral work in the twenty-first century, see below.

132 Smith, "An International History of the Black Panther Party"; Yohuru Williams, "American-Exported Black Nationalism: The Student Non-Violent Coordinating Committee, the Black Panther Party, and the Worldwide Freedom Struggle, 1967–1972," *Negro History Bulletin* (July-September 1997): 13–21; Ogbar, "From the Bottom Up."

133 The complex nature of Panther gender relations, exposed most famously in Elaine Brown's autobiography, and treated most carefully in Tracye Matthews's dissertation, continued to be a subject of interest to scholars, though not necessarily historians. E.g., Joy James, *Shadowboxing: Representations of Black Feminist Politics* (New York: St. Martin's, 1999); Margo V. Perkins, *Autobiography as Activism: Three Black Women of the Sixties* (Jackson: University Press of

Mississippi, 2000). See, too, from another angle, Steve Estes's discussion of manhood and the Panthers in *I Am a Man! Race, Manhood, and the Civil Rights Movement* (Chapel Hill: University of North Carolina Press, 2005).

134 Craig Peck, "Educate to Liberate: The Black Panther Party and Political Education" (Ph.D. diss., Stanford University, 2001).

135 Joel Wilson, "Free Huey: The Black Panther Party, the Peace and Freedom Party, and the Politics of Race in 1968" (Ph.D. diss., University of California, Santa Cruz, 2002); Devin Fergus, "The Ordeal of Liberalism and Black Nationalism in an American Southern State, 1965–1980" (Ph.D. diss., Columbia University, 2002).

136 Matthew Countryman, "Civil Rights and Black Power in Philadelphia, 1940–1971" (Ph.D. diss., Duke University, 1998); Rhonda Williams, "Living Just Enough in the City: Change and Activism in Baltimore's Public Housing, 1940–1980" (Ph.D. diss., University of Maryland, 1998). Countryman provides a brief treatment of the Philadelphia Panthers at the end of his masterful published study, *Up South.*

137 Rose Thevenin, "'The Greatest Single Threat': A Study of the Black Panther Party, 1966–1971" (Ph.D. diss., Michigan State University, 2003); Curtis Austin, *Up Against the Wall: Violence in the Making and Unmaking of the Black Panther Party* (Fayetteville: University of Arkansas Press, 2006).

138 Y. Williams, *Black Politics/White Power* is still the only local monograph outside the Bay Area to focus on the Panthers. See also Yohuru Williams, "No Haven: From Civil Rights to Black Power in New Haven, Connecticut," *The Black Scholar* 31, no. 3–4 (fall/winter 2001): 54–66. For a substantial treatment of the Panthers in a larger urban study, see Winston A. Grady-Willis, *Challenging U.S. Apartheid: Atlanta and Black Struggles for Human Rights, 1960–1977* (Durham, N.C.: Duke University Press, 2006). Austin's work, though told from a national perspective, contains significant and sustained forays into the local history of a number of communities. In article form, there is Jon Rice's short and unevenly sourced "The World of the Illinois Panthers," in Theoharis and Woodard, *Freedom North.* Two other such essays have been published by scholars outside the history discipline: Judson L. Jeffries (political science), "Black Radicalism and Political Repression in Baltimore: The Case of the Black Panther Party," *Ethnic and Racial Studies* (London) 25 (January 2002): 64–98; Reynaldo Anderson (communication studies), "Practical Internationalists: The Story of the Des Moines, Iowa, Black Panther Party," in *Groundwork: Local Black Freedom Movements in America*, ed. Jeanne Theoharis and Komozi Woodard, chap. 12 (New York: New York University Press, 2005). One indication of continued avoidance of the local story is Patrick Jones's brilliant dissertation on Milwaukee, which *ends* just as the Panthers arrive in that midwestern city: "The Selma of the North: Race Relations and Civil Rights Insurgency in Milwaukee, 1958–1970" (Ph.D. diss.,

University of Wisconsin, 2002). Jeffries's edited collection, *Comrades: A Local History of the Black Panther Party* (Bloomington: Indiana University Press, 2007) —a volume once again dominated by authors outside the history profession— arrived too late for our consideration here.

139 Tupac Shakur's version of "Changes": "It's time to fight back that's what Huey said/2 shots in the dark now Huey's dead" (*2Pac Greatest Hits*, Interscope Records, 1998); more recently, The Game's "Song Dreams": "The Dream of Huey Newton, that's what I'm livin' through/The Dream of Eric Wright, that's what I'm givin' you!" (*The Documentary*, Aftermath Records, 2005). For an insightful commentary on the Panthers that ultimately loses its way partly because of its reliance on sources such as Seale and Newton, as well as its preoccupation with what went on in Oakland, see Scott L. Malcomson, *One Drop of Blood: The American Misadventure of Race* (New York: Farrar, Strauss and Giroux, 2000), 400, 434, 447–52. In 2002, David Hilliard and Donald Weise reproduced much of what had been in *To Die for the People*, with some additional pieces, in *The Huey P. Newton Reader* (New York: Seven Stories). Also, Hilliard, the executive director of the Dr. Huey P. Newton Foundation, produced a new biography of Newton, which is based mostly on Newton's memoirs and recent interviews with people who knew him, though it is told largely in the first person. Hilliard with Keith and Kent Zimmerman, *Huey: Spirit of the Panther* (New York: Thunder's Mouth Press, 2006). Largely hagiographic—indeed, a kind of mirror image of Hugh Pearson's scathing *The Shadow of the Panther*—the book's real value lies in its use of several unpublished manuscripts Newton wrote in the 1970s and 1980s. For a recent popular history, see Jim Haskins, *Power to the People: The Rise and Fall of the Black Panther Party* (New York: Simon and Schuster Books for Young Readers, 1997); for a whodunit collaboration by a journalist and a professor of urban politics, in the style of the early journalistic accounts of the party, see Paul Bass and Douglas W. Rae, *Murder in the Model City: The Black Panthers, Yale, and the Redemption of a Killer* (New York: Basic Books, 2006); for photographs, see Ruth-Marion Baruch and Pirkle Jones, *Black Panthers: 1968* (Los Angeles: Greybull Press, 2002) and Stephen Shames, *The Black Panthers* (New York: Aperture, 2006); for Panther art, see the recent coffee-table book, *Black Panther: The Revolutionary Art of Emory Douglas* (New York: Rizzoli, 2007).

140 Paul Alkebulan, "The Role of Ideology in the Growth, Establishment, and Decline of the Black Panther Party: 1966 to 1982" (Ph.D. diss., University of California, Berkeley, 2003). Though a full and careful reading of this thesis, which includes a chapter on "regional development," reveals the use of a wide range of printed materials, compare the author's argument in his abstract (esp., 2) to that advanced in Richard Ichord's foreword to CIS, *Gun-Barrel Politics* (esp., vii). His slim *Survival Pending Revolution: The History of the Black Panther Party* (Tuscaloosa: University of Alabama Press, 2007) arrived too late for inclusion. Austin,

Up Against the Wall does make use of new oral histories and even attempts some investigation of the local context. However, with the exception of the important New York case, the book adds little to what we already know. Moreover, the power of the new testimony is attenuated by the author's general acceptance of it as fact.

141 Robyn Ceanne Spencer, "Repression Breeds Resistance: The Rise and Fall of the Black Panther Party in Oakland, CA, 1966–1982" (Ph.D. diss., Columbia University, 2001). Recent work in other fields—ethnic studies, historical sociology, political science—exhibits a similar trend. See, e.g., Jason Michael Ferreira, "All Power to the People: A Comparative History of Third World Radicalism in San Francisco, 1968–1974" (Ph.D. diss., University of California, Berkeley, 2003); Chris Rhomberg, *No There There: Race, Class and Political Community in Oakland* (Berkeley: University of California Press, 2004); Judson L. Jeffries, *Huey P. Newton: The Radical Theorist* (Jackson: University Press of Mississippi, 2002).

142 Detroit was among the several chapters the U.S. House of Representatives Committee on Internal Security studied in 1970. *Black Panther Party*, vol. 3, *Investigation of Activities in Detroit, Michigan; Philadelphia, Pennsylvania; and Indianapolis, Indiana*, 91st Congress, 2nd sess., March 4–November 17, 1970 (Washington, D.C.: U.S. Government Printing Office, 1970–71). The lack of attention serious historians of the city have given to the group is evident in Heather Ann Thompson, *Whose Detroit? Politics, Labor, and Race in a Modern American City* (Ithaca, N.Y.: Cornell University Press, 2001). For a corrective, see Ahmad A. Rahman's penetrating study, "Marching Blind: The Rise and Fall of the Black Panther Party in Detroit," in this volume.

143 Joel P. Rhodes, *The Voice of Violence: Performative Violence as Protest in the Vietnam Era* (Westport, Conn.: Praeger, 2001), chap. 5 ("Revolutionary Commitment? The Detroit Black Panthers"), 155n3. Austin's most important source for the New York story in *Up Against the Wall* is anonymous as well, identified only as BJ in the text (see esp. 304ff.).

144 Jasmine Guy, *Afeni Shakur: Evolution of a Revolutionary* (New York: Atria Books, 2004); Evan D. Hopkins, *Life after Life: A Story of Rage and Redemption* (New York: Free Press, 2005); Abu-Jamal, *We Want Freedom*. In manuscript are the long-awaited autobiographies of Donald ("DC") Cox and Kathleen Cleaver. To this list might be added the authorized biography of Geronimo Ji Jaga (né Elmer Pratt), a fascinating book made frustrating by the absence of any source citations at all (Jack Olsen's *Last Man Standing: The Tragedy and Triumph of Geronimo Pratt* [New York: Doubleday, 2000]); also, the entirely uncritical and unsourced "biography" of Mumia by Terry Bisson (*On a Move: The Story of Mumia Abu-Jamal* [Farmington, Pa.: Litmus, 2001]), who is described on the book jacket as "the author of numerous science fiction novels, short stories, motion picture novelizations, and a biography of Nat Turner for young adults."

In a league by itself is Flores A. Forbes's memoir, *Will You Die with Me? My Life and the Black Panther Party* (New York: Atria, 2006), which tells a story without illusion—or bitterness. Unfortunately, that story is short of details of his experience as a young recruit in southern California in the late 1960s and long on his experience as a leader of the Panthers' military wing at national headquarters after 1971, rendering the book much more instructive about the Panthers' long decline than about their heyday.

145 Paul Ricoeur, *Memory, History, Forgetting* (Chicago: University of Chicago Press, 2004), 21.

146 Guy, *Afeni Shakur*, 2–4.

147 On Shakur's reasons for joining the party, see ibid., 62–64, 76, 79–80; on her current perspective on what explains the party's demise, see 66–68, 80; on the question of sexism and gender relations generally, see 72, 76–78, 90, 97, 102, 104, 111, 139; on the tollbooth story, see 79; on the split, see 108. There are also errors that escape Guy, probably because she is simply unfamiliar with the history. For example, Shakur twice (60, 75) tells of having been impressed in her first encounter with the Panthers—hearing Bobby Seale speak in Harlem in May 1968—by a photograph someone held up of an armed Huey Newton on the steps of the Sacramento Capitol Building. Newton, on probation at the time, was not in Sacramento. For apparent errors in dating, or simply looseness in dating that makes it impossible for the historian to pin down the precise order of events from this account, for example, on the cases of the 21, see 106 and 115.

148 Ibid., e.g., 49–50, 95, 114. The prospect of the Afeni Shakur story on film now seems a reality. "HollyHood Filmz to Bring 'Dear Mama: The Life Story of Afeni Shakur' to Silver Screen," August 27, 2007, http://www.prweb.com/releases/2007/8/prweb549279.htm.

149 The book is based on Mumia's Abu-Jamal's master's thesis, written while on death row, "A Life in the Party: An Historical and Retrospective Examination of the Lessons and Legacies of the Black Panther Party" (California State University, Dominquez Hills, 2000).

150 Occasionally, as at the outset, the reader can expect soaring phrasing: "It was in the mid 1960s, movements were circling the globe like fresh winds blowing through stale, unopened, darkened rooms. Waiting on those winds were the seductive scents of rebellion, resistance, and world revolution!" (ibid., 1). Or, toward the end, describing the role of the FBI: "Quietly, under cloak of darkness, the hunter lay, feeding poisons into the waters and death into the air" (226). For one glaring omission of historical context, see his discussion of the Seattle Breakfast Program: "Panthers gathered food (often from supportive neighborhood merchants), assembled the necessary personnel, and cooked breakfasts for neighborhood kids" (69). The controversial matters of coercion of local merchants or of precisely when such community programs began are unexplored. For uncritical use of sources such as Seale and Cleaver, see 2, 161; for lack of sources on critical matters such as numbers of members, see 46, 62; for lack of specific historical context, see esp., 70; for chronological problems, in addition to the general organizational scheme, which promiscuously mixes periods, see 104, 213; for repetitiveness, see 67 and 80, 106 and 114, 182 and 201, 138−39 and 22. In a sense, *We Want Freedom* mirrors Pearson's *The Shadow of the Panther*, though, like Hilliard's *Huey*, from a decidedly different political perspective.

151 Cleaver, introduction to Abu-Jamal, *We Want Freedom*, xv, xvi.

152 Ibid., xvii.

153 Ibid., xv−xvi.

154 See the discussion of Black House, ibid., 101−2.

155 Allessandro Portelli, "What Makes Oral History Different," in *The Death of Luigi Trastulli and Other Stories: Form and Meaning in Oral History* (Albany: State University of New York Press, 1991), reprinted in Robert Perks and Alistair Thomson, eds., *The Oral History Reader* (London: Routledge, 1998), 67; also, Elizabeth Lapovsky Kennedy, "Telling Tales: Oral History and the Construction of Pre-Stonewall Lesbian History," *Radical History Review* 62 (1995), reprinted in Perks and Thomson, 271−83.

Jama Lazerow

2

The Black Panthers at the Water's Edge

OAKLAND, BOSTON, AND THE NEW BEDFORD

"RIOTS" OF 1970

In the winter of 1970, a group of high school students in New Bedford, Massachusetts, who called themselves the Revolutionary Student Union (RSU) announced that they were "working toward basic human rights for all people."[1] Eschewing appellations that were common at the time, such as the "Black Student Union" or even the "High School Union," they explicitly rejected "asking for petty things like a change in the curriculum of a Black Studies Department," while embracing something much broader. "We are demanding our basic right to self-determination because we want freedom," they wrote. "We want the power to determine the destiny of our academic community." The language came directly from the platform of the Black Panther Party (BPP).[2]

In an article published in the BPP national organ, *The Black Panther*, in late December, the students referred to their "racist pig principal . . . and his lackeys," who had harassed and threatened the RSU because it represented "the threat of an armed student union with a revolutionary ideology." They also complained that at a meeting of the New Bedford School Committee in early November—in the "latest act of madness"—they had been refused permission to set up registration tables for the Panthers' Revolutionary People's Constitutional Convention planned for later that month. Flatly denying the insinuation of the chairman of the School Committee, "super pig" Mayor George Rogers, that the request had really come from the Black Panther Party, and seeking to raise their "right to alter or abolish the constitution," the RSU claimed that Rogers had "changed it [the School Committee] around to his fascist way of thinking and oinked some madness about killing people." Threatening "a political consequence for those who seek to deny [them their] rights," the students ended their short report by warning that "those power crazed pigs on the School Committee" would "experience the wrath of the armed people." Over their signature, they wrote in capital letters, "ALL POWER TO THE PEOPLE."

In making sense of such a document, one cannot discount the role of Panther editing at its national headquarters in California, where *The Black Panther* was published, nor can one be certain of precisely who composed the RSU, which does not appear in any other documents of the period.[3] Still, it is striking to find this kind of rhetoric over the byline of high school students in a place like New Bedford, a city of some one hundred thousand people about sixty miles south of Boston along the Atlantic coast, a community best known for whales, not Panthers. Yet, the Panthers had some resonance in New Bedford in late 1970, and not just among this one group. The RSU surfaced that fall in the aftermath of a cataclysmic event in New Bedford: the "riots" of the previous July. Typically, local political leaders and the press referred to these events as "civil disorder," "civil unrest," or "civil disturbance," often adding the adjective "racial"; the city daily, the *Standard Times*, at least once printed a reference to New Bedford's "month of turmoil."[4] But, in a filmed interview during the second week of July, which was taped for a public television program in Boston called, *Say, Brother!*—the first television program in the country produced for and by black people—Mayor Rogers referred to "this revolt." To be sure, the mayor quickly corrected himself, adding, "or, this riot." The show's host, Ray Richardson, was more emphatic: at the end of the program he pronounced the event a "justified rebellion," one of several reasons he was fired shortly after its airing. And, responding to an interviewer's request to define what was going on, an angry young black man in the city's predominantly black West End went further, declaring simply, "It's a *revolution!*"[5] Indeed, in the wake of this watershed community moment, the Black Panthers, the leading revolutionary group of the age, surfaced in New Bedford. In fact, they had been organizing in the city for more than six months before the events of July. And, in one guise or another, they would be there until they closed their office in the spring of 1972; moreover, their presence would be felt well beyond even that particular moment in time.[6]

The story of the New Bedford Panthers cannot be told in isolation from the regional and national contexts that helped define it. Both the violence of July and the presence of the Panthers were intimately linked to what was going on in Boston, the hub of Panther (and other black militant) activity in New England, and in Oakland, the national font of party policy, ideology, and rhetoric. This essay, then, though primarily concerned with tracing the origins, nature, and development of the Panthers in this one relatively small community, seeks historical perspective on what might be called the Panther "moment" by exploring some of the intersections of the local, regional, and national developments in the history of New Bedford in the 1960s and 1970s. The result demonstrates Sam Bass Warner's dictum that the local historian must "accept the authenticity of the particular" while seeking to draw together many stories into a coherent story.[7] In this case, New Bedford stands as testimony to how little we really know about the Black Panther Party.[8]

The story of the Panthers at the center of things in their birthplace and national headquarters in Oakland, California, is well known. After nearly four years of engagement in what they perceived as a worldwide revolutionary movement—in which they, in America, were the "vanguard" of that movement—they were on the precipice of two momentous, linked events: the release from prison of their founder, Huey Newton, for the first time since the fall of 1967, when the party had been in its infancy; and the subsequent internecine warfare that would, early in 1971, sunder the party and set it on the road to a decade-long national decline and its ultimate demise in the early 1980s. In contrast, the story of the Panthers in Boston is relatively little known. The Panthers there were remarkably successful at organizing and sustaining themselves and others in the region but not at drawing the kind of fire from local authorities that brought national, even international fame—or infamy, depending on one's perspective—and, thus, they have drawn little attention from historians.[9] Unlike chapters in New Haven, New York, Chicago, and Los Angeles, the chapter in Boston never won the dubious compliment of a police raid, never got a celebrated trial.[10] They were only an hour's drive from New Bedford, though, and some had family and political ties there; in the wake of the violence of July 1970, New Bedford would become a key arena of struggle for them. Here, they would get their "raid," and (almost) their day in court. The third, and arguably most important, story of all, however, is the one virtually unknown beyond the local community: the story of the Panthers in New Bedford itself. That story, when told in the context of the two others, constitutes a kind of "hidden history" of the BPP at a crucial moment in its development, in a place far from what we think of as the center of the action—a history, as it were, at the water's edge.

"Everything Comes Late to New Bedford"

"Everything comes late to New Bedford. Even a riot," the local community activist Claudette Blake told a reporter for the *Boston Globe* nearly a year after the disturbances of July 1970.[11] In fact, the explosion in New Bedford was part of a summer of "small city riots," with upheavals in nearly a dozen communities in nine states, including Asbury Park, New Jersey, Fort Lauderdale, Florida, Lima, Ohio, and Mathis, Texas.[12] Described in one retrospective as a "quaint doorstep to Cape Cod," New Bedford was much more than that, with a rich history of dissent.[13] Religiously tolerant, racially diverse, and socially progressive, even radical from its earliest days in 1787 when it was set off from Dartmouth township, New Bedford in the early nineteenth century was home to Quakers and Baptists, free people of color (including an especially large fugitive slave community), and temperance and anti-slavery advocates.[14] Already a maritime center by the late eighteenth century because of its deep harbor, created by the broad expanse of the Acushnet River emptying into Buzzard's Bay, by the 1820s New Bedford had replaced Nantucket as the nation's principal whaling port, claiming, "We light the world" with whale oil. By the late 1840s, when the first of many textile mills opened, New Bedford, then the country's fourth largest port, claimed to be its richest city.[15] Even then, though, there were two New Bedfords, as the historian Kathryn Grover points out: the mansions and gardens on the hilltop and the squalid boardinghouses and saloons for sailors below, a division that would remain when textiles replaced whaling in the late nineteenth century, and garments replaced textiles in the twentieth.[16]

More important for the future of class, ethnic, and race relations in the city, unlike shoe centers such as Lynn or textile centers such as Lowell, antebellum New Bedford relied on an international workforce of mixed cultures and colors. Among the most prominent in this mix were crews from Cape Verde, a crescent of ten volcanic islands and five islets off the coast of Senegal that the Portuguese settled in the mid-fifteenth century. An early outpost of the slave trade and a key transshipment point because of its strategic location along the trade winds to the New World, the archipelago became an entrepôt for trade and labor, especially in whaling. Populated by people from all over the world, but most crucially by free and enslaved West Africans, Cape Verde was the source of significant migration to New Bedford.[17] Indeed, New Bedford would become the capital of Cape Verdeans in the United States. Crucially, those who stayed, working, for example, in ancillary maritime trades, fishing, cranberry picking, textiles, and later the garment industry, did not always mix peacefully with the area's original inhabitants, the Wampanoag Indians, or with southern blacks, the descendants of local freed slaves, or West Indian immigrants. For most Cape Verdeans in New Bedford—who were the offspring of the only voluntary mass migration of Africans to North America, whose ancestors had helped administer the Portuguese slave empire—considered themselves a group apart. Because of extensive intermarriage, and depending on their home island, they ranged from dark-skinned, dark-eyed, and curly-haired to fair-skinned, blue-eyed, and straight-haired. In a double irony, the Cape Verdeans came to New Bedford, settling mostly in the city's South End, and found themselves shunned by "white" Portuguese who considered them "colored," just as they sought to distance *them*selves from what they derisively called "Americans de couer" (Americans of color) in the West End by seeking to identify themselves as Portuguese, even as "white."[18] Thus, throughout the nineteenth and twentieth centuries, the city was denominated predominantly Caucasian: English, Irish, French-Canadian, Polish, Finn, Italian, and, especially, Portuguese. In 1970, the City Planning Department identified only 3,335 "Negroes" (3.7 percent of the population), who were overwhelmingly concentrated in the West End of town.[19] The Cape Verdeans represented at least twice that number.

Still, from the late 1920s, New Bedford had entered a slow, secular economic and demographic decline that quickened after World War II.[20] With the exposure of some Cape Verdean males to American racism in the armed services during and after the war and the postwar Puerto Rican immigration into the South End, the combination of limited horizons with the confluence of race and ethnicity generated tensions. Then, in the 1960s, millions of dollars in federal money for urban renewal, the war on poverty, and the Model Cities program—disproportionate to New Bedford's population, thanks to the effective politicking of the mayor, Edward Harrington—failed to address high unemployment, a struggling school system, and a shortage of housing and recreational space.[21] Finally, a police force that seemed especially brutal to the young and dark-skinned sparked the conflagration. As early as 1964, the new head of the local chapter of the National Association for the Advancement of Colored People (NAACP) warned that New Bedford had all the ingredients that were generating riots that summer in Philadelphia, Rochester, and New York City.[22] More such warnings followed.[23] Yet, despite skirmishes, New Bedford did not explode until the summer of 1970.[24]

One reason is that the NAACP chapter, established in 1917 and long a membership organization more than anything else, was for most of the 1960s the "only show in town." It began to move more aggressively in the mid-1960s under the direction of its new president, the fiery West Indian social worker from Cambridge, Duncan Dottin. Despite Dottin's recruitment of several Cape Verdeans, he remained frustrated, as he told headquarters in a handwritten letter in 1966, "Very few Cape Verdeans identify with the Negro and champion our causes."[25] He had been working with his Cape Verdean protégé, Jack Custodio, to pressure local businesses for more equitable hiring practices.[26] He also helped establish the Labor and Industries Committee, which included African Americans, Cape Verdeans, and whites; the committee's secretary was the head of the local United Electrical Workers Union.[27] But, what Dottin called "the Cape Verdean-Negro problem" plagued him throughout his tenure in New Bedford.

One solution was to organize an NAACP Youth Council. To head it, he tapped Gloria (Clark) Xifaras, a local teacher and civil rights activist who had taught at the Holly Springs Freedom School during the Mississippi Freedom Summer. Organizing both Negro and Cape Verdean youth in the West End beginning in 1965, Clark sought to build links to the much larger Cape Verdean population in the South End. At the same time, she helped develop Working for Equality, an integrated group dedicated to ending the de facto segregation of housing in the New Bedford area, though the group's work was confined to meetings and newspaper advertisements.[28]

At the same time, Clark worked at the Rodman Job Corps Center, a program of the Office of Economic Opportunity (OEO) that brought together teenage "drop-outs" and idealistic young teacher-counselors at Clark's Point, the farthest southern part of New Bedford.[29] Spanning the critical years 1965 to early 1968, the experiment was a kind of radicalism incubator, in complex and sometimes unexpected ways. First, it brought hundreds of young, mostly male blacks, often from precisely those large urban centers that had experienced rioting during the decade, into a lily white, blue-collar and lower white-collar community of French-Canadians, Irish, Poles, Italians, and Portuguese homeowners. The result was immediate and sustained community opposition, whose locus was the all-white City Council.[30] In response, the NAACP sought, largely without success, both jobs at and leverage over a federally run project whose leadership was composed of liberal visionaries from outside the community. The group succeeded, however, in getting Mayor Harrington, after many years of urging, to create a Human Rights Commission for the city.[31] All the while, Clark and others sought to bring black and Cape Verdean youth together with the often more politically savvy corpsmen and some of their teachers. The latter included Ezell ("Easy") Blair, one of the four freshmen who sparked the sit-in movement that began in Greensboro, N.C., in 1960, and Lou Randall, a former gang member from Chicago and one-time associate of the Revolutionary Action Movement. Meanwhile, sporting events at Rodman, which were organized to build better community relations, naturally broadened the horizons of local youth. At the same time, there were tensions between the corpsmen and Cape Verdean boys, partly because of the competition over local girls, and partly because of differences of racial identity. As Dottin put it in 1966, "[Because the corpsmen were] unfamiliar with the Cape Verdean situation[,] seeing black people calling themselves white[,] several arguments ensued between the youths."[32] Geography played a role here: to get to the downtown area, the corpsmen had to walk through the predominantly Cape Verdean section of the South End. In sum, the battles over the very existence of Rodman always had a racial as well as a class and an ethnic cast.[33]

Still, when it closed in early 1968, in the shadow of scores of riots the summer before, Rodman went out with a whimper, not a bang. The one evidence of protest was a trip several corpsmen took to Washington to see the president and vice president, as well as OEO officials and the Massachusetts congressional delegation. Their leader, James Caldwell of Oklahoma City, told a local reporter, "We want to express ourselves in a peaceful and sensible way, without the violence that other protests by the younger generation have stirred." Though he did warn that cutting such programs "could be a cause for young teen-agers this summer who are rebelling," it is not clear if he was referring specifically to New Bedford.[34]

At that moment, unlike in larger cities such as Boston, there was no local chapter of the Congress of Racial Equality (CORE) or the Student Non-Violent Coordinating Committee (SNCC), nor was there any of the range of other organizations, homegrown or national, that dotted such larger urban centers.[35] Even New Bedford's peaceful civil rights demonstrations lay in the future. The first real sign of militancy was the creation, in the aftermath of Martin Luther King's assassination, of the Black United Front—typically referred to as simply the United Front. Moreover, although it was linked to a similar organization in Boston, in New Bedford its constituency was principally the more impatient members of the local NAACP. The city did witness some youthful skirmishes with police in the West End, but not until King was assassinated, and that violence hardly registered compared to what occurred elsewhere in the country.[36]

As for the Black Panthers, even most Panther scholars are unaware of their existence here. Most people at the time—even the most assiduous readers of *The Black Panther*—would not have known about their presence in New Bedford. That is, until an incident during the early morning hours of July 31, 1970, the middle of the Panthers' last year as a dynamic national organization.[37]

The New Bedford 21

Sometime around 6 a.m. on July 31, 1970, a local resident named Stephen Paul Botelho drove to police headquarters to report that he had been shot. He claimed that while he was driving home from work on Kempton Street in the heart of New Bedford's West End a sniper had shot at his car, wounding him in the right ankle.[38] He had just passed by the makeshift headquarters of the local National Committee to Combat Fascism (NCCF), essentially an arm of the BPP. Such organizations, established at a conference in Oakland the previous summer to address two related problems the Panthers faced by late 1968—too rapid growth and state repression—were front groups that also served as "organizing bureaus" for the BPP.[39] In New Bedford, the NCCF had been established with the sanction of the Boston Panthers, and staffed from the second week of July by several of them, but the idea and impetus were local.[40] Moreover, the headquarters emerged by late July as the focal point of attention for a community wracked by a series of violent events that had begun on the evening of

Wednesday, July 8—by the definition used by the Kerner (Riot) Commission of 1968, these events constituted a "serious," perhaps "major" civil disturbance.[41] Now, Botelho's report provided the pretext for a massive raid by local and state police designed to crush the Panther presence in the city and to end what some had begun to call an uprising.[42]

The raided building was the partially burned and looted remains of a local institution called Pieraccini's Variety, which had been looted on the third and fourth nights of the riot and partially burned on the fifth day; it was taken over by Panthers and their allies as early as the following morning.[43] During the month of July, it became a kind of cross-generational community center; the Panthers ran it, but people of varying degrees of politicization came to talk, debate, discover.[44] It also functioned as a kind of on-the-spot liberation school, with outdoor political education classes (what the Panthers called PE); the text was usually *Quotations from Chairman Mao* (the so-called *Little Red Book*). It being the middle of the summer, the classes were often held under an oak tree behind the building.[45] Pieraccini's was also a distribution center for Panther materials—leaflets, pamphlets, newspapers, posters. Most crucially, though, for the local political and business establishment, the storefront was a fortress of sorts, complete with sandbags, gun slots, and a cache of weapons—thanks largely to the expertise of local radicalized Vietnam veterans.[46] Some of the guns may have come by way of Joseph "The Animal" Barboza, a local mob hit man of note who was well-known to many of the black radicals in the area.[47]

The arrest of nearly two dozen people in and around Pieraccini's that day gave birth to the New Bedford 21. Later, because one was immediately released, the label New Bedford 20 became common; even after charges were dropped against several, and ten were subsequently indicted by a grand jury, that name stuck. From the beginning and throughout, they were associated with the Panthers, for they were allegedly arrested in a Panther building, which was occupied by several people known to be members of the Boston chapter of the Panthers. In fact, some of those who were arrested were merely community supporters, some unaffiliated activists, and some complete innocents. Even excluding these, however, there is enough dispute among some of the principals about who was a Panther and how one became one to raise the issue as a historical problem.

Johnny "Butch" Viera, one of the people from Boston, was actually still denominated a community worker at the time of the raid. He had been working with the Boston Panthers for the better part of 1970 and was trusted enough to "go upstairs, go to the gun room," typically the mark of a member. He thought of himself as a Panther. But he only became a member, he says, when Audrea Jones, the captain of the Boston area Panthers, visited him in the Dedham County Jail after the raid on July 31, yelling up at him from outside, "Hey, Johnny, you're a Panther!"

Meanwhile, Viera is particularly dismissive of those arrested who were part of the Ad Hoc Committee, which was negotiating with city officials, after a fashion, in the wake of the rioting. Because Viera suspects that the group may have betrayed those inside Pieracinni's, he does not count them among the Panther ranks. Two committee members were among those arrested—Richard "Dickie" Duarte, who insisted he was a Panther at the time (because he was accepted as such in Boston), and Robert "Bobby" Stevens, who insists he never was. Viera associates Russell "Buffalo" Rebeiro with the committee, which he was not, and rejects the idea that he was ever a Panther, which others insist he was. For his part, Rebeiro says he was "abandoned" by the Boston Panthers after the raid.[48]

Precisely *how* someone became a Panther, then, varied considerably, in different places, at different times, and from individual to individual—adding somewhat to the confusion about the New Bedford 21. The formal process involving a certain specific probationary period described by the former Oakland Panther Billy X (Williams) in his newsletter, *It's About Time* . . . seems not to have been the standard procedure in either New Bedford or Boston.[49] As Viera asserts, "A lot of this becomin' a Panther was on how people felt in their gut about you." In this period, 1969–72, in Massachusetts, that gut seems to have been Audrea Jones's.[50] Meanwhile, the FBI, having long tracked the Boston group and compiling information from a range of sources on New Bedford from the moment of the raid, had no trouble identifying, every month, the number and names of leaders, members, and community workers in both locations.[51]

In any case, the charges against those arrested were dramatic, even shocking: they included conspiracy to commit murder and anarchy, and to incite riot. Moreover, the original total bail was over one million dollars. The prisoners were questioned by the FBI, which immediately opened a file on the NCCF and all associated with it.[52] One of the twenty-one claims to have been maced in his cell by frustrated police, because, he says, "We kinda took over that part of the city, . . . made fools out of 'em."[53] The 1960s had finally come to New Bedford, and in a big way.

"We've Taken off Our Shufflin' Shoes"
The New Bedford Conflagration

For many—in the predominantly white North End, in business and political circles, in the local press—it had come out of nowhere. As one white reporter for the *New Bedford Standard Times* put it in a column that appeared two days into the rioting, "Things like this only happen in Detroit, Watts, Newark and other places, but not in New Bedford."[54] The sentiment captured the local sense that the city had long ago fallen out of the mainstream. Nevertheless, the sense of foreboding that Duncan Dottin had articulated in 1964 appeared in the paper's "Black Views" column the morning before the rioting began. Opening with one local proclaiming, "We've taken off our shufflin' shoes," the reporter continued, "The new black is convinced his government and his community have not responded to his needs and where he once argued in the confines of a quiet city hall chamber, his arguments now also are presented in the streets . . . and when he feels there is still no respect, he brings the streets into that chamber. [The new black is ready to] take over a building and tell the police, 'Shoot me, but we're not leaving until we solve the problem.' "[55]

Just who was this "new black," and what, precisely, was the problem? Neither can be answered definitively. First, as became clear the first night of the riots, many of those in the streets were Cape Verdeans. Second, while the rhetoric of black power and the symbols of black nationalism were scrawled on the walls and doorways of the West End, many of the more politically sophisticated—and not just among the Panthers—insisted that this was not a race riot. Dr. Herbert Waters, for example, the first black administrator in the New Bedford school system, and a self-identified Afro-Indian, maintained later that "it was never a race riot; it was a social movement."[56] "It was between the have-nots and the people in authority. The poor and disenfranchised were showing their displeasure with those in power who overlooked their basic human and civil rights."[57]

It is no easier to determine precisely what started things on that night of July 8, though it appears that, like most "ghetto riots" of the period, it was spontaneous, initially unorganized, and precipitated by police action.[58] Once begun, though, the lid seemed to have come off New Bedford. By 1:00 a.m. on the July 9, the city had witnessed clashes between scores of youths and police and firefighters, with injuries on both sides, the first of scores. The young people chanted the now popular Panther slogans "Off

the Pig" and "pigs out of the community," built homemade street barricades composed of overturned and burning cars, threw rocks and other
debris, started numerous fires, and even began sniping at vehicles, including police cruisers. In response, on more than one occasion, police drew
their guns; they also arrested three men in their early twenties, the first
crop of hundreds who would be taken in during the month. The first to be
arrested on July 8 was Warren Houtman. Well-known locally as a militant
black, Houtman was perhaps arrested for driving with a defective car light,
a police action that may have been an escalation of tensions that had
already begun earlier in the evening.[59] Some early press reports suggest
that something happened before Houtman was arrested, as that altercation
came when police were allegedly removing barricades blocking the inter-
section of Kempton and Ash Streets. But, Frank "Parky" Grace, a Cape
Verdean born and raised in the South End, was hanging out on the streets
of the West End that night, as he did most summer nights. He insisted that
the violence began with a routine police stop of Houtman for demonstrating the sound and speed of his souped-up car in front of the West End
Social Club, a local hangout just off Kempton on Cedar Street. Grace,
already a member of the Black Panther Party, though there was no branch
yet in the city, categorically rejected the story that police were already in
the area to remove barricades ("it's all in their minds"), as he did the claim
that Houtman was stopped for a defective tail light. From Grace's perspective, what happened that night happened all the time, as the police regularly harassed those hanging out on the street.[60]

Arrested next was Charlie Perry, another Cape Verdean and a good
friend of Grace's, who, like Grace, was known for his street-fighting abili-
ties. He would soon become a Panther, too; that night, though, he was
taken in for helping a black girl escape police clutches in the troubled
aftermath of Houtman's arrest. And, finally, there was Jimmy Magnett,
with family roots in Cape Verde and the American South. He was another
associate of Grace's, though already more politically engaged than Perry.
Well-known as a firebrand voice at local meetings and in the letters-to-
the-editor column of the *Standard Times*, Magnett was identified in press
reports as the defense minister of a local veterans' group called the Black
Brothers Political Party, to which Grace also belonged. If press reports of
the evening are accurate, Magnett was arrested just for being there.[61]

The violence that night was spontaneous, but several blacks told a local reporter that it had been "slowly, but surely, building to that pitch for months, probably for years." There was little dispute about the *underlying* causes: local residents consistently mentioned high unemployment, poor and limited housing, lack of adequate educational and recreational facilities, and especially police brutality. Thus, it followed, as another local interviewed on the street that night said: "Tonight won't be the end of it."[62] And it was not. By the next day, the violence had escalated and spread to the city's South End, which meant significant involvement of both Cape Verdeans and Puerto Ricans. Soon, Panthers such as Dickie Duarte would use a megaphone taken from Burns Electric on Kempton to proselytize young people at Monte's Park in the heart of the South End. The local newspaper, consumed by the news of the fast-paced and unexpected events, could only characterize the conflagration in its July 10 edition as "the worst civil disturbance in decades."[63] One rookie cop, recently returned from Vietnam, said later, "It reminded me of the war."[64] In the coming days and weeks of July, sympathetic white radicals and antipathetic white vigilantes joined the fray, as did civil rights activists of all stripes, a new mayor of particularly liberal bent, a rather conservative City Council, the state police, and state political leaders. Even Ed Brooke, the first black Republican U.S. senator since Reconstruction, came to town and appointed the Ad Hoc Committee to negotiate with the mayor and police.

Drawn in, too, were the Boston Black Panthers, seen by the mayor, the City Council, and the police as the quintessential "outside agitators," the cause of the trouble itself. Even some of the street militants saw it that way. Indeed, the nature and extent of local support for the Panthers in the summer of 1970, even who they were precisely, is not easily assessed.[65] The memories of those closest to the story sometimes unintentionally reveal the complexity of the moment. Johnny Viera, who grew up in New Bedford, got involved with the Panthers in Boston, and returned with a few cadre after the rioting began, described their reception this way: "When we came, I'll never forget, when we came, people were like, wow! Y'know, yeah! You're here; they were very anxious to know—we were like heroes, y'know?" But, when confronted with evidence that some local militants recall a sense of having been invaded, he qualified that statement: "There was Parky [Grace] and his group that were receptive. . . . But, don't forget, there was this ad hoc committee; and there was this, other groups, of people, and they did, y'know, they felt that, hey, we don't need the Panthers. . . . There was only a small group of people that actually wanted us to be there." Clearly, too, there was a significant difference for many between Parky Grace, a local who had become a Panther, and Robert "Big Bob" Heard, the Panther from Boston. Unsurprisingly, Viera himself seems to have fallen somewhere in between: "We *were* looked upon as outsiders, because that's what we were. Even I, though I was born in New Bedford, I can remember conversations with them, they would tell me, y'know, 'You ain't been here, Johnny, you haven't been here in X amount of years.' Right? But I was known there, and I would tell them, 'It makes no difference; I was born here; this is my home.' " Grace verified the problem when he was asked why, given his links to the Boston Panthers, and his involvement with the Black Brothers Political Party, which had a lot of the Panther trappings, he hadn't just formed a Panther branch out of that. "The neighborhood," he said flatly. "There's a mistrust. And I, get your own, you know? We don' need them to come in and tell us what to do. . . . They're outsiders."[66]

So, on July 14, nearly a week into the uprising, the *Standard Times* carried a UPI story, "Black Panthers Called Worst Extremists," which quoted J. Edgar Hoover telling Congress that the Panthers "continued to be the most dangerous and violence prone of all extremist groups."[67] He had been saying as much since the fall of 1968. No wonder that many locals—then and now—would see the raid on Pieraccini's on July 31 as the solution to New Bedford's problem in the summer of 1970.

Cape Verdean Roads to Pieraccini's

Inside the building that morning, in bed but awake, Viera heard one of his compatriots yell from the roof, "They're coming!"[68] At first, he thought it was another of the "runners"—the vigilantes who drove by trying to provoke them—or perhaps a police provocation, but this time it was for real. Viera turned to Cathy Perry, the Boston Panther in bed with him, and said, "This is it." Quickly armed and ready, he claims today to have been unafraid: "We were pumped. . . . We were *political*. We understood this would happen one day. . . . Like Mao said, the greatest thing that the revolutionary has to give to the revolution is his life."[69]

Viera had been sent to New Bedford because he had been born and raised there. Like many local Panthers, he was of Cape Verdean descent—a matter that would both facilitate and complicate Panther politics. Close family and community connections facilitated organizing as a younger generation of Cape Verdeans came to identify as "black" or "Afro-American" in the late 1960s.[70] Their parents' chagrin at such a turn complicated matters, as did the presence of the Boston Panthers, who simply could not make sense of the Cape Verdean culture. Viera, of course, was different. He had grown up in the South End, considering himself Portuguese—until he moved to Boston and felt the sting of racism. In the sixth grade at the John Winthrop School, he remembered later with great bitterness, he was engaged in a debate on the Civil War with the smartest white boy in the class. Suddenly, his teacher turned to him and said, "*Your* people were slaves." Viera says now, "It really crushed me. So what he did, what the teacher effectively did—and I can see his face to this day, right?—what he did, he basically was saying to me and to the rest of the class, right?—'You're just a nigger. Sit down. You're just a nigger. This is a white boy, and what he's saying weighs more than yours.'"

By 1963, having lived for several years in predominantly black Roxbury, Dorchester, and Mattapan, he was back in New Bedford's South End, seventeen and on his own. Only now he thought of himself as black—for which he was called "nigger lover" by some of his friends. Meanwhile, because he lived in the *South* End, inevitably he got into scrapes with black kids in the rival *West* End. One fight led to his nearly killing another boy his age named "Parky" Grace—indeed, Grace was given last rites and, he claimed, a sheet was pulled over his head before he regained consciousness, protesting that he was still alive.[71] Thus began a feud that would eventually lead to an enduring if sometimes rocky relationship. Now, many years later, after a stint in the army and another in jail, where he became attracted to the Nation of Islam, and then out on the streets of Boston in 1970 where he developed a very different attraction to the Black Panther Party—in some measure, at least initially, to the Panther Cathy Perry, who was half Cape Verdean and half Chinese—Viera would find himself linked *politically* to his old friend Parky in a life-and-death struggle on the streets of their native New Bedford.

On that morning in July 1970, while preparing to defend Pieraccini's from atop the building, Viera saw people from the community marching up Kempton Street—the people who had frequented the "headquarters" over the past weeks—and he called out, "Get Parky!" After all, locals sometimes referred to the Panthers in town as "Parky's Panthers." Parky was born in New Bedford and, like Viera, he was a Cape Verdean who had been raised in the South End.[72] When he was a young teen, though, he and his family moved to the *West* End, and he began "running" with black kids, for which, he, too, would be chastised by his family: why was he hanging out with "niggers"? Frequently in trouble with the law, he entered the army in 1965 to avoid serious jail time, fought in the jungles of Vietnam as a combat engineer, and came home in 1968 with a new outlook on life. Now, he identified with the National Liberation Front (NLF), harboring an even deeper animus toward authority than the one he had gone away with. He returned to a city whose younger Cape Verdeans had become "black."

Accepted into the New Careers program for returning students at nearby Bristol Community College (BCC), he encountered an antiwar demonstration on his first day. He traveled to Washington for the massive November 1969 antiwar march with some of the leaders of the campus demonstrations. They were young radical professors, "Mother Country Radicals" (Panther terminology for revolutionary whites); some, like Gloria Clark, were the very professors who taught in his program. As it happened, Parky returned with them by way of Boston, where *they* introduced *him* to the Boston branch of the Black Panther Party. It was an impressive group. There, at the Panthers' office on Blue Hill Avenue in Roxbury, he met Audrea Jones. Because she was energetic, tough, and sometimes abrasive, some of the Panthers under her command called her "Stalin," though Viera insists the label was applied with respect. Parky also encountered "Big Bob" Heard, who stood six feet seven inches (though everyone *said* he was six feet eight inches) and weighed well over three hundred pounds, and who was later Huey Newton's bodyguard. And, too, he met Donna Howell, who in the 1970s was an administrator, with Elaine Brown and Erika Huggins, of the Panthers' last project, the Oakland Liberation School.[73]

The Boston Panthers "We Were Talking Socialist Ideas"

In Boston, the previous spring, a group of Young Turks led by Doug Miranda, Audrea Jones, Gene Jones, Greg Jones, and Floyd Hardwick had expelled the original leadership, derived from area SNCC members and established in the summer of 1968 by Stokely Carmichael, then the prime minister of the BPP.[74] Among their political crimes as of May 24,

1969, were "propagating cultural nationalist madness inside our Party instead of class struggle" and "racism."[75] At the time, the Panthers had emerged nationally as an avowedly revolutionary socialist party dedicated to Marxist-Leninist principles, a process with roots deep in the party's history (and prehistory) and sharpened by its bloody battles with the US Organization early that year. By July, Carmichael, who was never ideologically compatible with the national Panther leadership on the thorny issue of race and class, resigned from the party ostensibly over precisely that issue, prompting an open letter from Eldridge Cleaver the following year condemning him retrospectively for having been "unable to distinguish your friends from your enemies because all you could see was the color of the cat's skin."[76]

But the story of the Panthers in Boston had its own logic. Though they were sharply aware of ideological struggles going on in Oakland—they read *The Black Panther*, after all—the new leaders were also generally younger, more indigenous to the community, more deeply and personally tied to one another, and, in their view at least, worked harder, studied more, and hungered more to make revolution than the leaders they ousted. "We were teenagers," Doug Miranda remembers, but "we outgrew them." Part Cape Verdean and a distant cousin of Parky Grace, Miranda was a product of Boston's Dorchester neighborhood. He became the area captain after the purge and, subsequently would hold ranking positions in New Haven, New York, Winston-Salem, and ultimately Oakland, becoming an important national presence in the party. The story he tells is of a movement in flux, offering a useful corrective to the standard one-dimensional portraits of the Black Panthers.

You see . . . the Party was a spontaneous development. . . . People would put on berets and black leather coats, and say, "we're Panthers." So . . . it wasn't this like equal development in growth that was going on. . . . It was in different cities, *within* cities. So . . . things would sort of filter down from . . . Oakland, and . . . in terms of how later on you talk about "Party line" . . . I mean, there might have been fifty. . . . Oakland didn't know what it was doing. We were doing something, but we didn't know what we were doing. . . . How do we bring all this stuff together? How do we create something so Oakland can relate to Boston, Boston can relate to New York, New York can relate to Detroit . . . ?

Still, there was an ideological fault line in Boston, at least by early 1969, dividing the group into what Miranda calls "two clearly identifiable blocs." As Greg Jones, another of the new leaders, remembers it:

> We started reading. And we knew where it was basically going. First of all, we had the Red Book. . . . All Panthers carried the Red Book. . . . And when you read some of the sayings of it . . . that right there makes you know that you was headed more towards Marxist-Leninist. The other Panthers, I guess that they carried it, but they didn't read it. But, we started reading it, you know, from the front to the back. And then we started internalizing what they were saying inside. You know, like trying to make those things we were reading *happen.* You know, like, trying to treat your brother like a brother.

"We were talking socialistic ideas," he says, while the leaders were more interested in their guns ("they were always cleaning their guns") and "thought it was a black struggle."[77]

The precise nature, order, and timing of events in the Boston chapter leading to the May 1969 purge are murky, but this much seems clear: the Young Turks asked for help from Oakland, and Field Marshal Don Cox ("DC") of the Central Committee came to Boston, presided over a climactic meeting at which both factions were armed, and expelled the old leadership. Cox was on the East Coast that spring organizing for the United Front against Fascism Conference, which produced the NCCF, and, in the process, he oversaw the reorganization of several chapters.[78] About Boston, he remembers in particular hearing reports that the area captain, Chico Neblett, who was also a Panther field marshal for the country east of the Continental Divide, had shown up one day in a Corvette. "Naturally," DC says now, "people want to know what the fuck's going on." But he also remembers that a younger group in Boston embraced what he sees as having been natural for the Bay Area Panthers from the beginning: unity with people of all colors if they were ready "to get down." The change in the Boston BPP in mid-1969 was palpable, not only in its adoption of a much higher public profile, including the establishment of a host of community projects such as the Breakfast for School Children Program, but in its public repudiation of the old leadership's rhetoric. As Miranda told the *Boston Globe* that summer, announcing the arrival of a new leadership on the scene, "This country propagates the race struggle to hide the class struggle."[79]

Parky Grace *"This Is What I Want"*

The party that Parky Grace made contact with the following fall, then, was a revolutionary socialist organization, claiming the ideology of "Marxism-Leninism-Mao Tse-tung Thought." As he told it thirty years later, it was exactly what he was looking for. "Just goin' in there, enterin' the door," he said, describing his first visit to the Panthers' headquarters in Boston, "there was Big Bob teaching a PE class. . . . And I knew right then: I said, *this is what I want.*" That day in November 1969, Grace brought back "newspapers and buttons and posters" to New Bedford; he would make many more trips to Boston by bus or by hitchhiking that school year, always bringing back material—and sometimes Panthers such as Audrea or Big Bob as well.[80] *They* would speak to gatherings of local young people—often at the African Church, one of the oldest in the country, sometimes at the teen hangout on Kempton Street they called simply, The Club.[81] Some in the audience came to identify as Panthers and formed the core of the future New Bedford party. Still, either because they were unaware of these meetings or they have forgotten, the mayor and the living city councilors insist today, as they did in 1970, that the Panthers were "outside agitators" who had kicked up the unrest that began in July.[82] In contrast, the police, who were paid to keep track of such things, knew about the Panthers meeting in town well before the summer.

They also knew about the other group Parky Grace and a number of military veterans had formed in the local Elks Club one night early that year: the Black Brothers Political Party. Meeting in houses and on street corners to talk—though, as Grace maintained later, this group's view of revolution was *fighting*—they also put up posters of revolutionaries across the street from the Elks at the West End Social Club—a bar for *adults*, also on Kempton.[83] Most did not become Panthers, at least in part because they were seen as outsiders. Still, by July, "without really knowing what we were doing," Grace insisted, they had created the kind of unity and dedication that would be revealed in the explosion of violence he always called "the Insurrection" or "the Rebellion." Just as for Herb Waters, for Parky Grace "it wasn't a race riot. There were blacks, Puerto Ricans, and whites in the crowd. We were fighting the government. It was just the people coming together." More than that, perhaps, it was about control of the community. As he maintained throughout his life, "The police didn't stop anything.

We did."[84] Thus, he always referred to the events of July 1970 as the *so-called* riots.

Grace was there when the violence started on July 8, he was in the streets throughout the month, and he was at the center of the effort to establish the "headquarters." Pieraccini himself, the longtime owner of the neighborhood variety store, testified later that Grace approached him on July 11 with a plan to make the store into a "community service center." Pieraccini's son told the police that Grace told him he wanted to establish a "youth center" there, and that his father had agreed to turn the electricity back on as long as he received a statement signed by several "reliable and responsible people in the neighborhood."[85] He would allow the installation of a phone in the name of the NCCF, as long as Grace's name was not on the contract. Meanwhile, on July 13, Pieraccini's son arrived from his home in South Dartmouth to assess the damage and found people on the site cleaning up. He told the police that when he asked them why they were there, they said, "The People told us to take over the building and we are doing so."[86] Grace, who always insisted that his efforts were entirely defensive, claimed later that he and other Panthers tried to stop the taking of Pieraccini's.[87] Once it was largely destroyed by rioters, however, the idea to make it the Panthers' headquarters was apparently Grace's. "We came down and we looked; I said, 'that over there would be good.'" About Pieraccini, he said, "Good people. I said, 'Look, man, I'm sorry about what happened.' Saved all his equipment, y'know, for cuttin' meat an' everything. People—we put out a call for it and they brought it back. The food, you know, that's gone. But all his equipment, I called him [and] I told him, 'You know, you don't want to open up no more here.' It's sad." Viera remembers clearly—and Grace confirmed—that Grace and "one or two other guys" then went to Boston and talked to Audrea. According to Viera, "Parky said, 'We have to have Panthers in New Bedford.' " "He says, 'I got a place,' he said, 'I've got a store front that we can have as a center; all of the stuff, you know?' He had things all lined up." Once in New Bedford, Viera says, "Parky took us over to this place that was an old store that they had gutted out . . . and everything, and he said, 'Here, man, this is *ours!* ' " The district attorney was thus not far off the mark when he explained in court that "they confiscated the store."[88]

A prominent presence in Pieraccini's, along with the Boston Panthers, Grace was there the night before the raid—but he had gone home to sleep the night of July 30 and so came on the scene after many of the arrested were already in the police wagon. In one of the moments in this drama most everyone remembers in the same way, he banged on the wagon's sides until they let him in, as he insisted—against all logic of self-preservation—that he belonged with his people and demanded to be taken. "I remember them," says Viera, "they came over and they grabbed me and handcuffed me and threw me into the, into the wagon, right? And, like I say, here comes my boy, Parky! Coming out of the crowd. 'Take *me!*,' right?" For that, Grace would spend several weeks in jail, with capital charges hanging over his head for another eight months.[89]

Kim Holland "Just a Kid"

Already in the wagon was Kim Holland, who had been grabbed as she exited the back door of Pieraccini's.[90] At fifteen, she was the youngest of the group, and she was released almost immediately for that reason; like Grace, though, she too seems to have been everywhere during those days—and later.[91] She was with Grace on the Washington trip, at the Panther office in Boston afterward (he remembers), and in the New Bedford branch. She was also a central player, of sorts, in that July's most dramatic, if horrific, moment, the incident that turned escalating street violence into a real conflagration. In the early evening hours of July 11, a Saturday and some three days into the "riot," Holland and scores of other young people, some as young as fourteen, others in their late twenties, were milling around on Kempton Street. They were just down the block from Pieraccini's at the green building called The Club where Grace and the Boston Panthers had proselytized local youth earlier in the year. Somehow, a gray and white 1957 Chevy containing three young whites from neighboring towns breached the barricades Grace and others had erected on the first night of trouble and stopped in the middle of the street. Ralph Brown, the twenty-year-old driver, and Gary DesLauriers, his eighteen-year-old backseat passenger, lived in Acushnet; sitting in the front passenger seat was George Rose, a nineteen year old from Fairhaven. Brown, the son of a popular local junior high school principal and a recent graduate of New Bedford High School, was the "quiet and somewhat strange" boy who had sat behind Lee Blake, Kim Holland's friend and later her co-worker in the Panthers' Free Breakfast Program, in math class. By the summer of 1970,

Brown had a wife and a young child, and he worked at White's Farm Dairy in Acushnet. Without any psychological or criminal history, he would be diagnosed as a "sociopathic personality" by a state psychiatrist assigned to evaluate him.[92] That night on Kempton Street, Brown got out of his car, laid his shotgun across its roof, and fired point-blank into the crowd to his right.

There may have been an altercation at just that spot involving the same car earlier in the evening, which suggests that revenge may have been a motive, but Brown told the police afterward that he thought it was "rotten what happened to Pieraccini's Variety Store."[93] Whatever his motive, dozens of shotgun pellets from Brown's weapon sprayed across the torso of seventeen-year-old Lester Lima, from his neck to his navel, riddling both arms and piercing his heart, lungs, aorta, liver, and intestines. He died on an operating table at St. Luke's Hospital at 9:40 p.m. The press reported it as the shotgun slaying of a black youth; Lima, from the South End, was Cape Verdean. Three others were seriously wounded, including a politically precocious twenty year old named Gordon Rebeiro, another Cape Verdean but from the West End. Years earlier, he had formed his own gang of sorts, which he called the Junior Panthers. Radicalized in part by his contacts with job corpsmen from Rodman with whom he played sports as a teen, in part by what he heard at local barbershops where older men such as John "Duke" Cruz, a supporter of the Panthers and a West End Cape Verdean, held forth, he was also very close to Parky Grace, his sister's boyfriend. Two older brothers and a cousin would join the Panthers, but his parents made sure Gordon stayed away from the action in the shooting's aftermath. Her family was unable to do the same for Kim Holland, who was also shot that night and who would say later that the shooter seemed to be pointing his weapon "in [her] direction, specifically at [her]."[94]

She was, in some ways, very different from the others. Born in Queens, New York, of professional parents (college professors), she moved to New Bedford at the age of nine, into an all-white neighborhood, though not far from the West End. Her parents were active in the local NAACP and later the United Front; her father can be seen holding forth for the cameras of *Say, Brother!* on Friday, July 10; her mother, a prominent force in New Bedford's anti-poverty program in the mid-1960s, was active in the Panther breakfast program in late 1970 and 1971. The Hollands passed their activism to their daughter when she was young, taking her to picket Kresge's and Woolworth's in 1960 when she was barely five and to the March on Washington three years later. Despite all of this—perhaps because of it—Kim never felt comfortable in New Bedford. She was of Caribbean descent, *not* Cape Verdean but "American de couer," and recalls being derided by Cape Verdean kids from the beginning for being black. Thus, early on, she sought refuge in the black communities of New York, where many of her relatives still lived, and of nearby Boston.

But then she fell in with the group of white radicals at BCC whom Parky Grace knew; they called themselves the Regional Action Group (RAG). Fresh from the university and the break-up of the Students for a Democratic Society (SDS) in the summer of 1969, they had come to the New Bedford and Fall River area to organize among the poor and the working class. Their first targets were white and black youth in the junior high and high schools, particularly around the war issue. They helped to organize the first antiwar demonstration in New Bedford—complete with guerilla theater, NLF flags, and chants for Huey Newton, Bobby Seale, and Ho Chi Minh—in early November 1969.[95] One local reporter called the scene "unreal," but it exhilarated people such as Parky Grace, who had lived to see the antiwar movement come to his own community, and Kim Holland, who had helped organize the event. A week later, the two went to Washington, got on the wrong bus coming back and ended up with Panthers in New Haven, then New York, and finally Boston. By then a runaway, she says now she knew only that she wanted to be a Panther.

She joined the party, working in both New Bedford and Boston during the early 1970s. She describes herself during this period as "just a kid," "always the kid"; others remember her as a significant force, even as an early teen. By 1970, she had persuaded the adults in RAG to move from antiwar demonstrations to a march in Fall River in support of the Panthers, which they scheduled for May 1 to coincide with demonstrations planned in New Haven for Bobby Seale, Erika Huggins, and others on trial there. The announcement of the action led to wild rumors of Panthers landing in boats along the Massachusetts coast, the cancellation of the march, and, ultimately, the dissolution of RAG over just what kind of action the group should take.[96]

Three members of the more militant faction—identified in the local press as SDS members, though by then that affiliation was largely in their past—would be arrested on the second night of the New Bedford disturbances for attempted arson. According to one, BCC instructor Mark Dworkin, who had cut his political teeth at Columbia University in the late 1960s, the goal was to provide a diversion to take some pressure off those in the streets. He came up with the idea of burning an abandoned building away from the action after calling the one person he knew best and trusted most in New Bedford—Kim Holland—and asking her how he could help in the "rebellion." Though the action was an utter failure, the press and local politicians played up the story of "outsider agitators" in their midst. The notion gained some credibility from the lawyer Dworkin managed to get to represent the three in court—the most famous Movement lawyer of the age, William Kuntzler.[97]

The "Liberated Territory" of New Bedford

The white radicals knew another in the arrest wagon: Russell Rebeiro, an older brother of Gordon, the Junior Panther who had been shot in front of The Club. Called "Buffalo" because of his military bent, he joined the Marines in 1962 fresh out of high school. Cape Verdean, he did not think of himself as black—until he encountered a military that defined him as "colored," not Portuguese. Here, like Gordon's experience with the Rodman corpsmen, Buffalo learned from black Marines who hailed from large urban centers such as Philadelphia, though the experience did not make him "political." That part of his development came with Vietnam, for, on his way back from Okinawa to his home base in Hawaii in the late winter of 1965, his company was diverted to Indochina with the first wave of official combat troops. He returned to New Bedford in early 1969, worked, and entered Southeastern Massachusetts University the following fall—just in time for a student strike against a college president widely perceived as racist by black students. They formed the Black Student Union, and Buffalo would eventually become its head. During the school year of 1969–70, he saw the "so-called black leadership" as "played out," but he did not see an alternative.

One was the Nation of Islam. He learned about them from a new friend, "Easy" Blair. Blair had not advertised his past when he came to town; indeed, that only became known when he was publicly identified by Jackie Robinson, who visited the Job Corps Center in the fall of 1966. By the time Rebeiro got out of the service, Blair had become Jibreel Khazan, a Muslim with close connections to civil rights activists in Boston. Rebeiro also met local white communists from a group that called itself the People's Party, one of whom passed him a Red Book. He went to some meetings, he had informal conversations, but he was, as he put it later, "kind of lost." He cannot now even identify precisely when he decided to join the Panthers. He had known Parky Grace "since forever," which surely made a difference, but, as things festered on the streets of New Bedford in April and May and into June of 1970, he still felt "left out." Until July 8, the taking of Pieraccini's, and the subsequent arrival of the Boston Panthers. Just what *was* he by then? A socialist, a revolutionary, a radical, a black nationalist, a black militant? A combination of all, he says now, but he also admits that he "didn't go to that level." For him, what happened in New Bedford was indeed a rebellion, and he was ready for it—but just what kind he cannot say.

He remembers most that he was ready to defend the territory he and his compatriots had won: early on, they had blocked off the West End from the police, and Pieraccini's for him was merely an outpost in that "liberated territory." Grace maintained the same position, also from a military point of view. Thus, for example, one of his first activities was to shoot out the streetlights in the Kempton Street area.[98] Some later belittled such efforts as evidence of a lack of seriousness. For Grace, though, it was simply a first step in controlling the community. His old friend, Viera, remembers it the same way. "The whole West End area that we were in was a totally liberated area. At night, you know, we would organize patrols, and we would patrol the community with shotguns and stuff like that—y'know what I mean? So.... It was really the Utopia, really, now that I think about it." One of the reasons the murder of Lester Lima caused such shock was precisely because that evening's gathering along Kempton was a kind of celebration of community control. Thus, virtually everyone there that night insists the police had to have connived with the three to allow them onto Kempton Street.[99] At the same time, once raided, the Panthers called New Bedford "occupied territory."[100]

The Retaking of Pieraccini's

The pressure on city authorities to act was intense just before the raid, particularly after renewed arson and rioting in the South End sparked more of the same in the West End during the last week of July. The morning of July 30, for example, the local newspaper ran a front-page editorial that ended with the warning, "New Bedford is in trouble. It is inviting more. Stiff measures must be taken to stop it, and stop it now." On the editorial page, the headline demanded, "The Violence Must Stop."[101]

There are countless stories about who ordered the raid that followed—when, why, and who knew about it. They include Senator Ted Kennedy telling Jimmy Magnett and his brother, the local firebrand Peter Antone, days before the event that the building was about to be retaken.[102] Ex-Panthers claim to have been tipped of an imminent raid, suggesting that perhaps the police were simply waiting for the pretext that the Botelho shooting offered.[103] A desire to avoid just such an eventuality apparently explains why the Panthers called a press conference the day before inviting the police in, as long as the media and their lawyers were present; the police declined the invitation.[104] George Rogers, the former mayor, adamantly insists he ordered the raid, while several city councilors remember the idea emanating from within the City Council, which then pressured Rogers to act—because the status quo was untenable. Sergeant Gauthier insists police at the scene made the decision in response to the Botelho shooting.[105]

In any case, Buffalo Rebeiro, who now works for the sheriff's department in New Bedford, was prepared to defend what he had helped secure with his seven years of military experience. Given the number of other veterans involved, the Panthers' military posture, and Viera's contention that he believed then that "the greatest thing that the revolutionary has to give to the revolution is his life," that the Panthers did not defend Pieracinni's presents an intriguing historical puzzle, stretching the historian's ability to get to the "truth" to its limits. Perhaps the surrender was merely an expression of what Jibreel Khazan refers to as the "soft people" of New Bedford; perhaps, as for the militant Ronnie Cruz, the veteran who shot *above* passing motorists that month, the taste for blood was not there that morning; perhaps it was simply the absence of the more daring Parky Grace.[106] But, Pieraccini's was under the control of forces beyond New Bedford.

According to Johnny Viera, as he took up his position in the back of Pieraccini's in preparation to defend the building just after dawn on July 31, the ranking Panther on site, the Boston Panther Orlando Vaughn, was on the phone to Audrea Jones in Boston, who was simultaneously on the phone to national headquarters in Oakland. Given the stakes, and the outcome, it is likely the person on the other end of the line was David

Hilliard, the Panther chief of staff—or perhaps his brother June, the deputy chief of staff.[107] They constituted the top party leadership in the absence of Huey Newton (in jail), Eldridge Cleaver (in exile), and Bobby Seale (tied up in legal cases in Chicago and New Haven). Meanwhile, Newton's release from prison on bail was just days away. His reappearance on the streets for the first time since the fall of 1967—that is, since the Panthers had become a national organization—would quickly bring into the open a festering internal conflict over the complicated question of political versus military activity in making revolution.[108] Within a mere six months, that division would lead to a bloody split between Newton and Cleaver, and, at least from the perspective of the Panthers as a national movement, the beginning of the end of the party. Viera insists that Oakland ordered a surrender, and Jones communicated the order; he was, he says, "livid": it was "the beginning of my demise in the BPP."[109]

In any case, Boston now had its raid and, although no lengthy trial, there were plenty of courtroom theatrics, jailhouse protests, and "political prisoners."[110] Though only ten of the original twenty-one were indicted by the grand jury the following October, the name New Bedford 21 (or 20) would stick, and Boston invested much time and effort in freeing the five Boston Panthers among those waiting to stand trial. Forgetting for a moment the others involved, Viera recalls, "Me 'n Big Bob are the only political prisoners Boston ever had." As for his "demise," it was a relatively long one. Though increasingly disillusioned, and sympathetic with those who wanted "to really take the struggle to the next level," he stayed through the traumas of meeting what he quickly concluded was a drug-addicted Huey Newton in the fall of 1970 and the bloody split of early 1971. He would even return to New Bedford for a time to head up the group there whose vitality was assured in part because of the raid. That is, so long as there was the issue of the trial, set for late March 1971, Boston would take a keen interest in New Bedford.

The Fruits of July 1970
The New Bedford Black Panthers

The rest of the story, which local officials thought the raid had ended, can be glimpsed in the life of someone who was *not* in the police wagon that July morning in 1970, Dukie Matthews. A member of the Boston chapter and for a short time the head of the New Bedford branch—at seven-teen, probably the youngest leader the Panthers ever produced—Matthews spent much of late 1970 selling Panther newspapers in New Bedford, and late 1971 living and working out of the Boston headquarters. In July 1970, when he was barely fifteen, he was in a nearby reformatory. The night the four kids were shot—he knew them all from hanging out in West End—he and thirty other boys broke out of the facility and tried to make their way south to join the action. Within hours, though, all were caught.[111]

Matthews, however, represented the future of the New Bedford party, a younger cohort that had come of age with the Lima shooting and the raid. And yet, his life experiences were remarkably similar to those of other local Panthers. A Cape Verdean from Wareham, Massachusetts, at ten he moved to New Bedford when his mother divorced. Her boyfriend was Cape Verdean and dark-skinned, but he considered himself Portu-guese (thus, white) and lived in the predominantly Portuguese, French-Canadian, and Italian North End. On Matthews's first day in town, he claims, a gang of boys attacked him for being "colored," which made no sense to him. He fought back, won the grudging respect of this gang called the Wild Cats, and became a member. He insists that he first began to identify as black out of sympathy for those his new buddies derisively referred to as "the niggers," about whom he kept thinking to himself: "What did *they* do?" Soon, he was hanging out in the West End and running with the Lane Gang, through which a number of local radicals including Panthers had passed (among them, Parky Grace). Eventually, Matthews would grow an Afro, which took a lot of work because his hair was fine and relatively straight. For that act, he remembers receiving a slap from his mother's boyfriend and chastisement from his father for "looking like a nigger." By the time he was in the eighth grade, in 1969, his agitation against police brutality—his primary entry point into the struggle, his focus entirely local—had caused a near riot at his school, and he was put in the hands of the state Department of Youth Services, eventually serving two six-month terms in reform school. Here, he met black kids from the Bos-ton area, whom he quickly began organizing against the authorities.

Out on the street for a short period in the aftermath of New Bedford's summer of discontent, he began selling Panther papers and hanging out with Kim Holland, Parky Grace, and Buffalo Rebeiro. Later, during his second stint in reform school, he was recruited into the party one day during a visit by Parky Grace and Audrea Jones, a typical way that members were "made" in this area of the country. When he got out in the fall of 1971, he went straight to the Boston BPP office and began working full time. The following year, Jones sent him to New Bedford to head up the branch there, though he would shortly shut it down.

In the intervening period, Panthers and community workers had been operating openly in the city. After the raid on Pieraccini's, early work focused on getting the criminal cases lifted. At least that seems to have been the particular interest of the Boston leadership, especially because a number of Boston Panthers were held for months at high bail. The original capital charges were thrown out the weekend before the trial was to begin in late March. All that remained were possession of stolen goods and illegal weapons charges against Dickie Duarte, Parky Grace, and Bobby Stevens. In the end, only Stevens served any time. Just then finishing his term as the first student trustee at Southern Massachusetts University, he had the support of the governor and was soon released. These cases are forever linked to the one brought against the three whites charged with murder, attempted murder, assault with a dangerous weapon, and, in the case of the shooter, unlawful possession of a firearm in the shootings on July 11 of Lester Lima, Gordon Rebeiro, Kim Holland, and Randy Robinson. The notion persists, though there is no concrete evidence to support it, that a newly elected district attorney abandoned the case against the Panthers as part of a deal to keep things cool during the murder trial set to begin the following month.[112] In that trial, Ralph Brown admitted to the shooting in court, albeit during a hearing on suppression of evidence with the jury out of the room, telling the same story he had told police. The jury, all whites, deliberated for forty-five minutes and voted to acquit on all charges. There were some scattered fires, and lots of talk, but New Bedford did not erupt.[113] Still, one local civil rights leader ten years later called the Lima killing "a scar that's never going to get healed."[114]

There was much more to the New Bedford Panthers than the legal cases, however. By early September, Grace, out on bail in the 21 case, had secured a new headquarters up the street from Pieracinni's, in Ernie's drugstore (Ernie, a local bookie, was persuaded to move his operation across the street).[115] The place was clearly identified as a Panther building, with NCCF signs, the Panther insignia, and posters of prominent Panthers such as Huey Newton and Bobby Seale. But an FBI informant reported that several days after moving in an unidentified member of the group told the realty company that owned the property that "he had taken over the building to establish a community clubhouse for the youth of the West End section of New Bedford."[116] The apparent subterfuge, if the account is accurate, is not far off the mark, for the New Bedford Panthers immediately established a breakfast program, first at a local church and later at an anti-poverty center in the West End. In both cases, the program had significant community support, including from many whites. Also popular were the special events at which food was given away—mixing "soul" food like ribs with Cape Verdean dishes like "jag." Typically, these were all-day affairs, with live music, dance, and political films. Especially successful was the Free Clothing Program, organized initially by Grace and run out of the Kempton Street office. Perhaps in part because of the city's apparel industry, as well as Grace's early work in it, the program seems to have succeeded in some measure because of frequent donations provided by local residents and merchants. At the headquarters, too, the group established a liberation school and ran regular PE classes, which were also held at the South Central anti-poverty center.[117] Ernie's was also, as the children of Panthers recall, a neighborhood hangout where adults mixed with teenagers and even the very young.[118] Crucially, the group made repeated attempts to draw in others, especially Cape Verdeans in the South End, just as they had done during the July Days.

By late 1971, the New Bedford Panthers had added health care to their community programs, with free sickle cell anemia testing in area schools thanks to the assistance of the Free Medical Program in Boston. Indeed, it is hard to separate the two histories here: from the start, Boston exercised authority over New Bedford, determining its leadership, moving people in and out, even controlling its finances. Of course, the Boston group clearly had a much greater reservoir of talent and skill. With some Boston Panthers still in jail, Kim Holland still in high school, Parky Grace and Charlie Perry lacking the discipline of seasoned Panthers, Audrea Jones herself came down to oversee the operation sometime during the first fall. By the early part of 1971, just after the split between Newton and Cleaver, Viera persuaded Jones to send him back as area captain. "The morale was very low [in New Bedford]," he remembers. "By this time, the, y'know, the party is really fragmented, y'know? Eldridge an' them're doin' their things, I mean, y'know, the party is beginning to fall apart." He says he concentrated on community programs, PE classes, and, especially, speaking at area colleges and high schools. He left in the spring—New Bedford and the party—and Boston Panther Tony Marshall, already working in town, took over. In addition, Viera notes, as things became more chaotic at the national level, Oakland drained not just people but money from Boston, and Boston did the same with New Bedford.[119] In a sense, Boston had colonized an already existent movement and would try to exploit it for its own purposes.

Ultimately, for the twice-transplanted Viera, the real weakness in New Bedford was the failure of local activists to attend to those things that had made Boston so strong. "What happened was, is the branch started to fall apart. And the reason why the branch started to fall apart is because they weren't you know, they weren't politically educating themselves; they weren't, you know, they had stopped studying." Press reports, FBI documents, and personal reminiscences of local Panthers tell a different story, certainly for the spring and summer of 1971. New Bedford took its own path despite Boston's efforts to direct it from afar. Membership and community programs appear strong until the late winter of 1972. Even the closing down of the Panther office in the spring of that year seems to have been at least partly a result of the building's scheduled demolition as part of the local Redevelopment Authority's urban renewal program. For a time, the Panthers worked out of the United Front office across the street, as they made plans to raise funds for a new office by sponsoring an event called the Freedom Fund Dance.[120] As late as February 29, 1972, FBI sources reported sixteen members and thirteen community workers for the branch.[121] Here, in this much smaller place, the numbers and programs at times were nearly comparable to those in Boston. Of course, it was the Boston leadership, for its own reasons, that made the decision to close New Bedford and transport its furniture and equipment to the Winthrop Street office in Roxbury.[122] Some, such as Parky Grace, were ordered to Boston. Most refused, seeing their struggle as they always had, as a community project in New Bedford. Grace, too, who thought of himself as a Panther for the rest of his life, would return within months.

This attachment to place—the Cape Verdean capital of the United States—explains a lot about the Panther success in New Bedford. Arguably, the Cape Verdeans—precisely what had made the civil rights movement relatively weak there in the 1960s—helped the Panthers sink roots so deeply in the Whaling City's soil. Ironically, as the transplanted Boston Panther Tony

Marshall emphatically maintains, the Boston leadership never understood that. In his view, they wanted to get their people out of jail, and "get the hell out of Dodge."[123] Once the anarchy and attempted murder charges were dropped, New Bedford became a place to dump people as punishment, or to exploit for whatever economic resources it might yield.[124] In fact, there is corroborating, if problematic, evidence that the Boston group was confused by the Cape Verdeans, who supplied most of the support for the Panthers in New Bedford, from Parky Grace to Dukie Matthews. The Boston leadership seems to have been well aware of the independence movement then being waged by the PAIGC, the African Party for the Independence of Guinea Bissau and the Cape Verde Islands. Indeed, Audrea Jones had named her first child, born just before the New Bedford conflagration, after its leader, Amilcar Cabral.[125] But, Jibreel Khazan, who knew all the players in both Boston and New York, says he heard in 1970 that the Boston Panthers were leery of the New Bedford group because of their questionable racial identity. A Cape Verdean police detective, Guy Oliveira, insists that he knew from his Boston sources, though he would not name any, that the Boston group was interested only in stealing headlines because of what he called "the disturbances." Tony Marshall says Jones and several other Boston leaders came to New Bedford one day and had a restricted meeting in an upstairs room at the local headquarters. Marshall was excluded, but he claims he overheard the conversation through the porous ceiling. At the time, March 1971, ten of the original New Bedford 21 were still facing serious charges, with the trial to begin shortly. According to his account, Jones said, "I'll be glad when this is over so we can get the fuck out of here; we should never o' came down to New Bedford in the first goddamn place. . . . Because, they said, These goddamn Cape Verdeans, they don't think they're black anyway. . . ." Not long after, in a different circumstance, Jones expelled Marshall from the party, and, according to his account, put a contract out on his life.

Hearsay, a story without a specific source, and a tale from a potentially tainted source do not add up to conclusive evidence. But there is more. Egidio Mello, one of the policemen who stood guard during the removal of the materials from Pieraccini's after the raid, could recall little about the sights and sounds of that building on that day. Without any prompting, though, he did recall one thing. There were these notes, he said, on lined paper. It was "strange," he mused: the notes talked about these people being a "mixed breed," "not worthy of being Black Panthers."[126] Those notes could only have been written by one of the Boston Black Panthers.

Thus helped and hurt by the Boston connection, causing friction with some in the older generation of Cape Verdeans, the New Bedford Panthers hung on, sometimes thriving, typically relying on family and community connections among West End Cape Verdeans. The larger New Bedford context was difficult, however. First, in the troubled aftermath of the July violence, the New Bedford establishment was newly awake to the need for concessions, for integrating at least some militant elements into the city system. As different individuals and groups scrambled for position in this new and often more welcoming political environment, the Panthers held onto their politics—sometimes appearing in their signature uniform of black leather jackets and black berets, sometimes brandishing their guns, but mostly developing those community projects as "survival programs pending revolution."[127] Moreover, at public meetings, in their flyers, and in their articles in *The Black Panther* they maintained, too, their fiery, revolutionary rhetoric that is so much on display in the prose of the Revolutionary Student Union. The hope that they would finally be heard as a result of July 1970 carried them further than they perhaps might ordinarily have gone.

The other side of this new context, though, was more ominous. As the Panthers declined nationally—indeed, as the 1960s radical fervor dissipated in the early 1970s—the New Bedford Panthers, over time, lost the dynamism and sense of urgency of their earlier, heady days. It did not help, either, that in the immediate aftermath of the July Days New Bedford was, for the first time in its history, flooded with heroin.[128] The New Bedford Panthers and many of their youthful supporters, often from the streets, maintained an ambiguous relationship to the drug trade in 1970 and 1971, officially and ideologically opposed but sometimes using its profits to finance their operations. By 1972, especially after the closing of the local Panther office, many had become heavily involved in dealing heroin while maintaining a rhetorical stance as Panthers.[129] At the same time, at least in 1971 and 1972, some would move to armed activities in a kind of informal radical underground, stealing weapons and robbing banks.[130] The latter did not last; the former typically led to prison. Since many, such as Parky Grace, would maintain their politics in jail, while others, such as his cousin Gerald Ribeiro, would become community activists after getting out, these too are part of the history of the Black Panthers "at the water's edge."[131]

Notes

1 "New Bedford School Board Rejects Revolutionary People's Constitutional Convention," *The Black Panther*, December 16, 1970, in FBI Freedom of Information Act release to author, Boston Office, March 1, 1971, Field Office File # 157–654, Bureau File # 105–165706-Sub 5, 123.

2 Point 1 of the Panther Ten-Point Platform and Program, October 1966 ("Black Panther Party for *Self Defense*: What We Want, What We Believe"), in its original, read in all capitals, "WE WANT FREEDOM. WE WANT POWER TO DETERMINE THE DESTINY OF OUR BLACK COMMUNITY." The first draft of the document referred to black communities, rather than community. Dr. Huey P. Newton Foundation Papers, Greene Library, Stanford University.

3 Several Panther sympathizers in the area were of high school age; at least one local Panther, sixteen-year-old Kim Holland, was then at New Bedford High and had been organizing there for over a year. Telephone interviews, Dr. Kim Holland, June 8, 2000, February 11, 2001; Dan Gilbarg, January 27, 2001.

4 E.g., *New Bedford Standard Times*, August 12, 1970; Jack Stewardson and Carol Lee Costa-Crowell, "Simmering Tensions Finally Erupted in City Turmoil," ibid., July 9, 1995; H. D. Quigg (UPS senior editor), "City's Problems Are Rooted in Economic Concerns," ibid., September 13, 1970.

5 WGBH, "Special: New Bedford," *Say, Brother!* July 16, 1970, tape in possession of author.

6 According to the New Bedford Panther Frank "Parky" Grace, the Boston Panthers authorized him to organize locally well before the events of July, though there was no branch until later. Interview, Jamaica Plain, March 18, 2000. A local newspaper retrospective of the events claimed the presence of Panthers in New Bedford in 1969. Jack Stewardson and Carol Lee Costa-Crowell, "1995: Progress Recorded, but a Fearful Time Uneasily Recalled," *New Bedford Standard Times*, July 19, 1995. The local activist James "Jimmy" Magnett, who did not like the Boston Panthers intruding, remembers organizing activity in the winter of 1969–70. Interview, New Bedford, June 2, 1970. Parky Grace claimed, "When I used to leave Boston, I used to leave with newspapers, buttons, and posters, leaflets, y'know, different information—stimulate the community, educate the community. So, people would say that there was Panthers in New Bedford; they sold posters of Huey and Bobby on the streets. . . . [There were] people wearin' buttons, 'Off the Pigs!' buttons. . . . And then, people wearing Panther gear—leather jackets 'n' berets, in people's minds were the Panther Party." In mid-July 1970, after a Boston Panther delegation arrived, a branch of the National Committee to Combat Fascism (NCCF) was officially established; the following spring, Boston's Tony Marshall became area captain of a New Bedford BPP branch as part of the Massachusetts state chapter. *NAACP News* 1, no. 3 (May 14, 1971), NAACP, New Bedford.

7 Sam Bass Warner, introduction to *Spinner: People and Culture of Massachusetts* (New Bedford, Mass.: Reynolds-DeWalt, 1984), 3:1, 3.

8 For the current state of the literature, see "Bringing the Black Panther Party Back In: A Survey" in this volume.

9 The strength of the Boston chapter was stressed in virtually every interview I conducted—e.g., the Central Committee's Don Cox ("DC") (Sur Agly, France, June 28, 2000); Boston Panthers Michael Fultz (telephone, June 5, 2001), Donna Howell (telephone, June 11, 2000), Greg Jones (Roxbury, April 17, 2000), Doug Miranda (Dorchester, March, 29, 2000; May 24, 2000), Charles "Cappy" Pinderhughes (Brookline, August 17, 1999; telephone, June 13, 2000), and Johnny "Butch" Viera (telephone, October 22, 2000—all subsequent Viera quotations are from that four-and-a-half-hour interview); Parky Grace (Charlestown, July 14, 1999; Medford, July 28, 1999; Jamaica Plain, March 18, 2000). Viera, for example, claimed, "The Boston chapter was one of the best chapters. I mean, we were the most political, and, I mean, I'm not saying it because I was a member, but it's a *fact.*" The theme showed up again in at least two interviews with Boston Panthers who claimed that, in the wake of the split in 1971, Boston became a key recruiting ground for assassins, partly because of the chapter's reputation as an intellectual group (and thus unlikely to draw attention), and partly because it had a reputation for being disciplined (anonymous in-person interviews). A hint at such activity—impossible to determine with any certainty, though, given the number of deletions—can be found in the FBI memorandum, to SAC 157–654, August 12, 1971, 2. For a brief mention of the Massachusetts Panthers, unfortunately riddled with errors, see Michael Newton, *Bitter Grain: Huey Newton and the Black Panther Party* (1980; repr., Los Angeles: Holloway House, 1991), 156.

10 On the *desire* for a police raid, see interviews with Pinderhughes, Fultz, and especially Viera, who said, "They always wanted to get vamped on [i.e., attacked] in Boston; they wanted to get raided, right?" "Keep in mind, the Boston chapter was struggling to come into their own, y'know. Though we were known as a very disciplined chapter and a very intelligent chapter, we had never had a raid; y'know what I mean? That's what sets you with the elite. If your center was vamped on, and raided, you were the crème de la crème." Indeed, according to Viera, in the Boston chapter "there was [*sic*] attempts like some, well, not overt, but covert attempts" essentially to bait the police into "moving on" them. The goal, he says, was to draw community support—that is, the tactic was conceived as an organizing tool—and, as such, whatever action they took could not appear to be offensive.

11 Andrew Blake, "Riot Scars Have Yet to Heal," *Boston Globe*, April 18, 1971.

12 Monroe W. Karmin, "Dissecting a Riot: New Bedford's Trouble Laid to Unemployment, Lack of Aid for Slums," *Wall Street Journal*, August 11, 1970. For government fears of rioting in "ghettos of densely populated big cities" that summer, with specific reference to "increasing support for the Black Panther Party," see Isabelle Hall, "Potential Trouble Seen in Big Cities," *Afro-American*

(Baltimore), July 25, 1970. An overview of the race riots of the 1960s is Joe R. Feagin and Harlan Hahn, *Ghetto Revolts* (New York: Macmillan, 1973), esp. chap. 3; for a broader historical perspective, see Paul A. Gilje, *Rioting in America* (Bloomington: Indiana University Press, 1996), esp. 151–61.

13 H. D. Quigg, "City's Problems Are Rooted in Economic Concerns." Also, Jack Custodio (Cape Verdean activist) videotape, 1993, in possession of author.

14 See Kathryn Grover's excellent *The Fugitive's Gibralter: Escaping Slaves and Abolitionism in New Bedford, Massachusetts* (Amherst: University of Massachusetts Press, 2001). As the reformer Samuel J. May would remark later about Frederick Douglass's initial escape to New Bedford, it was "the best place, on the whole, to which he could have gone" (quoted in ibid., 16). See also Zephaniah W. Pease, ed., *The Diary of Samuel Rodman: A New Bedford Chronicle of Thirty-Seven Years* (New Bedford, Mass.: Reynolds, 1927); Pease, ed., *History of New Bedford*, 3 vols. (New York: Lewis Historical, 1918); Earl Francis Mulderink, III, " 'We Want a Country': African-American and Irish-American Community Life in New Bedford, Massachusetts, During the Civil War Era" (Ph.D. diss., University of Wisconsin, 1995), esp. chap. 1; *Know New Bedford* (New Bedford: League of Women Voters, 1964); Judith A. Boss and Joseph D. Thomas, *New Bedford: A Pictorial History* (Norfolk/Virginia Beach: Denning, 1983).

15 Some claimed it had the highest per capita income of any city in the *world*. C. Eric Linden, "New Bedford Is in Transition—If We Help," *New Bedford Standard Times*, February 5, 1994. For the claim that it moved more whaling vessels from its port than from all the world's ports combined during the 1850s, see Boss and Thomas, *New Bedford*, 41.

16 Grover, *The Fugitive's Gibralter*, 28.

17 Elmo Paul Hohman, *The American Whaleman: A Study of Life and Labor in the Whaling Industry* (New York: Longmans, Green, 1928); Everett S. Allen, *Children of the Light: The Rise and Fall of New Bedford Whaling and the Death of the Arctic Fleet* (Boston: Little, Brown, 1973).

18 "Cape Verdeans thought they were, I can't say all, they were white, they were different." Grace, interview, March 18, 2000. See also Raymond Anthony Almeida, comp. and ed., *Cape Verdeans in America, Our Story* (Boston: The American Committee for Cape Verde, 1978); Barry Glassner, "Cape Verdeans: The People without a Race," *Sepia* (November 1975): 65–71; Marilyn Halter, *Between Race and Ethnicity: Cape Verdean American Immigrants, 1860–1965* (Urbana: University of Illinois Press, 1993); African Information Service, ed., *Return to the Source: Selected Speeches by Amilcar Cabral* (New York: Monthly Review, 1973); "Cape Verde," in *Africana: The Encyclopedia of the African and African American Experience*, Kwame Anthony Appiah and Henry Louis Gates, Jr., eds., 368–70 (New York: Basic Civitas, 1999).

19 *Statistical Profile for the City of New Bedford and Surrounding Area: Industry, Population Programs, and Economic Indicators* (n.p., 1970), 9.

20 Ross Gittell calls the entire half-century after World War II, despite re-peated attempts to arrest the decline, an "extended period of economic stagna-tion," with population and employment falling by double digits from 1950. Gittell, "A Critical Analysis of Local Initiatives in Economic Revitalization" (Ph.D. diss., Harvard University, 1989), 170; Gittell, *Renewing Cities* (Princeton, N.J.: Prince-ton University Press, 1992), chap. 5.

21 City Planning Department, *Statistical Profile*. Boss and Thomas claim that New Bedford received "more federal funds per capita for urban renewal than any other American city." Boss and Thomas, *New Bedford*, 206.

22 Duncan Dottin, on a panel discussing that summer's Mississippi Freedom Project, "NAACP Aid Says Racial Tension Exists in City," *New Bedford Standard Times*, August 31, 1964.

23 "Harrington Talks Walk on Two from NAACP," *Taunton Daily Gazette*, June 8, 1967, for a warning by the NAACP's Jack Custodio. Deploring the late riot in Boston, he advised action "before such a thing happened elsewhere." Also, regarding the always contentious issue of the Job Corps program at Fort Rodman (discussed below), see Robert Martin, "City Prepares Plan to Meet Any Riot Here," ibid., August 2, 1967; "Rights Ordinance Favored Here," ibid., June 30, 1967.

24 Why ghetto riots occurred in the 1960s—and why they occurred where they did—is perceptively discussed in Robert M. Fogelson, *Violence as Protest: A Study of Riots and Ghettos* (Garden City, N.Y.: Doubleday, 1971), esp. chap. 1.

25 Report to Headquarters, n.d. (ca. May 1966), NAACP Papers, Group IV, Box C15, Library of Congress.

26 Interviews, Gloria Clark, telephone, June 13, 2000, New Bedford, June 27, 2002; Carl Cruz, New Bedford, May 30, 2002.

27 Meeting Minutes, New Bedford NAACP Labor and Industries Committee, March 28, 1965–May 29, 1967, copy in possession of author; interview, Douglas Perry, Dartmouth, July 1, 2002.

28 "Equal Housing Unit to Meet," *New Bedford Standard Times*, September 12, 1963; "New Group Seeks Plan to Avoid Racial Problem," ibid., September 13, 1963; "Workshop Unit Takes Teen-Agers to Job," ibid., October 10, 1963; "Law-yer Heads Group: Joseph S. Vera Elected President," ibid, February 10, 1964; "Brotherhood Goal of New Organization," ibid., March 18, 1964; "Equality Unit Names Dubin as Leader," ibid., June 25, 1965. For their full-page ad in the *New Bedford Standard Times*, "Closed Doors in New Bedford," see ibid., June 20, 1965. Among the activists in this group were the NAACP's Duncan Dottin and Earle Carter; the Reverend Richard A. Kellaway of the First Unitarian Church; the Cape Verdean Fermino J. Spencer of the New Bedford Council of the Mas-sachusetts Committee Against Discrimination; and the war on poverty worker (and wife of a prominent local labor leader), Barbara Dubin.

29 A story unto itself, Rodman is discussed in detail in my forthcoming book,

30 Ironically, Samuel Rodman, for whom the fort was named and on whose grounds the Job Corps was based, was a radical Quaker frustrated with what he saw as the timidity of New England Quakerism on the slavery question. Meanwhile, the boulevard separating the Rodman gate from the community nearby was named for Rodney French, a New Bedford merchant whose vessels were boycotted by North Carolina because of the claim that he had advocated that fugitive slaves and free blacks arm themselves to prevent the return of runaways in the aftermath of the Fugitive Slave Law of 1850. See Grover, *The Fugitive's Gibralter*, 33, 14–15.

31 The catalyst was the near riot at the Rodman gate in late May 1966, which prompted Dottin's letter to Washington.

32 Report to headquarters.

33 This was true, even though, in some instances, there were fights between corpsmen and West End blacks.

34 Dan Hurley, "Rodman Students Take Protest to Washington," *New Bedford Standard Times*, February 1, 1968. The students managed to get an audience with Sargent Shriver, the head of the OEO. Dottin protested, too, but in a letter to the editor in the local paper, calling the closing "a victory for bigotry" (ibid., February 6, 1968).

35 Custodio, telephone interview, April 12, 2000; Robert C. Hayden, *African-American and Cape Verdean-Americans in New Bedford: A History of Community and Achievement* (Boston: Select, 1993). Indeed, one reason for the strength of the BPP in New Bedford, which appears to have rivaled Boston for much of its lifetime, may have been the lack of organizational competition in the former. For that suggestion, I am indebted to Tony Marshall, telephone interview, January 5, 2005.

36 See Hayden, *African-American and Cape Verdean-Americans*, 16, 32; and Greg Stone's two articles "Race Demands Presented: United Front Pressures Major" and " 'Eighty-Point' Plan Offered for City," *New Bedford Standard Times*, May 6, 1968. On the United Front, see coverage in the *New Bedford Standard Times* on May 7, 10–13, 15, 17, and 25 in 1968. On the United Front and the NAACP, see Dan Hurley, "NAACP Leaders Split on United Front Issue," ibid., May 16, 1968; Hurley, "United Front Granted Use of NAACP Building," ibid., May 18, 1968; also, interviews with the United Front activists Antone Cruz (telephone, May 1, 2000), Marlene Tavares (New Bedford, May 26, 2000), and James Magnett. By contrast, the FBI reported, Boston SNCC sought support for a front within the city's black moderate organizations such as the NAACP only because of local militant opposition to Stokely Carmichael, the principal author of the "front" idea. Airtel, February 1, 1968, to Division, from Special Agent in

Charge, Boston, Re Bureau Letter to Albany, August 25, 1967, "Newspapers," Roz Payne Archives. On the Boston connection, see "Blacks Rally in West End: Boston Speakers Hail United Front," *New Bedford Standard Times*, June 16, 1968. On public civil rights protest in New Bedford, see "City Has First Protest March," ibid., May 14, 1968. The May "protest" was not the first march, however. See Bob Hall, "Orderly March Downtown Marks Dr. King's Death," ibid., April 5, 1968. And on violence in New Bedford in the aftermath of King's murder, see "Breaks, Broken Windows Probed," ibid., April 6, 1968. Interview, Ronnie Cruz, Dorchester, June 8, 2002. For "skirmishes" with police before New Bedford's July Days, see Nancy McCarthy, "Youth Program Called Success: 150 Kept Active, Useful," *New Bedford Standard Times*, October 13, 1968; "Nine Arrested in Center Fracas," ibid, April 18, 26, May 4, 12, 1969; "Statement of Attorney General Quinn in New Bedford Police-Community Relations," typescript, January 26, 1971, New Bedford File, 1971, *Boston Globe* offices, Dorchester.

37 The local police knew, as did the FBI. Detective Guy Oliveira had an FBI liaison early on for such surveillance (interview, June 15, 2000). No FBI records prior to July 31, 1971 have been released, however.

38 Jack Stewardson, "Police Raid West End, Arrest 20, Seize Guns," *New Bedford Standard Times*, July 31, 1970; Criminal Offense Report, Supplementary Report, New Bedford Police Department, H-8919, July 31, 1970.

39 A purge and moratorium on new members began officially in January 1969, with perhaps as many as one thousand expelled and several locals disbanded. In July, the "United Front Against Fascism" conference established the NCCF. *The Black Panther*, January 4, 1969; U.S. House of Representatives, Committee on Internal Security, *Gun-Barrel Politics: The Black Panther Party, 1966–1971*, 92nd Congress, 1st sess. (Washington, D.C.: U.S. Government Printing Office, 1971), 54–59, 76–78; Bobby Seale, *Seize the Time: The Story of the Black Panther Party and Huey P. Newton*, ed. Art Goldberg (New York: Vintage, 1970), 370, 389–90.

40 An initial reconnoiter by Boston Panthers may have occurred during the latter part of the first week of rioting, according to a telephone interview with Pinderhughes, June 13, 2000.

41 The New Bedford eruption fulfilled three of the four criteria used by the commission to denote a "major" disturbance: "(1) many fires, intensive looting, and reports of sniping; (2) violence lasting more than two days; (3) sizeable crowds." It was not characterized by the fourth: "use of National Guard or federal forces," which, in the case of the National Guard, was frequently urged on the mayor and the City Council. At the same time, the New Bedford disturbances clearly exceeded the criteria for "serious" disorders: "(1) isolated looting, some fires, and some rock throwing; (2) violence lasting between one and two days; (3) only one sizeable crowd or many small groups; and (4) use of state police though generally not National Guard or federal forces." *Report of the National Advisory Commission on Civil Disorders* (New York: Bantam Books, 1968), 113. The city contemplated using the National Guard, placing the unit at the Fall River armory on alert several days into the violence, but never did. Alan Sheehan, "Brooke in New Bedford: Blacks List Demands," *Boston Globe*, July 13, 1970.

42 In response to a question about the Botelho shooting, one of those arrested explained to police, "They have been getting shot at all night (meaning the Panthers' headquarters), and 'we are not going to take it any more.'" The same individual, whose name is expunged in the police report, is alleged to have "stated that one white male in a truck was doing the shooting at the building," and further "that they must arm themselves from the 'PIGS' because the Pigs have guns and they were going to have them also." New Bedford Police Department, Criminal Office Report, H-8919, July 31, 1970, 3. Oliveira, who testified that the individual he interviewed was Parky Grace, related the exchange in similar fashion in court. "Sixteen Defendants in Raid Held for Grand Jury," *New Bedford Standard Times*, August 14, 1970. At the same hearing, one of the leaders of the raid, Det. Sgt. Clovis "Toby" Gauthier, claimed that the police received a call from Botelho, who arrived at police headquarters at 6:20 a.m. Interview, Toby Gauthier, New Bedford, June 7, 2000; all references to Gauthier are to this interview. No one I talked to would take credit for shooting Botelho, though Grace, who was not at the scene, acknowledged that "we" shot at the tires of Botelho's vehicle, evidently from inside, beside, or on the roof of the "headquarters." All of those who were arrested in the raid are convinced that the event was staged. According to Grace, "In the morning there was a milk truck. Came down Kempton Street the wrong way. Y'know? It came up Cedar; I mean, they [the police] had let this milk truck through." Interview, Grace, March 18, 2000. Russell "Buffalo" Rebeiro, who was there, verifies that gunfire came from the building, though he would not identify the shooter. He says that Botelho was "cruising up and down Park Street. . . . If [it were not] a deliberate provocation, then a reconnoiter or a scouting action prior to what they [the police] did." Telephone interview, December 28, 2000. Alfred "Page" Roderick, one of those arrested outside the building during the raid, says he had been hanging around the "headquarters" all month, that he had gone there that morning to "check in, say 'hello,' you know if there was anything I could do before I went to work." While he was standing outside, he noticed what he remembers as "one o' those big Ford cars" pass by several times. He says that one of the Panthers, Peter Almeida, noted the same thing: "There goes that car again." After yet another appearance of the car, Bob ("Big Bob") Heard, one of the Boston Panthers, came out of the building. "There was some discussion," Roderick says, "I can't remember who said what, but it was to the effect that, 'There it is again. There's that damn car again. I wonder who it is. Let's find out.'" With that, Heard "just took his rifle and shot at the car." Telephone interview, Page Roderick, May

30, 2002. As for the raid itself, witnesses testify to state police helicopters over-head, and the Panthers wrote often of police from surrounding towns participat-ing, but the New Bedford Police Department Report mentions only "approxi-mately 75 New Bedford police," a huge force, given the size of the building and the numbers inside. Criminal Offense Report, H-8919, July 31, 1970, 2.

43 Burned and looted in the uprising's first phase, then, the store is mis-identified as having been attacked only the day before the raid in "Bail Cuts Denied for Four Held in Riot," *Boston Globe*, August 18, 1970. Grace estimated they occupied the building for about two weeks.

44 Interviews, Viera; Grace (March 28, 2000); Roderick; Holland (telephone, February 11, 2001).

45 In the raid's aftermath, City Councilor Paul Mathieu retrieved what ap-pears to have been the Red Book belonging to the Boston Panther Cathy Perry. It bore the notations on the inside, "reactionaries/reve[revolutionary?] cul[ture?] + reac[tionary?] cul[ture?]/Hitler's fas[cism?] + here to chauvinism." Interview, Paul Mathieu, New Bedford, May 11, 2000; book in Mathieu's possession.

46 The district attorney called the building a "bunker." "Atkins Blasts Panther Bail Ruling," *Boston Globe*, August 19, 1970. Whether Pieraccini's was fortified before the Boston Panthers arrived is in dispute, but there is no doubt that once on the scene, they—particularly people such as Heard, whom Viera claims was part of the Panthers' military wing—systematized the operation. At the same time, the operation benefited from the experience of several local Vietnam vet-erans. Rebeiro insists that what the Boston Panthers did was to provide ideologi-cal coherence to something that was already happening. The city was "fertile territory," he says; the Panthers "finally [gave] a sense of direction . . . to the movement."

47 Barboza, who had grown up with several principals in the July events, was in the witness protection program at the time, having turned state's evidence in 1968 in a case involving the Rhode Island crime boss Raymond Patriarca. Relo-cated in early 1969 "to another part of the world," as the FBI put it later, he was ordered to stay away from Massachusetts. Known locally as "the Baron"—a name associated with his short-lived boxing career—Barboza told a reporter just before his arrest on weapons and narcotics charges that he had come to town at the request of the Federal Organized Crime Strike Force "to help restore law and order" because he had influence with local black militants. The FBI denied the assertion. "Informer Baron Arrested in City: Held on Gun, Drug Charges," *New Bedford Standard Times*, July 18, 1970; "Sent to Cool City's Strife, Baron Report-edly Claims," ibid., July 18, 1970; "FBI Denies Baron Acting for U.S. When Ar-rested in New Bedford," *Boston Globe*, July 19, 1970; "Baron Charges Dropped, but He's Not Free," ibid., July 20, 1970; Associated Press, "F. Lee Bailey Seeks Baron's Prison Release," ibid., August 12, 1970. Grace, who had known him since childhood, claimed Barboza was running guns to local radicals; Viera remembers hearing the same thing. Gauthier says Barboza was in town to "hit" a local bookie. "Later, I received information—and it was good information—that they were casing a known bookie's house in the North End of the city. . . . I had information—and it was good information—that they were going to hit a bookie." For Barboza's life, see his obituary, *New Bedford Standard Times*, February 12, 1976.

48 Interviews, Buffalo Rebeiro; Grace; Stevens (Cambridge, December 13, 2000).

49 "When I Joined the Party: Panther in Training," *It's About Time . . .* 3, no. 3 (fall 1999): 6; also, on Winston-Salem, see Evans D. Hopkins, *Life after Life: A Story of Rage and Redemption* (New York: Free Press, 2005), chap. 3.

50 In a report to the Boston FBI SAC, January 24, 1972, an unidentified agent communicated an oral report received from one of his informants (3): "—— held the position of Area Captain at the BPP in New Bedford, Mass. Before being expelled by —— in the latter part of 1971. Source advised that BPP membership is determined by ——. She has the power to appoint and remove members."

51 See, e.g., Boston SAC (157–654) Airtel to FBI Director (105–165706 Sub 5), Monthly Summary, February 3, 1971. Released FBI documents evince a large body of regular informants in New Bedford at least: agents on the scene, police, local businessmen, community residents, and, it appears, several people inside the Panther group itself.

52 Several were held on $100,000 bail. The Panthers reported two figures for the total. In "New Bedford Pigs Kidnap 21," typescript flyer, n.d., in "New Bedford," Folder 2, Box 469, Senator Edward Brooke Collection, Collections of the Manuscript Division, Washington, D.C., they claimed a $1.26 million "ransom." In "New Bedford: Gestapo Pig Force Raids NCCF: 21 NCCF Members Kidnapped," *The Black Panther*, August 15, 1970, the figure is $2.35 million. Regardless, New Bedford had never seen anything like this before. Of the twenty-one, eight recall interrogation by the FBI (telephone interview, Dennis Cruz, June 17, 2001; Richard "Dickie" Duarte, New Bedford, May 6, 2000; Lloyd Haddocks, telephone interview, August 31, 2000; Grace, March 28, 2000; Holland, February 11, 2001; Buffalo Rebeiro; Viera; Roderick). Freedom of Information Act releases to author verify that the FBI kept close—and remarkably accurate—tabs on New Bedford Panthers from August 1970 until at least 1974.

53 Interview, Buffalo Rebeiro.

54 Rick Bragg, "Lay Brothers Work in World" (mistitled), *New Bedford Standard Times*, July 10, 1970. Councilman Hughes, quoted in Daniel P. Judah, "Compromise Called Key to New Bedford Program," *Boston Globe*, July 26, 1970.

55 Dick Bigos, "Black Views," *New Bedford Standard Times*, July 8, 1970.

56 Quoted in Stewardson and Costa-Crowell, "1995."

57 http://www.providence.edu. Waters emphasized the same sentiments in an interview with the author in New Bedford, June 6, 2002. He used the same language in an interview with local reporters in 1995. See Stewardson and Costa-Crowell, "Twenty-five Years Later, Just How Far Have We Come?" *New Bedford Standard Times*, July 19, 1995.

58 Fogelson, *Violence as Protest*, 18. Jack Stewardson, "Reasons for West End Conflagration Evasive," *New Bedford Standard Times*, July 10, 1970.

59 "Three Are Arrested in West End Fracas," *New Bedford Standard Times*, July 9, 1970; "Fires, Violence Flare for Second Day in New Bedford's Black Section," *Boston Globe*, July 10, 1970; Dick Bigos, "Blacks Halt Meeting with City, Vow Revolt," *New Bedford Standard Times*, July 13, 1970. One retrospective in 1984 declared flatly, "To this day, no one knows exactly what caused the week-long West End racial disturbances of 1970," a reference to the first phase of the violence. Other reports identified Houtman's arrest as the precipitating event, as do at least two people on the scene that night. Margaret A. Charig, " 'Parky' Grace: A Story of Black Pride, Anger," ibid., October 7, 1984; "Three Are Arrested in West End Fracas," ibid., July 9, 1970; "Sixteen Hurt in New Bedford's Second Night of Violence," ibid., July 10, 1970; "Fires, Violence Flare for Second Day in New Bedford's Black Section," ibid.; William A. Davis, "Kempton Street Cool Now, but the Anger Simmers," *Boston Globe*, July 10, 1970; interviews, Grace, March 18, 2000; Magnett. Also, Jack Stewardson, "Reasons for West End Conflagration Evasive," *New Bedford Standard Times*, July 10, 1970. The *Globe* identified Houtman as a "local black leader" in a July 13 news report. Alan Sheehan and Daniel Juda, "Mayor Clamps Curfew to Calm New Bedford." Grace called him a "bad dude," an "hombre," "a tough . . . a bad mukky-muck," but also a "resister." Interview, Grace, March 18, 2000.

60 On Grace's life and politics, see my " 'A Rebel All His Life': The Unexpected Story of Frank 'Parky' Grace," in *In Search of the Black Panther Party: New Perspectives on a Revolutionary Movement*, ed. Jama Lazerow and Yohuru Williams, 104–57 (Durham, N.C.: Duke University Press, 2006).

61 Magnett identified himself as "Black Brother" in letters to the local newspaper as early as January 24, 1969; in one, he wrote of a party (March 11, 1970). In the *Say, Brother!* tape, which includes an extensive interview with him, the group is identified as an "Action Committee."

62 Dick Bigos, "West End Tension High," *New Bedford Standard Times*, July 9, 1970.

63 Greg Stone, "Disorders Erupt Again in New Bedford, 23 Hurt," ibid., July 10, 1970; "Fires, Violence Flare for Second Day," *Boston Globe*, July 10, 1970.

64 Stewardson and Costa-Crowell, "Summer of Discontent: Changed a City and Its People Forever," *New Bedford Standard Times*, July 20, 1995. The Vietnam analogy was not unusual. One resident told a reporter the following September that for a few days in July New Bedford was "like downtown Saigon." Quigg,

"City's Problems Are Rooted in Economic Concerns." Charig ("'Parky' Grace") characterized mid-July 1970 as a period of "open warfare."

65 Notably, when crosschecked with the memories of ex-Panthers, other activists, and local residents, the FBI documents, despite abundant redactions, constitute one of the most reliable and complete sources of information on the personnel and activities of the New Bedford Panthers.

66 Interview, Grace, March 18, 2000.

67 "Anarchy Takes a Setback," *New Bedford Standard Times*, August 1, 1970.

68 Viera's story of the raid was verified in substance in a telephone interview with former Boston Black Panther Cathy Perry (Lotus Hsu), July 29, 2002.

69 "You know, it's all about dying and, I mean . . . we actually lived every day, every day was our last day."

70 Telephone interviews, Jackie Ramos, May 11, 2000; Jack Custodio, April 12, 2000; Holland, June 8, 2000.

71 "Xiarhos Case Jury Drawn," *New Bedford Standard Times*, November 4, 1964; Diane Hinchcliffe, "They Were Never the Same after July 1970," ibid., July 20, 1980. "[Y]eah, he stabbed me. He killed me," Grace told me (March 18, 2000).

72 "Seven Youths Held on Bail in Aftermath of Fight," *New Bedford Standard Times*, January 8, 1963; "Court Decides Assault Cases," ibid., June 28, 1963; "New England Motorist Faces Two Charges in Accident Case," ibid., April 27, 1964; "False Name Results in Fine," ibid., October 10, 1965; Charig, "'Parky' Grace"; ten interviews with author: July 14, 1999, Charlestown; July 28, 1999, Medford; March 18, 29, 2000, Jamaica Plain; May 6, 2000, New Bedford; and by telephone, May 1, 5, 10, 12, June 8, 2000. Maintaining the politics he had as a Black Panther in 1970, Parky Grace died in October 2001.

73 Telephone interview, Howell, June 11, 2000. On Jones's "Stalin" appellation, Viera says it was "a term of endearment, y'know, and also a term of, y'know, fear. Like, and, you know, you didn't mess with Audrea, man. . . . I mean, Big Bob was in our chapter, too, you know. She would sit him down. I mean, she, really, y'know, . . . and that's why we called her 'Stalin.' 'Cause she ran the chapter with an iron hand." FBI documents from early 1971, however, though redacted, appear to suggest demoralization in the Boston chapter as a result of her leadership. Boston Office, March 1, 1971, Field Office File # 157–654, Bureau File # 105–165706-Sub 5, 15, from an informant reporting on February 3, 1971: "It seems that [short blank—Jones?] is so unpleasant and hard to get along with that she is breaking up most of the BPP membership at 23 Winthrop Street" (then the headquarters of the Boston Panthers).

74 To the Director, from SAC, Boston, November 14, 1968, "Factionalism, SNCC, CORE," Roz Payne Archives; Dan Queen, "Who Are the Black Panthers?" *Bay State Banner*, December 5, 1968; James B. Alexander, "Black Panthers: A Yardstick?" *Christian Science Monitor*, December 18, 1968; Victor Chen, "Boston's Panthers Stalk New Goal," *Boston Globe*, July 6, 1969. Miranda says the chapter "may have been" originally a chapter of SNCC (interview, Dorchester, March 29 2000). As several who were purged—Frank Hughes, Chico Neblett, Rene Neblett—did not respond to or refused requests for interviews, what follows is the story of the ousters, not the ousted. At the same time, two of the latter—Floyd Hardwick and Audrea Jones—also refused repeated requests for interviews.

75 *The Black Panther*, July 19, 1969. Most of the charges involved the failure of the ousted leadership to accept the primacy of class struggle.

76 "An Open Letter to Stokely Carmichael" (July 1969), *Ramparts* (September 1969), in Philip Foner, ed., *The Black Panthers Speak* (1970; repr., New York: Da Capo, 1995), 104–8, quotation, 106.

77 Interview, Greg Jones, April 17, 2000.

78 Cox claims never to have taken orders from the Central Committee (indeed, he describes himself as something of a "contract agent" from the beginning of his Panther involvement in 1967), but he did come to Boston shortly after a call was placed to the West Coast, probably by Floyd Hardwick, the oldest of the new group and something of an intellectual mentor to them. Interviews, Miranda; Cox.

79 Chen, "Boston's Panthers Stalk New Goal." Interviews, Ronald Addison, telephone, June 12, 2000; Cox; Miranda; Greg Jones.

80 Interview, Grace, March 18, 2000. Grace also talked of his New Bedford-to-Boston travels in Stewardson and Costa-Crowell, "Summer of Discontent." At the same time, according to Viera, Parky was "doin' certain, m'see how I can put this, certain covert work for the Panthers.... He had connections that we needed. And without getting into too much detail . . . he was doin' some things that we needed to do."

81 The Club was identified as Black Panther headquarters before the taking of Pieraccini's in "Bail Denied Three in Slaying," *New Bedford Standard Times*, August 26, 1970.

82 Telephone interview, George Rogers, the former mayor, May 5, June 14, 2000; Bob Hall, "City Will Act on Black Demands: Council Meetings Continue; Brooke Flying In," *New Bedford Standard Times*, July 13, 1970; F. B. Taylor, "New Bedford Imposes Eleven P.M. Curfew," *Boston Globe*, July 30, 1970; Quigg, "City's Problems Are Rooted in Economic Concerns"; Stewardson and Costa-Crowell, "Summer of Discontent." Interviews with former city councilors expressing similar views: Richard Bachand, telephone, May 25, 2000; Rosalind Booker, telephone, June 7, 2000; George Clark, telephone, May 31, 2000; Daniel Hayes, New Bedford, June 10, 2000; Walter Hughes, telephone, June 4, 2000 and New Bedford, June 9, 2000; Paul J. Mathieu, New Bedford, May 11, 2000; Michele Merolla, telephone, June 12, 2000; David Nelson, New Bedford, June 9, 2000; Ralph J.

Saulnier, New Bedford, May 11, 2000. Local businessmen saw it the same way. E.g., Karmin, "Dissecting a Riot." Local civil rights leaders saw it in a more nuanced way. The NAACP's Howard Baptista, for example, noted at the time that the violence had local origins, "but shortly after outsiders started to come in." Quigg, "City's Problems Are Rooted in Economic Concerns."

83 The day of the Pieraccini raid, police stormed the place, which was just doors away. Charig, " 'Parky' Grace." Information on the Black Brothers Political Party came from interviews with Grace; Magnett; Stevens.

84 Quoted in Stewardson and Costa-Crowell, "1995."

85 "Judge Dismisses Three Raid Cases," *New Bedford Standard Times*, August 13, 1970; Criminal Offense Report, H-8917, August 3, 1970, 2.

86 Criminal Offense Report, H-8917, August 3, 1970, 2.

87 Stewardson and Costa-Crowell, "Summer of Discontent."

88 Interviews, Grace; Viera. "Bail Cuts Denied for Four Held in Riot," *Boston Globe*, August 18, 1970. In an odd construction, Mario Van Peebles, Ula Taylor, and J. Tarika Lewis, *Panther: A Pictorial History of the Black Panthers and the Story Behind the Film* (New York: New Market Press, 1995), 72–73, refers to Pieraccini's as "what police called the New Bedford, Massachusetts, Black Panther Headquarters."

89 Interviews, Grace; Viera; Duarte; Oliviera.

90 Interviews, Holland, telephone, February 11, June 8, 2000. A police report on the raid (Criminal Offense Report H-8918, August 5, 1970) indicated that all twenty-one were arrested as they exited the "headquarters," either by the back or front. Interviews with many of the principals (e.g., Grace; Viera; Stevens; Duarte; Dennis Cruz; Barbara Texiera [Sullivan], telephone, February 6, 2001; Buffalo Rebeiro; Haddocks) suggest otherwise.

91 In a letter that appeared in *The Black Panther* ("Letter from One of the New Bedford 20"), Holland refers to having been "kidnapped," along with the others, kept at the "city pig sty" for "at least eight hours," and deprived of food, knowledge of the charges against them, or the right to make a telephone call. The piece suggests she is still being held. It also contains language strikingly similar to that found in the RSU article discussed at the outset of this essay. Article in Freedom of Information Act material, to SAC, Boston, from Legal Section (190-BS-90690).

92 Barrows to Grant, February 8, 1971, Docket # 34563, *Commonwealth v. Ralph D. Brown*, State Archives for Courts, Bristol County, Taunton, Mass.

93 The police reports of the incident, which include the three telling essentially the same story, indicate an earlier incident. However, those at the scene I interviewed (Holland, Buffalo Rebeiro, Magnett, Page Roderick, Ronnie Cruz, Dennis Cruz) recall only the shooting. Whatever happened that night, some person or persons severely damaged the automobile, from the right and rear. Police found seven bullet holes in the trunk, ten "bullet marks" on its right side, the rear window smashed, and a red brick on the rear seat. "Bail Denied in Slaying for Trio Charged in Lima Death," *New Bedford Standard Times*, August 19, 1970.

94 Criminal Offense Report H-7978, July 11, 1970, which includes the Certificate of Death; also, "Bail Denied in Slaying"; Holland, court testimony, quoted in "Bail Denied in Slaying." The fourth victim, Randy Robinson, like Holland, was African American. Only fourteen at the time, like the others, he was enamored of the Panthers. He would sell papers with Parky Grace in coming years, though he never joined. A generation later, having taken shotgun pellets to the left neck, cheek, upper abdomen, and small intestine that night in 1970, he died of respiratory problems stemming from those wounds.

95 The only disruption occurred when two servicemen grabbed one of the NLF flags, for which they were charged with disorderly conduct. In court the next day, Judge Margaret Scott, the bête noire of local activists, declared that charges should be brought against the bearer of the flag. Dick Bigos, "March on Center Peaceful, Attendance 75–100 in Rain," *New Bedford Standard Times*, November 7, 1970; "Observers Noted March in City," ibid.; Larry Moniz, "NLF Flag Foes in Court," ibid.; Ron Bouchard, "A Tense Few Moments," ibid. Bigos identified RAG as a coalition of SDS chapters, the Women's Liberation Front, and "radical high school students."

96 Interview, Holland; Hattie Bernstein, "Black Panthers or Medicine, Her Aim Is to Help People," *New Bedford Standard Times*, May 2, 1976; on RAG, interviews with Gilbarg; Gloria Clark, telephone, June 13, 2000.

97 Dick Bigos, "Violence Less on Third Night of Disorders," *New Bedford Standard Times*, July 11, 1970; Keith Bromey, "Three Arrested in New Bedford," *Boston Globe*, July 11, 1970; "Black Youth Killed, Three Hurt in New Bedford," *Boston Globe*, July 12, 1970; Don Fraser, "Sessions to Resolve Unrest Tonight," *New Bedford Standard Times*, July 14, 1970; "No Disciplinary Action Set for Bristol Community College Teacher," *Boston Globe*, July 15, 1970; "Arson Charged, Three Indicted in New Bedford," *Boston Globe*, September 30, 1970; "Kuntzler Defends Couple in New Bedford Arson Case," *Boston Globe*, November 11, 1970. Also interviews, Dworkin; Marilyn (Dworkin) Abrahamson, telephone, July 10, 2002; Susan (Reeves) Hagedorn, telephone, August 15, 2002. Reeves had been briefly involved with the radical SDS splinter group, Weatherman, in Boston, but dropped out and moved to Fall River after the group went "underground" in the late winter of 1970.

98 Police refer to "youths" shooting out streetlights with "small caliber weapons" in Thomas Shepard, "Black Youth Killed, Three Hurt in New Bedford," *Boston Globe*, July 12, 1970.

99 In fact, the explanation all three gave police—that they simply moved the barricades that blocked their way—seems just as logical.

100 "New Bedford: Gestapo Pigs Force Raids NCCF."

101 Jack Stewardson, "Councilors Rap Curfew Decision," *New Bedford Standard Times*, July 30, 1970; Hall, "Sanctuaries Ruled Out by Mayor," ibid.

102 Interview, Magnett.

103 Interview, Grace, Buffalo Rebeiro. The tipster, according to Rebeiro, was an ally in the "government establishment"—not an African American—who was to secure dynamite for a planned bombing of the Central Police Station. On police brutality as the principal catalyst for the violence that month, e.g., Bigos, "Blacks Hit Police Role in Coalition," *New Bedford Standard Times*, July 10, 1970; "Text of Atkins Report to Sargent Tells of New Bedford Trouble," ibid., August 19, 1970; Taylor, "Atkins Urges Probe of Bias by Police, Courts in New Bedford," *Boston Globe*, August 19, 1970; "Statement of Attorney General Quinn." In turn, Gauthier claims the police had several sources inside Pieraccini's, but he will not identify any. Meanwhile, Botelho, with family in the New Bedford Police Department, would have at least one more scrape with Panther weaponry. In late August, he told the police he had been shot—again, while driving—this time in front of the Tropicana Café in the South End. The press reported no arrests, but a police report identified the shooter as Parky Grace. "South End Man Shot in Arm Near City Café," *New Bedford Standard Times*, August 30 1970; Grace FBI file.

104 "New Bedford Pigs Kidnap 21"; "New Bedford: Gestapo Pig Force Raids NCCF."

105 Of the other three officers in charge that morning, two are dead and one refuses to talk about the incident, though the police report of the raid names Sergeant Joe Vincent as the one who ordered his men in, and several New Bedford policemen support that story. The mum policeman is Raymond Eugenio; interview, Octavio Pragana, New Bedford, June 1, 2002. For his part, Viera asserts, without evidence, that the Panthers developed information later verifying that the raid was "orchestrated" by the FBI.

106 The "restrained and selected" nature of the New Bedford violence in July 1970, though, aimed mostly at property and not people, conforms to the pattern in most ghetto rioting of the period. Fogelson, *Violence as Protest*, chap. 1, esp. pp. 16, 18.

107 In a telephone conversation, Vaughan refused to answer any questions without Hilliard's approval. Hilliard agreed to an interview only if his literary agent in New York approved it; she did not return repeated phone calls and letters. As already noted, Jones refused all entreaties for an interview.

108 For the long-simmering tensions in the party, see David Hilliard and Lewis Cole, *This Side of Glory: The Autobiography of David Hilliard and the Story of the Black Panther Party* (Boston: Little, Brown, 1993).

109 Buffalo Rebeiro, who says he was in the building all night, says simply, "There wasn't enough people who wanted to [defend the building]. Or who felt the need to."

110 For an example of jailhouse protest, see "Lowell Jail Fire Blamed on City Men," *New Bedford Standard Times*, September 6, 1970.

111 Interview, Duke Matthews, Cape Cod, April 1, 2001. The story is not unique. Gerald Ribeiro, Gordon's and Russell's cousin, was in the army in July 1970, stationed in Germany. Having already been exposed to Panthers traveling in Europe, he wanted desperately to return to his hometown when he learned of the rioting on Armed Forces Radio. The report was of the Lima shooting, and there was mention of his cousin, Gordon, and of Kim Holland. Immediately, he called his brother, Bruce, who told him, "The Panthers were coming down and I was like, 'Wow!' There's Panthers out here!" He made his way back by the early fall, immediately taking up residence at the new NCCF headquarters just up the block from Pieracinni's. "First thing I did was walk right to the Panther Headquarters and join up. I think I came home, ate a meal, you know, with my mother and father, and that same night I was right there. Right over there." Interview, Gerald Ribeiro, New Bedford, May 14, 2002. Jean Beaubian of the New Bedford Historical Society remembers hearing about the violence on Air Forces Radio while in Madrid with her husband; she also recalls reading about the events in the *Stars and Stripes.* Her response to the news was typical: "Hmm, *New Bedford?!*" Interview, New Bedford, July 1, 2002.

112 Buffalo Reberio: "We always got the inkling, but never any concrete proof, that a deal was made with the so-called black leaders."

113 "Brown Admits Firing Shotgun Blast That Killed Lima," *New Bedford Standard Times*, May 13, 1971; "Three Defendants Acquitted in Lima Shooting," ibid., May 19, 1971. On the muted response to the verdicts, see "Fire Chief's Car Stoned in West End; Two Fires Set," ibid., May 19, 1971; Taylor, "New Bedford Feels Acquittal Effects," *Boston Globe*, May 22, 1971. One of the twenty-one, Black Brother Bobby Stevens claims that he and several others planned to kill the three, suggesting that they did not because of a general hopelessness that descended on the community in the aftermath of the trial. Interview, Stevens.

114 Donald Gomes, quoted in Hinchcliffe, "They Were Never the Same after July 1970." Local activists tried unsuccessfully for months to get the U.S. attorney in Boston to bring a civil rights case against the three.

115 Grace's story about how Ernie's Drugs was secured for the new NCCF headquarters is verified by an FBI informant's report of September 22, 1970 (regarding Grace's having been given a key to the building on August 27), File Office (Boston) File # 157–654, Bureau File # 105–165706-Sub 5, March 1, 1971, 125.

116 Ibid. On the building's appearance, at the date of its closing, though consistent with reports from September 1970, see "Photos of BPP, New Bedford Branch, 352 Kempton St., New Bedford, Mass.," FBI File No. 157–1932, April 25, 1972.

117 Classes were held every Monday, Wednesday, and Saturday afternoon. E.g., report (January 13, 1971) and accompanying flyer in Boston Field Office File # 157–654, Bureau File # 105–165706-Sub 5, March 1, 1971, 142, 143. Report (October 21, 1970) from the New Bedford Police Department, with flyer, in ibid., 144, 145. New Bedford's official community action agency, under the OEO, was the Organized New Bedford Opportunity and Resource Development (or Onboard).

118 Interviews, Grace; Holland; Gerald Ribeiro; Charlie Perry Jr., New Bedford, May 21, 2002.

119 Marshall verified the fact (telephone interview, January 5, 2005), as do some FBI documents. One, dated March 24, 1971, to Boston SAC, refers to an informant's report of an unidentified Panther being assigned to New Bedford. "The BPP is keeping the New Bedford office well staffed inasmuch as New Bedford is taking in more money from donations than the Boston office."

120 E.g., FBI Special Agent Lawrence G. Gettings to Boston SAC 157–1932, February 17, 1972; Boston SAC 157–654, March 4, 1972, 55.

121 Boston SAC 157–654, March 4, 1972, 57. For the first time, however, an FBI informant in New Bedford stressed the presence of a criminal rather than a political element in the group. The leadership at present, one reported in January 1972, largely "believe[s] in the criminal element rather than the philosophical or idealistic views of the BPP" (ibid.).

122 Howard Baptista, executive director of the New Bedford Redevelopment Authority, to person unknown, April 13, 1972; Adalberth S. Rozario, director of Relocation and Property Management, to Baptista, April 4, 1972; Claim for Relocation Payment from New Bedford Redevelopment Authority, re West End Urban Renewal (Mass. R-143), by New Bedford Branch of the Black Panther Party, filed by person unknown with address at 23 Winthrop Street, Roxbury; Supporting Data—Moving Expenses (from Andrade's Trucking Co., Fairhaven, Mass.); Claim for Moving Expenses for $500 or Less, March 21, 1972, signed by unknown person identified by title, "Captain"; handwritten receipt from Andrade's Trucking Co., March 21, 1972, for moving "personal property of the New Bedford Branch of the Black Panther Party" to 23 Winthrop Street—all contained in Freedom of Information Act release.

123 Telephone interview, Tony Marshall, January 5, 2005.

124 Interviews with Howell; Grace; Holland; Fultz; *NAACP News*, May 14, 1971; David Branco, "Panthers Tell Center Merchants of New Policy," *New Bedford Standard Times*, May 27, 1971.

125 Robert A. Jordan, "'You Can Jail a Revolutionary but Not a Revolution'— Black Panther," *Boston Globe*, July 26, 1970.

126 Interviews, Khazan, telephone, May 31, June 7, 2000; Oliveira, telephone, June 15, 2000; Marshall, telephone, May 24, 2002; Mello, New Bedford, June 20, 2002.

127 Interviews, William Carmo, New Bedford, May 3, 2000; Holland; Texiera.

128 Interviews, Holland, Buffalo Rebeiro, Stevens. Charig noted the influx of drugs into New Bedford in 1971–72 in "'Parky' Grace." The notion that "the authorities" deliberately flooded the black community with drugs "to destroy the Panther power base" is advanced in Van Peebles et al., *Panther*, 228, and in the movie based on the novel (Polygram Filmed Entertainment and Gramercy Pictures, 1995). FBI documents, like released police reports, reveal increasing involvement in the (heroin) drug trade by ex-Panthers as early as late 1971.

129 Interview, Vern "Black Rudy" Rudolph, New Bedford, April 26, 2003. Among the materials seized from Pieracinni's on July 31, 1970 was marijuana belonging to Parky Grace, for which he was charged with possession with intent to sell (a charged dropped along with most of the others the following spring). See, too, FBI SAC 157–654, March 8, 1972, 3, which contains a written report taken orally from an informant who named people among the Panthers— typically hanging out at the West End Citizens' Club (more commonly, the West End *Social* Club)—who were involved with pushing drugs in the New Bedford area. The street outside West End Social would be the scene of a shooting during that summer of 1972, sending Parky Grace to jail for first-degree murder. On that incident and case, as well as more on the Panthers and drugs in New Bedford, see Lazerow, "'A Rebel All His Life.'"

130 Gerald Ribeiro talked of planning robberies with Parky Grace and unnamed others as an escalation of revolutionary activity. Interview, Gerald Ribeiro, New Bedford, June 13, 2002. Marshall talked of bank robberies outside political purposes, but with ex-Panthers, in a telephone interview, July 2, 2002.

131 On Gerald Ribeiro, see his posthumously published *This Path I Took*, ed. Robert French (New York: Universe, Inc., 2005).

3

"The Power Belongs to Us and

We Belong to the Revolutionary Age"

THE ALABAMA BLACK LIBERATION FRONT AND

THE LONG REACH OF THE BLACK PANTHER PARTY

On November 1, 1970, a crowd of some 175 to 200 people marched from Kelly Ingram Park in Birmingham, Alabama, to the courthouse downtown.[1] According to police reports, "Upon arriving at the Court House, [protestors] threw up their right fists in the air, giving the power salute, and repeated over and over, 'The power belongs to the people. The power belongs to us and we belong to the Revolutionary age.'" Protestors had organized the event as a demonstration of support for two black men imprisoned in a nearby jail—Wayland "Doc" Bryant and Ronnie Williams —who were among the leaders of an organization known as the Alabama Black Liberation Front (A B L F). Modeled on what its members knew of the Black Panther Party (B P P), the A B L F had been active in Birmingham since late May 1970, focusing on issues of concern to the city's black poor.[2] From that moment, area law enforcement, including the local F B I, had waged a campaign to discredit and eliminate the organization. On September 15, 1970, the campaign led to a confrontation in Birmingham's Tarrant City section at the home of Bernice Turner, a black domestic whose eviction the A B L F was trying to prevent. Charges stemming from that confrontation— termed a "shootout" by local law enforcement—caused Bryant's and Williams' incarceration.[3]

The immediate events sparking the confrontation had begun a day earlier when Turner received a "first notice" of eviction; having fallen behind on her mortgage payments, she would have to vacate the house where she and her children had been living for over a decade.[4] Turner testified later that she then spoke with members of the ABLF, including Bryant, about her situation. At that point, she and Steve Meriweather, a member of the ABLF, went to see Arthur Shores, a local attorney and Birmingham's first black city councilman, about obtaining a three-day postponement.[5] During the evening, the situation still unresolved, Turner invited Bryant, Williams, and several other representatives of the ABLF to dinner at her home.[6] They discussed plans to raise the necessary funds to cover her payments, and several members of the ABLF went back and forth from the home during the night.[7] The next morning, Turner sent her two children to school and departed for work, along with the boarder who lived with them.[8] The ABLF members left as well to attend a neighborhood meeting and distribute a leaflet intended to "politicize" the surrounding community.[9] Five returned to the house around mid-morning and, according to their testimony at trial, gathered in a front room to listen to records.[10]

Meanwhile, aware of the presence of the ABLF, the Jefferson County Sheriff's Department dispatched at least sixteen deputies to the house, each of them, according to Sheriff Mel Bailey, "prepared for resistance."[11] Deputy Sheriff Major David Orange testified later, "I, along with about 15 other officers, arrived . . . at about 11:50 a.m. . . . We were armed with tear gas guns, shotguns, and rifles, along with our regular side arms."[12] According to Orange, the deputies knocked on the front door. Receiving no answer, Orange kicked in the door to find Bryant holding a shotgun. Orange claimed that Bryant pointed the gun at him, though Bryant swore he had a telephone in his hand and "at no time did he wave the shotgun."[13] In any event, all the while sheriff's deputies were bombarding the house with tear gas canisters. Bryant, Williams, and the others crawled out to the sidewalk and were arrested.

Although deputies did find guns inside the house, including a twenty-two caliber rifle belonging to Turner, none had been discharged.[14] This fact, of course, contradicted law enforcement's characterization of the event as a "shootout."[15] Nevertheless, all five representatives of the ABLF were arrested and taken to the county jail on charges of assault with intent to murder.[16] A month and a half later, Bryant and Williams remained imprisoned—awaiting trial—the ostensible reason for the protest at the courthouse on November 1.

The confrontation at the Turner house and its aftermath marked a turning point in the history of the ABLF. Forced to divert energy and resources from issues such as police brutality, housing, and poverty to keeping its members out of jail, it became increasingly difficult for the group to operate in Birmingham. It was not simply the arrests of September 15, for in the aftermath police arrested additional members of the ABLF in a coordinated attempt to disrupt the organization. Even under these trying circumstances, however, the ABLF did continue to work in the community. In its efforts to free Bryant and Williams, for example, it allied with a broad cross section of people and groups, including white leftists, traditional civil rights groups, clergy, and black labor organizations.[17] This diverse array of activists mobilized defense committees to publicize the case, raise funds on behalf of the two men, and coordinate events such as the protest march and rally in November. The coalition the ABLF assembled also provided valuable assistance to others facing wrongful imprisonment and did much to publicize rampant racism and abuse in Alabama's prison system.[18] Still, by 1974 the cumulative effect of arrests, trials, and imprisonments, along with the internal stresses they exacerbated, meant that the ABLF was no longer able to function as a viable organization.[19]

Although its organizational life was thus brief, and its impact was largely local, the story of the Alabama Black Liberation Front is crucial to our understanding of the late 1960s and early 1970s. In both the issues it addressed and the methods it employed, it exemplified much of what defined that particular historical moment. For young African Americans like those in the ABLF—frustrated by what they perceived as the limited impact of the early civil rights movement, inspired by an emerging sense of black consciousness, and radicalized by their personal experiences with racial oppression—groups that offered a more forceful response to the problem of race in America became increasingly attractive.[20] To the extent that the ABLF merely exemplified that shift, which historians have long emphasized, it was not exceptional. When it is examined more closely, though, it carries added significance because it sheds critical light on an almost entirely unexplored aspect of that shift: the dramatic impact of the Black Panther Party on local groups that, while never taking on its name, were essentially part of the same movement.

Recent scholarship has done much to recover the BPP's organizational history, but not the centrality of the Panthers to the larger historical moment of the late 1960s and early 1970s.[21] The ABLF underscores the importance of the Panthers by demonstrating their long reach, even in an area where there was no official chapter, and in a region—the Deep South—not often associated with the Panthers.[22] Moreover, exploring the Birmingham story in depth reveals an intertwined history—local and national, ABLF and BPP—rendering the Black Panthers' moment more significant still.

The impact of the BPP on the ABLF was evident in a variety of ways. First, the ABLF's work in Birmingham mirrored the approach taken by the BPP in other cities. In both the issues they addressed—housing, poverty, and, most important, police brutality—and the tactics they employed—police patrols, breakfast programs, and investigative reporting—the ABLF drew inspiration from the Panthers. For example, not only did members of the ABLF sell copies of the Panther paper—whose full title was *The Black Panther: Black Community News Service*—they produced their own publication under a byline that mimicked the BPP, calling it the *Alabama Community News Service.* In the course of its work, the ABLF also engaged in the type of masculinist posturing that would be attached permanently to the Panthers' image. Indeed, Washington Booker III, an early recruit into the ABLF, recalls that he was attracted initially by the image of the Panthers as "some cool, tough, brave dudes who were confronting the police."[23]

Second, and arguably most significant, the ABLF sought to become an official affiliate of the Black Panther Party. Although it never achieved that goal, the ABLF did receive guidance from the party's headquarters in California and even sent a representative to the West Coast for training. Moreover, at least one of the ABLF's founders, Doc Bryant, had prior experience with the Panthers in Greensboro, North Carolina, and he incorporated that experience into the organization's training and recruitment process. On at least one occasion, Bryant would refer to Huey Newton, the co-founder of the BPP, as "our leader."[24] He also attempted to attach the party's insignia to the back of the jackets of the ABLF's members.[25] Critically, such connections were not lost on local police who identified members of the ABLF as Black Panthers and used that association to negatively affect the ABLF's reception in Birmingham.

That reception itself reveals the long shadow cast by the BPP over the period. First, that the Birmingham police responded as swiftly and as forcefully as they did to early reports of Panther-related activity in Alabama testifies to the BPP's visibility and impact. Indeed, local law enforcement's familiarity with the BPP was itself confirmation of the party's national impact. In September 1970, for example, the Jefferson County Sheriff's

Department even sent representatives to the Panthers' Revolutionary People's Constitutional Convention in Philadelphia.[26] Second, the ability of law enforcement in the Birmingham area to provoke fear in the community by simply connecting the ABLF to the BPP in public pronouncements illustrates further the Panthers' influence on the historical moment. Examples of such efforts include an article in the *Birmingham Post-Herald* in July 1970 in which, under the headline "Panther Threat Here," Sheriff Bailey of Jefferson County informed readers, "The Black Panther Movement, which has as its goal the overthrow of the United States government and which has been responsible for the deaths of numerous law enforcement officials throughout the nation recently, is organizing in Birmingham."[27] Clearly, law enforcement had a preconceived notion of what the Panthers represented and wanted the general population to share that assessment.

The ABLF, then, is an important piece of the larger story of black activism in the late 1960s and early 1970s. As the last twenty years of civil rights scholarship have made clear, though, the story of the ABLF—and the role of the BPP in that story—cannot be divorced from its local setting. The critical context is the history of black activism in Birmingham during the 1960s.[28]

Birmingham, 1963–70

Unfortunately, historians have paid relatively little attention to that history. The traditional narrative ends, effectively, in 1963, when Martin Luther King Jr.'s Southern Christian Leadership Conference coordinated a series of marches and protests that catapulted the city to the forefront of the modern civil rights movement and into the national spotlight.[29] If discussed at all, the period from the mid-1960s is typically treated as an epilogue to the story of Birmingham in the early 1960s.[30] The lavish attention paid to 1963 is understandable. That year, Americans across the country were shocked by images of nonviolent protesters—including schoolchildren—being attacked with fire hoses and by police dogs. The events in Birmingham, which included black people rising up in retaliation against violence by the police and the Ku Klux Klan, and which sparked hundreds of demonstrations across the nation that summer, injected new energy into the civil rights movement. Birmingham set the stage for the March on Washington that August, and, perhaps most important, played a critical role in persuading President John F. Kennedy to propose what would become the landmark Civil Rights Act of 1964.[31] As a result, civil rights scholars regard Birmingham as the site of one of the civil rights movement's greatest successes. From a national perspective, that characterization is indisputable.

At the same time, as historians Glenn Eskew and J. Mills Thornton have argued, the Birmingham campaign was something less than a panacea when viewed from a local perspective.[32] In particular, the 1963 demonstrations ended with concessions that left unresolved many of the issues of importance to a working-class base acting as "foot soldiers" in the effort. These unresolved issues contributed to the emergence of groups such as the ABLF.

That Birmingham proved resistant to change should come as little surprise to anyone familiar with the city's troubled racial history. King once described it as "the most thoroughly segregated city" in the country. In the 1950s, its public parks were closed and its professional baseball team disbanded to avoid compliance with judicial desegregation orders.[33] Birmingham had even found itself at the forefront of the effort to reverse the most tangible success of the 1963 campaign—the Civil Rights Act of 1964. Ollie's, a local barbecue restaurant, challenged the public accommodations provisions of the act all the way to the Supreme Court.[34] Most troubling, of course, was the city's propensity for violence as a means of maintaining the segregated order. Birmingham garnered the dubious distinction "Bombingham" because of the frequency with which black homes and churches were targeted. Indeed, an entire section of black homes was dubbed "Dynamite Hill."

By 1970, the year the Alabama Black Liberation Front emerged, deindustrialization, urban renewal, and persistent white racism had rendered lack of jobs, scarce housing, and poor medical care a continuing plague on Birmingham's African American community. As little as five months after the campaign of 1963, Fred Shuttlesworth, one of its lead organizers, was already threatening renewed protests around employment opportunities for black citizens.[35] Birmingham would not hire a single black police officer until 1966; the first black fireman was not hired until 1968.[36] In fact, throughout the remainder of the 1960s, the city continued to resist hiring African Americans in any capacity other than maintenance or custodial positions.[37] Employment opportunities for African Americans were limited outside the municipal arena as well. In Birmingham's coal, iron, and steel plants, African Americans had to file lawsuits to gain access to higher-paying jobs commensurate with their experience and years of service.[38] Although many of these cases would eventually prove successful, lengthy appeals, hostile judges, and company resistance meant that compensation did not arrive until well after deindustrialization had rendered many of the advances moot. Black service workers, particularly those working in Birmingham's newest industry—health care—also complained of low wages and benefits, discriminatory treatment, and lack of advancement opportunities.[39]

As the case of Bernice Turner revealed, African Americans in Birmingham in the late 1960s continued to encounter obstacles in their search for decent housing as well. Turner had turned to the ABLF for assistance because, despite holding down a steady job and renting out a room to a boarder, she still could not keep up with her mortgage payments. Eviction was only one facet of a larger set of concerns, however. By the late 1960s, for example, urban renewal, in the form of a new medical center and the downtown Civic Center, had displaced many poor blacks.[40] In a bit of tragic irony, the medical center had even displaced a valuable source of temporary housing, the Help One Another Club's Rescue House.[41]

Housing was a concern even for those who did not find themselves evicted or their homes demolished. Black citizens complained of a lack of recreational opportunities, deteriorating buildings, and an influx of drugs in their neighborhoods.[42] They also complained that Little League teams and others were denied use of those parks and recreational services that *were* available.[43] Escaping such circumstances was not easy, nor did escape mean an end to the problem. Those African Americans who could afford to purchase homes in the "over-the-mountain" suburbs of Vestavia Hills, Mountain Brook, or Homewood had to file lawsuits in order even to be shown a home.[44] Meanwhile, African Americans who had surmounted such obstacles and successfully moved their families into previously all-white neighborhoods faced harassment and intimidation from their new neighbors. In June 1970, for example, the Birmingham police dispatched officers to the home of Mattie Reese on Fayette Avenue. Reese's white neighbors had thrown rocks at her five children and then built a "ten foot solid wood fence" to separate the families from one another. Mary Francis Hobson, the white woman for whom Reese worked as a domestic, told the officers that her neighbors' son, a white man named Skipper Smith, had warned her that he was planning to bomb Reese's house.

Despite having sacrificed their homes to facilitate the city's new commitment to the medical industry, as well as filling many of the low-wage jobs necessary to keep the city's medical facilities running, by 1970 African Americans still found it difficult to obtain adequate, accessible, and affordable health care. Conditions were so bad that, in March 1965, the NAACP filed suit in federal court on behalf of Birmingham's black residents, charging that University Hospital maintained segregated facilities and offered "inferior service" to black patients.[45] Davis Jordan and Edward Hicks, residents of Birmingham who had helped organize a committee to document such discrimination, recall: "All black folks had to go in the basement. Our wives, when they had babies and things, they had to go in the basement. With the other sick folks and all the pipes and everything around. All the good rooms and everything were upstairs."[46] Although the lawsuit proved successful, desegregation was only part of the problem. Into the 1970s, African Americans faced problems of both access to medical facilities and the quality of health care received.

In 1971, for example, a survey of health-care needs conducted by black activists in Roosevelt City, a predominately black town on the outskirts of Birmingham, revealed the lack of prenatal, preventive, and dental care available to African Americans.[47] The absence of such services had persisted for more than three decades following the closing in the 1940s of the Slossfield Community Center, the only local facility that recognized the licenses of black doctors and nurses.[48] The problem would be addressed only in 1974 when, in response to the survey, a community-run mobile health center was created. But, that stopgap measure, too, was short-lived.

African Americans faced these fundamental quality-of-life issues in Birmingham, despite the 1963 campaign. But, what remained especially alarming—so glaringly evident in that campaign—was the pervasiveness of police brutality, a long-standing problem in a city where the local police force had well-established ties to the Ku Klux Klan.[49] In the years after 1963, violence by police against African Americans actually increased, with repeated interactions ending in officers filing reports of "justifiable homicide."[50] The prevalence of such cases was revealed in February 1967 when black leaders petitioned the city and county governments for greater police accountability. The effort began following the deaths of ten African Americans over the previous fourteen months.[51] In a letter addressed to various government officials, the petitioners wrote that it was "difficult to describe the growing anger, fear, resentment, and distrust these shootings have caused among thousands of citizens."[52] The following month, Fred Shuttlesworth called for the "non-violent movement" to "regroup and reorganize" around the issue.[53] As part of that effort, local civil rights groups attempted to organize a boycott to protest the situation. A flyer distributed by Shuttlesworth's Alabama Christian Movement for Human Rights called for a "60-Day period of mourning for the dead" in which black citizens would stay away from both downtown stores and area shopping centers.[54] Such tactics, however, did little to remedy the problem.

That was evident two years later, in 1969, when many of the same leaders, making many of the same demands, mounted a new campaign. This effort *did* result in a grand jury probe of police conduct, but the jury returned no indictments. Instead, it recommended that police "make a special effort to be somewhat more diplomatic in their contact with the public." Police were also directed to disregard "race, creed, or color" in their work.[55] According to the seventeen-member jury, although Jefferson County's law enforcement had been guilty of "some instances of discourtesy," there was "no basis for the charge of widespread police brutality."[56] Members of Birmingham's black community—including future members of the ABLF—knew otherwise. For them, the only truth in the grand jury report was its reinforcement of the city's unwillingness to act. Indeed, concerns about police brutality would remain so salient that nine years later Richard Arrington would ride a wave of resentment about the issue to become the city's first black mayor.[57]

The persistence of these concerns—jobs, housing, medical care, and especially police brutality—meant that the Alabama Black Liberation Front emerged in an environment in which Birmingham's black poor, despite the real successes of the early civil rights movement, grappled with multiple concerns and sought leadership that was prepared to address them.[58] Such was the case around the country—a set of circumstances that, in fact, had contributed to the emergence of the Black Panther Party in the first place. Because these issues seemed so intractable—and because marches, boycotts, and political appeals were becoming increasingly less effective—Birmingham, as much as any other city, was open to the ideas of a BPP-inspired organization such as the ABLF.

To be sure, many, if not most, African Americans remained committed to nonviolence as a tactic and integration as a goal. There was, however, a substantial population for whom the basic ideas of groups such as the ABLF—the right to self-defense, an end to police brutality, and the importance of community control of services and resources—were appealing. In short, while they may have disagreed tactically, most of Birmingham's African Americans were sympathetic to the issues the ABLF raised. As Washington Booker III, a member of the ABLF, recalls: "The ground was much, much more fertile than what the FBI, and the sheriff, and some people in the media, and even white folks who wanted to feel comfortable would like to believe. And so when we met folk, they would talk to us. . . . The times and the treatment that these people had received *made* them receptive. They weren't that sure about whether they wanted to go with us into battle, but they basically embraced the things we said and what we talked about."[59] Rita Anthony, an activist involved in the Welfare Rights Organization and other local efforts in the Birmingham area, recalls that the ABLF was well-known in the black community. Although she did not support the group's tactics, Anthony remembers holding meetings with Bryant and Williams and notes that the ABLF and activist groups with which she was involved offered each other mutual support.[60]

Even Birmingham's usually conservative black newspaper, the *Birmingham World*, although also critical of the "methods" of the ABLF, nevertheless editorialized that it understood the group's "grievances." "In this city there are many angry with what they conceived to be injustice, double standards of treatment, civic brutality, and economic evils."[61] And, although the *Birmingham World* may not have agreed, traditions of self-defense remained strong in Birmingham and across the black South. Groups espousing philosophies grounded in self-defense would not have been as alarming to members of Birmingham's black community as one might assume from the traditional narratives of the 1963 campaign. In fact, although these protests had established Birmingham as a symbol of the strategy of nonviolent direct action espoused by King, many local African Americans were not committed to nonviolence. "Onlookers" and "bystanders" in 1963 had thrown rocks and bottles at police and questioned the wisdom of allowing officers to strike citizens without retaliation.[62]

Even many of Birmingham's most devoted disciples of nonviolence viewed it more as a strategy than as a way of life. To this day, many black

residents remember organizing night watches and armed patrols throughout the 1950s and 1960s to protect their neighborhoods from bombings
and other forms of racial violence.[63] In 1951, African Americans in the
Smithfield neighborhood actually received federal authorization to form a
"civil defense unit."[64] According to J. Mills Thornton, the "Smithfield District Civil Defense Reserve Police" was on duty every night for fifteen years
and, by 1963, had expanded to four additional black districts.[65] Thurgood
Marshall recalled black men patrolling outside Arthur Shores's home with
machine guns when he spent the night there in 1955.[66] After his home was
bombed in 1963, Shores himself would later lament not having been able
to retaliate. In an interview in 1974, he commented: "Well, the only thing
[the bombing] did was to anger me that I couldn't at least get a potshot at
the persons who were perpetrating these bombings . . . I wasn't of the
nonviolent type. I had sufficient arsenal there at my house that if I had
gotten a chance, I would have retaliated in kind."[67]

Such memories, though, are not part of the Birmingham story with
which most people are familiar. Nor is the work of the Alabama Black
Liberation Front and other "militant" organizations usually included in
discussions of "the movement" in Birmingham. Birmingham does not typically conjure up shootouts, revolutionary rhetoric, and Panther-styled
organizations—just as the city does not factor into most discussions of the
Black Panther Party. As we shall see, though, the ABLF challenges the
conventional narrative. Its history began with the meeting of two local
activists, Wayland "Doc" Bryant and Michael Reese.

The Origins of the Alabama Black Liberation Front

Although the ABLF emerged within the specific context of post-1963 Birmingham, its origins were in the neighboring state of Georgia. There, in
early 1970, Wayland "Doc" Bryant and Michael Reese first met, beginning a
long collaboration in black radical politics. The two men were members
of an Atlanta-based group known as the Georgia Black Liberation Front
(GBLF), which operated out of the Vine City neighborhood, a center of
black power activism best known for its connection to SNCC's Atlanta
Project.[68] In both its name and its programs, the GBLF prefigured the ABLF,
leading Birmingham police to contact their Atlanta counterpart about the
organization as part of its surveillance effort. Responding to these inquiries,

Atlanta police identified Bryant as the GBLF's leader and painted a negative picture of the group. "They advocate violence, also described as ignorant and dangerous, their only source of income is selling and distributing hate literature. . . . Bryant teaches his followers to hate and kill police."[69] According to a flyer produced by the GBLF, though, there was more to the organization than what the Atlanta police allowed. Members maintained that their group's focus was countering the effects of poverty in Vine City, where they had established a program to provide "free breakfast[s] for school children." They also alleged that at least three of their members had been imprisoned because of their participation in that program.[70]

Although sources on the GBLF are few, this flyer alone makes it clear that the group constituted an early attempt by Bryant and Reese to incorporate the programs and ideas of the BPP into their activist work. It was not mere coincidence, for example, that the GBLF initiated "free breakfast[s] for school children." Rather, the program and its title reflected the influence of Bryant, who, prior to arriving in Atlanta, had forged a relationship with the Panthers in Greensboro, North Carolina.[71] From at least April 1969 until his departure for Atlanta in the spring of 1970, Bryant had operated a black bookstore in Greensboro that the FBI linked to the BPP.[72] According to the FBI, Bryant stocked, among other items, "artifacts, publications, books, and African regalia," including "both paperback and hardback" books about Malcolm X. Of greatest concern, though, were the Panther newspapers Bryant carried, and, according to FBI sources, the frequenting of his store by North Carolina Panthers.[73] Although not necessarily "the center for militant activity in Greensboro," as the FBI asserted, Bryant's bookshop had been an important resource for that activity.[74]

Beyond these references to his bookstore, Bryant appears elsewhere in FBI surveillance documents on the North Carolina BPP, suggesting, at the very least, some tangential involvement with efforts to establish an official Panther branch in the state. In February 1970, for example, according to FBI documents, an attorney in Jacksonville received a "Black Panther Party Greeting Card" sent from a post office box registered to the Office of Economic Opportunity in Greensboro and signed "Doc." Agents believed "Doc" was Bryant and requested an investigation.[75] Bryant appeared as well in a thirty-seven-page memo of the FBI dated May 23, 1969. Here a source, whose name has since been redacted, reported that Greensboro Panthers had gone to Winston-Salem to speak at a rally. The memo portrayed

Bryant as an organizer of the event, noting that he had attended a planning meeting, and "stated that Chico Neblett, the BPP leader for the East Coast, had been in Greensboro on April 22, 1969, and had given Eric Brown [a member of the BPP] permission to have the rally at Winston-Salem."[76]

Police in both Birmingham and Atlanta also connected Bryant to the BPP, although they likely relied, at least in part, on information provided by the FBI. Police in Atlanta noted that he had "at one time tried to gain control of a 'Black Panther' unit in North Carolina."[77] In a memo of October 19, 1970, shortly after the "shootout" at Bernice Turner's home, an unidentified Birmingham police official reported that Bryant had attempted to join the BPP in Fort Bragg, North Carolina, after getting out of the army. He was allegedly refused membership and instructed to "go out and form a group which show[ed] that he was worthy and well qualified."[78] Of course, the motivation behind Bryant's relocation outside North Carolina and his exact relationship with the BPP may well have been misunderstood—even deliberately misconstrued—by the FBI and other law enforcement officials. That the Birmingham police were talking about a Fort Bragg chapter of the BPP suggests that ignorance played some role; that the Panthers were the most feared of all black radical groups of the era offers the tantalizing possibility that authorities sought to make someone they suspected appear more dangerous than he was—a kind of "bad jacketing" in reverse. The type and amount of FBI documents, as well as Bryant's activities in Birmingham, however, suggest he had at least some experience with the BPP and knew how to contact it. And, as we shall see, this experience would not only inform the work of the GBLF but also have an even greater influence on that of the ABLF.

The Atlanta police described the GBLF as "very successful." Their correspondence with the Birmingham police, for example, noted that the organization had attracted a significant number of recruits, estimating that they had at least twenty-five members by the mid-summer of 1970.[79] Despite such success, in the spring of that year, Bryant and Reese left Atlanta for Birmingham. In an interview with the *Southern Patriot*, Reese attributed the move to a "rash of police killings of black people in Birmingham" that had led the two men to conclude they were needed there.[80] Reese was a native of Birmingham; so the opportunity to return home was likely also a draw. The success of the GBLF may also have led both men to believe they could safely start work in another southern state, eventually building a region-wide network of like-minded organizations. That they would maintain regular contact with the GBLF suggests as much, as do brief mentions in police surveillance records of Bryant being in contact with the South Carolina Black Liberation Front.[81] Whatever the full set of motivations, the two men arrived in Birmingham in May and began to put together another organization styled after the Black Panther Party: the Alabama Black Liberation Front.

The Alabama Black Liberation Front Comes to Birmingham

On their arrival, Bryant and Reese immediately began seeking support in the black community. With that, the organization could then work to increase its profile and more effectively disseminate its ideas. Knowledge of the surrounding area and available resources would also allow the ABLF to identify local issues. Bryant appears to have taken the lead in this effort. He kept a personal notebook filled with observations about local events and lists of potential sources of support.[82] Unsurprisingly, given his experience in Greensboro and the role his store played in the Panther effort there, among his priorities was finding bookstores or "afro shops" to serve as community bases.[83] Bryant also sought to forge connections with sympathetic people and groups in Birmingham. Among those were "all Revolutionary Women's Liberation Movements" and "the lumpen proletariat, workers, rank and file soldiers, progressive youth, students, intellectuals, urban petty bourgeoise [sic] and conscientious national capitalist[s]."[84] More important than establishing the ABLF in the community, though, was the need to recruit and train members.

To that end, Bryant and Reese began contacting potential allies. By June 1970, they had assembled a core group of at least six men, including Washington Booker, Larry Watkins, James Colbert, and Ronnie Williams.[85] Although this core was small, its number was not indicative of the group's eventual scope and influence.[86] Numerous others would spend a week or two in training with the organization, participate in specific efforts, or offer other means of support. Precise membership numbers are difficult to assess, as police do not appear ever to have confiscated any sort of membership roll, and none seems to have survived in any other hands.[87] Throughout their files on the ABLF, though, police regularly cite names outside of those considered the ABLF's core.[88] At a news conference in July 1970,

Sheriff Bailey estimated that by then the ABLF had recruited some twenty-five to thirty members. Booker also recalled a steady stream of supporters, whether official members or not. At the very least, support for the ABLF was strong enough to allow it to open as many as three separate offices across the city.

What inspired these men to dedicate themselves to the black freedom struggle? And why did they look to the BPP for inspiration in doing so? Such questions are crucial to understanding the specific history of the ABLF, as well as the broader dynamics of the period. Thus, before exploring specific activities of the ABLF, it is worth examining the experiences that contributed to its founding in the first place. Fortunately, a number of the organization's founding members are now willing to share their personal stories of recruitment and radicalization. Beyond their importance to the ABLF's history, those stories offer important insights to scholars seeking to understand the ways that African Americans, and black southerners in particular, discovered the Black Panther Party, as well as the reasons they were receptive to its platform and programs. Significantly, prior to the ABLF's formation, several of its founders experienced a radicalization process similar to what Panthers elsewhere have described.

Wash Booker reflected upon his recruitment in a series of interviews in both 1995 and 2002. In May 1969, at the age of twenty, he had returned to Birmingham from military service in Vietnam.[89] Although born in Demopolis, Alabama, he had spent the bulk of his childhood in Birmingham, mostly in Loveman's Village, a public housing development. Having participated as a teenager in the 1963 Birmingham campaign, Booker was disappointed to discover upon his return from Vietnam that African Americans still did not "share equally in the American dream."[90] He also despaired of the lack of unity he perceived among Birmingham's blacks. Those who had benefited from the early civil rights movement, he now says he felt then, had not continued that effort for those still struggling. Most disheartening, though, was the conduct of the Birmingham police. Booker remembers officers who would brag about how many "niggers" they had killed.[91] Reflecting on his return, Booker recalls: "So . . . then you come back and as you get back into the neighborhood you realize that the police brutality is really just as rampant as it was when you left. You're thinking that you're coming back to a whole different kind of society—that things have changed, that everything, that folk are together, and it ain't."[92] At the same time, Booker had found it difficult to readjust. The training he

had received as a marine, as well as his combat experience, had not prepared him for life as a civilian. As a result, Booker was receptive when
approached for help in organizing what he was told was to be a Birmingham chapter of the BPP.[93]

Michael Reese told his story, as noted above, in a 1972 interview piece
for the *Southern Patriot.* Twenty-three years old when he helped found the
GBLF and then the ABLF, he was also a native of the Birmingham area. He
had been raised in a coal mining camp, where both his father and grand-
father were employed by the Tennessee Coal and Iron Company.[94] Having
seen his family "working all their lives and having nothing," Reese articulated a strong desire as a young man to do something different with his life.
He enrolled in college but left school when he married, eventually spend-
ing fourteen months in the Marine Corps, including time in Vietnam.

By 1969, Reese had left the military and settled in Atlanta. Inspired by
what he knew of the BPP—calling it the only thing he could relate to—he
began to search for a means of contacting the organization, but knew of no
way to do so in the South.[95] In what he described as the effort to build
"black liberation fronts," though, Reese found what the *Southern Patriot*
called "a model of contact for people looking to organize." It is unclear
what Reese meant by the "building of black liberation fronts" or what his
experience with them had been.[96] We do know, however, that Reese's
efforts to contact the Panthers led him to "Doc" Bryant and, ultimately,
the ABLF.

Although one had sought out the BPP and the other had been found by
it, Booker and Reese described similar experiences. Both had grown up
surrounded by poverty and had seen its effects on their families. Both
come of age at the height of the civil rights movement—in a city that had
played a primary role in that movement. The most significant experience
these men shared, however, was service in the Vietnam War. Booker,
Reese, and other members of the ABLF would apply lessons they learned
on the battlefield in Vietnam to their experiences with racial oppression
back home, a process that made them receptive to the ideas expressed by
the BPP. For these men, military service had a transforming effect similar
to that experienced by black soldiers in previous conflicts. Just as these
earlier generations had done, Booker and Reese returned home prepared
to take the struggle for black equality into the streets, employing armed
resistance if necessary.[97]

Booker links his membership in the ABLF explicitly to his experience in

Vietnam, describing the latter as nothing less than a "revolutionary education." He recalls: "When I first got to 'Nam, I was gung-ho [about the United States and its commitment to equality] . . . [but] little by little it started to erode, and I started to turn the corner until a revolutionary came back . . . a young man bent on changing everything. . . . I was a different person. I was ready for the Panther Party."[98] Reese made similar observations. Describing himself as "outraged" by what he had seen at the front, Reese recalled: "I soon realized I was fighting people, some of whom were darker than me, people who were poor like my people at home. It shocked me."[99] He also began to connect the war to larger forces such as corporate capitalism. "The first thing I saw in Vietnam," he remembered, "was a Shell Oil Plant."[100]

Other members of the ABLF, including Larry Watkins and Charles Cannon, expressed similar sentiments regarding Vietnam. Cannon, for example, told a reporter for the *Southern Patriot*, "I got into the [Alabama] Black Liberation Front because of my Vietnam War experience. It was sickening."[101] An ABLF flyer later contrasted Charles Cannon's service in Vietnam to his work with the organization. The flyer informed the community that Cannon had come home to Birmingham to fight for "real freedom."[102] In Booker's words, the men of the ABLF came back from Vietnam "more militant, more conscious, and more aware."[103]

The crucial role of Vietnam military service was not exclusive to the members of the ABLF, of course. Across the country, returning black soldiers expressed similar ideas, demonstrating again the broader significance of the ABLF's story.[104] Haywood Kirkland of Washington, D.C., remembered "getting more of a revolutionary, militant attitude," which he intended to put to use as "part of the struggle of black people."[105] Reginald "Malik" Edwards of Phoenix, Louisiana, a Washington Panther, recalled: "I had left one war and came back and got into another. Most of the Panthers then were veterans. We figured if we had been over in Vietnam fighting for our country, which at that point wasn't serving us properly, it was only proper that we had to go out and fight for our own cause."[106] Harold Bryant of East St. Louis remembered a new perception of whites, just as Booker did. "I got to find out that white people weren't as tough, weren't the number one race and all them other perceptions that they had tried to ingrain in my head. I found out they got scared like I did. I found out a lot of them were a lot more cowardly than I expected."[107] Radicalized, then, by their experiences in Vietnam and able to draw on their interactions with other black soldiers, returning veterans, including future members of the ABLF, responded to the oppression they and other African Americans encountered back home in a new way.[108] For a significant number of these veterans, that response was shaped by the BPP.

For Reese, Booker, Watkins, and Cannon, Vietnam acted as a catalyst, introducing them to the BPP and preparing them for membership in a Panther-styled group such as the ABLF. What remained was to find an outlet for their newly radicalized perspective. When they encountered someone like Bryant—who had direct experience with the BPP—their newly formed ideas turned into action. According to Watkins, Bryant, who was about twenty years older than the others, served as the group's intellectual mentor. He was the driving force behind the early ABLF, at least in terms of its philosophy and strategies, and in that role he pointed its members toward the BPP.

Yet, though Bryant had provided the means for the ABLF to incorporate Panther programs and ideas into its work, he was not the reason the BPP was attractive. As noted earlier, for the ABLF, much of the initial appeal of the Panthers lay in their reputation as "some cool, tough, brave dudes who were confronting the police."[109] Although at least the Oakland-based wing of the national BPP was, by late 1970, trying to distance itself from such an image, as George Katsiaficas notes, "The Panthers' notoriety initially turned on their overt practice and explicit advocacy of armed self-defense."[110] The Panthers, then, offered a well-known example of black citizens confronting police brutality in ways the ABLF considered more effective than the marches and petitions familiar to residents of Birmingham. That the BPP's approach provided an outlet for the skills they had acquired as soldiers certainly did not hurt, either.[111]

Behind the Panthers' appeal as a group willing to stand up to the police, of course, was a larger reality: they spoke to the issues of most immediate concern to African Americans at the time—police brutality, but also housing, medical care, and other problems related to poverty and racial discrimination. These issues, moreover, were as salient in Birmingham as they were in Oakland, Chicago, or New York. Indeed, once they moved beyond police brutality, the cadre of the Alabama Black Liberation Front discovered that the BPP's free breakfast programs, medical clinics, clothing giveaways, and other "survival programs" were as necessary in the cities of the Deep South as they were in the North or the West. In short, the ideas expressed in the BPP's Ten-Point Platform and Program were arguably the clearest articulation of the concerns faced by most black citizens of the period, regardless of the region where they lived. Thus, the ABLF used the platform in its flyers and other publications, often highlighting a particular plank and relating it to a specific local event. In all these ways, the aplicability of the BPP's ideas to local circumstances was a major reason for its appeal.

The BPP's national visibility was an additional factor that contributed to its appeal. It was not just in Vietnam, but also back home, that the BPP had made a name for itself among African Americans. As the historian Charles Jones has noted, "The BPP was a mainstay of the national media and a frequent headline maker of both the mainstream and dissident press."[112] If Bryant was intent on starting an affiliate of the BPP, he did not need to explain to recruits who the Panthers were. Recall that when Michael Reese returned from Vietnam and began looking for an organization to join, his thoughts turned first to the Panthers. The national circulation of their newspaper contributed further to the Panthers' accessibility. Not only did the paper provide a ready means for members of the ABLF to communicate with the Birmingham community, it also gave them a way to remain connected with a larger organization. Thus, if the Panthers were not the only choice available to these aspiring black revolutionaries, they were, at the very least, a well-known and recognizable one.

Having settled on the BPP as its model and hoping to receive recognition as an official affiliate, the ABLF incorporated the Panthers into nearly every aspect of its work: in its training of new members, its response to police brutality, its production of alternative news sources, and its community service programs. In each of these areas, the ABLF emulated what it knew of the BPP. Unfortunately, as noted earlier, that work would be stymied by a final way in which the ABLF came to resemble the BPP: the hostile reception it received from local law enforcement. Before addressing that reception, though, a more detailed look at the influence of the BPP on the ABLF's activities in and around Birmingham is necessary.

From the beginning, members of the ABLF set about the task of educating themselves. Members read Frantz Fanon's *Wretched of the Earth* and *Dying Colonialism*, as well as the writings of Che Guevara, Mao Tse-tung, and Amiri Baraka.[113] An entry on June 17, 1970 in Bryant's notebook reflected the BPP's influence on that process. "An active day. Things moved in the interest of the people. Read articles from Ramparts on Revolution and concepts of Revolution. Read book by Minister of Information Mr. Eldridge Cleaver on the Social, Educational and Political structure of (Babylon) America and its illegal existence."[114] The ABLF also obtained copies of the BPP newspaper, and members committed the BPP's Ten-Point Platform and Program to memory.[115] In fact, the ABLF would later produce its own statement that was almost identical to that of the BPP platform.[116] The influence of that platform, as well as other BPP documents, was reflected in an application for membership in the ABLF, which required adherence to the following pledge.

> A membership in the ABLF requires you to support (1) The Black Panther Party. (2) The Black Laws. (3) The Universal Declaration of Human Rights and United Nations. (4) Support the Peoples Army. (5) Read Evolutionary and Revolutionary Phamphlets [sic] newspapers and books. (6) Learn Self-Defense. (7) The Three Main Rules of Discipline are 1. Okay [obey?] orders in all your actions 2. Do not take a single needle or piece of threads [sic] from the Humans. 3. Turn in everything captured. (8) Volunteer 8 hours a week to Party Business. (9) Think Military, Political and Economical in [what] so ever you do.[117]

Members were then required to affirm that they would "learn truth and How to fight by any means necessary for Human Rights."[118]

Once trained, ABLF members' actual involvement in the community also took its cue from the BPP. Initially, the influence was most evident in the ABLF's approach to police brutality, which remained a central focus of its work throughout. As the Panthers had done early on, members of the ABLF began by monitoring police activity in Birmingham.[119] One way they did so was by taking advantage of a shortwave radio. Tuned into police channels, they knew when officers were responding to a call. The ABLF would then appear on the scene to observe police conduct and cite city codes.[120] In July 1970, Lieutenant Robert Harper of the Birmingham police submitted an intelligence report to Chief Jamie Moore apprising him that in responding to two calls, Car 62 had arrived on the scene only to find Wash Booker already there.[121] During an incident in which Booker and several others were pulled over, police claimed that the men had cited "some jail house law" upon being approached by officers. Officers also noted that, although they did not find any weapons in the car, they did locate "articles indicating some connections with the Black Panther Party."

The ABLF also sought to reduce incidents of brutality by playing on the fears of police officers.[122] They reasoned that the sight of armed black men refusing to back down would have a deep psychological effect on the officers.[123] The idea was to make them think twice before harassing or beating a black suspect. Such sentiments were displayed in one of the ABLF's early flyers, which was produced after police had shot and killed a young black man named Eugene Brown. Paraphrasing the BPP's incorporation of Mao Tse-tung's ideas, the flyer proclaimed, "But the pen is not respected only the gun is respected. We must bear arms to ensure and gain our Human Rights."[124] The ABLF put this idea to the test after it discovered a wiretap in a wall of its headquarters. Knowing that police were listening, members made exaggerated claims about the arms they possessed and discussed fake ambushes.[125] On another occasion, police reported that members "alledged [sic] to be members of the Black Panther Party" were harassing deputies who had been called to assist in a home eviction.[126] Officers reported that they had pursued and pulled over a white Buick with Gregory Watkins, Barry [Larry?] Watkins, and Wash Booker after the car had driven past the site of the eviction and stated, "They would be back just as soon as they could get some guns."[127] Although influenced as much by the predominant *image* of Panthers as by their *programs*, such attempts still revealed the deep and abiding influence the BPP had on the ABLF.[128]

The ABLF also kept tabs on police activity by publicizing the issue of police brutality in the hope that it would force city officials to take action. A police surveillance memorandum noted, "Presently they have a recording device on their phone and are soliciting any complaints from Negro citizens about police brutality."[129] On receiving word of an alleged incident of police brutality, the ABLF would dispatch members to conduct an investigation. Through a connection with Richard Arrington, then a city councilman, some of these investigations were, in fact, brought to the attention of city hall.[130] Booker recalled in an interview in 1995: "Let's say the police was going to somebody's house in [Collegeville], kicked the door in and roughed their momma up and their sister and just kind of beat up everybody . . . and we would get a call. We would shoot over there. We'd talk to everybody who was a witness. We'd get their story. . . . Doc would take [Arrington] the information, and he would get up in the council meeting . . . and he would blast them."[131]

Here again, the ABLF incorporated the BPP's ideas and tactics in making their investigations public via newsletters and bulletins published under the byline of the Alabama Black Community News Service (ABCNS), a name that mimicked the BPP's Black Community News Service (BCNS). In fact, the ABLF's office in Roosevelt City featured a sign identifying the building as the Black Community News Service and later police reports indicated that the group was considering the title as a name for the organization instead of ABLF.[132] The similarities between the ABLF's ABCNS and the BPP's BCNS went beyond their names, though. On at least one occasion, the results of an ABLF investigation appeared in the BPP newspaper itself. That story—which appeared in the *Black Panther* on August 15, 1970—was taken from a bulletin published by the ABLF in June 1970.[133] The bulletin had reported that, after a thirty-day "intensive investigation in the black community of Alabama," the ABLF had uncovered twenty-four instances of police brutality, of which nine had been "successfully documented." Among the documented cases in Birmingham were

—1 Brother Lynched[,] Bessemer, Alabama Jail.
—1 Brother Shot In His Grandmothers [sic] Apartment.
—1 Brother Shot 12 times On May 10, 1970 Between 2−5 A.M.
—1 Brother Beaten To Death On Or About the 12th Of June 1970.
—1 Brother Beaten So Bad He Lost one Eye.
—1 Brother (A Free Bleeder) Beaten To A Pulp[,] On Critical List At Hospital.

The bulletin noted further that the ABLF was forming a "defense fund" to help uncover the truth about the incidents and provide aid to the victims.[134] Later, in September, Doc Bryant expressed his desire "to write an article for the Panther magazine" about segregation in Birmingham's jails.[135]

The production of alternative sources of news had been an effective tactic for the BPP, and the ABLF deliberately incorporated it into its own work. Not only did members of the ABLF distribute copies of the BPP's national newspaper, they also posted flyers and handbills with details of local injustices, just as the Panthers did. Although the ABLF's publications were not as professional in appearance as the BPP's, they served the same purpose. Moreover, these postings often highlighted a plank of the BPP platform and followed it with a local story related to the issue.[136] One such flyer opened by stating, "Point Number #3 of the Black Panther Platform: We want an immediate end to the robbery by the capitalist of our Black Community." The flyer then detailed the story of a woman with six kids who was facing eviction because she had opted to pay for medical needs ahead of her rent. At the bottom were the phrases, "All Power to the People" and "All Power to Motherhood."[137] Another flyer highlighted "Point #10 of the Black Panther Party's Platform and Program," regarding the need for "land, bread, housing, education[,] clothing, justice and peace" and listed the names and addresses of seven individuals allegedly standing in the way of their respective communities' attempts to merge with the all-black town of Roosevelt City.[138] Yet another publication, about the ABLF's "Free Breakfast for the Children" program, informed readers that "the [ABLF,] as revolutionaries following the example set by the Black Panther Party, must always go forthh [sic] to answer the needs and desires of the people."[139]

As these flyers indicate, beyond the ABLF's work on police brutality and alternative news production, the group's other community work bore the mark of the BPP. Issues such as the loss of utility service, the lack of recreational options, the inability to make mortgage or rent payments, and the availability of health care and other services were all addressed by the organization.[140] And, the way in which the ABLF did so was, once again, borrowed from the BPP.

The ABLF, for example, attempted to initiate a variety of community assistance programs, each modeled after survival programs of the BPP, the first being free breakfasts at the Loveman's Village housing project.[141] One flyer read: "Following the example of the Black Panther Party, the vanguard organization of the Human Rights struggle, the [ABLF] has organized the Peoples' Free Breakfast For Children Program. A study of the human needs and a survey of our community has confirmed the conditions as expressed in a Black Panther report."[142] Run out of one of the residents' homes, the program served as many as twenty-one kids each day.[143] Eventually, the ABLF attempted to expand to other neighborhoods, approaching local institutions such as the South Elyton Baptist Church about hosting the breakfasts.[144] Other projects included a free clothing giveaway in Kelly Ingram Park, which the ABLF publicized during an appearance on a local radio station's community call-in program.[145]

In all of the ABLF's activities, then, the influence of the BPP was evident.

The ABLF, however, did more than simply model itself after the Panthers. Eventually, the organization hoped to gain recognition as an official branch of the BPP, arguably the strongest indicator of the party's impact on the broader historical moment. Although it never realized this goal, the ABLF did establish contact with the national BPP and received some guidance. Items confiscated by Birmingham police document these connections. One such item was a handwritten note with an address and a phone number attributed to Sam Napier, who was in charge of national distribution of the Panther newspaper and was based in San Francisco. The note—evidently meant as a form of instruction regarding how to approach the national party—read: "It would be best to send Sam a letter and ask him for the prices of the Party material—telling him you want to sell the material in hopes of forming a branch in Ala." Also included in the note, in different handwriting, were an address and a phone number for the BPP in New York, along with the name "Brother D.C."[146] Phone logs obtained from the ABLF's headquarters by Birmingham police included multiple calls to the BPP's office in California, as well as at least one to the BPP's office in the Bronx.[147] Contact with the national organization was also necessary to obtain copies of the BPP newspaper. Police records include notations documenting that members of the ABLF signed for deliveries of the BPP newspaper at the Birmingham airport.[148]

Contacts with the national BPP were not just made by phone or mail. In July 1970, Michael Reese traveled to California for direct training at the party's national headquarters. According to the same unnamed source that provided the Birmingham police with details on Bryant's interactions with the North Carolina BPP, Bryant had been in contact with the BPP's headquarters and sent Reese and at least one other member to learn how to form an official chapter. According to the source, the second man returned to Birmingham after only a few days, but Reese remained in California for about a month, returning after the Tarrant City "shootout." The same police memo reported that Reese had been "accepted" by the BPP and sent back to Birmingham to operate the group. An additional memo claimed that Bryant had spoken with Reese while he was in San Francisco and learned that he was "studying how to solicit new members[,] which they need to get a charter." Bryant apparently told the rest of the ABLF that "to get a charter for the Black Panther Party, they must have so many members and so much cash."[149]

Upon his return, a police memo claimed, Reese "ran into trouble" with Perry Carlisle, the local black businessman who had aligned himself with the ABLF, and a split between groups loyal to Reese and one loyal to Carlisle and Bryant developed.[150] The memo further noted that a "small group in Ensley" had formed a third group separate from both Reese and Bryant.[151] Another police memo in October 1970 referred to an "Ensley section" thought to be "under the leadership of a negro named Danny Prickett." This latter group was reported to have ordered their own shipment of Panther newspapers, which they intended to sell "without any help of the Birmingham branch of the Alabama Black Liberation League."[152] The memo contended that the Ensley section had "gotten tired of waiting and listening to Michael Reese" and that Reese, Watkins, and others spent most of their time and money on drugs.

It is unclear what, if anything, should be made of such reports. In a later interview, Watkins did recall that Reese had learned printing skills from the BPP and had attempted to make the ABLF's publications more professional.[153] He did not indicate that any splits had emerged as a result. Other police documents suggest that whatever splits occurred were not permanent. By December 1970 police had obtained copies of letters sent to the "West Coast headquarters of the Black Panther Party" in which Bryant and Reese were both listed as officers.[154] The letters also mentioned an "Alabama office" of the group, suggesting that, if there had been factions, they may have decided to cooperate as branches of a larger organization. That rival groups may have wished to claim to be the true Panthers in Birmingham, of course, only underscores the party's influence and appeal.

Whether official factions formed or not, by the end of 1970, the ABLF did, in fact, find it increasingly difficult to operate in the city. Any tensions that might have arisen between members were surely exacerbated by law enforcement's campaign to discredit and disrupt the organization. That campaign represents one final way the Black Panther Party left its mark on the Alabama Black Liberation Front. Almost as soon as the ABLF had begun to organize in Birmingham, law enforcement had targeted the group.[155] Law enforcement instituted regular surveillance of the group's offices and relied on a network of informants to keep tabs on their activities.[156] In fact, so confident was Sheriff Bailey in public support for such measures that he announced the strategy at a news conference.[157] Members of the ABLF were subject to harassment by officers, with fines and arrests for posting flyers or selling BPP newspapers.[158] Just one week prior to the incident in Tarrant City, Bryant and Williams had been jailed and fined for "failing to obey the lawful command of an officer."[159] Sheriff Bailey and District Attorney Morgan also revealed plans to prosecute members of the ABLF under laws pertaining to groups "advocating anarchy."[160]

Law enforcement officials also used the local press in an effort to frighten the public about the goals and intentions of the ABLF, referring to them as terrorists intent on killing police officers. District Attorney Morgan told the *Birmingham Post-Herald* that "the organization 'poses a big threat.'" Sheriff Bailey announced that "[members of the ABLF] are known to be accumulating firearms, such as shotguns and rifles, and talking about explosives and ammunition." Conflating the two organizations, he added that the BPP had been responsible for killing two Chicago police officers only two weeks prior to his news conference. Morgan and Bailey also released copies of the ABLF's literature that referred to police as pigs and called for an end to police brutality lest police "'face the wrath of the armed people.'" Local businesses were enlisted in the effort to disrupt the ABLF as well. A memo of July 1970 regarding the effort to evict the ABLF from its office on Center Street noted that police had "talked to the man who owns the house and the rental company and they are both willing to cooperate in any way that we want them to."[161]

Such was the Panthers' reputation, however much deserved, that Birmingham police exhibited concern at the very first hint of BPP activity, caring little whether it was official or unofficial. Law enforcement assumed that anyone associated in any way with the Panthers was intent on instigating violence, particularly toward police officers. An early police memo regarding the ABLF reported an attempt by Agent Starley Carr of the FBI to "interview" a member of the ABLF after he was discovered taking photographs of the office in Roosevelt City. According to the memo, the only response by the ABLF to Carr's questions was silence and a "deep stare of hate."[162] Reports from other law enforcement agencies reinforced the single-minded view of the Birmingham Police Department. Most telling was a letter dated July 13, 1970 to Chief Moore of the Birmingham police in which Agent Ralph Miles of the FBI wrote, "It is my hope that by a city-county-state-federal cooperative effort, it may be possible to contain, if not eliminate entirely, the new threat to the peace and tranquility of the Birmingham area."[163]

The Demise of the Alabama Black Liberation Front

All of this, of course, contributed to the "shootout" in Tarrant City that fateful fall evening in 1970. The confrontation, coming some four months after the ABLF began its work, provided the justification for the first in a series of arrests involving members of the group. Police relied on their earlier characterizations of the ABLF to garner public support following the incident. The *Birmingham News*, for example, ran a story about the event that featured a photo of Sheriff Bailey with two guns. The caption read: "Weapons found in home after shooting. . . . Both were fully loaded, Sheriff Bailey said." Although no shots had been fired from the house, the article noted uncertainties about who had "fired first." Having repeatedly warned the public about the violent nature of the ABLF, though, law enforcement surely knew what conclusion most people would draw.[164]

Almost all of the core members of the ABLF were arrested or detained at some point. Several were convicted on serious charges. After eight months in prison, in May 1971, Bryant and Williams were tried on charges stemming from the confrontation in Tarrant City. A mistrial based on prejudicial statements by a juror forced a retrial in the fall, but the two men remained in prison.[165] Ultimately, an all-white jury convicted the two after only two hours of deliberation. On October 7, 1971, Bryant and Williams were each sentenced to five years in prison.[166]

As their lawyers began the appeals process, supporters of the two men, working through an organization called Concerned Citizens for Justice (CCJ), raised enough money to bail them out by hosting events to publicize the case and piecing together donations and small loans from residents of Birmingham.[167] One event was a " 'covered dish' dinner" at Miles College in December 1971. Jack Drake and Ralph Knowles, attorneys for Bryant and Williams; the Reverend Charles Hutchison, the chairman of the CCJ; Lewis White, a fund-raising organizer; and Josh Lewis (Stephens), a representative of the ABLF, were scheduled to participate in a panel discussion. Supporters unable to attend were asked to send pledge cards to the Reverend Jesse Douglas, the treasurer of the CCJ. A dinner had been held the previous June featuring a similar panel.[168]

In August 1971, the CCJ managed to raise sufficient funds to bail Bryant out of jail. Following his release, he held a press conference at St. Paul's Methodist Church.[169] According to the *Birmingham-Post Herald*, about

150 people attended the gathering.[170] Police put the number at about two hundred, noting that about one-third were white, most of whom were "long haired, wearing hippie type clothes."[171] Bryant thanked his supporters and asked them to continue working until Williams was also able to make bail.[172] He took the opportunity to describe conditions in the Jefferson County jail, likening it to a "Nazi concentration camp" and detailing middle-of-the-night beatings. He spoke of the use of a "punishment block" where prisoners were confined to six by eight foot cells with no bed. He said that guards had confiscated his writings in which he kept track of such abuses. He also called for investigations into "justifiable homicides" by police, counseled residents to keep firearms for protection from the police, and drew attention to the case of jailed black Communist and Panther supporter Angela Davis, who had grown up in the "Dynamite Hill" neighborhood of Birmingham. The last remarks prompted the crowd to applaud Sallye Davis, Angela's mother, who was in attendance.[173] Bryant concluded by asking his audience to follow Huey Newton, whom he identified as "our leader," and touched on other cases involving the BPP, including the trial and release of party members in New Orleans.

On January 31, 1972, the CCJ was able to bail out Williams with monies collected from such events. On February 14, the CCJ hosted a coffee and cake get-together at the home of Annie and Frederick Kraus, where Williams was scheduled to speak about his case, the conditions in the jailhouse, and the work of the ABLF. Supporters were asked to bring friends and other potential allies.[174] Police identified Frederick Kraus as a professor at the University of Alabama's dental school and noted that he and his wife lived in the suburbs and had been "very active coordinating legal affairs of the CCJ, dealing specifically with legal aspects of bailing out the two members of the ABLF."[175] Present at the dinner were Williams and other members of the ABLF—Josh Stephens, Charles Cannon, and Richard Parnell—as well as Caliph Washington, a black man recently released after fourteen years of wrongful imprisonment in Bessemer, one of Jefferson County's two jails. Williams also participated in other efforts intended to expose conditions in Alabama's prison system, working with, among others, the Southern Conference Educational Fund (SCEF).

The following June, Bryant's and Williams's final appeal was denied a hearing by the U.S. Court of Appeals for the Fifth Circuit.[176] Rather than surrender himself to authorities, however, Williams fled with his new wife,

Susan Hamerquist, to Oregon, where she had family connections. Alabama attempted to have Williams extradited, but a well-coordinated letter-writing campaign and appeals to Governor Tom McCall allowed Williams to remain safe out west. Those who had contributed to Williams's bail fund supported his decision to flee, even though it meant the loss of their money. Letters urging the governor not to extradite Williams arrived even before the formal extradition papers arrived in late November 1973.[177] The former member of the Alabama Black Liberation Front lived out the rest of his life in the Portland area, passing away in 1982. Bryant served his time and, in the late 1970s, resurfaced in Birmingham working with a group called Operation Human Rights (OHR). Significantly, OHR organized around the enduring issue of police brutality in the city. Indeed, Mayor Richard Arrington's papers contain a number of references to the work of Bryant's group.[178] Like Williams, Bryant, too, has since passed away.

Bryant and Williams, however, were not the only members of the ABLF to be imprisoned because of their radical activity. In the fall of 1970, after the Turner affair, Michael Reese and Jamel Colbert were stopped by police and charged with possession of sawed-off shotguns. Although the circumstances of the arrest were questioned, even by a federal judge called to hear one of their appeals, the two men were sentenced to five years in federal prison. While incarcerated at a federal facility in Texas, Reese forged a relationship with Walter Collins, an organizer affiliated with SCEF. Together, the two men continued to organize, instigating food and work strikes to protest conditions in the prison.[179] After his release, Reese returned to Birmingham, where he currently resides. In 1972, Charles Cannon found himself framed on murder charges in connection with the shooting death of the son of Birmingham's acting police chief, Jack Warren. After serving several years in prison, a federal appeals court finally granted Cannon a new trial, based on withheld evidence, and he was released.

Despite such focused attempts to disrupt the work of the ABLF, the group tried to remain active through at least 1972.[180] Police records contain documentation of Charles Cannon's arrest in February of that year for "selling paper w/o license."[181] In April, Sergeant C. M. Cates filed a report that he had responded to a complaint called in by Bryant about an arrest near what Cates referred to as the "Black Panther headquarters."[182] Additional breakfast programs were established in other Birmingham neighborhoods.[183] Efforts to support imprisoned members were instigated as the need arose.[184] Members also continued to distribute the Panther news-paper around the city and state. Ultimately, though, the group was unable to withstand the onslaught of police repression, and its members moved on to other work.

For many African Americans during the late 1960s and early 1970s, the BPP represented the most authentic expression of their political, eco-nomic, and social concerns. The story of the Alabama Black Liberation Front suggests elements of the Black Panthers' national appeal, as well as ways in which African Americans, in this case southerners, discovered the Panthers' ideas and organizing strategies. The story of the ABLF also re-veals that the concerns articulated by groups such as the BPP—the need for decent food and housing, the need for black self-determination, the need for an understanding of black history, and, most important, the need to address police brutality of black people—were salient across the country, not just in Chicago, Detroit, or New York. In addition, the response of law enforcement in Birmingham to the ABLF demonstrated that at least the white power structure there understood the potential "threat" posed by the ABLF's inspiration, the Black Panther Party. The crowd at the Birmingham courthouse in November 1970 had proclaimed, "We belong to the Revolu-tionary age." If they were correct, then the story of the Alabama Black Liberation Front demonstrates that the Black Panther Party was one of the primary reasons why.

Notes

1 Information on the rally comes from the files of the Birmingham Police Department, which surveilled people, groups, and events deemed associated with agitation, especially about race. See also files in several collections in the Depart-ment of Archives and History at the Birmingham Public Library (BPL). If treated critically, such sources are invaluable for detail unavailable in traditional sources such as newspapers. Moreover, much of the material consists of activist docu-ments confiscated by police. Finally, the files themselves illuminate the environ-ment of police repression in which protest groups operated. A report on the rally of November 1, 1970 is in the papers of George Seibels, a city councilman and later the mayor. "Memo Notes, Re: Birmingham Coalition Against War, Racism, and Repression," Police Department Intelligence Reports, November 2, 1970 to December 29, 1970, File 37.32, George Seibels Papers, 1963–1975, BPL (here-after, Seibels Papers).

2 For model surveys of Birmingham's black poor after 1963, see Robin D. G.

Kelley, "The Black Poor and the Politics of Opposition in a New South City: Birmingham, Alabama, 1929–1970," in *The Underclass Debate: Views from History*, ed. Michael B. Katz (Princeton, N.J.: Princeton University Press, 1993); Kelley, "Birmingham's Untouchables: The Black Poor in the Age of Civil Rights," in *Race Rebels: Culture, Politics, and the Black Working Class*, 293–333 (New York: Free Press, 1994).

3 Jack Drake, one of Bryant's and Williams's attorneys, characterized the event as more of a "shoot-in"; at trial, he and his co-counsel demonstrated that all of the shots came from sheriff's department weaponry, as the defendants' supporters claimed. Interview, Drake, spring 2002; Anne E. Braden, " 'Law and Order in Birmingham': Two Black Liberation Front Leaders Jailed," *Southern Patriot*, March 1971, 4–5; "Ronald Williams and Doc Bryant," Box 14, "Concerned Citizens for Justice" folder, Social Action Vertical File (SAVF), Wisconsin Historical Society (WHS), Madison; "Birmingham Police Stage 'Shoot-In' Against Alabama Black Liberation Front," *The Great Speckled Bird*, March 22, 1971. An editorial in the *Birmingham World*, an African American paper, raised questions about the precise manner in which Bryant and Williams were involved in the shooting. "What Is a 'Shoot-Out'?" *Birmingham World*, September 26, 1970.

4 Testimony of Bernice Turner, *Wayland Earl Bryant and Ronald Elliott Williams v. State*, Court of Criminal Appeals of Alabama, No. 6, Div. 339, November 21, 1972 (hereafter, *Bryant and Williams v. State*).

5 Ibid. A memo to Mayor Seibels indicates that Turner had also been in contact with the ABLF at least two weeks prior to receiving the eviction notice. "Doc Bryant and three of his Black Panther group" went to Turner's house and discussed the case over a "snapper fish supper." "Memorandum, August 28, 1970," File 37.31, Seibels Papers. Of more importance than the precise timing of Turner's contact(s) with the ABLF is the indication in an earlier police memo that Meriweather was actually a police informant. On August 12, 1970, Lt. C. V. Garrett reported that Officer Moss suspected that the ABLF was aware of the police affiliation of "Merriwether," who evidently reported to police sergeant Harry Deal. "Memo, 7/28/70," File 2.18, "Police Department Surveillance Files, 1947–1980," BPL (hereafter, Birmingham Police Files [BPF]).

6 Turner testimony, *Bryant and Williams v. State*.

7 Police officers tracked ABLF movements throughout the night and had at least one informant (Meriweather) in Turner's house, producing detailed information about the comings and goings of specific ABLF members, as well as the topics of their conversations. They promised to "keep [Major Orange of the Jefferson County Sheriff's Department] up on what [had been] learned from inside the house and also from Black Panther Party headquarters." "9/15/70 Memorandum," File 2.18, BPF.

8 Turner, Bryant, and Williams testimony, *Bryant and Williams v. State*.

9 Ibid.

10 The five were Bryant, Williams, Harold Robertson (or Robinson), Robert Jakes, and Brenda Joyce Griffin. *Bryant and Williams v. State*; Braden, "Law and Order in Birmingham."

11 Quoted in Harold Kennedy, "Negroes Held after City Shootout," *Birmingham News*, September 16, 1970. Bailey's assistant, David Orange, testified (*Bryant and Williams v. State*) that Sergeant C. C. Gillespie of the Sheriff's Department and Sergeant Marcus Jones of the Birmingham Police Department had alerted him to the ABLF's presence in Turner's home. This testimony is corroborated by "Memo Notes, September 26, 1970," File 37.31, Seibels Papers: "The Jefferson County Sheriff's Office . . . had received advance information that members of the Black Liberation Front were going to be present and armed to resist the eviction."

12 *Bryant and Williams v. State.*

13 Ibid.

14 "[Bryant and Williams] admitted taking an Italian make rifle to Mrs. Turner's home with ammunition, but denied there had been any discussion as to an ambush of any police officers. They further testified they had Brenda Griffin go by and pick up a shotgun which was brought to the premises in question. . . . Examination of the shotgun and rifle indicated that neither had been fired." *Bryant and Williams v. State.*

15 After the incident, Sheriff Bailey further mischaracterized the incident when he told local press that his deputies had successfully thwarted an "ambush," thus inferring that the ABLF had been the instigators. *SCEF News*, March 18, 1971, File 1.28, David Vann Papers, BPL (hereafter, Vann Papers).

16 Prosecutors later reduced the charges against Bryant and Williams to assault with a deadly weapon rather than assault with intent to murder.

17 "Open Letter on the Case of Members of the Alabama Black Liberation Front Unjustly Imprisoned in the County Jail: Birmingham, ALA," File 2.15, BPF.

18 The Alabama prison system would eventually be declared in violation of the constitutional protection against cruel and unusual punishment. Larry Yackle, *Reform and Regret: The Story of Federal Judicial Involvement in the Alabama Prison System* (Oxford: Oxford University Press, 1989).

19 The precise moment when the ABLF ceased to exist is impossible to determine. Individual members either remained in Birmingham or returned later in the decade, often participating in various activist efforts. Others may have gone underground or lent their support to efforts in other places. Because so much of what we know about the ABLF comes from documents confiscated by the Birmingham police, the best indicator of the group's demise may be the date when police ceased tracking them (or at least submitting reports on them).

20 The black power movement with which these tendencies have been identified was not based simply on disillusionment and anger, although those emotions were certainly part of the equation. African Americans drawn to groups such as the ABLF, for example, were also motivated by a desire for more effective strategies and tactics and new understandings of the way American society functioned. Peniel E. Joseph, introduction to "Black Power Studies: A New Scholarship," ed. Peniel E. Joseph, special issue, *The Black Scholar* 31 (fall/winter 2001): 3–4; Jeffrey O. G. Ogbar, *Black Power: Radical Politics and African American Identity* (Baltimore: Johns Hopkins University Press, 2004).

21 For anthologies, see Charles E. Jones, ed., *The Black Panther Party [Reconsidered]* (Baltimore: Black Classic Press, 1998); Kathleen Cleaver and George Katsiaficas, eds., *Liberation, Imagination, and the Black Panther Party: A New Look at the Panthers and Their Legacy* (New York: Routledge Press, 2001). For the limitations in the current scholarship, see Lazerow and Williams, "Bringing the Black Panther Party Back In: A Survey" in this volume.

22 Birmingham was not the only southern city with groups of Panthers and Panther sympathizers. In addition to New Orleans and North Carolina, affiliates, both official and unofficial, could also be found in Louisville, Atlanta, and Houston. For Louisville, see Box 6, "Black Panther Party" folder, SAVF, WHS; for Atlanta, see Winston A. Grady-Willis, "A Changing Tide: Black Politics and Activism in Atlanta, Georgia, 1960–1977" (Ph. diss., Emory University, 1998); for a Houston-based group known as the "People's Party No. 2," described as "a militant group similar to the Black Panthers," see Preston F. Kirk, "Black Militants Battle Police in Ghetto Gun Fight in Texas," *Birmingham World*, August 1, 1970. A police memo also made mention of a "black militant organization in Jacksonville" called the "Florida Black Front." File 1.8, BPF. Another police memo on Birmingham's leftist groups mentions that members had "met with members of the Black Liberation League here and [have] communicated with members of the Black Panther Party and Black Liberation group in other cities, including the West Coast, *Arkansas*, and New York." "Memo Notes, 4/12/72," File 1.8, BPF, emphasis added.

23 Interview, Washington Booker III, September 24, 2002. Unless otherwise noted, all interviews were conducted by the author in Birmingham. Tapes and interview transcripts are in the author's possession, except when the interview was not recorded (denoted "conversations" here).

24 "Memorandum," September 2, 1971, File 4.23, BPF.

25 "Memorandum, undated," File 2.18, BPF. Other information in the memo suggests composition in late August or early September 1970.

26 Orange reported to Sheriff Mel Bailey that he, Frank Rogers, and Earl Robins had attended the convention. They had also met with Philadelphia police and received a tour of the city. Orange regarded the trip as a success, writing, "As you know, we have been for sometime and are currently keeping a close surveillance on the Black Panther Party in our area. I believe that this trip to Philadelphia has caused us to have an even better awareness of the danger of this group of people." "Memo," September 14, 1970, File 1.8, BPF.

27 Elaine H. Miller, "Panther Threat Here—Bailey," *Birmingham Post-Herald*, July 28, 1970.

28 For the importance of local history in civil rights scholarship, see Jeanne F. Theoharis and Komozi Woodard, eds., *Freedom North: Black Freedom Struggles Outside the South, 1940–1980* (New York: Palgrave, 2003); Theoharis and Woodard, *Groundwork: Local Black Freedom Movements in America* (New York: New York University Press, 2005).

29 Glenn Eskew, *But for Birmingham: The Local and National Movements in the Civil Rights Struggle* (Chapel Hill: University of North Carolina Press, 1997); J. Mills Thornton, *Dividing Lines: Municipal Politics and the Struggle for Civil Rights in Montgomery, Birmingham, and Selma* (Tuscaloosa: University of Alabama Press, 2002); Diane McWhorter, *Carry Me Home: Birmingham, Alabama; The Climactic Battle of the Civil Rights Revolution* (New York: Simon and Schuster, 2001); Taylor Branch, *Parting the Waters: America in the King Years, 1954–1963* (New York: Simon and Schuster, 1988); David J. Garrow, *Bearing the Cross: Martin Luther King, Jr. and the Southern Christian Leadership Conference 1955–1968* (New York: Morrow, 1986); Garrow, ed. *Birmingham, Alabama, 1956–1963: The Black Struggle for Civil Rights* (Brooklyn: Carlson, 1989); Andrew Manis, *A Fire You Can't Put Out: The Civil Rights Life of Birmingham's Reverend Fred Shuttlesworth* (Tuscaloosa: University of Alabama Press, 2000).

30 Eskew includes a short epilogue, but his focus is the demonstrations of 1963. Moreover, his overview of Birmingham after 1963 relies mainly on census data from 1980. Thornton also includes discussion of Birmingham after 1963, but his primary interest is electoral politics. The most recent chronicle of the 1963 demonstrations, McWhorter's *Carry Me Home*, refers to 1963 as the "climactic" battle of the civil rights movement, implying (perhaps unintentionally) that what came after was part of an overall decline. Notable exceptions to this scholarly pattern include Jimmie Lewis Franklin, *Back to Birmingham: Richard Arrington, Jr. and His Times* (Tuscaloosa: University of Alabama Press, 1989); Kelley, "Birmingham's Untouchables"; Kelley, "The Black Poor."

31 Eskew, *But for Birmingham*, chap. 9.

32 A more detailed overview of black Birmingham in the 1970s and 1980s, at least statistically, is Ernest Porterfield, "Birmingham: A Magic City," in *In Search of the New South: The Black Urban Experience in the 1970s and 1980s*, ed. Robert Bullard, 121–41 (Tuscaloosa: University of Alabama Press, 1989). Citing—among other figures—a 28 percent poverty level among African Americans, as well as a significant income gap between black and white families, Porterfield concludes that "black Birmingham in the 1980s suffer[ed] from many of the same problems that plagued it in the 1960s" (135).

33 Porterfield estimates that the city closed "more than sixty-eight parks, thirty-eight playgrounds, six swimming pools, and four golf courses." Ibid., 130.

34 *Katzenbach v. Mcclung*, 379 U.S. 294 (1964).

35 Thornton, *Dividing Lines*, 351–70.

36 Porterfield, "Birmingham," 135.

37 In 1966, only 9 of 1,698 city employees were African American; by 1975, the figure was 155 of 2,233. In 1970, African Americans constituted 42 percent of the population. Ibid.

38 In 1966, for example, the Committee for Equal Job Opportunity (CEJO), a group of employees at the American Cast Iron Pipe Company (ACIPCO) filed suit against the company, charging racial discrimination in hiring and advancement. Similar efforts, many encouraged by the CEJO, soon emerged at other plants in the Birmingham area. *Pettway v. American Cast Iron Pipe Company*; interview, Davis Jordan and Edward Hicks, April 2003.

39 In 1972, these workers organized their own union, the Public Employees Organizing Committee (PEOC). A white student activist involved in the PEOC effort would later marry Ronnie Williams, one of the ABLF members arrested at Bernice Turner's home. Seibels Papers; BPF, Boxes 37–38, File "Police Department Intelligence Reports."

40 "A School Superintendent Speaks," *Birmingham World*, June 27, 1970; "Hidden Racism Halts Birmingham's Growth," ibid., July 4, 1970. Kelley discusses the negative impact of urban renewal, noting that at least a thousand families were displaced by the medical center project, in "The Black Poor."

41 "Club Seeks Funds for Rescue Home," *Birmingham World*, July 11, 1970. Such a disruption was surely felt all the more acutely in a city that was historically reluctant to devote substantial resources to social services. Indeed, the Help One Another Club was refused assistance by several city, county, state, and federal agencies. Edward Shannon LaMonte, *Politics and Welfare in Birmingham, 1900–1975* (Tuscaloosa: University of Alabama Press, 1995).

42 "ACIPCO Residents Form Action Organization," *Birmingham Post-Herald*, June 27, 1970.

43 "Roosevelt Park Bias Charged by Negroes," *Birmingham Post-Herald*, June 27, 1970.

44 "Negroes Seek Home in Vestavia," *Birmingham Post-Herald*, June 17, 1970. A feature in 1968 in the *Birmingham World* titled "You and Your Housing" suggests that the problem was widespread. It counseled black homebuyers on their rights under Title VIII of the Civil Rights Act of 1968, encouraging them to file complaints with the Department of Housing and Urban Development.

45 Similar suits were filed across the state and region in an effort to force compliance with Title VI of the Civil Rights Act of 1964. Tim L. Pennycuff, "'Offering Inferior Service to Negro Patients': Unequal Healthcare in Birmingham, Alabama" (paper presented at the "Race and Place III" Conference, University of Alabama, March 2004, in possession of the author).

46 Interview, Jordan and Hicks, April 2003.

47 "Action at the Grass-Roots," *Southern Fight-Back*, February 1978, 3.

48 The clinic had been opened in 1939, but after World War II federal funding dried up, and local leaders were unwilling to dedicate the funds to keep the facility running. Pennycuff, "Offering Inferior Service."

49 McWhorter documents such connections in *Carry Me Home*.

50 Kelley, "Birmingham's Untouchables," 90–92; "Two Police Shootings Are Ruled 'Justifiable,'" *Birmingham World*, May 16, 1970.

51 Interdenominational Ministerial Alliance, et al. to County Commission et al., February 22, 1967, "Birmingham, AL Misc.," Box 6, SAVF, WHS.

52 Ibid.

53 Fred Shuttlesworth, "Opening Statement to Statewide Civil Rights Leaders' Meeting on Law Enforcement," March 13, 1967, ibid.

54 "NEGROES Are Calling a 60-Day Period of Mourning for the Dead!," ibid.

55 Tom Gibson, "No Indictments: Jury Urges Change in Police Attitudes," *Birmingham News*, May 15, 1969.

56 Ibid.

57 Franklin, *Back to Birmingham*, chap. 5.

58 My current research has uncovered people and groups in addition to the ABLF who helped sustain Birmingham's activist tradition outside of the more established leadership. As we shall see, the ABLF attracted significant support because of its willingness to tackle the everyday concerns that others disregarded.

59 Interview, Booker, November 20, 2002.

60 Interview, Rita Anthony, May 7, 2003.

61 "What Is a 'Shoot-Out'?"

62 Booker recalls being among those "participating" that way (interview, May 7, 2003); Kelley, "Birmingham's Untouchables"; Charles M. Payne, "Bibliographic Essay: The Social Construction of History," in *I've Got the Light of Freedom: The Organizing Tradition and the Mississippi Freedom Struggle* (Berkeley: University of California Press, 1995).

63 Conversations with a number of Birmingham residents revealed the depth of commitment to self-defense in the face of racial violence, with some remembering sleepless nights of watch duty. Colonel Stone Johnson, a stalwart advocate of nonviolence, nevertheless carried a shotgun in his car, even when he went to the airport to pick up representatives of the Kennedy administration in 1963. Interview, spring 2003; conversation, Fredna Coachman, spring 2003. Generally, see Timothy Tyson, *Radio Free Dixie: Robert F. Williams and the Roots of Black Power* (Chapel Hill: University of North Carolina Press, 1999).

64 Thornton, *Dividing Lines*, 164.

65 Ibid.

66 Juan Williams, *Thurgood Marshall: American Revolutionary* (New York: Times Books, 1998), cited in Tyson, *Radio Free Dixie*, 153.

67 Shores interview with Jack Bass, July 17, 1974, transcript housed in the Southern Oral History Collection, University of North Carolina, Chapel Hill.

68 "Georgia Black Liberation Front" (GBLF) File 2.17, BPF. On Vine City, see Clayborne Carson, *In Struggle: SNCC and the Black Awakening of the 1960s* (1981; repr., Cambridge, Mass.: Harvard University Press, 1995); Grady-Willis, "A Changing Tide."

69 Atlanta police also described the GBLF "philosophy" as "live off the land and raise an army." File 1.24, Moore Papers, BPF.

70 "Georgia Black Liberation Front," File 2.18, BPF (handwritten date, June 26, 1970). Atlanta police claimed that the men, one of whom was Reese, had been arrested for stealing from a grocery store near their headquarters. "Memorandum, Re: Alabama Black Liberation Front . . . ," File 2.18, BPF.

71 Beyond FBI surveillance records, few sources detail Bryant's experiences before arriving in Greensboro. He provided some detail in an interview with the *Southern Patriot*, in which he noted that, prior to his work with the ABLF, he had been active in "so-called civil rights movements" since at least 1948, when he tried to integrate his military base in North Carolina. Braden, "Law and Order in Birmingham." Atlanta police claimed he had been in the army for fourteen years, but they did not provide dates. "Letter to Jamie Moore," File 2.15, BPF. Birmingham police files contain a photocopy of Bryant's North Carolina driver's license, which was issued in 1966. The license indicates residence in Jacksonville, N.C., a city surrounding the Fort Bragg military base. File 8.28, BPF. Other police records assert that Bryant had been raised in Pennsylvania. File 2.18, BPF. Information on Bryant's activities in Greensboro and his connection to the BPP can found in the FBI document, "Black Panther Party—Winston-Salem, NC," downloadable as a PDF file from the FBI's Electronic Reading Room (http://foia.fbi .gov/foiaindex/bpanther.htm).

72 "It was determined that W. E. M. Bryant, Jr. has opened a Black-African store on the corner of Market and Benbo[r?] Road in Greensboro and calls his place the 'house of Umivesimoja.' This is supposed to be an African term; and Bryant has artifacts, publications, books, and African regalia for sale." FBI, "Black Panther Party—Winston-Salem, NC," Section 2b, 15. Further, "On [blacked out] reported that W. E. M. Bryant's bookstore is now the center for black militant activity in Greensboro, North Carolina. Bryant sells mainly paperback books and hardback books about Malcolm X, the Muslims, and so forth. The only BPP publication he sells is the Black Panther Newspaper." Ibid., Section 2b, 18.

73 "On April 12, 1969, CE T-9 advised that W. E. M. Bryant has opened a shop on East Market Street, Greensboro, where BPP members hang out. At this shop, Bryant sells all sorts of literature, including the BPP newspaper and various

publications and material of black culture. . . . On May 6, 1969, CE T-13 reported that W. E. M. Bryant, Jr. calls his bookstore 'Wesui Umoja.' This means Black Power in Swahili." Ibid., Section 1a, 45, Section 2a, 30.

74 On the role of black bookstores in the black power movement, see Colin A. Beckles, "Black Bookstores, Black Power, and the F.B.I.: The Case of Drum and Spear," *The Western Journal of Black Studies* 20, no. 2 (1996): 63–71.

75 The greeting card was attached to a Naval Intelligence Service Information Report from the Marine base at Camp Lejeune, N.C., January 26, 1970, according to FBI documents, but the naval report has been removed from the FBI folder. FBI, "Black Panther Party—Winston-Salem, NC," Section 4b, 23–25. During the same period, federal officials expressed concern about charges that the OEO and other poverty agencies had been infiltrated by black power groups like the BPP. See, e.g., *Birmingham News*, October 13, 1970.

76 Evidently Neblett was traveling to a number of cities in North Carolina (Fayetteville and Durham were also mentioned) and speaking about the BPP. FBI, "Black Panther Party—Winston-Salem, NC," Section 1, 57, Section 2b, 17. Neblett, a founding member of the Boston chapter, would shortly be purged from the party. See Jama Lazerow, "The Black Panthers at the Water's Edge: Oakland, Boston, and the New Bedford 'Riots' of 1970" in this volume.

77 "Memorandum, Re: Alabama Black Liberation Front . . . ," File 2.18, BPF.

78 The information came from what the reporting officer called "a source that we have never received information from before." "Memorandum, Re: Alabama Black Liberation League, 10/19/70," File 2.18, BPF.

79 "Memorandum Re: Alabama Black Liberation League 10/19/70," File 2.17, BPF.

80 Reese, in "Fellow Prisoner Responds," *Southern Patriot*, April 1972, 5.

81 In October 1972, for example, police noted that Bryant, out of prison, "is now in Greenville, South Carolina, running the South Carolina Black Liberation League there." "Memorandum, 10/19/72," File 1.8, BPF.

82 These documents were confiscated from Bryant's briefcase, and are included in the police surveillance files at the BPL. A page inserted into the files reads, "The following documents were contained in a separate notebook and the notebook was in the possession of Dr. Wayland Bryant at the time of his arrest [on minor charges prior to the Tarrant City confrontation]." File 2.17, "Black Nationalists," BPF.

83 The ABLF would eventually hook up with Perry Carlisle—"Mobile Fats"— who operated a variety store in the black business district along 4th Avenue North. Carlisle was already known to police for his participation in a variety of protest activities and for wearing a black power fist around his neck as a pendant. He appears regularly in the BPF. Police noted, for example, that Carlisle's store was "plastered with Panther signs and pictures." Police would also later surmise that Carlisle had ulterior—that is, monetary—motives for his involvement. What-

ever his motivations, Carlisle's store did serve as a meeting place for the ABLF. "9/10/70 Memo," File 2.18, BPF. Bryant also noted a desire for local maps, including land use maps showing housing values, locations of public facilities such as sewage and gas, and census data. Other necessary materials included tapes and tape recorders, a shortwave radio, a record player, and everyday items such as dishes, pots, and a hot plate.

84 Bryant notebook, File 2.17, BPF.

85 James "Jap" Moseley and Cleveland "Cleve" Carlton appear regularly in early police files as well, suggesting that they too were active members. Charles Cannon was particularly prominent following his arrest in 1972, but I have been unable to determine whether he was with the organization from the beginning.

86 There are numerous indications that the membership reached well beyond this number, if people who were in contact with the organization or participated in at least one of its programs are counted.

87 Unfortunately, at least for historians, any central record-keeping system that might have existed was not part of the materials confiscated by Birmingham police. An additional complicating factor in determining the numbers involved with the ABLF is the desire by the original members to differentiate themselves from others as the only "true" members of the group.

88 Bryant, for example, was reported by police to have discussed the existence of cadres in North Birmingham, Kingston, High Chapperell, Ensley, and Roosevelt City in July 1970. "Memo Notes, July 28, 1970," File 2.18, BPF.

89 Booker related the story of his return to Birmingham in an interview with Dr. Horace Huntley, Archives Division of the Civil Rights Institute, Birmingham, on January 5, 1995.

90 Ibid.

91 Ibid.

92 Interview, Booker, September 24, 2002.

93 Ibid.

94 "Fellow Prisoner Responds."

95 Ibid.

96 For avenues of future research, see Akinyele Umoja, "Repression Breeds Resistance: The Black Liberation Army and the Radical Legacy of the Black Panther Party," in *Liberation, Imagination, and the Black Panther Party: A New Look at the Panthers and Their Legacy*, ed. Kathleen Cleaver and George Katsiaficas, 3–19 (New York: Routledge Press, 2001).

97 For the historiography of African American war veterans returning determined to claim their full citizenship rights, see, e.g., Payne, *I've Got the Light of Freedom*; George Lipsitz, *A Life in the Struggle: Ivory Perry and the Culture of Opposition*, rev. ed. (1988; repr., Philadelphia: Temple University Press, 1995); Tyson, *Radio Free Dixie*.

98 Interview, Booker, September 24, 2002.

99 "Fellow Prisoner Responds."

100 Ibid. Reese may have been embellishing his awareness at the time; at some point, though, he did make the connection between Vietnam and the freedom struggle back home.

101 "Southern Conference Educational Fund Record Papers, 1958–1985," Box 3389, Folder 1, "SCEF Political Prisoners, 1972–1980," Southern Labor Archives, Special Collections Department, Pullen Library, Georgia State University.

102 Ibid.

103 Interview, Booker, September 24, 2002.

104 Indeed, that the experience was not exclusive to members of the ABLF suggests that, as historians explore the appeal of the BPP among the rank and file, they should look closer at service in Vietnam as a catalyst for radicalization.

105 Quoted in Wallace Terry, *Bloods: An Oral History of the Vietnam War by Black Veterans* (New York: Random House, 1984), 105. Citing Terry's earlier articles on African Americans and Vietnam, William Van Deburg notes that "some 30 percent of Wallace Terry's respondents planned to join a militant group like the Black Panthers upon their release from the service." Van Deburg, *New Day in Babylon: The Black Power Movement and American Culture, 1965–1975* (Chicago: University of Chicago Press, 1992), 105.

106 Terry, *Bloods*, 13–14.

107 Ibid., 25; interview, Booker, September 24, 2002.

108 The shift in returning soldiers' response to racial discrimination back home was not lost on contemporary observers. In August 1970—the summer the ABLF began—a white country club in Homer, Louisiana, was torched in retaliation for recent white violence against blacks. A local (white) attorney observed, "Black veterans back from Vietnam say they are not going to take any more of this." Quoted in "Louisiana Negroes to Stop Reign of Terror," *Birmingham World*, August 1, 1970. Official surveys of returning soldiers confirmed the attorney's observation. Describing the findings of a Pentagon investigation into racial tensions among black troops in Vietnam, a deputy assistant defense secretary reported, "[Black soldiers] said their place was back in the United States: New York, Chicago, Atlanta, Detroit, Jacksonville, where they could fight to liberate and free their black sisters and brothers from the dirty, stinking teeming ghettoes and from all forms of racial bigotry and oppression." Quoted in Darrell Garwood, "Pentagon Officials Told: Discrimination Irks Blacks in Armed Forces," ibid., December 26, 1970.

109 Interview, Booker, November 20, 2002.

110 Katsiaficas, introduction to Cleaver and Katsiaficas, *Liberation, Imagination, and the Black Panther Party*, vii.

111 For example, an informant told police that at one ABLF meeting someone

said the "best recruits" were Vietnam veterans, in part because they "knew all about gorilla [*sic*] warfare, as they had been well trained." "Memorandum, July 20, 1970," File 2.18, BPF.

112 Jones, introduction to *The Black Panther Party*, 1.

113 Interview, Booker, September 24, 2002. In December 1970, police confiscated materials following the arrest of three ABLF members; among the items were *Lenin on the National and Colonial Questions*, the *Pyongyang Declaration*, and *Guerilla Warfare and Marxism* by William J. Pomdroy. File 37.32, Seibels Papers.

114 Note Bryant's identification of Cleaver by his BPP title, as well as his incorporation of concepts that would have been familiar to BPP members.

115 Police observed, "Doc Bryant has been holding different meetings with young children as low as eight and nine years of age and teaching them the Ten Point Program, which is identifying the Black Panther platform and program and getting these children to memorize this." "Memorandum, Re: Alabama Black Liberation Front located at #9 Center Street South . . . ," File 2.18, BPF.

116 ABLF's list, "What We Want," September-October 1970, in "Background of the Situation," File 1.8, BPF.

117 Bryant notebook, File 2.17, BPF.

118 Ibid.

119 Although by 1970 the Bay Area BPP no longer engaged in this practice, it had been an effective recruitment tool, and this consideration likely influenced the ABLF's decision to implement it.

120 A police memo of August 1970 noted that the ABLF had acquired a "police monitor, a six channel citizens band radio, and 2 Army type radio telephones." "Memorandum, August 28, 1970," File 2.18, BPF.

121 "Memo, 7/25/70," File 1.8, BPF.

122 For a related phenomenon among the Detroit Panther underground, at about the same time, see Ahmad A. Rahman, "Marching Blind: The Rise and Fall of the Black Panther Party in Detroit" in this volume.

123 Interview, Booker, September 24, 2002.

124 File 37.31, Seibels Papers.

125 According to Booker, reacting to an accusation that they were only talkers, the group planned an ambush of the police. When the accuser was convinced they intended to follow through, he left, calling them crazy. The ambush never materialized. Interview, Booker, Huntley, January 5, 1995.

126 File 1.24, Moore Papers.

127 "Memo," August 4, 1970, File 1.8, BPF. A similar incident was reported a day later when police learned that a woman cleaning up after an eviction at 845 Goldwire Street—near the ABLF office on Center Street South—had been threatened by "two men claiming to be Black Panthers." "Memo," 5 August 1970, File 1.8, BPF.

128 Intimidation worked to the ABLF's advantage. Booker remembered a night when he was caught alone by a patrol car as he walked along Goldwire Street. The police said something to the effect, "We've got you now." Bluffing, Booker asked the police, "Do you really think I'd be out here all alone?" According to Booker, the implication that others were hiding in wait was enough to make the officers reconsider their plans; they drove away without incident. Conversation, Booker, November 2002.

129 "Memorandum," undated, File 2.18, BPF.

130 The papers of Birmingham mayors George Seibels and David Vann both contain letters from Arrington regarding specific instances of alleged brutality. For details on the campaign and the Carter shooting, see Franklin, *Back to Birmingham*, chap. 9.

131 Interview, Booker, Huntley, January 5, 1995.

132 "Black Panther Investigation, Lt. C. L. Limbaugh to Chief Jamie Moore, June 18, 1970," File 2.18, BPF.

133 "Alabama Black Liberation Front Investigates Cases of Pig Brutality; Also Starts Drive for Defense Funds," *The Black Panther*, August 15, 1970.

134 "Alabama Black Liberation Front Starts Drive for Defense Funds," *Alabama Black Community News Service*, File 2.17, BPF.

135 "Memo Notes," September 10, 1970, in File 2.18, BPF.

136 File 1.24, Moore Papers.

137 File 2.18, BPF.

138 Ibid.

139 "Alabama Black Liberation Front: Of the People, by the People, for the People," File 2.18, BPF.

140 At a meeting of the Loveman's Village Citizens Committee for Community Improvement, for example, four members raised concerns about the lack of adequate recreational programs. File 1.24, Moore Papers.

141 File 1.8, BPF.

142 "Alabama Black Liberation Front: Of the People, by the People, for the People," File 2.18, BPF.

143 "Memo Notes, the Free Breakfast Program," September 28, 1970, File 2.18, BPF.

144 Bryant notebook, July 3, 1970.

145 WJLD broadcast, tape in BPF.

146 File 2.18, BPF.

147 Phone logs in File 2.18, BPF. "Memorandum, August 28, 1970," ibid., reports phone contact with the BPP's "Minister of Information" in San Francisco.

148 Instances of members of the ABLF selling the BPP newspaper or signing for deliveries at the airport may be found throughout the surveillance files. One such report, for example, noted that "the Black Panther Newspaper is being distributed by [Bryant, Watkins, and "Milinzi"] to small teenage negro boys who have been selling them in downtown negro areas, Southtown Project, Loveman's Village Project, and at Roosevelt City." The ABLF's use, in this case, of surrogate distributors appears to have been in an effort to avoid harassment by police, as the memo further noted, "an effort will be made to make an arrest if any adult or any leader of the Black Liberation Front is caught selling them." "Memorandum, Re: Alabama Black Liberation Front . . . ," File 1.8, BPF. The same memo that discussed the ABLF's use of local teenagers to distribute the Panther paper also noted, "This organization has received the following shipments of the Black Panther newspaper. These were sent from national distributors. 1336—Fillmore Street, San Francisco, California . . . On Saturday July 11 . . . there was ninety pounds of newspapers received and signed for by Perry Carlisle. . . . On Thursday July 23 . . . one hundred fifty pounds of newspapers were received by Mike Milinzi [an alternative name used by Reese]." "Memo, Re: Alabama Black Liberation Front," File 1.8, BPF.

149 A police memo of September 1970 identified Reese as "the person who went to San Francisco with others and was in contact with the National Black Panther Headquarters there," returning five weeks later. "Memo Notes, Alabama Black Liberation Front, Re: Black Panther Newspaper," September 25, 1970, File 2.18, BPF. The identity of Reese's companion (or companions) is not clear. Another memo in September named Warren Vaughn as having gone to California, noting that he claimed to have "carried one member of Doc Bryant's party." Back in Alabama, Vaughn had been attending meetings, but he was reportedly unhappy about the ABLF's fund-raising capability—the group had not sold enough BPP material to pay for the return of the member who had accompanied Vaughn. "Memorandum, undated," File 2.18, BPF. "Memo, August 28, 1970," File 2.18, BPF also identifies Warren Vaughn as the man who accompanied Reese, noting he had returned to Birmingham with various BPP merchandise to sell. In February 1971, police investigated an Anthony Williams, who said he had gone to California with " 'Luonzo Michael' in a station wagon" and stayed for three weeks before returning with a "load of Black Panther papers and some marijuana." "Memo Notes Re: Anthony Williams possibly a member of the Alabama Black Liberation Front, February 8, 1971," File 2.18, BPF.

150 The memo referred to a statement by Bryant that "some of the so called friends left him in time of need and followed Michael Reese" and went on to surmise that "Reese might be in trouble if he is released from jail." "Memorandum, Re: Alabama Black Liberation League, 10/19/70," File 2.18, BPF. Back in Birmingham, Reese was arrested and sent to jail on weapons charges. For details, see below.

151 "Memorandum Re: Alabama Black Liberation League 10/19/70," File 2.17, BPF. I have not been able to confirm the existence of such a split or of competing factions within the organization. The connection between these reports and the police, however, would be consistent with how law enforcement approached the BPP in other areas of the country. That is, if such a split (or splits) developed, police informants were likely at least partially involved in their instigation or exacerbation.

152 "RE: Alabama Black Liberation League. It is a branch from the Black Panther Party," 10/13/70, File 37.31, Seibels Papers.

153 Conversation, Larry Watkins, spring 2004.

154 "Memo Notes," December 16, 1970, File 37.32, Seibels Papers.

155 On July 23, 1970, Jamie Moore, the police chief of Birmingham, wrote to the police chief of Atlanta, stating they had been tracking the ABLF since June 15. File 2.15, BPF.

156 Police filed a four-page report on July 20, 1970 based on information provided by an informant who had dropped by the ABLF's office on Center Street. "Memorandum, July 20, 1970," File 2.18, BPF. Atlanta police, in their correspondence regarding the GBLF, had also recommended to their Birmingham counterparts that the best way to keep tabs on such groups was through paid informants. "Memorandum, Re: Alabama Black Liberation Front . . . ," File 2.18, BPF.

157 "We are keeping them under constant surveillance, Bailey said . . . and we're feeding information to law enforcement people. Key personnel at all levels are being kept informed in the interest of stopping them." Quoted in Miller, "Panther Threat Here."

158 Again, such treatment was publicly announced, albeit with a different slant. At his press conference, Bailey noted that ABLF members "have been arrested for such charges as possessing stolen automobiles, failing to identify themselves and resisting a law enforcement officer." Quoted in ibid.

159 "Alabama Black Liberation Front and News Service," File 2.18, BPF.

160 "Black Panther Activity Revealed," *Birmingham News*, July 28, 1970. For the use of "incitement to anarchy" charges against Panthers elsewhere, see Jama Lazerow, "The Black Panthers at the Water's Edge: Oakland, Boston, and the New Bedford 'Riots' of 1970" in this volume.

161 "Notes, July 17, 1970," File 2.18, BPF.

162 Lt. C. L. Limbaugh to Moore, June 18, 1970, "Black Panther Investigation," File 2.18, BPF.

163 Ralph J. Miles to Moore, July 13, 1970, File 2.18, BPF.

164 As an indication of the wider context, the article appeared next to one in which President Richard Nixon was quoted telling a college audience, "The time has come for us to recognize that violence and terror have no place in a free society, whoever the perpetrators and whatever their purported cause. In a system that provides for peaceful change, no cause justifies violence in the name of change."

165 Concerned Citizens for Justice (CCJ) letter, June 21, 1971, File 4.23, BPF.

166 "Application for Extradition, State of Alabama, Jefferson County," Item 5,

Carton 6, Extradition Records, Governor Tom McCall Records, Oregon State Archives, Salem, Oregon (hereafter, McCall Papers).

167 Unfortunately, the files maintained by Bryant's and Williams's attorneys were destroyed several years prior to the beginning of my research. Interview, Jack Drake, spring 2002. On the CCJ, see Letter, November 15, 1971, File 1.28, Vann Papers. Members included a broad cross section of Birmingham, including many activists. Among these were Davis Jordan, a black steelworker and founding member of the Committee for Equal Job Opportunity; Asbury Howard, an activist from the Bessemer jail and the son of the famous labor organizer of the same name; Alex Hurder, a white member of the Southern Conference Education Fund who was instrumental in organizing hospital and nursing home workers in Birmingham; Jim Bains, a local white organizer for the Communist Party; and Merulrine "Rita" Watkins, also known by her married name, Rita Anthony, the welfare rights advocate.

168 "Dear Friend," December 1971 letter from CCJ, File 1.28, Vann Papers.

169 "Memorandum," August 31, 1971, File 4.23, BPF.

170 "Afraid to Sleep in Jail Bryant Says," *Birmingham Post-Herald*, September 2, 1971.

171 "Memorandum," September 2, 1971, File 4.23, BPF.

172 "CCJ Press Release, 1 Sept. 1971," File 4.23, BPF.

173 "Afraid to Sleep in Jail Bryant Says," *Birmingham Post-Herald*, September 2, 1971.

174 "Dear Friend: Good News!" File 1.28, Vann Papers.

175 Police letter (with handwritten note to Captain House), February 23, 1972, File 4.23, Police Surveillance Files.

176 "Application for Extradition," McCall Papers.

177 Letter from legal counsel Bob Oliver to District Attorney Harl Haas, November 26, 1973, McCall Papers.

178 Among Mayor Arrington's papers is a document titled "Research Report C," which Bryant produced in 1979. Bryant described the report as a "Study of Police Reports Not Publicly Released to All Citizens of Birmingham, Alabama" and included detailed information regarding shootings and other incidents of police brutality. "Research Report C," File 51.32, "Operation Human Rights, 1978–79," Richard Arrington Papers, BPL. Also, File 51.33, "Operation Human Rights, 1980–81," ibid.

179 "Fellow Prisoner Responds."

180 Telephone conversation, Steve Whitman, fall 2003.

181 Document in File 2.18, BPF.

182 "Sgt. C. M. Gates to Deputy Chief W. J. Haley," April 30, 1972, File 2.18, BPF.

183 "The Alabama Black Liberation Front Black Community News Bulletin," File 2.18, BPF; conversation, Whitman.

184 Conversation, Whitman.

Ahmad A. Rahman

4

Marching Blind

THE RISE AND FALL OF THE

BLACK PANTHER PARTY IN DETROIT

After the Japanese attacked Pearl Harbor in December 1941—and, quickly, the United States was at war in both the Pacific and Europe—the Packard automobile plant in Detroit retooled to mass-produce bombers and patrol boats. On the shop floor, with workers now facing a common, foreign enemy, long-simmering racial tensions cooled. The apparent harmony was short-lived, however: in June 1943, when management promoted three black workers, some twenty-five thousand of their white counterparts immediately protested by going out on strike.[1] Reporters heard one white worker shout, "I'd rather see Hitler and Hirohito win than work beside a nigger on the assembly line."[2] The hatred resonated in greater Detroit. Indeed, later that month, a thirty-six-hour race war erupted between Detroit's white and black citizens, one of the worst "race riots" of the century. President Roosevelt had to send in federal troops to restore order. But it was black people who bore the brunt of the violence, typically at the hands of local authorities. Thirty-four citizens died, twenty-five of them black, seventeen of those at the hands of local white police officers. Most of the eighteen hundred people arrested for looting and other offenses were African American.[3]

A governor's commission tasked to investigate the causes of the strife blamed it on the recent influx of southern black migrants, who, according to the commission, exhibited a propensity toward violence and lawlessness that the city's black leadership had actually encouraged by fanning unrealistic expectations of equal rights in the North.[4] Following that logic, Francis Biddle, the attorney general, advised Roosevelt that he could prevent rioting in Detroit if he simply stopped black migration into the city by invoking the same emergency war powers used to intern the Japanese.[5] Meanwhile, on the other side of the Atlantic, pro-Nazi radio in occupied France reported on the events in Detroit as evidence of "the internal disorganization of a country torn by social injustice, race hatreds, regional disputes, the violence of an irritated proletariat, and the gangsterism of a capitalistic police."[6] Though the Nazis hardly possessed the moral authority to criticize America on this score, their analysis of the causes of Detroit's racial violence was much closer to the mark than that found in the governor's commission report. More important for my purposes here, the German pronouncement of 1943 offers a prescient catalog of what motivated local black people during the far worse violence that engulfed the city twenty-four years later in what many called the Detroit rebellion of 1967. It also neatly encapsulates much of what produced, a year later, a local variant of the Black Panther Party (BPP) in the heart of the riot-torn area.

Demography, economy, and politics comprise the necessary context, well described in recent historiography. By the late 1960s, continued black migration combined with white flight and deindustrialization to severely exacerbate ongoing problems of housing, education, jobs, and especially police brutality. During the 1950s, Detroit's population of whites declined by 23 percent, while the population of people of color increased from 16.1 percent to 29.1 percent; by 1967, African Americans constituted fully 40 percent of the city. The dramatic shift in population was especially noticeable in the Twelfth Street neighborhood, where rioting broke out in 1967 and which would be the epicenter of the rebellion. As Thomas Sugrue put it in his now classic study of the riot's origins, "Whereas virtually no blacks lived there in 1940 (the area was 98.7% white), the area was over one-third (37.2%) non-white in 1950. By 1960, the proportion of blacks to whites had nearly reversed: only 3.8 percent of the area's residents were white. Given that the first blacks did not move to the area until 1947 and 1948, the area underwent a complete racial transition in little more than a decade."[7] Given the numbers involved, the rapid turnover in neighborhood population predictably gave rise to other social ills, such as an increase in crime, which in turn fed an already virulent white racism and system of institutional discrimination. Sidney Fine, the author of an exhaustive treatment of the events of 1967, described the situation this way.

The transition from white to black on Detroit's near northwest side occurred at a remarkably rapid rate. . . . In a familiar pattern of neighborhood succession, as blacks moved in after World War II, the Jews moved out. The first black migrants to the area were middle class persons seeking to escape the confines of Paradise Valley. They enjoyed about "five good years" in their new homes until underworld and seedier elements from Hastings Street and Paradise Valley, the poor and indigent from the inner city, and winos and derelicts from skid row flowed into the area. Some of the commercial establishments on Twelfth Street gave way to pool halls, liquor stores, sleazy bars, pawnshops, and second hand businesses. Already suffering from a housing shortage and lack of open space, Twelfth Street became more "densely packed" as apartments were subdivided and six to eight families began to live where two had resided before. The 21,376 persons per square mile in the area in 1960 were almost double the city's average.[8]

Fine's use of pejoratives here, such as "seedier elements," betrays a class bias about those who were not among the middle class enjoying those "five good years"; the entire second wave of black newcomers was not composed of winos and derelicts. Nevertheless, along with Sugrue, he provides the relevant socioeconomic dynamics of the district that gave birth to the rebellion and, subsequently, the BPP.

In the summer of 1967, as elsewhere in this era, the flashpoint was the relationship between blacks and a police force that was nearly 95 percent white.[9] George Edwards, the police commissioner in 1961–63, predicted a coming conflagration in the *Michigan Law Review* in 1965.

Although local police forces generally regard themselves as public servants with the responsibility of maintaining law and order, they tend to minimize this attitude when they are patrolling areas that are heavily populated with Negro citizens. There, they tend to view each person on the streets as a potential criminal or enemy, and all too often that attitude is reciprocated. Indeed, hostility between the Negro communities in our large cities and police departments is the major problem of law enforcement in this decade. It has been a major cause of all recent race riots.[10]

Two years later, at approximately 3:45 a.m. on July 23, 1967, police raided an illegal after-hours drinking establishment known as a "blind pig."[11] Five days of violence ensued: looting, burning, sniping, and death.

In fact, police violence against unarmed black Detroiters framed the beginning and end of the event like bloody bookends. On the final day of the insurrection, for example, white police officers shotgunned to death three unarmed black teenagers—two while either kneeling or lying prone—at the Algiers Motel. The youths, the last of forty-three citizens of Detroit to die that week in July, had incurred the wrath of the police for their alleged involvement with white female prostitutes.[12] In all, like the 1943 riots, three-quarters of the dead were black men killed by either police or National Guardsmen; most of the seventy-five hundred arrested were African American.[13] And, like Roosevelt a quarter century before, President Lyndon Johnson sent in the army to stop what became the era's bloodiest domestic uprising.

A year later, researchers in the federal government released a surprising report, concluding that Detroit had not experienced a "race riot" because the crowds in the streets were racially integrated. Even though whites were only 12 percent of the arrestees, prosecutors charged white rioters with committing 27 percent of the arsons and 35 percent of the violent assaults.[14] Moreover, African Americans had attacked few civilian white Detroiters. Instead, the black rebels directed their wrath almost exclusively against the most visible symbols of capitalism and racism: first, property, and second, the firefighters and policemen who protected it.[15] Nine months later, in the spring of 1968, the Detroit branch of the Black Panther Party opened an ideological, armed assault on precisely those forces. The rise and fall of that organization in the city, following hard on the heels of the Detroit rebellion, can only be understood within the larger context of black Detroiters' preexisting animus toward these twin economic and social antagonists.

The Detroit Black Panther Party The Founding

Ron Scott and Eric Bell were the two principal organizers of the Detroit branch of the BPP. As a college student and graphic artist, Bell operated on the periphery of organized political movements during these years of increasing political and racial fervor—the open phase of the so-called black power movement—and his contribution came initially in statements he made on canvas. Still, living on the fourth floor of a building known as the Rappa House—with a jazz club on the first floor—he was exposed to the intense searching going on elsewhere in the building in discussions among young black people eager to learn about African American history, radical political theory such as revolutionary nationalism and black cultural nationalism, and especially the overseas revolutions then sweeping the globe.[16] By the time Bell participated in the 1967 rebellion, he considered himself a nationalist. Scott was a student at Highland Park Community College and then Wayne State University, where he and Bell organized the Afro-American History Club. Also a participant in the rebellion, Scott had witnessed the police murder and maim black Detroiters, barely avoiding the same fate himself, which, in turn, spurred his increasing social and political disaffection.[17]

In the aftermath of the rebellion, the legacy of student activism in the South, the burgeoning opposition to the Vietnam War, and the growing quest for "Blackness" in the North all crystallized the belief among youths such as Bell and Scott that they had to act. But they were dissatisfied with the traditional Negro leadership in the civil rights movement. They also felt that they could do more than they saw being done by the two black nationalist religious organizations—the Nation of Islam and the Shrine of the Black Madonna.[18]

In late 1967, Bell and Scott campaigned together for the re-election of George Crockett, a longtime political activist and attorney, to Detroit's Recorders Court. Crockett had gained both notoriety and support because he had released some black people from police custody during the rebellion. Also during this time, Scott began writing articles for the *Inner City Voice*, a community newspaper started by General Gordon Baker and black activists from the Student Nonviolent Coordinating Committee (SNCC), the Revolutionary Action Movement (RAM), and the *Uhuru* (Freedom) organization.[19] Baker and other members of Uhuru would soon constitute Detroit's Marxist-Leninist League of Revolutionary Black Workers (LRBW).[20] Meanwhile, they sharpened Scott's perception of the link between capitalism and racism in America. Scott now saw revolution as the solution.

Scott and Bell met regularly at the Rappa House with other activists— Aretha Hankins, Jackie Spicer, and William Chambers—who would form the nucleus of the Detroit Panther Party. Like others during this fertile period, they debated the relative merits of black separatism, cultural nationalism, revolutionary nationalism, Marxism-Leninism, Maoism—and various mixtures of each.[21] One day Bell came to a meeting carrying an issue of *Ramparts* magazine with photos accompanying an article about the Black Panther Party, which had been founded in Oakland, California, just a year earlier. Immediately, the militant revolutionary politics of the black-uniformed party members captured the group's imagination. Bell and Scott had already decided they wanted to institutionalize the 1967 rebellion and move the struggle in Detroit to a higher, organized level. They now concluded that the BPP was the way. According to Scott, that choice was directly linked to the trauma of the murderous repression of the previous July. The response of the police and the military had impressed upon him and others that only a militant, armed (as opposed to cultural nationalist) response would suffice. And, no other organization in America at the time took the kind of militant, self-defense stance the Panthers did.[22]

The two men called the party's office in Oakland and were informed that, coincidentally, two Detroiters—Victor Stewart and George Gillis—were already there, and, once they returned, would tell Scott and Bell what they needed to know. Stewart helped with some of the initial work of the organization, but his role, along with Gillis's, was more to introduce Bell, Scott, and the other future Panthers to sources such as Mao Tse-tung's *Little Red Book*.[23] The *Little Red Book* contained quotations from Mao's revolutionary philosophy on organization, political struggle, and women. The chapter, "Methods of Thinking and Methods of Work," for example, would provide a template for personal psychological and political discipline of a radical cadre. Mao's systematic enunciation of the proper inner and outer workings of a revolutionary party and movement would elevate the group above the eclectic blend of cultural and romantic nationalism that characterized their politics.[24] At the same time, the nascent Panther group also benefited from its connection to the John Brown Society, which consisted of white radicals who distributed literature to foster revolutionary black-white unity.

Then, in February 1968, Detroit's politically active St. Joseph Episcopal Church invited Panther leaders to speak for Black History Month. Scott and Bell were among the five to six hundred people who attended. Among the speakers was Kathleen Neal Cleaver, a member of the party's Central Committee and the party's communications secretary, who was on tour to gather support for Panther leader Huey P. Newton, whose trial for the killing an Oakland police officer was looming.[25] Cleaver's rendition of Newton's case was itself an inspirational recruitment vehicle, especially in Detroit's atmosphere of hostility between black youth and police.

Newton had been stopped early one morning, apparently because he was driving a vehicle known to be used by the Panthers. A confrontation ensued, ending with the serious wounding of Newton and two of the officers, one of whom died of a bullet wound from his own gun.[26] The prosecutor charged Newton with murder, but Newton's heroic survival of what was perceived as a police assault on him enhanced the Panthers' militant reputation.[27] Indeed, Cleaver's national speaking tour, and the "Free Huey" buttons and posters of Newton that became ubiquitous on campuses and in ghettoes in this period, helped make him a national symbol of black resistance.

Thirty-six years later, Ron Scott recalled the power of Cleaver's presence that night. First, her presentation was a more sophisticated version of the liberation language Scott and his fellow activists used at the Rappa House. Second, like all of the prospective Detroit Panthers, Cleaver and the entourage with her were between eighteen and twenty-two years old. "We were the same ages," Scott says. "They put our passion in a context that we knew we could replicate in Detroit."[28] Still, as Scott remembers it today, Cleaver only reinforced what he, Bell, and the others had already decided to do.[29]

Bell and Scott approached Cleaver after her speech and told her about their desire to become Panthers. She told them about an upcoming Peace and Freedom Party (PFP) convention in Ann Arbor, Michigan.[30] Her husband, Eldridge Cleaver, the Panthers' minister of information, was running for president under the banner of the mostly white PFP, with which the BPP had an alliance.[31] He and the Panther chairman Bobby Seale were coming to Ann Arbor to launch the campaign, she said. Scott, Bell, Victor Stewart, and several others then traveled to Ann Arbor and conferred with Seale, who consented to their establishing a branch of the party in Detroit.

In May 1968, Ron Scott, Eric Bell, Jackie Spicer, George Gillis, and Victor Stewart launched the Detroit branch of the Black Panther Party, holding their early meetings at an African cultural facility at Twelfth and Euclid Streets. From the beginning, the dynamics departed from all else they had known in the city. An incident during one early political education class, for example, illustrated for Scott and other male Panthers that gender relations in the party would be different from anything they had experienced before.[32] A young male named Khali demanded that Aretha Hankins show him the respect due him as a man and be silent while he spoke. Ron Scott recalled her response: "Sister Hankins jumped up on top of the table and pulled out a 38 caliber pistol. She stood over Khali and said that nobody was going to silence her. Khali got the point and apologized and shut up."[33]

The key *external* dynamic that determined the course of the Panther movement in Detroit, though, was the social and historical context of violence and extreme enmity between the black community and city police. Memories of the previous summer stung. Hundreds of burned-out buildings still scarred riot-torn neighborhoods. For their part, the police immediately viewed the new organization as an attempt to make lawlessness and violence against the police permanent in Detroit. The rhetoric in the first Panther newspaper distributed by Detroiters could only have fueled such police anxieties about an institutionalized insurrection. "Credo for Rioters and Looters" warned,

> America, you will be cleansed by fire, by blood, by death. We who perform your ablutions must step up our burning—bigger and better fires, one flame for all America, an all-American flame; we must step up our looting—loot, until we storm your last hoarding place, till we trample your last stolen jewel into your ashes beneath our naked black feet; we must step up our sniping—until the last pig is dead, shot to death with his own gun and the bullets in his guts that he had meant for the people. . . . We know that there are those amongst your people who are innocent, those who were brainwashed and manipulated out of their own humanity, out of their minds, out of their lives. We know who these are. These will help us burn you. These will help us loot. These will help us kill you. . . . [34]

Meanwhile, the Panthers' Afro hairstyle, leather jackets, and greetings of "power to the people" complemented their bold and fearless presentation of themselves as quintessential black militants.

While all this had a particular appeal for frustrated blacks in the Motor City, for the Detroit police it was an affront to their authority and a challenge to the racial status quo. Black Detroiters had always had a "place," and white policemen had confined and controlled them there, in their traditional role as protectors of the security and safety of whites and their property. The 1967 rebellion had been, in effect, an extremely destructive attempt by the black community to violate those boundaries of "place," raising the question of who would rule, and under what conditions.

The apparent sense of the police in the aftermath of July 1967 that they might be losing control was compounded by the activities in some of Detroit's factories by the black Marxist Revolutionary Union Movement (RUM). For May 1968 was not only the month when the dreaded Panthers established a beachhead in Detroit; it was also the month that the RUM at Dodge led a wildcat strike at the city's Chrysler plant. Automobile production fell nineteen hundred cars short. In turn, public knowledge that black workers had defiantly demonstrated their power in a traditional domain of their subservience led to the growth of RUMs at Ford, Cadillac, General Motors, and even the United Parcel Service.[35] Meanwhile, the Panthers opened their first office at Twelfth and Euclid, just two blocks from the epicenter of the 1967 rebellion. The police understood the symbolism. For them, driving past the new Panther office amid the charred storefronts was surely a reminder of the frightening days of the previous summer when black power flared beyond their control. Their response represented a concerted effort to regain the upper hand.

Across the street from the Panther office was a restaurant owned by a Mr. Hughes, the local numbers man, who regularly bribed police to stay in business.[36] According to ex-Panthers, Hughes was also a secret supporter of the BPP and a useful informant. Soon after the group opened its office, Hughes told Scott that police had told him that they planned to destroy the Panthers, vowing, he said, never to let them get a foothold in Detroit. Scott recalled the result. "From the very beginning, police were harassing us, sending in infiltrators. They had fresh memories of '67 and did not want to see rebellion institutionalized."[37] In fact, as a result, police harassment in this period was not confined to the Panthers.

Police fears of losing control of black Detroit were underscored the following spring in front of the New Bethel Baptist Church of the Reverend C. L. Franklin, the father of the soul singer Aretha Franklin. Members of the black nationalist organization Republic of New Africa (RNA) had rented New Bethel for the first anniversary celebration of its founding.[38] On that earlier day, March 31, 1968—barely a month before the founding of the Detroit Panther branch—over two hundred African Americans had signed a "Declaration of Independence," proclaiming that they were henceforth "forever free and independent of the jurisdiction of the United

States."[39] The RNA claimed five southern states for a future black nation in North America, demanding $400 billion in reparations for the establishment of a socialist Republic of New Africa. In the meantime, the group maintained an armed security force known as the Black Legion. The night of the RNA's first anniversary in March 1969, the Legionnaires wore black military uniforms with leopard epaulets and black combat boots and carried M-1 carbine rifles.

The police arrived at New Bethel at midnight as the Black Legion escorted Milton Henry, the president of the RNA, to his car. A former associate of the RNA described what happened next as a "ritualistic confrontation between two military organizations."[40] Armed white policemen in uniform viewed armed black nationalists in uniform as an affront to their monopoly on legitimate violence, while the black Legionnaires regarded themselves as the army of a newly founded nation. New African authority superseded white police authority and was legitimated by the African American right of revolution. The Black Legion thus epitomized a new black masculinity that reverberated from the cries of black power, the Legionnaires' erect clenched fists a defiant symbol challenging the masculine power of whiteness that had for centuries demanded obedience from dark-skinned people.[41]

That spring night in front of New Bethel far more was at stake than the life of President Milton Henry. Neither white nationalism nor black nationalism could back down. Reminiscent of the mythical showdowns in the old West, the Legionnaires beat the police to the draw. They wounded Patrolman Richard Worobec and shot Patrolman Michael Czapski to death. Worobec managed to radio an "officer down" alert. Scores of police converged on the scene; they later claimed they were shot at from inside the church. They opened fire, wounding four members of the RNA.[42] The conflict ended when the police broke down the front door of New Bethel and arrested 142 people, including many children, for murder.[43]

A few days after the shootings at New Bethel, police raided the Panthers' office on Euclid, claiming that the Panthers had stolen some police radios. With only two unarmed Panthers in the office during the raid, there was no resistance. There were no radios, either, though the police destroyed office equipment, including mimeograph copy machines and other objects of value.[44] A few weeks later, police arrested several Panthers and charged them with robbing some prostitutes whom the police had observed bringing donations to the Panthers' office. At trial, the prostitutes testified to the Panthers' innocence, and the jury found them not guilty. The harassment continued, however. Within a few weeks, police arrested several more Panthers for robbing local black businesses, many of whom had supported the BPP with donations.[45] When informed of the charges against the Panthers, most of these business leaders and community people expressed disbelief. Again, the community rallied around the Panthers, who were eventually released, and all charges were dropped.[46]

Evidently, the purpose of this repression was not to gain guilty verdicts. The process of raising bail money, the efforts to secure attorneys, the time spent taking care of the children and other family members of the arrestees, the hours working to get public support for the accused—all of these activities tied up Panther resources. Even court cases that ended in acquittals blocked Panthers from using their energies for goals not dictated by the police. The strategy—which was successful in the long run—was for the police to regain the control they had seen slipping away since the summer of 1967.[47] But the attempt to destroy the Panthers before they could fully establish themselves in the community was not successful.

By February 1969, the Panthers had already launched their Free Breakfast for Children programs at two locations on Detroit's West Side and at one on the East Side. They had started a free rat-removal extermination program as well as a free barbershop. They had recruited leftist doctors to staff a free health clinic in the Jeffries Projects, where they offered sickle cell anemia and blood pressure tests. Their assumption was that these altruistic and nonviolent programs would build community support and would not provoke the wrath of law enforcement. However, FBI documents show that the Panthers had misread the intentions of law enforcement. These community programs actually aroused more alarm in Director J. Edgar Hoover than did the Panthers' guns. That alarm was on display in a scolding letter Hoover sent to the FBI's office in San Francisco on June 6, 1969, apparently in response to resistance from the field. The letter commanded the city's agents to adhere to the FBI's policy.

You state that the Bureau under [COINTELPRO] should not attack programs of community interest such as the BPP "Breakfast for Children." You state that this is because many prominent "humanitarians," both black and white, are interested in the program as well as churches which are actively supporting it. You have obviously missed the point. The BPP is not engaged in the "Breakfast for Children" program for humanitarian reasons. This program was formed by the BPP for obvious reasons, including their efforts to create an image of civility, assume community control of Negroes, and to fill adolescent children with their insidious poison.[48]

Initially—perhaps for a year—the Detroit Panthers stayed away from guns or any activities that police might have considered illegal. But constant harassment forced the Panthers' hand. Sometime in the spring of 1969, Michael Baynham, the nineteen-year-old defense captain, went underground, leaving Detroit for military training. When he returned, he started preparing the group to defend itself with arms. One day in the summer of 1969, Panthers heard a gunshot in the house where they were assembled. "We ran downstairs and found Baynham's dead body with a bullet wound in his head," Scott recalled. "A twenty-two caliber pistol was beside him."[49] A door near Baynham's body was open. And, in the distance, Panthers heard fleeing footsteps. Scott and other Panthers pursued, but whoever it was had vanished.

The police quickly labeled Baynham's death a suicide and closed the case.[50] The Panthers recognized it immediately as a murder, which had revealed an obvious breach of security: they had been infiltrated. Indeed, Scott later estimated that at least half the members that summer were police agents. They also now had graphic evidence that no leader was safe from Baynham's fate. Under attack from both outside and inside, Scott and the other leading members decided to dissolve the Detroit Panthers. They planned to reconstitute the branch later after each incoming member had gone through a thorough security screening. Otherwise, the infiltrators could kill them one by one.

By the autumn of 1969, though, Scott and the others had not reconstituted the branch. Instead, Malik McClure, one of the younger Panthers who had opposed the dissolution, along with a number of prospective Panthers, appealed to the Central Committee for permission to reconstitute the organization as a branch of the newly established National Committees to Combat Fascism (NCCF). Essentially organizing bureaus generated by the Panthers' United Front against Fascism conference in the summer of 1969, the NCCFs were a way of dealing with too-rapid growth and concomitant infiltration by agents of the state.[51] In Detroit, though, the NCCF was, at least initially, a cover. McClure had actually been more than a junior member of the Detroit Panthers; he had been a participant in the clandestine founding of a Panther underground going on nationally. Like Michael Baynham, he too had left Detroit for several weeks and had been initiated into what amounted to a secret parallel organization that leading Panthers were then forming from coast to coast.[52] That is, the Detroit branch of the Black Panther Party would reconstitute itself, a year and a half after its founding, as an organization with a public face but with a clandestine core.

That core drew on an African American subculture of crime long predating the Panthers. Those who already had rebelled against the property relations of the capitalist system filled this realm. With their street skills they practiced what Huey Newton labeled "illegitimate capitalism," an apolitical act of defiance of the relations of production and the division of wealth in America. They were already outlaws because they literally lived outside the law. Guns were their regular companions, and they typically hated police more intensely than did regular, law-abiding African Americans. After all, their lives put them in a constant hunter/prey relationship with law enforcement. Death or long terms of imprisonment were frequently their fate when captured.

These elements constituted the lumpen proletariat—the so-called brothers off the block—that the Panthers had championed from the beginning and that has generated debate ever since about the party and its proposed path to revolution.[53] In the underground, though, that debate was a moot issue, for these revolutionaries knew from direct experience that those who had previously lived an illegal existence were best suited for conducting illegal, revolutionary actions. McClure was on friendly terms with such people in the community, in particular an underground cadre of Detroit men who lived by preying on dope houses. The apolitical ones would either sell or use the drugs themselves, but the more political among these raiders would confiscate money (and marijuana), keeping both for themselves, while later disposing of the hard drugs. From among this latter group, McClure would find recruits for the Detroit Panther underground.[54]

In late 1969, McClure became the chairman of the new Detroit branch of the NCCF. But the name change, intentions to the contrary, only made the Detroit Panthers more dangerous to the police than they had been before. Detroit was a hotbed of black radicalism in the late 1960s. In addition to the RNA, black Detroit had a growing trend of black Communist activism, exemplified by the LRBW, which had organized a growing base among the thousands of black autoworkers in the revolutionary union movement.[55] The city also had a cadre of RAM activists, the underground, military wing of the black liberation struggle for which Malcolm X's Organization of Afro-American Unity was to be the aboveground vehicle.[56] The heroic SNCC activists in the South, and the popularity of Stokely Carmichael and H. Rap Brown's black power advocacy, filled the Detroit chapter of SNCC with young militants.[57] Now, a new organization had arrived on the scene, calling itself the NCCF, but it was the BPP under a new guise. Moreover, it possessed a vibrant, growing, armed underground. Most important of all, perhaps, it aimed to unite all the disparate trends in Detroit's radical community—including white activists—under the Panthers' umbrella to combat what it termed *fascism*. The police, whom the Panthers unceasingly denounced as "fascists," regarded the entire prospect with profound dread.[58]

The *Tuebor*, the monthly newspaper of the Detroit Police Officers Association (DPOA), had run numerous articles in 1968 about area black militants representing a continuation of the disrespect for law enforcement and "criminality" of the 1967 "riot." More directly ominous for groups like the Panthers was the statement of Carl Parsell, the DPOA's leader, that critics of police racism and brutality were "part of a nefarious plot by those who would like our form of government overthrown."[59] The *Tuebor* also reflected the Detroit Police Department's dismissal of anything positive that might come of the Panthers' community survival programs, seeing the party in purely military terms.[60]

But the Detroit Panthers were not a wholly military force. If only as a response to police repression, McClure followed the Maoist line about serving the people. As the ex-Panther Eddie Irwin recalled, Malik would frequently say, "Our best protection is the people. If we serve the people, they will serve us."[61] Thus, as he built the underground, McClure reconstituted the party's survival programs, emphasizing the importance of spreading them into every black neighborhood. Thus, too, though taking direction from the Central Committee in Oakland, he crafted the NCCF as a base for local revolutionaries of all races who wished to be part of an international united front. Hence, McClure's initial focus was on presenting the Detroit organization as an instrument of political counterhegemonic influence, not as an armed opposition to the police.

Thus, the ex-Panther Tony Norman recalls that instead of carrying guns, he spent most of his time in early 1970 carrying and selling boxes of Black Panther newspapers.[62] McClure had acquired a mimeograph machine, and he kept the new recruit busy typing fliers to distribute with the newspaper. Norman remembers that when he first began working in the Detroit party, in late 1969, the Panthers used guns mostly to guard their doors. The slayings by police of Fred Hampton and Mark Clark, two leaders of the Panthers, in Chicago on December 4, 1969, had reinforced a siege mentality, with the Detroit Panthers on guard all night on four-hour shifts.[63] "We rarely took a gun outside our houses or offices," Norman recalls. "To do that and run into the police meant that you had to either shoot it out, or just surrender and let them kill you. Because any Panther found with a gun by the police was dead meat, even if he surrendered. We mainly pushed our community survival programs." But, despite McClure's best efforts to make the party's social programs the dominant party image, the police, once again, forced the Panthers' hand.[64]

The Rise of Armed Struggle in Detroit

And I hereby enjoin upon the people so declared to be free to abstain
from all violence unless in necessary self-defence.—ABRAHAM LINCOLN,
Emancipation Proclamation

Nadine Brown was a staff member of Detroit's African American newspaper, the *Michigan Chronicle*. She was also a leader of the Michigan Committee Against Repression (MCAP), an organization that comprised labor, church, community, and political leaders. In May 1970, MCAP filed an official complaint with the city against the Detroit police for having harassed and threatened members of the BPP on at least twenty-four occasions.[65] Mayor Roman Gribbs and Police Commissioner Patrick V. Murphy launched an investigation on May 22. By August, they had dismissed each complaint as "unprovable."[66] The whole affair deepened the impression inside the party and in the community that the Detroit Police Department had official sanction to act outside the law to suppress black uplift. With no legal recourse to stop police violence, the Panthers knew they would have to rely increasingly on extralegal means to protect themselves and their movement. Sometime in early 1970, therefore, Chuck Holt, a Panther with extensive military experience in the armed forces and an expert in small arms, explosives, and the martial arts, replaced Michael Baynham as defense captain in charge of security and of training the underground.[67]

In the process, as complaints of police beatings and harassment rose, the increased emphasis on armed struggle contributed to the militarization of the Detroit organization's public image—precisely what McClure had sought to avoid months earlier. Battles with police were not the sole cause of the Panthers assuming a more highly militarized profile, however. On March 9, 1970, for example, the Detroit NCCF distributed a leaflet throughout black Detroit announcing a "death warrant" on Ron Karenga and the black playwright LeRoi Jones, both of whom were to make public appearances in the city. Karenga was the leader of the cultural nationalist US (as opposed to "them") Organization—for over a year, an enemy of the Panthers—and Jones had once been associated with Karenga.[68] The leaflet called for both to be assassinated during their upcoming speaking engagements. The local press noted dryly, "Karenga cancelled his appearance but Jones appeared, heavily guarded by RNA adherents, but without incident."[69]

The "warrant" reflected growing antagonism between the cultural nationalist and the revolutionary nationalist wings of the black power movement. Neither knew at the time of the FBI program to destroy the movement—COINTELPRO—that promoted precisely such antagonism. Hoover had sent a memo to the Baltimore office of the FBI nearly a year and a half earlier, on November 25, 1968, demanding "hard-hitting counterintelligence measures aimed at crippling the BPP." He ordered that these measures should "fully capitalize upon BPP and US differences as well as to exploit all avenues of creating further dissension in the ranks of the BPP...." In the same memo, he gloated that already the conflict between the Panthers and Karenga's organization had "reached such proportions that it is taking on the aura of gang warfare with attendant threats of murder and reprisals."[70]

The militarization of the Detroit NCCF proceeded apace in early 1970. On May 1, the *Detroit News* reported, "About 200 black-garbed NCCF members marched outside the Federal Bldg. in sympathy with efforts to free Huey Newton, the founder of the Black Panther Party."[71] In part, the display reflected dissension bubbling up within the Detroit NCCF, with some openly complaining they had become "punching bags" for police.

Norman remembers, "We told Malik [McClure] that this was, after all, the Black Panther Party for *Self-Defense*. We got tired of *acting* tough on our enemies. We wanted to *be* tough."[72]

Then, in July, the police attacked McClure, his brother, his mother, and a family friend in front of McClure's mother's home.[73] McClure would later say that attacking his defenseless mother was for him the final straw. He could understand the police beating him and his brother; they were Panthers and expected such treatment. But the assault on his mother was a new low.[74] McClure was now ready to declare his own war with the full power of the underground organization he had been building for nearly a year. McClure freed the self-defense cells to take action, at their own initiative, against the police, to acquire explosives, and to step up their "expropriations" of the city's heroin dealers.[75]

What happened next is not, as yet, part of Panther historiography. Much of what is known about the BPP focuses on the aboveground features of the organization, including the social programs discussed above. At the same time, the story of the Panthers and gunplay is often told with the Panthers as victims of the government. There was, however, an underground arena of armed activism in which the Panthers were not always the victims. This was the case for a while in Detroit—until the authorities counterattacked. Indeed, at times in Detroit, aboveground Panthers did not participate in, did not even know about the activities that went on underground. Nzinga Mbote, who was active in the early 1970s, recalls, "I sometimes saw the other party members with guns going places. But I didn't know where they were going or what they were doing. And I didn't want to know."[76] Lawrence "Red" White, who led some of the group's underground activities, explained in the 1970s why many aboveground, daytime, members knew nothing about what was happening at night. "We functioned on a need-to-know basis," he said. "If you were not involved in an armed activity, then you had no reason to know about it. We did this to keep the possibility of infiltration and discovery by the police to the minimum."[77]

For Mbote's aboveground party work, Mao's *Little Red Book* was critical, for its admonitions to serve the people promoted the kind of community service in which Mbote was engaged.[78] Other texts by Lenin, Marx, Kwame Nkrumah, and Malcolm X composed the canon for the legal workers of the party. The canon of the underground extended from the works of these thinkers to other books. In fact, the party had two ideologies: one for the aboveground organization and the other for the underground activists. The aboveground members represented the party at news conferences and wrote the articles for the party's newspaper. For this reason, the history of the party tends to reflect their perspective and their ideology. Far less known are the works that comprised the canon of armed revolutionary activists. Without an understanding of those sources—and how they were used by the Detroit Panther underground—the story of the party in the Motor City remains radically incomplete.

The Seven Canons of Armed Struggle

Malcolm X's self-defense posture was the bedrock on which all else was built in Detroit. Having left the Nation of Islam in early 1964, in late June of that year he issued a "Statement on the Basic Aims" for a new organization, the Organization of Afro-American Unity.[79] Point number two noted forthrightly, "Since self-preservation is the first law of nature, we assert the Afro-American's right of self-defense."

> The Constitution of the U.S.A. clearly affirms the right of every American citizen to bear arms. . . . A man with a rifle or club can only be stopped by a man with a rifle or club. . . . Tactics based solely on morality can only succeed when you are dealing with basically moral people or a moral system. A man or system which oppresses a man because of his color is not moral. It is the duty of every Afro-American and every Afro-American community throughout this country to protect its people against mass murderers, bombers, lynchers, floggers, brutalizers and exploiters.[80]

The language was familiar to local activists. After all, Malcolm had lived in Detroit, where he had gotten his moniker, "Detroit Red." Albert Cleague, the future leader of the Shrine of the Black Madonna, Milton Henry, the future leader of the RNA, and longtime radical activists James and Grace Lee Boggs had provided Malcolm with a platform from which to speak.[81] They had been instrumental in bringing him to the city where he made two of his most famous speeches, "Message to the Grassroots" in 1963 and "The Ballot or the Bullet" in 1964.[82] There, Malcolm had exposed the blatant contradiction of black people's willingness to be violent overseas for America, but unwillingness to take up arms in Mississippi and Alabama in the face of Klan violence. In attendance at these speeches were activists from the city's nationalist and Marxist circles, but it was the Black Panthers who claimed to be his sons and daughters.[83] The first book on the "Black Panther Party Book List" in the *Black Panther* newspaper, for example, was the *Autobiography of Malcolm X*, which the Panthers considered a necessary first step toward revolutionary consciousness.[84] It was also a kind of bible in the Detroit underground.

A second, critical text was *The Wretched of the Earth* by Frantz Fanon, the Martiniquan revolutionary psychiatrist. Panthers extrapolated from his analysis of the polarized relationship between colonial settlers and colonized peoples, which he observed in the French colony of Algeria, and applied the analysis to African Americans and the white power structure in the United States. Fanon asserted that black people's sense of inferiority and their penchant for intracommunal violence stemmed from repressed rage at oppression and exploitation.

> The colonized man will manifest this tremendous aggressiveness that has been deposited in his bones against his own people. This is the period when the niggers beat each other up. . . .
>
> While the settler or the policeman has the right the livelong day to strike the native, to insult him and to make him crawl to them, you will see the native reaching for his knife at the slightest hostile or aggressive glance cast on him by another native; for the last resort of the native is to defend his personality vis-à-vis his brother.[85]

Here, Fanon exposed the psychological taboo that centuries of oppression had placed in black minds against striking back at the violent agents of white racism. He then wrote a prescription to cure black mental illness. "Violence is a cleansing force. It frees the native from his inferiority complex and from his despair and inaction; it makes him fearless and restores his self-respect."[86]

Various Panthers had grown up in the gangs of Chicago or in the hustler world of Detroit. When they fought gun battles with street rivals, the bullets whizzing by their heads when fired by black men just added to the thrill of the underworld experience. Indeed, they now describe gun battles in gang fights as fun. But, whenever they thought about fighting back against white policemen, who frequently humiliated, brutalized, and shot African Americans, they were overwhelmed with fear. Powerful feelings of dread and terror paralyzed them, even though police bullets were no more deadly than those from black gang bangers' guns.[87]

Black psychology thus permitted fighting fellow black gang members in American cities, even as it prohibited fighting against armed, racist white police. According to Fanon, this taboo was the visible manifestation of an inferiority complex vis-à-vis whiteness itself, a complex that, in turn, pent up a tremendous amount of aggressive energy. Breaking that taboo, then, would logically trigger a psychological catharsis, unleashing the power both to destroy and create. The resulting mental transformation would end the fighter's sense of inferiority and generate a new, free being. When vanquishing the oppressor, the fighter also vanquished the oppressed, for the oppressed could only exist as a binary of the oppressor. The formerly oppressed man arose from his taboo breaking reborn into full manhood.[88] Panthers such as Eddie Irwin, who participated in armed actions as part of the Detroit underground, claims to have experienced precisely that kind of catharsis.[89]

Third in the canon of the underground revolutionaries was Robert F. Williams's book *Negroes with Guns*, which was published in 1962. Here, in a series of essays, Williams popularized his own example, having created an armed, militant branch of the NAACP in Monroe, North Carolina. In doing so, Williams had challenged what the media called "responsible Negro leaders" who advocated nonviolence in the face of violence by the Klan. In *Negroes with Guns*, he refuted, point-by-point, the rationales of the black elite for denying black people the right to bear arms in self-defense. He wrote that whenever black people resorted to militant action, the responsible Negro leaders "complain that race relations may deteriorate to a point that many Negroes may lose their jobs. What they mean is that they [the black elite] may lose *their* jobs."[90] Roy Wilkins, the leader of the NAACP, removed Williams from his leadership position precisely because of such advocacy of armed black self-defense.[91]

Paralleling Malcolm X, in 1962 Williams exposed the contradiction between black people's pacifism in the face of Klan and police violence and support for the American military. "Of course, the respectable Negro leadership are the most outspoken exponents of non-violence," Williams noted. "But if these people, especially the ministers, are such pure pacifists, why is it that so few, if any, criticize the war preparations of this country?"[92] These kinds of arguments struck a chord among many, especially Panthers who saw self-defense as a way of making systemic change.

The Afro-American militant is a "militant" because he defends himself, his family, his home and his dignity. He does not introduce violence into a racist social system—the violence is already there and has always been there. It is precisely this unchallenged violence that allows a racist social system to perpetuate itself. When people say that they are opposed to Negroes "resorting to violence" what they really mean is that they are opposed to Negroes defending themselves and challenging the exclusive monopoly of violence practiced by white racists.[93]

A fourth treatise in this revolutionary canon was *Catechism of the Revolutionist*, which was written in 1869 by the Russian anarchist Mikhail Bakunin. According to Bakunin, revolutionaries take on their political role as "doomed" lives. They know they will inevitably die for their cause, so they erase from their minds all hope of a future with family, universities, and the comforts of middle and old age. Revolutionaries consciously enter the armed struggle having renounced life with the willingness to commit the revolutionary suicide that Huey P. Newton articulated in his autobiography. "My life had to come to an end sometime. But the people go on; in them lies the possibility for immortality . . . since each man eventually gives up his life, death can only be controlled through the ongoing life of the people. . . . By giving all to the present we reject fear, despair and defeat."[94] The psychological impact of such a total commitment was to suspend the ordinary reflexes of fear. The removal of the fear of death then enhanced the level of daring and bravery of the armed revolutionaries in the party. "Once you commit yourself and stop fearing death, you feel relieved," said Lawrence White. "That's a very powerful feeling. Imagine, for the first time in the hundreds of years since we were brought to America as slaves, we did not fear white folks. We stood in front of their armed men with our guns on terms of equals as men."[95]

Note the masculinization of the description of liberation here: to be a *man* required resistance. A common refrain among members of the Detroit Panther underground was that nonviolence before racist violence was unmanly. However, in this sense, "manhood" applied equally to the women warriors in the Detroit underground as it did to the men. The term "man" became a metaphor for the new being who arose from the catharsis of revolutionary violence. Manhood meant standing armed before armed white racism as an equal. Thus, in 1969, a female voice sings the lyrics of a Panther anthem on the record album, *Seize the Time*.

Have you ever stood
In the darkness of night
Screaming silently
You're a man? Have you ever thought
That a time would come
When your voice would be heard
In a new nation?
Have you waited for so long
Till your unheard song
Had stripped away your very soul?
Well, then believe it my friend
That this silence can end
We'll just have to get guns
AND BE MEN![96]

The Panthers were not the first to understand liberation in these absolutist terms of "manhood." W. E. B. Du Bois expressed it well. "The black man knows: his fight here is a fight to the finish. Either he dies or he wins. He will enter modern civilization here in America as a black man on terms of perfect and unlimited equality with any white man, or he will enter not at all."[97] Detroit Panthers such as Sundiata Akinshegun understood the point instinctively.[98] To the Panther underground, being "equal" meant an equalization of fear.

An incident in December 1970 in Ann Arbor, Michigan, illustrated this equalization of fear. Four Panthers were checking out the security of a building in which Huey Newton was to speak. A line of uniformed police from various departments had formed across the street, ostensibly in case Newton should incite a riot. Each of the Panthers carried at least two guns; one had a sawed-off shotgun dangling from a strap under his trench coat. Suddenly, Louis "Texas" Johnson told the other Panthers to "cover" him, and he approached the police. The three other Panthers walked behind him and faced the officers. Johnson opened his coat, exposing two pistols, and shouted in a loud voice, like a cowboy in a showdown, "Draw!"[99] The line of police officers stood stunned and silent. Although they outnumbered the Panthers, none would draw his gun.[100] Panthers in different locations understood the lesson of this experience in different ways. Most, however, came away from such confrontations with an appreciation for the effect on the equation of fear: for centuries all of the fear had been on the black side of the scale; now, some had shifted to the white side.[101]

The police here outnumbered the Panthers and had greater firepower. The officers knew the first one or two to reach for his weapon would most likely die. None wanted to take that chance. They were as afraid of armed black people in this instance as black people had been afraid of them.[102] It was an important revelation, and Panthers across the country experienced it.[103] As Akinshegun put it, "We had got to the point where we said that if we had to fear for our lives every time a cop stopped us on the streets, then they should fear for theirs, too. We could only make that a reality if we were determined to fight." Indeed, for many in the Detroit underground, this recalibration of the equation had been Huey Newton's greatest achievement—namely, showing that black people in cities could make armed white power back down. "This could only be shown by example," Eddie Irwin points out. "Somebody had to risk his life first. In spite of the problems Huey had later in his life, the comrades with the guns continue to this day to respect the example of courage he set for us back when he had his head on straight."[104]

A fifth author popular in the Detroit underground was Ernesto "Che" Guevara, the Cuban revolutionary, who was known especially for his essay "Man and Socialism in Cuba" and his book *Guerilla Warfare*. The essay offered an idealistic, even utopian view of Marxist revolution, in which Guevara described the production of a socialist "New Man" who would renounce capitalist selfishness and competitive social practices for a loving, sharing social ethos.[105] For Lawrence White, as a Detroit Panther and later as a prisoner seeking to maintain his revolutionary spirit, the essay was the most inspirational he had ever read.

In *Guerilla Warfare*, Guevara explained the actual techniques of fighting a guerilla war. At the same time, he also provided a valuable lesson to the Panther underground on gender. Che wrote, "The part that the woman can play in the development of a revolutionary process is of extraordinary importance. It is well to emphasize this, since in all our countries, with their colonial mentality, there is a certain underestimation of the woman which becomes a real discrimination against her. . . . The woman is capable of performing the most difficult tasks, of fighting beside the men; and despite current belief, she does not create conflicts of a sexual type in the troops."[106] According to several male Panthers, these teachings were important for men's struggles within themselves to overcome the sexism that was part of contemporary American culture. The equality between men and women in the underground went further than that in the aboveground organization precisely because, in situations of life and death, courage, competence, and commitment are the primary measurements of a comrade's value. These qualities have no gender. According to Akinshegun, "When your life is on the line, you're not thinking about what the persons who've got your back have got between their legs. You just want them to be strong, think fast, stay calm, and act with the highest level of efficiency."[107]

But, there was more to this issue. One incident in late 1970 stands out as pivotal in the struggle to overcome sexism among the Detroit Panthers and simultaneously reveals the intricate nature of the aboveground and underground elements in the party. Several women leveled charges against Malik McClure, the chairman of the NCCF, before the general body of the organization, charging him with practicing "Selfish Departmentalism." In Maoist vocabulary, the charge denoted the bureaucratic practice of favoritism in which the errant officer preferred his own particular bailiwick to the detriment of others. In this case, the women accused McClure of assigning light office duties to women who afforded him sexual favors, a violation of one of Mao's Eight Points of Attention ("Do Not Take Liberties with Women").[108] The women further charged that McClure punished women who resisted his sexual advances by sending them into the cold to sell newspapers.[109]

The Panther leading the "criticism and self-criticism" session on this matter sided with the women, adding that McClure had sent to distant duties in Flint, Michigan, those male Panthers whose wives and girlfriends he sought sexually.[110] These transfers and the subsequent friction caused disunity in the ranks, he argued, and should be judged foremost as hindrances to party unity. For, by then, all knew that government agents were observing and probing for weaknesses, and McClure's behavior had created the kind of intense resentments that could make a revenge-seeking Panther amenable to an approach by the government to turn informer. But, a formidable woman named Comrade Bahala, a leader of women and some men in the party, insisted that "male chauvinism" was the central issue in the revolutionary tribunal. Because of her legendary courage in the Panther underground, her words weighed heavily on the men who had been in self-defense squads with her. The majority of the collective body of

Panthers decided that McClure should accept the criticism and cease his chauvinistic practices.

McClure verbally accepted the criticism but reverted to his old behavior soon afterward, which resulted in a second general body meeting just three weeks later. By a majority vote McClure was then purged from the Detroit branch of the NCCF. Male and female Panthers recall his expulsion as a crucial point in realizing gender equality in the Detroit Panthers.[111] What most of those at the meeting did not know, however, was that McClure continued to play a leading role in the Panther underground, where the expulsion vote had no authority. The respect McClure had with the under-ground—including with Comrade Bahala—kept his expulsion restricted to the aboveground activities in which he had the power to supervise women and men.

A sixth key text for the Detroit underground, Samuel Greenlee's *The Spook Who Sat by the Door*, has received little attention from historians, perhaps because it is a work of fiction. Nevertheless, Greenlee wrote a realistic and inspiring thriller depicting an underground, organized black insurgency. The potency of its realism derived from its protagonist, Free-man, a veteran of the Korean War who joined the first group of black middle-class men at the Central Intelligence Agency. "Freeman read every-thing in the [CIA] library on gunnery, demolition, subversion, sabotage and terrorism," Greenlee wrote.[112] Freeman "sat by the door," a 1960s term for black people who assumed milquetoast personas to deceive white rac-ists for a higher purpose. But then he turned his training into a tool of black revolution. In the novel, he secretly organizes a revolutionary black under-ground to wreak destruction on the enemies of black Chicago.

Greenlee's novel was a template for what was an often-repeated goal of black radicals during the Vietnam War: turning the extensive combat experience and knowledge of weaponry and tactics of thousands of black veterans into a resource for black revolution.[113] Detroit Panther Eddie Irwin was a Vietnam veteran who was radicalized "in country," fighting in the 82nd Airborne Division. "Vietnamese people would come up to me and ask, 'Soul brother, why you here?' They would tell me that my fight was back in America. I felt ashamed that I was killing another people of color under orders of white officers from Mississippi and Alabama. Especially because I saw these same officers putting up Confederate flags in their hootches."[114] Irwin read Greenlee's book when he returned to the United

States in 1969. He then decided, like Freeman, that he would put the lessons he had learned fighting for Uncle Sam to work for the Detroit Panthers.

Lawrence White also joined the party in Detroit after a stint in the Marine Corps, where he experienced what he referred to as "true Americanism," the breach between the public propaganda image of America and the secret reality.[115] "In the media we were securing freedom for the Vietnamese from Ho Chi Minh. I saw that we were the ones actually stopping the freedom of the majority of them who wanted Ho Chi Minh to be their leader and wanted the Americans out of their country. We were torturing and raping them. We were like the Klan in Vietnam and the "gooks" were the niggers."[116] Like Eddie Irwin, this experience turned White into a revolutionary. He joined the Panthers in 1970 specifically so that he could "put [his] Marine Corps training in the service of the people.[117] I had killed all of those people in Viet Nam serving the wrong side.[118] But I woke up in Vietnam and decided to come home and be righteous."[119]

Finally, if one book encapsulated the armed struggle ideology of the underground, it was the *Minimanual of the Urban Guerrilla* by the Brazilian revolutionist Carlos Marighella.[120] Written in 1969, the *Minimanual* is a polished text of instruction. It details everything from the definition of the guerilla to a step-by-step description of each feature of urban warfare. On its first page, Marighella states: "The urban guerrilla is a person who fights . . . with weapons using unconventional methods. A revolutionary and an ardent patriot, he is a fighter for his country's liberation, a friend of the people and of freedom. The urban guerrilla, however, differs radically from the criminal. The criminal benefits personally from his actions and attacks indiscriminately without distinguishing between the exploiters and the exploited. The urban guerrilla follows a political goal, and only attacks the government, the big business and the . . . imperialists."[121] The definition applied to the Detroit underground, as did his admonition that revolutionaries be physically fit and train in the use of weaponry. Moreover, the *Minimanual* specifies that autonomous cells of four or five persons should carry out offensive operations against the enemy—in Detroit, the Panthers called these units "self-defense groups."

Of great tactical importance to Marighella was what he called "armed propaganda."[122] Media images of Panthers standing or marching with guns served this purpose; so did the famous poster of Bobby Seale and Huey Newton standing with pistol and shotgun. Armed propaganda also refers to any action that guerillas carry out that requires guns or violence. For the Panther underground in Detroit, armed propaganda was ideally retaliation against police or other government forces after they committed some atrocity against the people. When people's anger against the government was high, the retaliation needed no explanation—the deed spoke for itself. This covert combat was a form of psychological warfare the armed activists hoped the unorganized black masses would then emulate, at the same time that it would generate among the police second thoughts about repeating their violent, racist behavior.

Lawrence White described one such incident from the critical year, 1970. During the summer, police shot a black teenager in the back of the head, claiming he had attacked them with a broomstick. Though neither the media nor anyone in the city government asked how a person could be shot in the back of the head when he was moving toward a police officer, it was a question constantly asked in the black community. One night soon after this boy's death, a defense squad that included White ambushed a police car. After the armed action, which left two policemen wounded but not dead, the men split up. All got away from the scene safely, but, unfortunately for White, an elderly woman who lived downstairs from his residence in a two-family flat, peeped out the window when she heard his car in the driveway and saw him carry a rifle into the house. After seeing the news report of the two wounded police officers, she called the department.

White described how he was able to use his Marine Corps training to hold out for over ten hours against the ensuing onslaught. By shooting from multiple windows, he was able to give the impression that there were several men inside. With four gas masks, he fought long after the police canisters had saturated the entire flat with tear gas. White surrendered only when he ran out of ammunition and his gas masks ceased to work. The police nearly beat him to death.

Knowing that White had not acted alone, as more than one gun had been used in the attack on the squad car, the prosecutor offered a light sentence if he revealed the identities of his co-conspirators. He refused. For this one night of Fanonian taboo breaking, a judge sentenced White to spend the next fifteen to thirty years in prison. The other members of his self-defense group were never captured, however. And White never voiced any regrets about his actions, viewing his capture and imprisonment, philosophically, as part of what is known in military parlance as the "friction" of war.[123]

Marighella's *Minimanual* also provided a name for another key activity of the armed wing of the Detroit Panthers: "expropriation" of money from drug houses to support daytime, aboveground Panther activities.[124] Akinshegun remembered, "We regarded the heroin dealers as committing genocide against our community. Why shouldn't we have expropriated their money and used it to serve the people?"[125] The Detroit underground took seriously the formula, drawn from the colorful language of the New York Panther and ex-heroin addict Michael "Cetawayo" Tabor: *capitalism plus dope equal genocide.* Its members believed the federal government purposefully allowed the drug plague to spread in an effort to debilitate black America, and especially to weaken potentially rebellious communities. In their view, robbing dope houses located the Panthers within the realm of what the social historian Eric Hobsbawm called the "noble robber."[126]

One early member of the party, Earl Anthony, who later admitted to being an FBI informant from the moment he joined, also admitted that one of his many duties was to deal large quantities of marijuana. The statute of limitations for dealing heroin and cocaine had not yet expired when Anthony wrote his memoir, which could account for his silence about whether the FBI also supplied him with these hard drugs. In any case, what Anthony did reveal validated the Panther program of robbing drug dealers because of their conspiring with the government in what was essentially a chemical war.[127]

The rigorous use of the "canon" contributed to the rise of armed activism among the Detroit Panthers. Of course, books alone cannot explain why any one individual or group took up arms. We can, however, point to some material effects of the process, such as the apparent change in police recruitment and hiring. Previously, all-white squads had patrolled the city in twos, threes, and sometimes fours. After Panthers launched their "armed self-defense" campaign, white officers appeared reluctant to enter the black community without a black officer with them.[128] Norman observes, "While some folks might think it was nonviolent marching and singing that spurred the integration of the big city police departments, those of us who were there know that it was the white cops' fear of getting shot."[129]

The Turning Point Late 1970

Throughout the summer of 1970, the escalating tensions between Detroit's black militants and the city's white establishment augured an unpleasant climax; it came in October. Police pressure was so intense by the fall that on September 22, the Detroit NCCF and eight other black radical and nationalist organizations bound themselves to a "Self-defense Pact." They swore to oppose what they claimed was an impending mass incarceration in concentration camps.[130]

All summer, the police had heightened their self-declared war on the Panthers. Either as cause or consequence, by August their numbers had swelled to fifty-five active members, while uncounted dozens of community workers did party work without official membership.[131] Meanwhile, as elsewhere in the country, the primary points of tension between police and Panthers locally arose from the visibility of Panthers selling the *Black Panther*, which by 1970 had a national weekly circulation of 139,000.[132] The contents of the paper, which sold for twenty-five cents, were a constant affront to the armed representatives of the state. Not only did the paper highlight incidents of police murdering and brutalizing people of color throughout America, but it identified those police as "pigs," in part to denote the kind of creature that was capable of such violence. Defining a pig as "an ill-natured beast who has no respect for law and order, a foul traducer who's usually found masquerading as a victim of an unprovoked attack," the label enacted the Maoist tenet "From the masses, to the masses," for "pig" was a distillation of contemporary attitudes toward the police in black America.[133] Over time, the word's meaning expanded to include all forces that supported the status quo, and using the epithet came to mean that the user identified with an anti-establishment political culture. Too, the Panther paper employed the term promiscuously: the issue of October 24, 1970 referred to police as "pigs" 306 times in 24 pages.

In Detroit, the *Black Panther* had become an increasingly ubiquitous symbol of black power's transgression of place, and the police department worked daily to disrupt its sales. Numerous Panthers and community workers selling the paper reported being stopped, arrested, beaten, and charged with either assaulting the officers who beat them or resisting arrest.[134] One legal investigator noted on August 10, 1970, "17 year old [Black Panther] girl was ticketed for littering, witnesses said melee ensued & girl hit with blackjack."[135] On August 25, 1970, Patrolman Caldwell "bust[ed five] newspaper salesmen on Woodward & State for interfering with pedestrian traffic. . . . A woman tried to help & was beaten by Ptl. Colbert."[136] By October, police had issued twenty-four tickets to paper-selling Panthers for "impeding the pedestrian flow of traffic" on just one Detroit street.[137] The number of tickets, arrests, beatings, and other forms of harassment is, in fact, incalculable for all of the streets on which Panthers operated.

In this, police worked in tandem with local FBI officials, who proposed in a memo to Hoover dated October 13, 1970 that the campaign to disrupt the newspaper sales in Detroit intensify: "The Black Panther Party (BPP) in Detroit receives BPP publications from San Francisco. Detroit [FBI agents have] easy access to these papers after they arrive in Detroit. . . . The Bureau is requested to prepare and furnish to Detroit in liquid form a solution capable of duplicating a scent of the most foul smelling feces available. In this case, it might be appropriate to duplicate the feces of the specie sus scrofa."[138] The specific spray used seems to have been urinal rather than fecal, though it did its job. Benjamin Fondren recalls being dispatched to pick up the mid-October edition from the airport. "[The papers] smelled like somebody had pissed on them. I didn't want to touch them. Thousands of papers were unsaleable. We wouldn't even sign for them. We thought the airport people, maybe the pilots, had pissed on them. But to have messed up that many papers the whole crew would have had to do it."[139]

Meanwhile, *Tuebor*, the Detroit police journal, carried on a propaganda campaign against the Panthers. Its October 1970 edition, for example, printed a two-page screed titled "U.S. Police in a Cultural Crisis, How the Panthers Operate," which reflected a growing sense that a violent showdown with the Panthers was inevitable. "Intelligence officers have known ever since the Oleg Penkovskiy [sic] Case broke that Soviet strategy against the United States is headed toward a showdown in the early Nineteen Seventies. . . . J. Edgar Hoover made it very clear as to what FBI investigations have disclosed. . . . The subversive activities of the Communist-directed Black Panther party are spelled out in careful detail."[140] The article compared the "psychological climate" the Panthers had created to the era before the attack on Pearl Harbor, when law enforcement had ignored public indifference and prepared for the inevitable. "When it came time to do the job, we did it. Circumstances would strongly suggest that in the not too distant future we may have the job to do again."[141] The "job," of course, referred to the mass preventive detention of Japanese in American concentration camps. To drive home the point, the *Tuebor* offered an appeal from Patrolman Robert Olson: "Appoint a member of this department who has the rank and training to root out the headquarters of the Black Panthers at 14th and Indiandale.... There is a certain person in this Department who has had that training under General Patton and with the right time and the right equipment we could go in there and finish the job. The morale of the country suffers when the Police morale suffers and everyday at roll call we must be warned about this address or that address as the boss tells us there are Black Panthers here and there are [B]lack Panthers there." "I was in two victorious armies," Olson proclaimed, "and now I'm not used to being warned about the enemy. But to be given orders to chew them up."[142]

The Battle at Sixteenth and Myrtle

The bellicose rhetoric set the stage for the climactic event in front of the Detroit Panthers' headquarters at Sixteenth and Myrtle on October 24, when a Panther shot Patrolman Glenn Edward Smith to death. Unsurprisingly, the sale of the Panther newspaper provided the spark. Patrolman Frank Randazzo wrote the police version of the incident in his official report for the department's Homicide Bureau. According to Randazzo, while on routine patrol he observed Panthers blocking sidewalk traffic while selling their papers. He and his partner asked the Panthers to allow people to pass. As in numerous other confrontations between unarmed Panthers and armed police, the officer claimed that the Panther assaulted him. One Panther "grabbed writer and said 'It's all over now!' At this time this man swung at writer." Randazzo then placed two "thugs" in his squad car. Afterward, he heard an officer had been shot at Sixteenth and Myrtle.[143] On Myrtle, in front of the Panthers' headquarters, Patrolman Patrick H. Murray heard two shots. "I turned around & obs. Officer Smith . . . fall to the ground, wounded."[144] A hundred police officers sped to the scene in thirty patrol cars and an armored personnel carrier—one-third of the entire force on duty that Saturday night—and laid siege to the Panthers' office.[145]

From the Panther perspective came this eyewitness account: "I was upstairs [at the Panther headquarters] when I heard some comrades run into the office and shout that the pigs were chasing them. The pigs had hit one of them and tried to arrest them for selling papers. Then I heard a loud shot and a comrade yelled, 'I got him! I got him!' I shouted to him, 'You got who?' Then I looked out the window and saw the cop down on the sidewalk with his head bleeding. I was totally taken by surprise. But it was *on* then. The brother who shot the cop was fed up. He had been arrested and beaten one time too many. Nobody gave him an order. It was a spontaneous thing."[146] From the police came a different perspective, in a *Tuebor* editorial dedicated to Patrolman Smith: "Some people feel that some of those who were holed up in that building, were prepared to be martyrs to the cause most particularly the teenage girls just baiting and waiting for the Police to make a mistake. . . . Many hours have passed, tension is high, morale is low, everyone is on edge, guns are at ready, four scout cars are in flames. . . . You could cut the tension with a knife. Everyone is now waiting for the action. Waiting for the order to come. Everyone was tense and demanding that the order be given, asking when is the order coming."[147]

One Detroit Panther among the fifteen who defended the headquarters during the siege recalls, "We were shooting at them and their bullets were flying in at us. I thought for sure I was going to die. If we didn't have sandbags stacked we would have all been dead. The police shot *so* many bullet holes in the room where we were. It was like Swiss cheese."[148] The Panther Beverly Ann Fleming remembers that the spotlights the police aimed at the building lit up its every corner and made those inside vulnerable to police snipers. She also saw the armored personnel carrier in front of the house, which convinced her that no Panther would get out of the house alive.[149]

Suddenly, the police received an order to cease firing. Isaiah McKennon, then a junior officer and later Detroit's chief of police, insisted thirty years later that the only reason there was no order given to annihilate the Panthers inside was because thousands of black people from all over the city had converged on the scene.[150] They had surrounded the police who had surrounded the Panthers. These people had already firebombed police scout cars, and now they were loudly threatening to launch a war if the police attacked. Moreover, members of fraternal organizations such as the Black Legion of the RNA were mobilizing for war. Informants within the organization would have increased the police alarm that the battle might spread beyond the neighborhood of Sixteenth and Myrtle. Detroit's leading politicians and police officials were thus strongly motivated to end the siege without further bloodshed. "They didn't want to spark another riot like in '67," McKennon said. "If it wasn't for that concern, they would have wiped the Panthers out." For the survivors of the siege, that hesitation was affirmation of Huey Newton's "serve the people" strategy: the people whom the Panthers had served had arrived in the thousands and served the Panthers by saving their lives.[151]

At the same time, as one ex-Panther points out today, the police were not the only ones who could have ratcheted up the violence. "We had enough dynamite and pipe bombs in there to start throwing hell out the windows," he insists. "We just had to light some fuses and throw some footballs. They weren't going to kill us in our sleep like they did Fred Hampton. We were all wide awake." A police investigation three days later confirmed the Panthers' explosive capabilities.[152]

The siege of the Panther headquarters at Sixteenth and Myrtle lasted until the wee hours of October 25. Earlier that morning, the Panthers' gas masks began losing their effectiveness against police tear gas. Twelve of the young men and women surrendered at around 2:00 a.m. with the assistance of Nadine Brown, the columnist for the *Chronicle* newspaper. She had courageously and defiantly placed her body between the Panther building and the police that night, advocating for the Panthers before both police and the assembled white media. Panthers Benjamin Fondren, Erone Desaussure, and David Johnson held out for two more hours, exchanging gunfire with police who had surrounded the house, then finally surrendered at 4:00 a.m.

The failure of Panther counterintelligence played a critical role in the outcome. The Panthers had rented an apartment two blocks from their headquarters and stocked it with guns and ammunition. Their plan was to attack from the perimeter should police ever attack their headquarters. Such a counterattack would have represented a significant escalation of the Panther armed struggle in Detroit. Instead of a high point, however, it was a nadir. When Sundiata Akinshegun and other Panthers arrived at the apartment, they discovered that the guns and ammunition they had stored there had disappeared. The person in charge of the apartment claimed the arsenal had never arrived. Eddie Irwin, however, distinctly remembers personally moving the weapons into the apartment.

Some Panthers, such as Michael Dee, acquired guns elsewhere and approached the police perimeter via predesignated routes. They later reported being shot at by Panthers who held the guns believed to have been stored at the apartment. The shooters said the next day that they had fired on their comrades by accident, but Dee said the following year that he did not trust a single member of the Detroit Panther organization. Anybody could be, and probably was, an agent, he maintained.[153] This distrust—along with the arrest and imprisonment of the leaders of the underground self-defense groups—was a key to the demise of armed Black Panther activism in Detroit.

The fifteen Panthers who survived the siege were each charged with conspiracy to murder Patrolman Smith. Most would spend a year in jail awaiting trial. In the meantime, the Committee to Defend the Detroit Fifteen, led by the mother of one, secured a crack legal team that included Elliot Hall, a young attorney who would later become the first black vice president of the Ford Motor Company. The other principal attorney was Ernest Goodman, a founder of the National Lawyers Guild and a longtime proponent of progressive causes. The jury acquitted all fifteen Panthers on the murder charges, convicting only Benjamin Fondren, Erone Desaussure, and David Johnson of the lesser charge of felonious assault. Each man received "Three-to-Four Years at Hard Labor." A year after their conviction, however, the Michigan Court of Appeals overturned that sentence and set the men free.[154]

Throughout 1971, the Detroit Panthers were consumed and constrained by the campaign to free the Detroit 15. While the committee's propaganda work helped increase public support for the Panthers as the vanguard of the black community's resistance to continuing police racism and violence, the case and trial also exhausted the Panthers, in jail and out. In particular, raising defense funds and fending off police assaults depleted the time and energies of the Panther underground. At the same time, the death of Patrolman Smith spurred the Detroit police to intensify their harassment of party activists. Selling the Panther newspapers became more dangerous still. Only the most dedicated Panthers and community workers dared carry the paper on the streets. Police now viewed the Panthers as wounded prey and took advantage of every opportunity to effect their demise.

Meanwhile, on the national level, by early 1971 the party was wracked by internecine quarrels and violence, with groups coalescing around the now estranged leaders, Huey Newton and Eldridge Cleaver. On February 13, 1971, the FBI congratulated itself for fomenting strife that had already left several Panthers dead, even declaring its work in the matter done. "Since the differences between Newton and Cleaver now appear to be irreconcilable, no further counterintelligence activity in this regard will be undertaken at this time and now new targets must be established."[155] At the local level, though, the FBI's work continued apace. Among the bureau's new targets were the Detroit Panthers Larry Powell, Ronnie Irwin, Tony Norman, and Ronald Smith, four of the remaining members of the underground. By September 1971, all four would be in prison with sentences ranging from fifteen years to "Natural Life."[156] Their arrests and imprisonments would mark the end of the Detroit Panther underground.

The armed struggle in Detroit had risen with the underground activities and unsolved murder of Michael Baynham in the summer of 1969. It came to an end with the underground activities and imprisonment of Powell and the others in the summer of 1971. The party would continue its social survival programs in the Motor City for at least two more years. But, the chaos induced by the FBI at the national level, combined with the continued success of COINTELPRO at the local level, would leave the Detroit Panther Party a mere shadow of its former self.[157]

The Fall The Problem of Counterintelligence

In the long run, then, the Panthers who picked up the gun in Detroit failed. Many factors contributed to that failure. In retrospect, it now appears that from the moment of the Panthers' founding in the city, Panthers and police were heading toward a final, cataclysmic event, despite the nonviolent thrust of the NCCF's survival programs. The Detroit police demanded it, as did Panthers tired of police harassment, beatings, arrests, and incarcerations on phony charges. Panthers and police were opposing forces that could not simultaneously occupy the same space.

Wherever human beings devote their hearts and minds, shortcomings will inevitably come into play. In a political organization, leaders must have the foresight and will to sustain a protracted march toward the group's goals in the face of these deficiencies.[158] From a macro perspective, the reason for the fall of armed struggle in Detroit—and the eventual demise of the Black Panther Party itself—was a failure of the leadership to devise strategies and tactics to overcome challenges from within and without.[159] On a micro level, one dynamic that proved central to the Panthers' demise was a flaw in Marighella's *Minimanual.* Under the subheading "Guerrilla Security," he wrote, "The urban guerrilla lives in constant danger of the possibility of being discovered or denounced. The primary security problem is to make certain that we are well hidden and well guarded, and that there are secure methods to keep the police from locating us. The worst enemy of the urban guerrilla and the major danger that we can run into, is infiltration into our organization by a spy or informer."[160] What must revolutionaries do about this threat of infiltration, and how might they prevent it? Marighella offered instructions that were wholly unequal to the task: "The enemy . . . wants to know what steps we are taking so he can destroy us or prevent us from acting. In this sense, the danger of betrayal is present and the enemy encourages betrayal or infiltrates spies into the organization. The urban guerrilla's technique against this enemy tactic is to denounce publicly the traitors, spies, informers, and provocateurs. . . . For his part, the urban guerrilla must not evade the duty—once he knows who the spy or informer is—of physically wiping him out. This is the proper method . . . and it minimizes considerably the incidence of infiltration or enemy spying."[161]

The premise that public exposure of infiltrators would successfully counter this enemy tactic proved incorrect. In the spring of 1969, the *Black Panther* newspaper began regularly printing articles denouncing individuals, in bold letters, as "PIG[S]." The denunciation of a paid FBI infiltrator in one city, however, was ineffective in deterring infiltrators in other cities. Moreover, executing suspected informers and infiltrators was problematic, particularly because one tactic of the undercover agent was to cast suspicion on loyal party members by "bad jacketing." In more than one case, this FBI tactic caused party members to kill innocent people believed falsely to be informers.

And, what about the traitors, spies, informers, and *agents provocateurs* whose identities remained unknown and therefore could not suffer public denunciation or execution? How could revolutionaries have prevented their infiltration in the first place? Marighella provided no answers to this critical question. Evidently, he did not know the answers himself, because a Catholic priest whom he trusted informed on him to the Brazilian police, who ambushed and killed him. This critical shortcoming of Marighella's *Minimanual*, and the fact that Panthers had no knowledge of counterintelligence, left the them vulnerable to the infiltration that Marighella said was the urban guerilla's worst enemy.

The Panther underground thus collapsed for two reasons. First, the Panthers failed to realize the flaw in the *Minimanual* that left them open to penetration from within. Second, and perhaps more important, they failed to study those sources of intelligence and counterintelligence that would have taught them what Marighella could not teach. Marighella said, "The creation of an intelligence service, with an organized structure, is a basic need for us."[162] He offered no instructions on how to establish this intelligence capability or where to get training in establishing it.

According to Sun Tzu, in his celebrated study, *The Art of War*, an army without an intelligence wing marches blind. As a defensive measure, intelligence and counterintelligence had to be part of the structure of any organization that engaged in the work of the Panther underground. This was especially true in Detroit, where police declared war on the aboveground and the underground. In the parlance of the CIA, intelligence is the shield that accompanies the organization's sword. And, a principal goal of any intelligence operation is to infiltrate an agent into the enemy's office dedicated to preventing infiltration. Once an enemy intelligence service infiltrates an opponent's counterespionage or security office, it renders the entire enemy organization vulnerable to penetration. Thus, William O'Neal, who was working for the FBI while he was in charge of security and preventing infiltration of the Panthers' Illinois chapter, provided authorities with the map of the apartment in Chicago in which Hampton and Clark were slain by police. Likewise, Chuck Holt, the primary government infiltrator of the Detroit BPP, was in charge of its security. His misdirection was directly responsible for four core members going to prison for long stretches and may have assisted the police in killing two members of the Detroit Panther underground. Had the Panthers been as versed in the literature of spy craft as they were in third world liberation theories, they would have known that people like O'Neal and Holt, who seek the position of captain of security, should have been the first suspected. Moreover, had the Panthers studied the FBI and CIA, they would have known that the principal way to prevent infiltration or discover infiltrators is by in-depth background investigations and periodic lie detector tests.

Intelligence and counterintelligence are indispensable branches of warfare. The term "intelligence" denotes its value. The Panther aboveground and underground were "unintelligent" without the defensive shield of spy craft. The results, in Detroit and elsewhere, were catastrophic.

Conclusion

The rise of the underground wing conducting armed activism in the Black Panther Party marked an important moment in African American history. Youthful courage and black consciousness melded into a political program and ideology as armed black power challenged armed white power, with tangible and intangible benefits to black America. Fanon's psychological theories about the positive therapeutic affects of fighting back against tormenting oppressors proved true. But armed struggle as psychotherapy was a subjective phenomenon. It could not alone make activists invulnerable to the overt and covert counterattacks of the more skilled armed soldiers of the state.

Detroit's insurrection of 1967 bequeathed complicated political dynamics for those who established a Panther presence in that city. The Panthers' simplistic "off the pig" rhetoric did not meet the political challenge of the day. Youthful idealism and courageous dedication proved insufficient to the tasks of survival for a Panther underground. Without expertise in covert warfare, the Black Panthers' overt warfare headed for inevitable defeat from the start. They were, in fact, an army marching blind.

Notes

1 Winthrop D. Jordan, *The White Man's Burden: Historical Origins of Racism in the United States* (New York: Oxford University Press, 1974), 3–43.

2 Quotation, www.detnews.com/history/riot.htm. Also, Thomas Sugrue, *The Origins of the Urban Crisis: Race and Inequality in Post-War Detroit* (Princeton, N.J.: Princeton University Press, 1996); June Manning Thomas, *Redevelopment and Race: Planning a Finer City in Postwar Detroit* (Baltimore: Johns Hopkins University Press, 1997); Darlene Clark Hine, "Black Migration to the Urban Midwest: The Gender Dimension, 1915–1945" and Hine, "Black Women in the Middle West: The Michigan Experience," both in *Hine Sight: Black Women and the Re-Construction of American History* (Brooklyn: Carlton, 1994); Karen Tucker Anderson, "Last Hired, First Fired: Black Women Workers During World War II," *Journal of American History* 69 (June 1982): 82–97; Kevin Boyle, "The Kiss: Racial and Gender Conflict in a 1950s Automobile Factory," *Journal of American History* 84 (September 1997): 496–523; Megan Newbury Taylor Shockley, " 'We, Too, Are Americans': African-American Women, Citizenship, and Civil Rights Activism in Detroit and Richmond, 1940–1954" (Ph.D. diss., University of Arizona, 2000).

3 National Urban League, *Racial Conflict: A Home Front Danger; Lessons of the Detroit Riot* (New York: National Urban League, 1943); Robert Shogan, *The Detroit Race Riot: A Study in Violence* (Philadelphia: Chilton, 1964); George W. Beatty, "The Background and Causes of the 1943 Detroit Race Riot" (undergraduate thesis, Princeton University, 1954); Alfred McClung Lee and Nor-

man D. Humphrey, with new introductory essay by Alfred McClung Lee, *Detroit Riot, 1943* (ca. 1943; repr., New York: Octagon, 1968).

4 Reynolds Farley, Sheldon Danziger, and Harry J. Holzer, *Detroit Divided* (New York: Russell Sage, 2000), 36.

5 Robert Conot, *American Odyssey* (New York: Bantam Books, 1973), 497, cited in ibid.

6 Quotation, www.pbs.org/wgbh/amex/eleanor/peopleevents/pande10.html.

7 Sugrue, *The Origins of the Urban Crisis*, 244; Sidney Fine, *Violence in the Model City: The Cavanaugh Administration, Race Relations and the Detroit Riot of 1967* (Ann Arbor: University of Michigan Press, 1989), 4; *Report of the National Advisory Commission on Civil Disorders* (New York: Bantam Books, 1968), 89–90.

8 Fine, *Violence in the Model City*, 4.

9 Sheldon Joseph Lachman, *The Detroit Riot of July 1967: A Psychological, Social, and Economic Profile of 500 Arrestees* (Detroit: Behavior Research Institute, 1968); "Return to 12th Street: A Follow-Up Survey of Attitudes of Detroit Negroes," *Detroit Free Press*, October 7, 1968; Sheldon Danziger and Harry J. Holzer, *Detroit Divided* (New York: Russell Sage, 2000); Fine, *Violence in the Model City; Governor's Select Commission on Civil Disorders, Report for Action: An Investigation into the Causes and Events of the 1967 Newark Race Riots* (New York: Lemma, 1968, 1972); Max A. Herman, "Fighting in the Streets: Ethnic Succession and Urban Unrest in 20th Century America" (Ph.D. diss., University of Arizona, 1999); Hubert G. Locke, *The Detroit Riot of 1967* (Detroit: Wayne State University Press, 1969).

10 Edwards, quoted in Jerome H. Skolnick and James J. Fyfe, *Above the Law: Police and the Excessive Use of Force* (New York: Free Press, 1993), 77.

11 Such establishments were holdovers from the days of Prohibition, having survived by selling liquor after Detroit's legal clubs had to shut down at the city's mandated closing hour of 2:00 a.m.

12 John Hersey, with a new introduction by Thomas Sugrue, *The Algiers Motel Incident* (1968; repr., Baltimore: Johns Hopkins University Press, 1998).

13 Albert Bergson, "Official Violence During the Watts, Newark, and Detroit Race Riots of the 1960s," in *A Political Analysis of Deviance*, ed. Pat Lauderdale, 138–74 (Minneapolis: University of Minnesota Press, 1980).

14 John Hartigan Jr., *Racial Situations: Class Predicaments of Whiteness in Detroit* (Princeton, N.J.: Princeton University Press, 63).

15 *Report of the National Advisory Commission*, 107; also, Hartigan, *Racial Situations*, 63.

16 Robert Allen, *Black Awakening in Capitalist America* (Garden City, N.Y.: Doubleday, 1969).

17 *Eyes on the Prize II*, episode 3, "America at the Racial Crossroads," which contains Scott's eyewitness account of the deadly police attacks on Detroit's black citizens during the 1967 rebellion (Blackside Productions: PBS Video, 1990).

18 Louis Lomax, *When the Word Is Given: A Report on Elijah Muhammad, Malcolm X, and the Black Muslim World* (Cleveland: World, 1963); Albert B. Cleague, *Black Christian Nationalism* (New York: Morrow, 1972); Cleague, *The Black Messiah* (Trenton, N.J.: African World, 1989).

19 Dan Georgakas and Marvin Surkin, "Inner City Voice," in *Detroit: I Do Mind Dying; A Study in Urban Revolution* (1975; repr., Cambridge, Mass.: South End Press Classics, 1998), 13–22.

20 Robert Dewdrick, *Black Workers in Revolt: How Detroit's New Black Revolutionary Workers Are Changing the Face of American Trade Unionism* (New York: Guardian, 1969); Kuniko Fujita, *Black Workers' Struggles in Detroit's Auto Industry, 1935–1975* (Saratoga, N.Y.: Century Twenty One, 1980).

21 Ernie M. Mkalimoto, "Revolutionary Black Culture: The Cultural Arm of Revolutionary Nationalism," in *The Ideology of Blackness*, ed. Raymond F. Betts, 202–8 (Lexington, Mass.: D. C. Heath, 1971); Mkalimoto, *Revolutionary Black Nationalism and the Class Struggle* (Detroit: Black Star, 1970); Allen, *Black Awakening in Capitalist America.*

22 Interview, Scott, January 29, 2005. During the action in Sacramento in early May 1967—less than three months before the Detroit uprising—armed Panthers stormed the California state capitol building in protest of a gun control bill aimed directly at them; the event electrified black people all over the nation, including in Detroit.

23 On Mao, see Robin D. G. Kelley and Betsy Esch, "Black Like Mao: Red China and Black Revolution," *Souls* (fall 1999): 6–41. Stewart, despite his early interest in the Panthers, decided he wanted to go to college, and he put all of his time and energy into that. He later became active as "Brother Tariq" in the Shrine of the Black Madonna, where he functions today. Stewart and Gillis were in Oakland with a third man, George Sams, who would figure prominently, likely as a government agent, in the infamous murder of the Panther Alex Rackley in New Haven the following year. According to Scott, "Sams was overtly crazy." In Detroit, he was extremely erratic and played no role in helping to establish a new Panther organization there.

24 "Methods of Thinking and Methods of Work," in *Quotations from Chairman Mao Tse-tung* (Peking: Foreign Languages, 1967), 203–29.

25 Interview, Kathleen Cleaver, December 2004.

26 Bobby Seale, *Seize the Time: The Story of the Black Panther Party and Huey P. Newton* (New York: Vintage, 1970), 220.

27 Cover Story, "Huey Newton, the Story of a Black Man and the Gun," *Ramparts*, October 26, 1968.

28 Interview, Ron Scott, Detroit, November 5, 2004.

29 Interview, Scott, January 29, 2005.

30 Eldridge Cleaver, *Revolution in the White Mother Country and National Liberation in the Black Colony* (Oakland, Calif.: Black Panther Party for Self-Defense, 1969), a pamphlet version of the speech he delivered at the first convention of the Peace and Freedom Party (PFP) in Richmond, Calif., on March 16, 1968. Activists in California founded the PFP on June 27, 1967, their opposition to the Vietnam War represented by the "Peace" in the name of the organization, their opposition to the law-and-order campaign to suppress political dissent represented by "Freedom."

31 Newton explained his organization's alliance with the white activists of the PFP this way: "The Peace and Freedom Party has supported our program in full and this is the criterion for a coalition with the black revolutionary group. If they had not supported our program in full, then we would not have seen any reason to make an alliance with them, because we are the reality of the oppression. They are not. They are oppressed only in an abstract way; we are oppressed in the real way. . . . Many of the young white revolutionaries realize this and I see no reason not to have a coalition with them." Quoted in August Meier, Elliott Rudwick, and Francis L. Broderick, eds., *Black Protest Thought in the Twentieth Century* (New York: Macmillan, 1985), 502.

32 Mumia Abu-Jamal, "A Woman's Party" (chap. 7), in *We Want Freedom: A Life in the Black Panther Party* (Boston: South End, 2004), esp. 159; Tracye Matthews, " 'No One Ever Asks What a Man's Role in the Revolution Is': Gender and the Politics of the Black Panther Party, 1969–1971," in *The Black Panther Party [Reconsidered]*, ed. Charles E. Jones, 267 (Baltimore: Black Classic Press, 1998).

33 Interview, Scott, November 2004.

34 *The Black Panther*, May 4, 1968, 24.

35 Rod Bush, *We Are Not What We Seem: Black Nationalism and Class Struggle in the American Century* (New York: New York University Press, 1999), 207.

36 The numbers game was an illegal daily lottery popular in northern black communities. It was an intrinsic part of African American culture in many cities and was often viewed favorably because it was community controlled. In the 1970s and 1980s, legal state lotteries, along with police repression of numbers, led to the institution's demise.

37 Interview, Scott, August 2004.

38 Modibo M. Kadalie, *Internationalism, Pan-Africanism, and the Struggle of Social Classes* (Savannah: One Quest, 2000), 13, 203. Nationally, the Panthers sought fraternal relations with the RNA, although the two groups differed ideologically on black separatism. Huey Newton articulated the Panthers' position in "To the Republic of New Africa: September 13, 1969," in *To Die for the People: The Writings of Huey P. Newton* (New York: Vintage, 1972), 96–100, esp. 97–98.

In Detroit, though, the Panthers and the RNA worked together in public and on underground activities, mainly because area Panthers had known the RNA founders, who were local to the city, for years. An example of public collaboration, along with the League of Revolutionary Black Workers, which had been generated by RUM, is the National Black Economic Development Conference. James Forman, *The Making of Black Revolutionaries* (1972; repr., Seattle: Open Hand, 1985), 543–45. At the same time, underground activities by the Panthers were carried out jointly with the RNA's "Black Bazaar," so-called because it operated out of a store of that name which sold African artifacts. Most important, perhaps, Detroit police made little distinction between the groups, viewing all armed militant organizations in the city with the same trepidation and hatred.

39 Quoted in Alphonso Pinkney, *Red, Black, and Green: Black Nationalism in the United States* (New York: Cambridge University Press, 1976), 125.

40 Interview, Daniel Aldridge, Detroit, August 2004.

41 Robert Staples, *Black Masculinity: The Black Man's Role in American Society* (San Francisco: Black Scholar, 1982).

42 *Riots, Civil and Criminal Disorders*, Part 20 [microform]: Hearings before the United States Senate Committee on Government Operations, Permanent Subcommittee on Investigations, 91st Congress, 1st sess., June 26 and 30, 1969 (Washington, D.C.: U.S. Government Printing Office, 1969).

43 George Crockett, the judge of the Recorders Court and an African American activist, angered Detroit's white establishment when, the next morning, he released most of the arrestees on low bonds or on their own recognizance. *Detroit News* and *Detroit Free Press*, April 1 and 2, 1968.

44 Interview, Scott.

45 Charles R. Garry, "The Old Rules Do Not Apply: A Survey of the Persecution of the Black Panther Party," in *The Black Panthers Speak*, ed. Philip S. Foner, 257 (Philadelphia: Lippincott, 1970).

46 Interview, Scott.

47 Peter L. Zimroth, *Perversion of Justice: The Prosecution and Acquittal of the Panthers* (New York: Viking, 1974).

48 Quoted in Ward Churchill and Jim Vander Wall, *The COINTELPRO Papers, Documents from the FBI's Secret Wars Against Dissent in the United States* (Boston: South End, 1990), 145.

49 Interview, Scott.

50 Larry Powell, an early member of the Detroit Panthers, thought that Chuck Holt, who was later identified as a police informer, had assassinated Baynham. Scott, however, argues that Holt had not yet become active with the Panthers at the time Baynham was murdered. It is possible Holt had become active in the nascent Panther underground Baynham had been building separately and in secret. That is, Holt may have been involved, but Scott would have had no way of knowing it.

51 Seale's rationale for the new groups is in *The Black Panther*, August 30, 1969, 13. Newton theorized that the authorities would not attack branches of the NCCF as they had attacked the Panthers. At a meeting in Ann Arbor, Michigan, in December 1970, I remarked to him that the ruse had not worked. He expressed surprise and disappointment, explaining that he had hoped to replicate the Communist Party's tactic of employing "front" organizations that would not draw direct "heat" from a repressive state. I replied that we sold Black Panther newspapers, used all of the party's symbols, and had Panther survival programs. Thus, the Detroit police, seeing us walk and talk like ducks, reasoned we must be ducks. Newton appeared nonplussed and did not respond. His private secretary, Connie Matthews, then changed the subject to his preferences for dinner.

52 Interview, Geronimo Ji Jaga, November 2004.

53 For in-depth critiques of lumpen ideology, see Chris Booker, "Lumpenization: A Critical Error of the Black Panther Party," in Jones, *The Black Panther Party*, 337–62; Errol Henderson, "The Lumpenproletariat as Vanguard? The Black Panther Party, Social Transformation, and Pearson's Analysis of Huey Newton," *The Journal of Black Studies* 28, no. 2 (November 1997): 171–79.

54 Oliver Shows, Mark Bethune, John Percy Boyd, and Tommy Ross were four members of this Detroit underground. Shows, Bethune, and Boyd were killed by police in separate incidents in the line of duty. The circumstances of Ross's shooting death are unclear. For security reasons, there were no official, written membership rolls; belonging to the underground was based on personal relations, with cells of four to six Panthers operating autonomously. Thus, if the authorities compromised one cell, its members could not betray other cells even if broken under torture.

55 Luke Tripp, "D.R.U.M.—Vanguard of the Black Revolution, Dodge Revolutionary Union Movement States History, Purpose and Aims," in *The South End* (Detroit), 27, no. 62 (1969): 9.

56 Interview, Muhammad Ahmad (Max Stanford), Detroit, May 2004.

57 Clayborne Carson, *In Struggle: SNCC and the Black Awakening of the 1960s* (Cambridge, Mass.: Harvard University Press, 1981).

58 Heather Ann Thompson, *Whose Detroit? Politics, Labor and Race in a Modern American City* (Ithaca, N.Y.: Cornell University Press, 2001).

59 Quoted in *Tuebor*, November 29, 1968, 23.

60 Ibid., 26.

61 Interview, Eddie Irwin, Chicago, 2003. Seale, *Seize the Time*, 412, offered the national rationale for community programs; also, Newton " 'In Defense of Self-Defense' II: July 3, 1967," in his *To Die for the People*, 89.

62 Interview, Tony Norman, Detroit, December 2002.

63 Jeff Gottlieb and Jeff Cohen, "Was Fred Hampton Executed?" *Nation* 223 (December 25, 1976): 680–84; "A Collective Dedication: Ten Years after the Murder of Fred Hampton," *Keep Strong* (December 1979–January 1980): 41–

65. Hampton's voice: "Fred Hampton Speaks," in Foner, *The Black Panthers Speak*, 137. A chronology in late 1970 supports Norman's memory: "December 28, 1969, Members of NCCF piled sandbags in their headquarters at 2219 Indiandale against police attack they said was likely to come." W. H. Erickson, "Analysis," *Detroit News*, October 26, 1970, 16A.

64 Human Rights Watch, *Shielded from Justice: Police Brutality and Accountability in the United States* (New York: Human Rights Watch, 1998); Judson L. Jeffries, "Police Brutality of Black Men and the Destruction of the African American Community," *Negro Educational Review* 52 (October 2001): 115–31.

65 *Detroit News*, October 26, 1970, 16A.

66 Erickson, "Analysis."

67 On Holt, see n. 50.

68 The Panthers advocated the deaths of both Jones and Karenga in the apparent belief that they were still political collaborators. They did not know that their alliance ended in 1969. Amiri Baraka (né LeRoi Jones), *The Autobiography of Leroi Jones* (Chicago: Lawrence Hill, 1997), 389–94.

69 *Detroit News*, October 26, 1970. Karenga's failure to appear could not have been because the RNA refused him protection. Rather, he had failed to respond to the RNA's questions about his organization's responsibility for the murder of two Black Panthers, Alprentice "Bunchy" Carter and John Huggins, at the University of California, Los Angeles, on January 17, 1969. Less than three months later, on April 5, 1969, the RNA removed Karenga from his position as its minister of education. William Grattan, Republic of New Africa Minister of State and Foreign Affairs, "Republic of New Africa Denounces Ron Everett (Karenga)," *The Black Panther*, May 11, 1969, 7; Scot Brown, *Fighting for Us: Maulana Karenga, the US Organization, and Black Cultural Nationalism* (New York: New York University Press, 2003).

70 Quoted in Churchill and Vander Wall, *The COINTELPRO Papers*, 130.

71 *Detroit News*, October 26, 1970.

72 Interview, Norman, Detroit, December 2002.

73 "Three Members of Detroit N.C.C.F. and Mrs. Earlene McClure Brutally Beaten by Pigs," *The Black Panther*, July 25, 1970, 9.

74 Personal conversations with the author.

75 Cocaine was not a widely distributed drug in Detroit until years later.

76 Interview, Nzinga Mbote, Detroit, January 2002.

77 Quotations from Lawrence "Red" White are reconstructions of the author's conversations with him before he was stabbed to death in prison.

78 "Serving the People," in *Quotations of Mao Tse-tung* (Peking: Foreign Languages, 1971), 170; also, "On Practice," in *Selected Readings from the Works of Mao Tse-tung* (Peking: Foreign Languages, 1969), 65–85.

79 William W. Sales Jr., *From Civil Rights to Black Liberation: Malcolm X and the Organization of Afro-American Unity* (Boston: South End, 1994).

80 "Malcolm X Founds the Organization of Afro-American Unity," in Meier, Rudwick, and Broderick, *Black Protest Thought in the Twentieth Century*, 415.

81 Grace Lee Boggs, *Living for Change: An Autobiography* (Minneapolis: University of Minnesota Press, 1998); James Boggs, *Uprooting Racism and Racists in the United States* (Detroit: Radical Education Project, 1971); James Boggs, *The American Revolution: Pages from a Negro Worker's Notebook* (New York: Monthly Review, 1963); James Boggs, *Racism and the Class Struggle: Further Pages from a Black Worker's Notebook* (New York: Monthly Review, 1970).

82 George Breitman, ed., *Malcolm X Speaks* (New York: Grove, 1965), 3–17. Audio recordings of these speeches can be found at the Malcolm: What He Said Archive, http://www.brothermalcolm.net.

83 Julius Lester, *The Angry Children of Malcolm X* (Nashville: Southern Student Organizing Committee, 1966), 1–9.

84 *The Black Panther*, September 14, 1968, 5.

85 Frantz Fanon, *The Wretched of the Earth* (1961; repr., New York: Grove, 1969), 52, 54.

86 Ibid., 94. For an unsympathetic—indeed, counterrevolutionary—reading of Fanon, see W. W. Rostow, "Guerilla Warfare in Underdeveloped Areas," in *The Guerrilla and How to Fight Him*, ed. T. N. Greene, 65 (New York: Praeger, 1962).

87 Anonymous personal conversations with the author. Paul Adams, "The Social Psychiatry of Frantz Fanon," *American Journal of Psychiatry* 127, no. 6 (1970): 809–14.

88 B. Marie Perinbam, *Holy Violence: The Revolutionary Thought of Frantz Fanon—An Intellectual Biography* (Washington, D.C: Three Continents, 1982), analyzes Fanon's use of the term "violence" to convey seven different meanings. Perinbam criticizes him for writing about how violence creates a "new man" and detoxifies minds by eliminating inferiority complexes because Fanon cites the "impact without identifying the process or the power behind it" (8). See also, Hannah Arendt, *On Violence* (New York: Harcourt Brace, 1969), 70–75; Robert Blackey, "Fanon and Cabral: A Contrast in Theories of Revolution for Africa," *Journal of Modern African Studies* 12, no. 2 (1974): 191–209.

89 Interview, Irwin, Chicago, 2003.

90 Robert F. Williams, *Negroes with Guns* (1962; repr., Detroit: Wayne State University Press, 1998), 74; also, Timothy B. Tyson, *Radio Free Dixie: Robert F. Williams and Roots of Black Power* (Chapel Hill: University of North Carolina Press, 2001).

91 "NAACP Leader Urges Violence," *New York Times*, May 7, 1959, 22; "NAACP Unit Leader Fights His Suspension," ibid., May 8, 1959, 16; "NAACP Upholds Stand by Wilkins," ibid., May 12, 1959, 36.

92 Williams, *Negroes with Guns*, 75.

93 Ibid., 75, 76.

94 Huey P. Newton, *Revolutionary Suicide* (New York: Harcourt Brace, 1973), 189, 205.

95 Quotations from the author's conversations with Lawrence White in the 1970s.

96 *Seize the Time* (Vault Records, 1969).

97 W. E. B. Du Bois, *Black Reconstruction 1860–1880*, quoted in C. L. R. James, *The Future in the Present* (London: Ashby and Busby, 1980), 265; also, Mary Bucholtz, "You Da Man: Narrating the Racial Other in the Production of White Masculinity," *Journal of Sociolinguistics* 3, no. 4 (November 1999): 443.

98 Personal conversations with author.

99 The cowboy as a symbol of manliness was a recurrent metaphor used when male Panthers referred to gunplay. It transcends racial and class boundaries in the United States. Chris Blazina, *The Cultural Myth of Masculinity* (Westport, Conn.: Praeger, 2003).

100 Personal observations of the author.

101 "Psychological Armament," "The Psychological War," and "The Function of the Idea in Irregular Warfare," all in Friedrich August Freiherr von der Heydte, *Modern Irregular Warfare* (New York: New Benjamin Franklin House, 1986), 40–46.

102 In the incident in Ann Arbor, the officers may have been reluctant to engage in a confrontation so close to a university campus.

103 Numerous ex-Panthers have conveyed similar stories to the author.

104 "Huey Backs the Pigs Down," in Seale, *Seize the Time*, 107–16; Mario Peebles, screenplay author and director, *Panther* (London: Polygram Film International, 1995). Interview, Eddie Irwin, Chicago, 2003.

105 Ernesto Guevara, *Man and Socialism in Cuba*, trans. Margarita Zimmermann (Havana: Guairas, 1967).

106 Ernesto Guevara, *Guerilla Warfare* (Lincoln: University of Nebraska Press, 1998), 92.

107 First-person impressions on both aboveground and underground gender relations in the BPP are in Assata Shakur, *Assata: An Autobiography* (Westport, Conn.: Lawrence Hill Books, 1987).

108 Mao, *Quotations*, 257.

109 Safiya Bukhari-Alston, "On the Question of Sexism within the Black Panther Party." "In defining the work of the Party they [Panther leaders] looked to other struggles around the world and to Mao Tse-Tung's Red Book *Quotations of Chairman Mao* for direction. The Eight Points of Attention and the Three Main Rules of Discipline were lifted directly from this book. One of the Eight Points was Do Not Take Liberties With Women. This was a monumental step forward in addressing the issue of the treatment of women. The simple fact that the issue was placed in/on the books was a step forward. Now we had to make it a part of our everyday lives, the everyday lives of the lumpen who were the majority element of the Black Panther Party" (*Arm the Spirit*, March 9, 1995, http://www.hartford-hwp.com/archives/45a/014.html). Also, Regina Jennings, "Why I Joined the Party: An Africana Womanist Perspective," 257; and Angela D. LeBlanc-Ernest, "The Most Qualified Person to Handle the Job: Black Panther Women, 1966–1982," 305, both in Jones, *The Black Panther Party*.

110 At the time, the author was in charge of the Panthers' office in the eastside of Detroit and is the leader identified here.

111 Kathleen Cleaver relates a similar incident in Oakland in which the Panthers expelled a member whom a female Panther had accused of rape. In Cleaver's analysis, any abuse that women suffered in the party "was not something that arose from the policies or structure of the Black Panther Party . . . that's what was going on in the world. The difference that being in the Black Panther Party made was that it put a woman in a position when such treatment occurred to contest it." Kathleen Cleaver, "Women, Power, and Revolution," in *Liberation, Imagination, and the Black Panther Party: A New Look at the Panthers and Their Legacy*, ed. Cleaver and George Katsiaficas, 126 (New York: Routledge, 2001).

112 Samuel Greenlee, *The Spook Who Sat by the Door* (New York: Bantam, 1970), 22.

113 Stokely Carmichael, *Black Power and the Third World* (Nashville: Southern Student Organizing Committee, 1967), 1–10; Robert S. Brown, "The Freedom Movement and the War in Vietnam," *Freedomways* 5 (fall 1965): 467–80; Nat Hentoff, interview of Eldridge Cleaver, *Playboy* (December 1968): 89–108, 238.

114 Roland Snellings, "Vietnam: Whitey: I Will Not Serve," *Liberator*, March 9, 1966, 8–9; Lawrence P. Neal, "Black Power in the International Context," in *The Black Power Revolt*, ed. Floyd B. Barbour, 136–46 (Toronto: Collier-Macmillan, 1968).

115 The codified definition of Americanism that excluded and brutalized dissidents and people of color can be traced directly to the convening in 1938 of the Dies Committee by the House of Representatives to investigate un-American activities. Before that, the dominant culture's nativist and racist impositions of "Americanism" had been informal. The Dies Committee succeeded in formally labeling "American" the intellectual folkways and economic interests of the white majority. Citizens and organizations deemed outside this "norm" were criminalized, "un-American." Oliver Cox, *Caste, Class and Race: A Study in Social Dynamics* (New York: Modern Reader, 1970), 269–82.

116 "Paradox of the Black Soldier," *Ebony* (August 1968): 142; "The Returning Veteran," ibid., 145–51. Quotations from the author's conversations with Lawrence White in the 1970s.

117 In his New Year's statement of 1970, "To My Black Brothers in Viet Nam," Eldridge Cleaver wrote, "Organize all the Brothers around you and move. Force the pigs to understand that you will no longer be their slave and hired killer. Let

the pigs know that, instead, you want the persecution of your Black Brothers and sisters to stop, and that you intend help stop it." http://www.hippy.com/php/article-74.html.

118 See Herman Graham III, *The Brothers' Vietnam War: Black Power, Manhood, and the Military Experience* (Gainesville: University of Florida Press, 2003), which explores the black male bonding rituals that preserved the sense of dignity and nationalism of black soldiers during repeated crises in Vietnam. It also elucidates the crisis in black manhood there when Muhammad Ali denounced the war and refused induction into the military, stating, "I won't wear the uniform." See also, "Muhammad Ali: The Measure of a Man," *Freedomways* 2 (1967), in *Freedomways Reader: Prophets in Their Own Country*, ed. Constance Pohl and Esther Cooper Jackson, 176–78 (Boulder, Colo.: Westview, 2000).

119 From the author's conversations with Lawrence White in the 1970s.

120 The battles Panthers fought are more accurately described by the term "asymmetrical warfare."

121 Carlos Marighella, *Minimanual of the Urban Guerrilla*, 1.

122 Ibid., 14.

123 Carl Von Clausewitz, *On War* (New York: Random House, 1943), 54. Here, the great German military strategist described unexpected difficulties that arise in war as an "enormous friction . . . [that] is everywhere brought into contact with chance, and thus produces incidents quite impossible to foresee, just because it is to chance that to a great extent they belong." Story from author's conversations with Lawrence White in the 1970s.

124 Marighella, *Minimanual*, 3, 10.

125 In other cities, Panthers concentrated on robbing banks and businesses identified with American capitalism. In both cases, there are echoes of a very long history, chronicled by Eric Hobsbawm and others, of social banditry. Eric Hobsbawm, *Bandits* (New York: Pantheon, 1969), 42–43; Paul Chevigny, *Cops and Rebels* (New York: Irvington, 1972); James Green, *Grass-Roots Socialism: Radical Movements in the Southwest, 1895–1943* (Baton Rouge: Louisiana State University Press, 1978); Kent L. Steckmesser, "Robin Hood and the American Outlaw," *Journal of American Folklore* 79 (April–June 1966): 348–55.

126 During the 1960s and 1970s, the view of federal involvement in drug-dealing constituted a suspicion unsupported by evidence. "Conspiracy Theories Often Ring True: History Feeds Black Mistrust," *Washington Post*, October 4, 1991, A-1.

127 Earl Anthony, *Spitting in the Wind: The True Story Behind the Violent Legacy of the Black Panther Party* (Malibu, Calif.: Roundtable, 1990); Gary Webb, *Dark Alliance: The CIA, the Contras, and the Crack Cocaine Explosion* (New York: Seven Stories, 1998).

128 Personal observations by the author.

129 Interview, Norman, Detroit, December 2002.

130 *Detroit News*, Oct. 26, 1970, 1.

131 When I transported the membership lists, with photos, to a meeting of the West Coast Central Staff in New York in August 1970, the total was fifty-five. Community workers, whose numbers were constantly fluctuating in this period, were neither counted nor recorded in any way. However, they were always greater than the number of members, typically by a factor of two or three. As for the number of underground "self-defense" cells, which typically operated without knowledge of each other, the total is unknown. The author is aware of at least four in Detroit, having been pulled from one to fill a vacancy in another three times. There were rumors of an all-female cell, which cannot be confirmed, though there was at least one group that contained women as well as men.

132 Rodger Streightmatter, "Black Panther Newspaper: A Militant Voice, a Salient Vision," in *The Black Press: New Literary and Historical Essays*, ed. Todd Vogel (New Brunswick, N.J.: Rutgers University Press, 2001), 228–43. On circulation of the Panthers' paper, see Memo from FBI Headquarters, Washington, D. C., to Seven Field Offices, May 15, 1970. See, too, U.S. House of Representatives, Committee on Internal Security, *The Black Panther Party, Its Origin and Development as Reflected in Its Official Weekly Newspaper, The Black Panther, Black Community News Service*, 91st Congress, 2nd sess. (Washington, D.C.: U.S. Government Printing Office, 1970).

133 For the definition, see early issues of *The Black Panther*, May 1967. For the Maoist tenet, "Concerning Methods of Leadership," see *Selected Readings from the Works of Mao Tse-tung*: "In all the practical work of our Party, all correct leadership is necessarily 'from the masses to the masses.' This means, take the ideas of the masses (scattered and unsystematic ideas) and concentrate them (through study turn them into concentrated and systematic ideas), then go to the masses and propagate and explain these ideas until the masses embrace them as their own, hold fast to them and translate them into action, and test the correctness of these ideas in such action" (290).

134 During this period, the police arrested me for selling papers, handcuffed me, put me in their patrol car, and beat me on my knees with a blackjack. With each blow they shouted, "Here's some more power to the people!" The officers later testified that I had assaulted them. Judge John Murphy convicted me of misdemeanor assault and battery, though my face was bruised and a patch had been cut out of my afro to treat the knot on my head from a blow by a nightstick. Neither police officer had a scratch on him. The uproar in the courtroom following Murphy's pronouncement of my guilt obviously affected the judge. He sentenced me to ten days in jail, with credit for eight already served.

135 Ernest Goodman Collection, Box 18, Folder 18, Walter P. Reuther Library of Labor and Urban Affairs, Wayne State University, Detroit (hereafter, Goodman Collection).

136 Ibid.

137 *Detroit News*, October 27, 1970.

138 Churchill and Vander Wall, *The COINTELPRO Papers*, 212; also, U.S. Senate, 94th Congress, 2nd sess., "Efforts to Promote Criticism of the Black Panthers in the Mass Media and to Prevent the Black Panther Party and Its Sympathizers from Expressing Their Views," in *Final Report of the Senate Select Committee to Study Governmental Operations with Respect to Intelligence Activities*, Book III (Washington, D.C.: U.S. Government Printing Office, 1976), 22.

139 Interview, Ben Fondren, 2004.

140 *Tuebor*, October 1970, 41.

141 Ibid., 42.

142 Ibid., 29.

143 Official Detroit Police Department Incident Report of Patrolman Frank Randazzo, Goodman Collection, Box 12, Folder 10.

144 Patrolman Patrick H. Murray, Goodman Collection, Box 12, Folder 10.

145 *Detroit News*, October 25, 1970, 6A.

146 Interview (name withheld at request).

147 Patrolman Carl Parsell, *Tuebor*, November 1970, 2.

148 Interview, anonymous, August 2004.

149 Interview, Beverly Ann Fleming, November 2004.

150 McKennon, an African American, had himself been a victim of police brutality during the 1967 rebellion. His recollections were conveyed to me during a chance meeting at the Detroit Metro Airport in 1999.

151 Anonymous interviews.

152 Interview, anonymous; "Source of Dynamite in Panther Home Sought," *Detroit News*, October 27, 1970, 13A.

153 Author's conversations with Michael Dee, 1971.

154 Before his release from prison, Benjamin Fondren was visited by two FBI agents who attempted to recruit him as an informant. When he refused, the agents told him he had "a choice between being a live coward and a dead hero." Interview, Fondren, 2004.

155 "The FBI's Covert Action Program to Destroy the Black Panther Party," in U.S. Senate, *Supplementary Detailed Staff Reports on Intelligence Activities and the Rights of Americans, Book II: Final Report of the Select Committee to Study Governmental Operations with Respect to Intelligence Activities*, April 23, 1976, 16.

156 Herb Boyd, *The Black Panthers for Beginners* (New York: Writers and Readers, 1995), 42.

157 "The Effort to Disrupt the Black Panther Party by Promoting Internal Dissension," *Supplemental Detailed Staff Reports on Intelligence Activities*, 10–17.

158 "Transforming Leadership," in James MacGregor Burns, *Leadership* (New York: Harper and Row, 1979), 141–254.

159 Ollie Johnson, "Explaining the Demise of the Black Panther Party: The Role of Internal Factors," in Jones, *The Black Panther Party*, 391.

160 Marighella, *Minimanual*, 16.

161 Ibid., 18.

162 Ibid.

5

"Give Them a Cause to Die For"

THE BLACK PANTHER PARTY IN

MILWAUKEE, 1969–77

In 1990, after a series of particularly contentious meetings of the City Council about social services for African Americans, Alderman Michael McGee of Milwaukee made national headlines by announcing his intention to establish a group he called the Black Panther Militia.[1] Citing the city's failure to address the issues of crime, housing, employment, and police brutality, McGee threatened to unleash his new organization unless white legislators stopped squandering resources on skyscrapers and shopping malls. Pressed for details, he claimed he would enlist street gangs in the militia to participate in "actual fighting, bloodshed and urban guerrilla warfare." "They can fight and they already know how to shoot," he told reporters. "I'm going to give them a cause to die for."[2]

The rhetoric surprised few in Milwaukee. A former member of the Black Panther Party (BPP) who joined the City Council in 1984, McGee had already threatened to disrupt the city's annual summer festival "and other white people's fun" unless officials did more to reduce black joblessness.[3] Resulting in only peaceful demonstrations, that episode in 1987—and McGee—had left an indelible imprint on the community. Now, in 1990, he seemed ready to make good on his threats, holding a public recruitment meeting for his Black Panther Militia at a local school while dressed in black fatigues—"reminiscent of the original Panthers," in the words of one source.[4] Significantly, though, McGee told the crowd of approximately three hundred that he was "not advocating what the Black Panthers were advocating." Renouncing the original party's posture of *self-defense* and eschewing its emphasis on community programs, he proclaimed, "Our militia will be about violence."[5]

McGee's depiction of the Panthers here—largely accurate regarding their history locally—ran counter to their popular image while implicitly distinguishing the BPP from Milwaukee's black radical tradition. In the mid-1960s, most notably, the city became something of a poster child for northern black militancy when a white Catholic priest and an armed band of youth from the NAACP made national headlines by "picking up the gun." Such actions appealed to black residents who were tired of the ceaseless brutality of local police. However, even as the Detroit Panthers were nurturing a revolutionary underground in that city, the Milwaukee Panthers were sustained by community service, demonstrating once again the importance of local circumstances in Panther history.

Milwaukee The Civil Rights Movement in
the Heartland, 1958–67

Chartered in 1846, the territory that became Milwaukee arose from a scattered collection of settlements once occupied by Native Americans and French traders. Throughout most of its history, the African American population remained relatively small; the census of 1900, for instance, located only 862 blacks, or 0.3 percent of the total population. As in other places increased black migration to the city during and after the Second World War substantially swelled the number of black residents so that by the 1960s blacks accounted for 15 percent of the total population. But, if blacks hoped to find a better alternative to southern apartheid they found little comfort in Milwaukee. The majority were forced to live in the segregated near north neighborhood known as the Inner Core. Here, they faced the same limited social, political, and economic opportunities for advancement as elsewhere. And, like hundreds of such communities across the country in the late 1950s and early 1960s, black Milwaukee began hacking at the roots of this inequality.[6]

One turning point came in early 1958. On the evening of February 2, police shot and killed a twenty-two-year-old African American male named Daniel Bell as he fled the scene of a routine traffic stop, putatively over a missing taillight. Bell, police claimed, taunted them during the pursuit, purportedly identifying himself as a "hold-up" man while refusing to heed their warning shots. Commandeering a ride from a passing motorist, the officers caught up with Bell a few blocks away when he allegedly pulled a knife on Patrolman Thomas Grady. Grady fired one shot, which penetrated Bell's upper back, instantly killing the young man. Within hours, police ruled the shooting justified and produced a weapon—a large knife—while also pointing to Bell's arrest record, five previous citations and one arrest for motor vehicle violations, as proof of his criminal character. Over the next several days, however, the official story of what took place on the icy streets that evening began to unravel as key pieces of evidence failed to match the police version of the shooting. One of the most glaring was the discovery that Bell, who allegedly menaced the offices with a knife in his right hand, was left-handed. Furthermore, investigators determined, Bell had been shot at near point-blank range. These two facts, along with other inconsistencies in the officers' story, eventually led to the commission of a blue-ribbon panel to investigate the shooting. When that panel cleared the officers, an outpouring of protest from the black community forced a second investigation. In their efforts to secure that new investigation, various individuals and groups began discussing other issues, and a struggle was born. As the most recent historian of that struggle puts it, "The gunshot that killed Daniel Bell was the signal shot for the Movement in Milwaukee."[7] But, concerted, sustained activity across a wide front would not come until the early 1960s.

Then, the preeminent civil rights group in Milwaukee was the NAACP. Founded in 1919 with eighty members, by the 1950s the local branch had grown significantly, but its philosophy of combating discrimination through peaceful protest had not. In 1962, a lawyer from Tennessee named Lloyd Barbee arrived and eventually took over the reins of leadership. A tireless civil rights campaigner, Barbee nevertheless preferred negotiation to the direct action protest that was increasingly becoming the model of the 1960s. Following that latter path was a new local chapter of the Congress of Racial Equality (CORE). There were rumblings as well in the Youth Council (YC) of the NAACP. Constituted in 1947 to accommodate the NAACP's growing teen and young adult membership, by the early 1960s the Milwaukee YC was struggling against the NAACP's relative conservatism. A seemingly minor incident in the summer of 1963 provided the catalyst for increasing independence from the parent organization.[8]

On July 26, the local press reported the comments of Fred E. Lins, a member of the Mayor's Community Social Development Commission, who freely shared his thoughts on the city's black population. On crime, he purportedly remarked, "The Negroes look so much alike that you can't identify the ones that commit the crime." He also allegedly said, "An awful mess of them have an IQ of nothing." With the shooting of Daniel Bell five years earlier still fresh in the black community's mind, Lins's comments set off a firestorm of controversy, including calls for his dismissal. These fell on the deaf ears of Mayor Henry W. Maier. Born in Dayton, Ohio, in 1918, Maier had attended the University of Wisconsin before settling down in Milwaukee. Like most big-city mayors in the postwar urban north, he had worked his way up through the Democratic machine to capture the mayor's office.[9] He also proved generally insensitive to the plight of African Americans. Decisive action in censuring Lins might have quelled some of the ill will building in the city; Maier chose to support him, observing that Lins's remarks might have been taken out of context. Outraged by the mayor's position, the local CORE warned him, "Perhaps you underestimate the suspicion and resentment with which the whole commission will be tainted if Lins remains."[10] Maier, who ultimately served a record eighteen years in office, had not been mayor when Daniel Bell was killed in 1958. Elected the following year, though, he would inherit a city on the brink of chaos, partly of his own making. His comments were enough to reignite the tensions percolating just beneath the surface since the failed investigation into the shooting of Bell.

In response to the mayor's intransigence, CORE began a series of demonstrations that sparked a massive protest campaign—including sit-ins, which CORE had pioneered in the late 1940s, and which had produced the Student Nonviolent Coordinating Committee (SNCC) in 1960, essentially launching "the 1960s." The campaign deliberately sought to incorporate the entire range of concerns black Milwaukeeans had accumulated from years of neglect. After several CORE members were fined for their participation in demonstrations against the mayor in November 1963, Bob Heiss, a local white radio personality, observed, "The jury verdict of guilty in the first sit[-]in case . . . should cause second thoughts among Negro organization leaders who advocate this method of demonstrating for racial equality."[11] Perhaps he was thinking of other groups vying for support in the black community that fall. One, We-Milwaukeeans, a voluntary association composed of prominent African American and white civic leaders, was a consensus-seeking body that focused on finding solutions to unemployment, housing, and education through moderate means. But if Heiss thought the future of the struggle in Milwaukee belonged to the moderates, he was wrong. Even as CORE protestors were preparing to appeal, the local NAACP branch threatened sit-ins and marches if the school board did not take immediate action on school desegregation.[12]

Out of this struggle emerged an unlikely champion for black civil rights, the Roman Catholic priest James Edmund Groppi. One of the best-known and most controversial figures in the history of civil rights in Milwaukee, Groppi was born there in 1930. In 1963, the thirty-three-year-old priest was assigned to St. Boniface Parish, a predominately black parish in the inner city. The appointment was fortuitous. His youth, and his enthusiasm for the civil rights movement, helped him connect with the youth of the community. Initially, his attention focused on the southern civil rights struggle. He participated in several high-profile marches, including the March on Washington of 1963 and the Selma Campaign of 1965, the latter of which inspired him to become active in the local movement in Milwaukee. Soon, he became a regular on the local civil rights scene, earning the respect and admiration of many in the YC because of his stalwart activism. After he had been arrested twice for demonstrating in 1965, the group asked him to serve as their advisor. While the selection of a white priest instead of a black minister was curious to some, many in the YC saw Groppi as the answer to the group's restlessness with the staid tactics of the more conservative NAACP leadership.[13] Meanwhile, he challenged the YC in a myriad of ways to channel its energy into protesting second-class citizenship wherever it manifested itself. In 1965, that was predominately in the areas of education and housing.[14]

By the time Groppi turned his attention to Milwaukee, violence was an increasingly common response of local authorities to the rising tide of demonstrations in the city. Then, on the morning of August 9, 1966, someone bombed Freedom House, the local office of the NAACP, in the latest in a series of attacks targeting prominent civil rights advocates and leftists. While authorities blamed the explosion on the local Ku Klux Klan, others blamed the climate in the city as a whole. Even after Mayor Maier issued a strong statement condemning the violence, Father Groppi shared the concerns of many in the YC that public pronouncements were not enough. Shortly, the front page of a local newspaper featured a photograph of a member of the YC standing guard in front of Freedom House.

This new posture increased already sensitive relations between the YC and local police. For years, demonstrators had been complaining of rough treatment; now, they reported, among other things, police surveillance and harassment. Seemingly confronted with violence on all sides, in October, the same month the Black Panther Party for Self-Defense was established in Oakland, Father Groppi called a special meeting of the YC. Out of that gathering, the Commandoes were born. Formed, at least initially, as a defensive unit to help protect marchers (as well as Father Groppi) and prevent anti-black violence during demonstrations by the NAACP, the Commandoes raised the banner of armed self-defense in Milwaukee in an open and public way for the first time.[15] The idea itself was not new. At its fifty-fourth annual convention in July 1962, the NAACP made what one source described as a "dramatic move to accelerate integration" when it passed a resolution authorizing local chapters to form units called "Commandoes." The groups were to be composed of "college age youth, attorneys, teachers, clergymen and other persons" deployed as civil rights strike teams, which "could be sent into any area to lead local demonstrations such as sit-ins, economic boycotts and other action protests."[16] What Groppi and the YC proposed in 1966, though, was far more radical and threatening precisely because they were tinkering with the components of the entire movement's underlying philosophy. They claimed, for instance, that they were "not violent," rather than advocates of nonviolence. Moreover, they dressed in fatigues and berets. Although the uniform proved temporary, it helped to fix the image of the Milwaukee YC in the public mind as a violent, militant organization.[17]

The Commandoes' self-defense posture was consonant with national trends. Between 1965 and 1968, perhaps hundreds of local groups—east and west, north and south—adopted militant defensive postures, giving rise to their identification as "black power" organizations. Stokely Carmichael's use of the slogan in the summer of 1966 during the so-called March against Fear gave the media a convenient label for such militancy, even though many of these groups had been in existence, in some cases, more than two years before.[18] Indeed, these groups' angry rhetoric and paramilitary posturing, tailor-made for the television age, obscured the fact that black armed self-defense against white violence and governmental intransigence had a long history in the United States. Moreover, the Milwaukee Commandoes remind us that the Black Panthers, but for the publicity generated by their high-profile run-ins with police, and their ready-made Party Platform, including rules and party newspaper, might have remained but one among many similar groups operating throughout the country in the mid-1960s. Finally, the race of their leader and the presence of whites in their ranks challenge the media's depiction of the Commandoes as a black power group.

By 1967, the emergence of that movement, along with the injection of millions of dollars of urban renewal money, set fire to a movement in Milwaukee nearly a decade in the making. At least in the press, Groppi remained a central figure in that struggle, as did Mayor Henry Maier. Like other big-city mayors, Maier attempted to stave off violence by funneling money to community programs in the black community. Despite his efforts, though, in July the city joined the ranks of other urban areas when it experienced an outbreak of rioting. The disturbance, which lasted two days, was tame by comparison, but it raised the stakes for both protestors and police. Many publicly worried that calls for armed self-defense were morphing into strategic *offensive* violence aimed at crippling the nation. The Commandoes, who sold buttons with the slogan, "burn, baby, burn," emblazoned on the front, stoked these concerns. If their rhetoric had grown more extreme, though, the Commandoes remained firmly committed to a more traditional view of self-defense. August would again test that commitment.[19]

On August 28 and 29, two marches across the 16th Street Viaduct—long considered the dividing line between black and white Milwaukee—triggered a series of small riots on the South Side, resulting in dozens of injuries and arrests. As a result, the mayor issued a proclamation forbidding nighttime demonstrations in the city. The decree came too late to prevent violence. After the August 29 march, an arsonist set fire to Freedom House, rendering it uninhabitable. On August 30, Father Groppi and Alderman Vel Phillips held a rally at the burned-out Freedom House. When police arrived, they arrested 137 people and injured others. The following night, another clash took place at St. Boniface Parish, resulting in still more arrests and injuries. As usual, claims of police brutality peppered complaints to the mayor. In September, Roy Wilkins, the head of the NAACP, sent Maier a telegram to register his concern over "the excessive force used by the Milwaukee police" in subduing the marchers.[20] More significant, though, was the internal struggle over armed self-defense in Milwaukee's black freedom movement. The lightening rod was Father Groppi.

By the fall of 1967, Groppi remained the recognized leader—by the local media, at least—of the "Negro Movement" in the city. Now, he faced a challenge from within, though it came before a national audience and in the form of two outsiders: Marion Barry, a former chairman of SNCC and an activist in Washington, D.C., and Rufus (Catfish) Mayfield, a twenty-year-old youth organizer in Washington. Mayfield, who ran a publicly funded community outreach outfit called Pride Incorporated, under Barry's United Planning Organization (Washington's anti-poverty program), had recently received a two-million-dollar grant from the federal government to establish a jobs training project. He had garnered the public support of Vice President Hubert Humphrey, who praised Pride Incorporated, in the words of the columnist Drew Pearson, for its "valiant" work in "cleaning up Washington, D.C. slums, killing rats, removing rubbish and showing pride in the Negro community."[21] Now, in September 1967, at a conference on the church and urban tensions sponsored by the Department of Social Justice of the National Council of Churches in the nation's capital, Mayfield blindsided Groppi. During a session at the Nash Memorial Methodist Church, the young organizer reminded those in attendance that "Father Groppi's done a wonderful job in Milwaukee but [a] . . . Negro should be leading. Father Groppi should be pushing and putting Negroes into the role of leadership." Castigating those Commandoes who chose to remain with Groppi, Mayfield proclaimed, "It's the same old case of the white power structure using the Negroes. After they're through with Negroes then they throw us back." Caught off guard by the attack, the Commandoes at the meeting fired back that Groppi was "only an adviser." As the Commando Raymond Blathers put it, "The commandoes decide what we're going to do."[22] Only half-convinced, Mayfield continued the debate with Blathers while Barry met privately with Groppi in a back room of the church. The priest declined to comment on the meeting, but Mayfield and Barry told reporters that he had agreed to restrict his role. The two even claimed that Groppi had acquiesced to their demand that he not participate in a march in favor of open housing to be held later that evening near the Lincoln Memorial. He showed, anyway.

Far from restricting his civil rights activity over the next few months, Groppi continued marching; by March 1968 he had led nearly two hundred demonstrations in support of fair housing, the centerpiece of the YC's agenda. Still sounding like a proponent of black power, Groppi made headlines in December after he dismissed the Common Council's proposal for a fair housing ordinance that he deemed "crumbs from the white man's table." In late April, the city finally passed an open housing ordinance. However, the assassination of Martin Luther King and the failure of the Poor People's Campaign that spring signaled a winding down of the movement, both nationally and in Milwaukee. There had been considerable change in certain key areas—housing and education, for example—but less tangible and easily identifiable areas of concern such as hunger and health care remained a problem. Most important, though, police brutality, the issue that had catalyzed the Milwaukee movement in the first place, remained perhaps the most pressing issue of the day.

With legislation to deal with matters of inequality, the need for widespread demonstrations eased. Groppi acknowledged as much when, on his thirty-eighth birthday in November 1968, he resigned from the Youth Council to "devote more time to militant social action involvement within the St. Boniface parish."[23] Groppi was not dropping out as much as moving in a different direction. He had come to see that rights on paper did not necessarily translate into equal opportunity for people without economic means. He now sought to ground his work more deeply in the community. Lamenting the inability of the "parish structure" to "reach people," in August 1969 Groppi hired six young men, all from the community and all with criminal records, and employed them as community workers in his newly opened parish, which he ran out of a dilapidated house in the heart of Milwaukee's Inner Core. "We are trying to reach people in the community," Groppi explained, particularly "street people stumbling on skid row, and those ostracized from society, addicted to dope and drugs."[24] In moving in this direction, already in the spring of 1969, he had the example of a new defense-minded organization in front of him, the Black Panther Party.

Panthers in the Heartland

The Milwaukee Panthers defy easy characterization. They tapped several ideological traditions deeply entrenched in the black community. Before founding the party, for example, founders Huey Newton and Bobby Seale had links with Max Stanford's Revolutionary Action Movement, which wedded the philosophy of Malcolm X to calls for armed self-defense by Robert F. Williams, the former leader of the NAACP, in Monroe, North

Carolina. At the same time, as the Milwaukee activists divided over what ideology to pursue, by the close of 1968 the Panthers had undergone an internal transformation that put them at odds with the larger black power movement. The Revolutionary Action Movement, which had always been critical of the Panthers' highly visible media posturing, now questioned the party's putative decision to "put down the gun" and concentrate on community projects such as the Breakfast for School Children program. Meanwhile, the Panthers' election-year alliance with the predominately white Peace and Freedom Party invited criticism from other black power advocates such as Ron Karenga of the US Organization and Stokely Carmichael, the former chairman of SNCC turned black power advocate. By the time the party emerged locally in early 1969, its emphasis on what it now called "survival programs" and its willingness to ally with white radicals helped move it closer, in theory at least, to the model already established by Father Groppi and the Commandoes. But there was a critical difference: while the BPP accepted white allies and supporters, it rejected white leadership, considering the party the American vanguard of a world revolutionary movement led by people of color. There were other differences as well that put the Milwaukee Panthers squarely in the camp of black power. As Peniel Joseph has observed, black power was a movement "cynical about American democracy's willingness to defend black citizenship." But it was also political and intellectual. In Joseph's words, it "stress[ed] racial pride, the connection between civil rights in the United States and the third world, and political self-determination through bruising and at times deliberatively provocative protests."[25] If the Commandoes demonstrated a brand of northern militancy in its clearest expression, the Panthers who followed them would illustrate the black power model not only in their defense of self-defense but in the social and economic programs they pursued as a means of serving the black community.

Along with their survival programs and their belief in self-defense, the Panthers' emphasis on revolutionary struggle made them an attractive alternative to some who rejected the ideas of nonviolence pushed by the mainstream civil rights movement and even the "not violent" YC. Indeed, ex-military men (Vietnam veterans Ronald Starks, Donald Young, and Booker Collins) founded the party in Milwaukee. Moreover, some of their recruits recall the powerful pull of the Panthers' militancy. Born on the anniversary of the Boston Massacre, March 5, 1946, Hubert Canfield saw himself as the reincarnation of Crispus Attucks. Active in electoral politics at a young age, "handing out fliers and stuff," he helped elect Milwaukee's first black state representative, Isaac Cobb. By the time the civil rights movement came to Milwaukee, however, Canfield was more interested in "pimping and playing." "I know a lot of brothers and sisters who were involved at that time," he explained, "but I was into a whole different thing." Shortly after his twenty-first birthday in 1967, though, Canfield experienced a political reawakening after reading Malcolm X's autobiography. "I was opposed to nonviolence, because I figured if somebody hit me I was going to hit them back," he says now. Thus, when "the Black Panther Party came with their concepts, I supported that also," especially "after reading Malcolm in 67 . . . I always supported his philosophy."[26] He became a Panther in April 1969. Others echo Canfield's reasons for joining. Kenny Williamson, who saw the BPP's program as the next logical step in the movement's progression, remembers, "You had a couple of things going on here. You had disfranchised young black people who really gravitated toward that part of the platform of the Panther Party that said we had a right to defend ourselves." There was "nothing too terribly radical about that actually, and the Panther Party nationally and internationally picked that up from the Deacons of Defense, which predated us, and Malcolm X, who called for us to only be nonviolent with those who were nonviolent with us, and Huey Newton and Bobby Seale in continuing in that vein along with community control of community institutions and the adoption of some kind of cooperative economic endeavors took it to the next level."[27]

Williamson's and Canfield's awareness of these larger trends illustrate the intellectual components of black power. Canfield's youthful campaigning on the part of a black candidate for the mayor's office underscored his skepticism about the ability of whites in power to solve the problems of the African American community. Thus Canfield's rejection of Groppi and the YC was an extension of his view that whites in power were naturally inclined to see blacks as little more than children in need of their guidance and protection. For the men and women who formed the Milwaukee Panthers that responsibility would be taken over by black men and women.

Despite a program that pushed *community* control of community institutions, the local party's reception in the community was mixed, in some measure because of its military aura. As Canfield remembered, "Some people were accepting of it, and some people were frightened of it." Despite Milwaukee's tradition of armed self-defense and the rise of black power in the city, guns could get in the way. In the summer of 1969, for example, the Panthers contacted a local minister, the Reverend Joseph Ellwanger, in hopes that the Lutheran clergyman would allow them to use his church for their Breakfast for School Children program. The initial meeting, which was cordial, soon degenerated into a war of words; the result demonstrated both the value and liability of the Panthers. Enamored of the idea of a breakfast program, if not of its originators, Ellwanger denied the Panthers' request and then started his own version in Milwaukee's public schools under a new organization called the Citizens for Central City School Breakfast Program. Ultimately morphing into the Hunger Task Force of Milwaukee, the program eventually won support for government-subsidized free breakfast in the city's school system. Significantly, in the short term, Ellwanger and his associates faced many of the same difficulties the Panthers had faced while trying to secure resources and funding for the program. For the first couple of years, Ellwanger recalled, "The only alternate was this basic plan the Black Panthers were following, and which we followed in a couple of instances, namely, to have the breakfast program at a site other than the school, and to get as much community support and contributions as possible." While fully acknowledging that he had taken the idea from the Panthers, then, Ellwanger nevertheless excluded them from participating. For "the board was concerned that the BPP" might push "its ideology" along with serving breakfast.[28] The Panthers responded in the pages of their national newspaper, *The Black Panther*. Referring to Ellwanger as a "punk, racist, fascist, pig preacher," they accused the minister of pandering to the press by telling the media his church would not be used by "anyone advocating the violent overthrow of the capitalistic, racist, imperialistic, fascist country."[29] Name calling aside, the Panthers were at least partly responsible for helping to establish the later citywide program through the force of their ideas and their willingness to share them. While they were easy to dismiss ideologically, few could doubt the strength of many of their other social programs, which sought to tackle complex social problems in new ways. With the breakdown of the black family a subject of public discussion, for instance, the Panthers created a free prison busing program, allowing families to maintain contact over a distance of forty miles from the city.

More problematic was the Panthers' relationship with the Milwaukee police. Like the Commandoes, the BPP targeted police brutality, employing a confrontational approach. But, the party had a *national* reputation, and police moved swiftly to an aggressive arrest and harassment campaign to drive the group out of the city. The police were assisted by federal law enforcement agencies that had already identified the BPP as an unlawful menace. Only a few months before the chapter's emergence, in the fall of 1968, Director J. Edgar Hoover of the FBI declared the Panthers, "The number one threat to the nation's internal security."[30] Their arrival in Milwaukee also coincided with the first wave of congressional investigations into the party in its various manifestations throughout the country. In opening the hearings on the Des Moines and Kansas City chapters, Richardson Preyer, the chairman of the congressional commission, laid out the government's chief interest in the Black Panthers. "During the 10-year period, 1960–1969," he observed, "there were 561 law enforcement officers feloniously murdered while protecting life and property." "In 1969, the last year for which complete statistics are available," he emphasized with some alarm, "there were 35,202 assaults on police officers, 11,949 resulting in injury. Eighty-six police officers, a 34-percent increase over 1968, were killed." While noting that "no complete statistics" were available for 1970, the commission nonetheless concluded that "the trend, if anything, would appear to be increasing." "New accounts have alleged that certain of these killings and assaults have resulted from Panther activities. Statements by Panther leaders and remarks in their newspaper would seem to leave little doubt that the Panthers attempt to encourage physical attacks on police."[31] Moreover, during his testimony before the house Appropriations Committee in 1970, Hoover estimated the Panthers' strength at between "800 and 900 hard-core guerilla type members with many thousands of supporters." Hoover further testified that "authorities uncovered 125 machine guns, sawed-off shotguns, rifles, and hand grenades, together with thousands of rounds of ammunition. They also found 47 Molotov cocktails plus home-made bombs, gunpowder, and an accumulation of bayonets, swords and machetes."[32]

The media was quick to seize on the fear such statistics generated of the black power movement, despite what Panther supporters consistently described as overwhelming evidence of government repression of the organization. The image of the party as a group of murderous revolutionary guerillas intent on fomenting a race war by sniping police in the back was difficult to overcome, despite some valiant efforts, even for sympathetic writers. In January 1969, for instance, *Ramparts* magazine, which once employed Eldridge Cleaver, the Panthers' minister of information, ran a story entitled "The Persecution and Assassination of the Black Panthers." In it, the reporter Gene Marine questioned the legality of the assaults on the Panthers by police.[33] A year later, Marine published his now classic book on the party, *The Black Panthers*. "As a reporter," he wrote in the introduction, "I try to be sympathetic to anything I want to understand and write about." "But the more I work on the subject," he continued, "the more I know that sympathy is not my primary feeling." Rather, it was fear.[34] The drawing on the back cover of a black man with a clenched fist and a tattered American flag in the background augmented the description of the book that was meant to entice readers. "The Black Panthers," it read, "are revolutionaries and rebels who have sworn to liberate their 'nation' from the oppressive 'mother country.' Their nation? The Negro ghettos of New York, Chicago, San Francisco. The mother country? The United States of America!" As Milwaukee Panther Kenny Williamson conceptualized the problem, the BPP's emphasis on armed self-defense "was the piece that got the most attention." "People all over the world remember Huey Newton sitting in the wicker chair with the spear and the shotgun and so the part they got was the Black Panther Party for Defense. What we often don't remember is that when Huey started that effort they not only . . . [had] weapons which they had a constitutional right to carry but a law book as well. But somehow we forget the law book and that was very much a part of this effort."[35]

The Panthers anticipated problems with the Milwaukee police. Chief Brier had a well-earned reputation for brutality extending beyond state boundaries. As Canfield put it, "Going south I thought police were going to be tough down there, but they wasn't nothing compared to Harold Brier."[36] Furthermore, attempts at drawing attention to police brutality immediately put the Panthers in police cross hairs. In February 1969, with the chapter barely a month old, Walter Chesser, the Panthers' deputy minister of defense, accused the Milwaukee police of roughing him up after identifying him as a Panther. By June, tensions had heightened. That month, Tomie Chesser, a cousin of Walter Chesser and not a Panther himself, was killed by police in an incident that was not related to the Panthers. A few days later, Panther Nate Bellamy was injured after police rammed his car while pursuing him for carrying a concealed weapon. Reminiscent of Huey Newton's treatment in the aftermath of the shootout with Officer John Frey in the early morning hours of September 28, 1967, Bellamy was handcuffed to a hospital bed, denied visitation, and placed under twenty-four-hour guard. Over a four-day period, the police rounded up more Panthers in what the Panther national newspaper described as an effort to "bust as many people as they possibly can." Bellamy was only one of eleven Panthers charged with possession of weapons.[37] The arrests were local, but many Panthers complained that they were part of a national assault on the party, which they claimed was clearly reflected in the nature and scope of the arrests. Within a three-month period, from May to August 1969, police raided the Panthers' headquarters across the country, presumably in search of a fugitive Panther named George Sams, who was wanted in connection with the torture-murder of a New York Panther named Alex Rackley in New Haven, Connecticut. Nine Panthers, including Bobby Seale, the Panthers' chairman, stood accused of varying degrees of participation in the crime.[38] A few days after the mass arrests in Milwaukee, police raided the Chicago chapter of the party and arrested eight Panthers on weapons charges. After a similar incident in Sacramento, California, James E. Mott, the deputy minister of education of the local chapter, declared that the police and the FBI were using "gestapo tactics against us in an attempt to wipe us out."[39] Likened by some Panthers to a war of attrition, the range of police harassment ran the gamut from the serious to the mundane. On August 1, 1969, for example, Milwaukee police arrested Panther Richard Smith for jaywalking and selling the BPP's newspapers. Typically, however, these smaller incidents built up to larger and larger ones until violence erupted.[40]

Much of Hoover's and law enforcement's animosity toward the BPP was predicated on the belief that the party encouraged armed rebellion. Despite the Panthers' "defensive" origins on the West Coast, it would be a violent confrontation between black militants and police in the city of Cleveland that would serve as the catalyst for congressional investigations into the party between 1969 and 1971. Although Milwaukee was not directly involved, the incident had important consequences for the Milwaukee chapter as well. More important, that violent confrontation was emblematic of the Panther story—however unique to local circumstances—in the Midwest generally.

"Black Folks Got a Right to Have a Little Piece of Earth" The Cleveland Catalyst

On July 23, 1968, the city of Cleveland, Ohio, burst into gunfire after a black militant named Ahmed Evans was denied entry into an old tavern he had arranged to rent for a community cultural center. When his white landlady found out what the building would be used for, she promptly terminated the agreement, leaving Evans with few options. After diligently working to secure the location, Evans and his supporters were unceremoniously escorted from the property by police. Shortly thereafter, Evans returned home to find an eviction notice attached to his apartment door and two police cars watching his home. With police milling around the neighborhood, he purportedly told a black city councilor who had come to discuss the situation, "You know black folks got a right to have a little piece of earth. I'm not going to be shoved off this earth." As the council member drove away, shots rang out. Authorities would later claim that Evans just snapped, but the story was far more complex than that.[41]

Evans had actually received a grant from the Office of Economic Opportunity to start his "Cultural Store." His proposal had the blessing of Cleveland's newly elected black mayor, Carl Stokes, who believed such an initiative might actually help keep his city, a major center of racial violence two years earlier, quiet in the aftermath. Evans joined a host of other black militants such as Rufus Mayfield of Washington, D.C. in partaking in what one conservative source described as a one-billion-dollar attempt by the government to stave off urban rioting. The Cleveland police, unfortunately, did not share Stokes's enthusiasm and began a harassment campaign against Evans and his supporters.

That campaign surely would not have surprised the black residents of Cleveland. As in other cities, their police had a poor reputation on civil rights. In May 1965, the outgoing chief, Richard Wagner, made national headlines after he publicly urged the state legislature not to abolish the death penalty, explaining, "We need capital punishment to keep the Negro in line." The following year, an independent commission called the department's professionalism into question. Furthermore, while blacks comprised more than one-third of Cleveland's population (300,000 of 800,000), only 165 out of 2,186 police officers in the city was African American.[42]

"There is no satisfactory history of the Negro in Ohio," complained the historian James Rodabaugh in an article in the *Journal of Negro History* in

1946.[43] Thanks to a host of doctoral dissertations and a number of books, historians know a lot more today. What we have learned demonstrates that, in many ways, the circumstances of blacks in Ohio during the post-war era were similar to the conditions of blacks in other states. In 1946, for instance, African Americans comprised approximately 5 percent of the population in Ohio, but 6.5 percent of the total urban population of the state. Moreover, African Americans made up 6 percent of the total of Ohio's servicemen in World War II. The hypocrisy of fighting for democracy abroad while being denied the same on the home front weighed heavily on some veterans like Ahmed Evans, who served in Korea before being discharged for striking a white officer. Military service seemed to increase black veterans' desire for democracy and equality while making them cynical about the government's ability to deliver the same.

Yet, in 1950, *Ebony* recognized the state's largest city, Cleveland, as the "most democratic city" in the United States, with race relations better than any other big city in the country. First, Cleveland had never experienced a race riot. Second, so-called restrictive covenants did not require a legal challenge. Third, by establishing a community relations board, the city became "the first American city to promote inter-racial understanding with public funds." Fourth, Cleveland's Federal Employment Practices Committee had the support of the Chamber of Commerce. Fifth, there was "virtually no discrimination" at Cleveland's leading white hotels and restaurants. And, finally, "no major committees formed in committee-conscious Cleveland in the last twenty years has [sic] failed to include at least one Negro on its board."[44] By 1966, *Ebony*'s optimistic forecast for the future of Cleveland seemed to be confirmed when the city became the first to elect a black mayor. But Stokes's ascendancy to the mayor's office did little to forestall the racial turmoil sweeping the nation in the mid-1960s.

Thus, in the aftermath of the Cleveland shooting, responsibility for which was never determined and which led to rioting that claimed the lives of six people, the media and the FBI speculated that the violence in Cleveland was the beginning of a new pattern in which armed and highly trained black assault teams would engage police in violent attacks in the hopes of inspiring a race war. Despite Stokes's insistence that the event was an isolated incident, his own police force implicated the mayor in the violence for "paying" off Evans and his armed comrades in an exchange to *prevent* violence. Police surmised that the whole community program had been a front and that Evans had used federal money to purchase weapons and planned the action. Cleveland seemed the least likely place for such an attack, unless the intent was also meant to drive Mayor Stokes from office. In any event, the shooting had the opposite effect; in October 1968, Stokes dismissed Cleveland's police chief for lack of professionalism.

As for the shooting and subsequent rioting, the Civil Violence Research Center at Case Western Research Center found little merit in the claim that the violence had been part of a conspiracy and determined that the fighting in Cleveland "could have happened in any American city." But the speculation that the violence had been a part of "a nationwide, armed Black revolution" that "signaled the end of the nonviolent phase of the black revolution" and would be spearheaded by highly organized black militants wholly committed to bringing about armed revolution in America won the day.[45] Indeed, police used the rather tenuous connection between black power, the Black Panthers, and the violence in Cleveland as a justification for repression. Most of the Panthers' chapters and branches established between 1969 and 1971—such as the Milwaukee local—experienced violent encounters with police and the FBI, both of whom sought to take full advantage of each situation. It appears, in fact, that midwestern cities were singled out precisely because of their proximity to Cleveland. The Evans episode coincided with the emergence of Black Panther formations throughout the Midwest, all of which experienced significant confrontations with police that ultimately drove them out of existence or underground.[46] For a combination of reasons, including nationwide conflict with law enforcement and attempts by the party to bring renegade chapters under greater control, these new Panther chapters also had to contend with changes in national Panther policy that removed one of its potentially attractive features—namely, its free-flowing organizational style. In Milwaukee, all of these forces combined to render the Panthers' initial foray into the city particularly nasty, brutish, and short.

The Milwaukee Panthers

Tensions between Panthers and police back in Milwaukee reached a crescendo on the morning of September 22, 1969. Patrolman Robert Schroeder claimed that someone in a passing car shot at him shortly before 1 a.m. while he was walking his North Side beat. Dropping to the sidewalk just in time to avoid the deadly impact of what Schroeder said was shotgun pellet spray, he somehow managed to retrieve paper and a pen and hastily scribble the license number and a description of the automobile.[47] A few minutes later, Lieutenant Raymond Beste radioed police headquarters for backup after he and his partner, Officer Thomas Lelinski, spotted a Volkswagen matching the description given by Schroeder. Not waiting for help to arrive, however, and despite the fact that the occupants of the vehicle had allegedly just fired on a policeman, the officers executed a felony stop on the car. Following standard police procedure, they ordered the occupants, Black Panthers Jesse Lee White and Earl Walter Leverette, and the founder of the chapter, Booker Collins, out of the car. With Beste standing a short distance away pointing a shotgun at the suspects, Patrolman Lelinski searched them. What happened next became the subject of bitter contention. As he handcuffed the men, Officer Lelinski maintained, White shoved him in an effort to escape. They scuffled, police contended, and the other Panthers joined the fray. At that precise moment, the officers further claimed, the first of several backup units arrived on the scene. Those police waded into the battle and quickly subdued the suspects using appropriate force. The Panthers claimed that they were already handcuffed when the police arrived and were not only beaten by the arresting officers—with fists, firearm butts, and blackjacks—but also by more than twenty other policemen who subsequently arrived on the scene.[48]

Within a month of the incident, Father Groppi was once again in the spotlight after he led a "welfare mother's march on hunger" to the state capitol, culminating in a mass demonstration of more than one thousand people.[49] Meanwhile, the Panthers' violent interactions with police overshadowed their community programs, which were specifically designed to address problems such as welfare. The arrests of Collins, White, and Leverette, coupled with the earlier cases, drained the local party of resources and energy. If it was able to sustain some of its efforts—the November 15, 1969 issue of *The Black Panther*, for instance, listed Milwaukee as one of some twenty-three chapters with a functioning Breakfast for Children program—local media attention on the chapter focused on the members' confrontations with the police.[50]

By the time the three Panthers went to trial that November the local membership had been decimated. The trial itself became a spectacle. In sentencing the men on the misdemeanor charge of resisting an officer in the course of an arrest, Judge Christ T. Seraphim asked each of the defendants if they were revolutionaries. With each responding in the affirmative, Seraphim declared, "Well certainly I do not approve of revolutionaries with guns. So let the message go out to revolutionaries of this community. One year of Correction as to each defendant."[51] Although the men later appealed their convictions based on the judge's arbitrary sentencing and prejudicial behavior—an appeal they lost—the case had the desired effect, at least from the perspective of law enforcement. Within a few weeks of the trial, the local chapter, by then mired in political infighting and facing unceasing police repression, was disbanded by the national offices of the Black Panther Party.[52]

Years later, Huey Newton, the co-founder of the party, complained that the party "grew far too rapidly" and that many chapters were founded by those more attracted to the Panther uniforms and guns than to its program.[53] At least initially, the party did not have a reliable mechanism for chartering or recognizing new chapters, which allowed groups sporting the Panther banner to spring up across the country. In one sense, this was a real strength, in that it allowed local issues to predominate. Organizationally, however, it was a serious liability that left the party open to infiltration, provocation, and affiliation with individuals with little real knowledge of the party's goals and programs beyond what they read in the newspapers and saw on television, which often emphasized the Panthers' violent revolutionary image. Ironically, in Milwaukee, where the survival programs were at the forefront of activity from the beginning—as McGee claimed later—police and FBI succeeded in driving out the BPP within a year after its establishment, and prospects of a revival seemed slim. However, once again, an alleged shootout in another midwestern city would, in vindicating Panthers' claims of police repression, usher in a new wave of Panther-inspired activism that eventually helped to bring the party back to Milwaukee.

Redemption Song

Just as the Milwaukee Panthers cannot be understood outside events in nearby Cleveland, so they cannot be separated from events in neighboring Chicago, in whose shadow Milwaukee often lived. As Kenny Williamson recalled, "We were affiliated with Oakland," but "we did most of our training in Chicago with Bobby Rush . . . who was the chair of the Panther Party in the Chicago area, and we had some training and exposure to Fred Hampton and Mark Clark and some of those other gentlemen. But it was through Chicago [that we were oriented] because they were the local midwestern hub, because Detroit had pretty much been decimated and Chicago remained a strong and vibrant chapter."[54] Thus, the controversial police killing—some call it an execution—of two Chicago Panthers, Mark Clark and Fred Hampton, in an early morning raid in December 1969 would help reinvigorate the party in Milwaukee, validating its claims of systematic persecution and its insistence on community control of the police.

The event also raises the unexplored role of black officers, who were involved in the raid, in the suppression of black militant organizations. At some point, all of the major civil rights groups, from the NAACP to CORE, in Milwaukee as elsewhere, pushed for minority representation on the police force. The Black Panthers challenged the myth behind the demand: that black officers would be more sympathetic to black citizens. Given their day-to-day interaction with the law, the Panthers perhaps best understood the pressure to conform black officers faced. More than eighteen years before the horrific events of December 1969, one of the most notorious lawmen in Chicago was the black officer Sylvester "Two-Gun" Washington. For sixteen years, Washington patrolled the streets of the Windy City, earning the nicknames "The Terror of the South Side" and "Two Gun Pete, the trigger-happy policeman." In fact, black officers were assigned the toughest precincts, such as Chicago's outlaw district, sometimes called the "Bucket of Blood." In 1950, *Ebony* ran an article on Townsend in which he justified his slaughter of some eleven men. "Being a policeman in Chicago is a dangerous, rough-and tumble business," he explained. "If it weren't, our station-house walls wouldn't be covered with pictures of my slain fellow officers—grim reminders that death lurks in every darkened doorway[,] that a routine call might spell out careers [*sic*] end for another detective or patrolman." "There's only one way to deal with hoodlums, thugs, cheap prostitutes and stick-up men," he concluded, "get tough and keep your guns handy."[55] Townsend's attitudes betrayed the deep-seated animosity many police felt toward the communities they patrolled, and, more important, helps explain how, years later, police would be none too sympathetic toward a national organization pushing for community control of police.

In January 1972, the Wisconsin State Supreme Court denied the appeal of the three Milwaukee Panthers charged with resisting arrest back in November 1969. But, as the court issued its ruling, events were taking shape that would eventually bring the Black Panther Party back to Milwaukee. After their chapter was disbanded, several now ex-Panthers created the Milwaukee chapter of the National Committee to Combat Fascism (NCCF), the party's training arm.[56] Under the NCCF's banner, these Milwaukee Panthers continued many of their survival programs, including the breakfasts that now competed with Ellwanger's operation for hungry schoolchildren. Others went on to pursue other, sometimes related goals. Hubert Canfield, for instance, went south to attend Malcolm X Liberation University in North Carolina. Two years into his studies, he met a young woman, married, and decided to return to Milwaukee. His experience in North Carolina, where he worked for the Student Organization for Black Unity (SOBU), had deepened his political consciousness. As he explains, "I was the publisher of the school newsletter, and then we changed it to the *African World*." Enamored with pan-Africanism, Canfield returned to Milwaukee with his new bride in the spring of 1972. He was full of new ideas and new energy. He became part of a study group that regularly met to discuss and debate ways of improving the conditions of blacks in Milwaukee.[57]

Among its twelve core members were some familiar faces. Ronald Starks, an original member of the 1969 Panthers, was one of its leaders. Another was Michael McGee, the future alderman and leader of the NBPP. While some members worked with the Milwaukee NCCF, though, there was still no new BPP chapter in Milwaukee. Things would change in April 1972, when the group joined forces to create the People's Committee to Free Jan Starks in the hopes of winning the release of Ronald's brother, then in a U.S. military prison in Taiwan for the possession of opium. After Starks was released, the group decided to keep the organization going, forming the People's Committee for Survival (PCS). That group modeled itself on the Black Panther Party and its program of community service.[58] Without any official BPP ties, for example, in June the PCS started its Free Busing to Prison program.[59]

In the meantime, a fierce debate had developed over what direction the PCS should take. Some, including McGee, joined Starks in his calls to reconstitute the Milwaukee BPP, though initially without official sanction. Others thought the group should go in a different direction. Fresh from his experience with SOBU in North Carolina, for example, Canfield initially rejected the idea. "I though it was too premature," he says now. "We were supposed to be studying and finding what direction we were going to go in, whether we were going to be a pan-African organization, or we were going to organize the Panther Party, or were we going to join the Nation of Islam."[60] After McGee and Starks won over the majority, Canfield, as well as some of the others who did not join, did not actively oppose them. From the beginning, the men and women who coalesced around the PCS determined that even if they did not agree, they would not indulge in public criticism in order to maintain black unity. Moreover, Canfield remained committed to continuing many of the community service initiatives that ex-Panthers had started under the PCS, evident in a local conference the PCS held. "We had 12 workshops that we ran," Canfield recalls, "dealing with everything from drugs and alcohol to prisons to veterans to politics and education. Later on, we started an organization called the United Black Community Council (UBCC). The council grew out of the conference, and the council often worked with Ronny Starks and the Panthers."[61]

The UBCC set up shop in what became known as the Red, Black, and Green House at 2636 North King Drive. Working jointly with the Panthers, Canfield remembers, "We formed project RESPECT, organizing block clubs; we organized a basketball league for youth." The group also continued the programs the PCS had started, including the breakfasts and the free busing, the latter funded by a grant from the state's Department of Corrections. Both the Panthers and the UBCC also became involved in prison issues, with support from others. As Canfield explains, "A group of us used to go to penitentiaries with a group called 'Instant Wisdom,' bring actors, poets, and do different things in the penitentiaries. We had support from the Nation of Islam and the Commandoes and different things."[62]

In August 1973, after having functioned as Panthers for over a year, Starks's and McGee's group received the imprimatur of national headquarters, which chartered a second Milwaukee Black Panther Party chapter. As in its first incarnation, though now with apparently greater success, the chapter financed its activities by embedding itself in the community. As Kenny Williamson recalls, "We actually solicited in the community, we sold Black Panther newspapers, the white left was often willing to help us out by way of donations, we would speak and be part of panels for pay and those kinds of things and would always roll that money back into the Black

Panther Party; and then we lived communally as well and so all the resources we were able to develop individually we pooled that to ensure that we were all able to live from that." In essence, he concluded, "We created a mini-economic arrangement whereby we were pouring our resources into this effort and also in some modest ways taking care of ourselves."[63] That is, the Panthers sought to live the communal existence they envisioned for the larger community.

One of the issues the new group sought to address was the city's inadequate health-care system. In May 1970, the city had closed its emergency hospital, which had serviced the city's poverty-stricken and predominately African American North Side. The closing catalyzed waves of protest that generally went unheeded beyond a few temporary measures designed to ease the burden while failing to address the underlying need. When the city finally reopened a health-care facility on the North Side in August 1972, many residents of the neighborhood found the cost beyond their means. In order to alleviate this problem, in 1975 the Milwaukee Panthers established the People's Free Health Center, which offered all medical services free of charge. Writing in *The Black Panther* in June of that year, Panther Geneva McGee, Michael's mother, explained the rationale of the party's initiative. "We believe," she wrote, "that good health care is the right of all people and not a privilege of the wealthy."[64]

Despite the Panthers' hibernation of the last three years, their most successful and long-running project remained the Breakfast for Children program. Ironically, thanks to the Reverend Ellwanger, the Panthers' erstwhile enemy, by 1973 the BPP was only one of several groups offering morning meals for schoolchildren, though the Panthers' methods for soliciting donations remained controversial. In September, they initiated a successful two-week boycott of Kohl's food store after the chain refused to contribute anything more than fifty dollars a year toward the expense of the program. In addition to their call for larger and more regular donations, the group also called for the grocery chain to employ more black staff and managers. In solidarity with the United Farm Workers, the group further demanded that the store remove all non-union produce (grapes and lettuce) from their stands. When Kohl's agreed to make a few concessions two weeks later, the boycott ceased.[65]

When the Milwaukee School Board finally approved a school breakfast program in 1973, the Milwaukee Panthers encouraged the community to partake, though with caution. In a flyer, the Panthers reminded their constituents that "after much pressure from the Black Panther Party, that faggot uncle of ours is going to get off his ass, and give the poor hungry children a chance to go to bed with a full belly." "Just beware of what you eat," the handbill continued. "Be sure that what you eat is eggs and bacon, and not some of Uncle Sam's bullshit. Be constantly on the alert for the strings somewhere." The flier further warned, "Sam is slick; he's been tricking people with so called FREE programs for years. But this time we Black folks are going to be ready. Go to his breakfast program, and eat to your hearts content." "However remember this warning from your Black Panther Party. Sam gives nothing completely free, so be Alert!"[66] But, consistent with the Panthers' ability to maneuver the government into action through its social programs—locally as well as nationally—the Milwaukee group upped the ante with its own free grocery give-away. Williamson explained how it worked: "We had a grocery give away one thousand bags of groceries with a piece of meat in each bag in an attempt at both replicating what had been done nationally with the Panther Party and to draw the attention of folks and to let them know we were interested in meeting some of their fundamental needs."[67]

The Panthers also called for community control of the police. Along with its social programs, the demand clearly linked the party's first incarnation in the city with its more successful second run, especially in its continued attention to police brutality. However, while acknowledging that there may have still been some surveillance of the party in Milwaukee, Panthers were now less inclined to see it as part of organized repression, and rather as the continuation of brutality visited on them because they were black. In an effort to address the situation in May 1974, the BPP drafted a police decentralization plan that called for, among other things, a fifteen-member citywide police commission. This racially and ethnically diverse body, the Panthers proposed, would be a kind of watchdog agency to monitor police practices and provide both input and oversight for the department. Hammering away at the issue of poverty as well, the Panthers proposed that candidates running for election to the commission be provided a small stipend by the city to ensure equality of opportunity in the citywide race to fill the seats, and also to prevent wealthy politicians from wresting control from the poor.[68] The Milwaukee BPP of the mid-1970s then, had not lost its radical perspective.

Conclusion

While the gun-toting, tough-talking Panthers were easy to dismiss in their first incarnation, their programs, it seems, were not. For these were the next logical steps after the passage of the Civil Rights and Voting Rights Acts and the failure of the Poor People's Campaign. If the government would not address problems of poverty, literacy, health care, or hunger, the people would act on their own, not on a national or even a local stage through marches and demonstrations, but in the community itself in programs designed to meet popular needs. In this sense, Groppi and the Panthers were not so different. Groppi sought accountability in the Roman Catholic Church; when that seemed impossible, he moved into the arena of community building. Even after his tenure with the Youth Council Commandoes, much of Groppi's work seemed rooted in black power rather than civil rights ideology, perhaps because he understood black power to be a call for people power, or, as the BPP put it, "Power to the People." And, like Groppi, the BPP sought to serve the whole community.

In the final analysis, the Milwaukee Panthers, born of police violence as well as a rising tide of local militancy, did more building than threatening in their tenure in that city in the late 1960s and the 1970s. As Michael McGee would later claim, they did more picking up of "the hammer" than "the gun."[69] But McGee himself may have learned a critical lesson from that period—about the importance of the latter over the former. Even though he would rise to elective office as a city councilman, he apparently never forgot the volatile equation for achieving success in militant black politics in the 1960s: that fear equals power, and that power, no matter how fleeting, generally represents opportunity. Fearful that the black community was about to be cut out of the governmental pork and corporate largess involved in the creation of a new downtown, McGee employed the rhetoric of violent revolution in order to cow the city government. Nevertheless, he was quick to dispel the enduring notion that every Black Panther had been waiting in the wings to distribute not only breakfast to children but also buckshot in the backs of police. He understood that such angry rhetoric generally gets attention but also can lead to unintended consequences. More important, he understood the history of the Black Panther Party in his city: the Milwaukee Panthers, rhetoric aside, had been about self-defense and, especially, community programs, not insurrectionary violence. In their efforts to create new programs, such as the prison visitation initiative and the Breakfast for Children program, and by "building" on preexisting programs and community initiatives, such as the push for the decentralization of the police, the Panthers became important agents for social, economic, and political change in the community—if only for two brief moments. This, perhaps, was the real legacy of the Panthers in Milwaukee, as in many other communities.

As for McGee himself, his story suggests one of the problems that plagues scholarship of the black power era: the need to evaluate what activists said in the context of a careful examination of what they actually did. The more attractive side of the story of angry black revolutionaries and their white leftist sympathizers, armed to the teeth and ready to shoot it out with the police, obscures the constructive activities of groups such as the BPP and similar organizations such as the UBCC. All too often, getting a "little piece of this earth" for so-called minorities has involved threatening to destroy everyone else's piece. Perhaps not the most endearing or socially acceptable means of garnering attention, the threat has been effective primarily because it has allowed those oppressed by fear and violence to create the same climate of fear and violence that permeated the invisible struggles of the urban poor. The problem is this: rhetorical threats tend to invite harsher forms of state repression, and, perhaps more important, they obscure the "building" that political activists such as the Black Panthers did in the real world beyond their rhetoric.

Notes

1 This essay should not be read as, nor is it intended to be, a comprehensive study of the Milwaukee branch of the Black Panther Party or the struggle for civil rights and black power in that city. Instead, it is my aim by offering a thumbnail sketch of the local party to complicate the way historians look at and evaluate the Panthers' significance at the local level. By situating them in the larger movement and activities of the period, I hope to reinforce what historians such as John Dittmer, Peniel Joseph, Jeanne Theoharris, and Komozi Woodard have offered in their works—that local people mattered and that national movements are born of local struggles. This concept has been most eloquently articulated by John Dougherty in his efforts to come to grips with segregation and education in Milwaukee. As he observed, "I finally settled upon a richer and more historically appropriate research question for this study: How did different groups of black

Milwaukee activists define struggles over race and schooling, on their own terms, from the 1930s to the 1990s." John Dougherty, "More Than One Struggle: African American School Reform Movements in Milwaukee, 1930–1980" (Ph.D. diss., University of Wisconsin, Madison, 1997), 3. Although education is not the focus of the present essay, the BPP was one of many groups seeking to define struggles for equality and independence on their own terms in this period. Perhaps more important, the Milwaukee Panthers' roots in a much larger black power movement demonstrate that movement's intellectual and political legacy beyond the angry rhetoric and chronicle of failures often used to describe it. The local activists who made up the party saw their struggle as part of a much larger movement and only after much study and soul searching did they settle on the BPP model as a means toward achieving greater community control and autonomy that characterized the black power movement. See John Dittmer, *Local People: The Struggle for Civil Rights in Mississippi* (Urbana: University of Illinois Press, 1995); Peniel Joseph, *Waiting 'Til the Midnight Hour: A Narrative History of Black Power in America* (New York: Henry Holt, 2006); see also Joseph's salient essay, "Black Power's Powerful Legacy," *Chronicle Review*, July 21, 2006; Jeanne Theoharris and Komozi Woodard, eds., *Freedom North: Black Freedom Struggles Outside the South, 1940–1980* (New York: Macmillan, 2003); Theoharris and Woodard, *Groundwork: Local Black Freedom Movements in America* (New York: New York University Press, 2005); John Dougherty, *More Than One Struggle: The Evolution of Black School Reform in Milwaukee* (Chapel Hill: University of North Carolina Press, 2004); Yohuru Williams, *Black Politics/White Power: Civil Rights, Black Power, and Black Panthers in New Haven* (2000; repr. Oxford: Wiley-Blackwell, 2006).

2 Barbra Dolan, "Eruptions in the Heartland," *Time*, April 23, 1990. Also, Jonathan Coleman, *Long Way to Go: Black and White in America* (New York: Atlantic Monthly Press, 1997); "Milwaukee Militia Scares Some," *Intelligencer Record* (Doylestown, Pa.), May 6, 1990, A16; "Milwaukee Grapples with Crisis as Ills of Poverty Grip Inner City," *Syracuse Herald American*, January 27, 1991, B7; "Milwaukee Alderman Censured," *Chronicle Telegram* (Elyria, Ohio), June 30, 1990, A8; "Alderman Threatens to Form Ghetto Militia," ibid., March 2, 1990, 3.

3 McGee—and his inflammatory rhetoric during the late 1980s—sparked the so-called New Black Panther Party (NBPP)—a subject beyond this essay's scope and part of an entirely different historical moment. For the NBPP's evolution and current state, see its website at www.newblackpanther.com. For its opponents among the original BPP leadership, see http://www.blackpanther.org/newsalert .htm. Also see http://www.answers.com/topic/new-black-panthers; "Fire Kills Six Children; City's Second in Three Weeks," *Frederick* (Md.) *Post*, October 16, 1987, A3.

4 On the 1987 incident, see "Fire Kills Six Children, City's Second in Three

Weeks," *Frederick* (Md.) *Post*, October 16, 1987, A3. On the BPP Militia in the 1990s, see http://www.adl.org/learn/ext—us/Black—Panthers.asp.

5 For McGee's comments, see http://www.adl.org/learn/ext—us/Black—Panther.asp.

6 For the most comprehensive and engaging account of the civil rights movement in Milwaukee to date, see Patrick Jones, "The Selma of the North: Race Relations and Civil Rights Insurgency in Milwaukee, 1958–1970" (Ph.D. diss., University of Wisconsin, 2002). For a more general accounting of the movement with emphasis on education, see Dougherty, *More Than One Struggle*. The Wisconsin Historical Society maintains one of the best online research sites on the history of Wisconsin, including the history of the civil rights movement in Milwaukee. To access this outstanding collection, go to http://www.wisconsin history.org/turningpoints/.

7 For an account of the Bell shooting, see Jones, "The Selma of the North," 38–62; for a more bare bones account, see *Patrick Bell, Sr. vs. City of Milwaukee* (1984).

8 Jones, "The Selma of the North," 123–219.

9 Register of Milwaukee, Records of the Henry W. Maier Administration, 1960–88: Milwaukee Series 44, Milwaukee Tape 125 A; Henry Maier, *The Mayor Who Made Milwaukee Famous: An Autobiography* (Lanham, Md.: Madison Books, 1992); Martin Gruberg, *A Case Study in U.S. Urban Leadership: The Incumbency of Milwaukee Mayor Henry Maier* (Aldershot, U.K.: Avebury, 1996); "Milwaukee Mayor Boosted by Daley for '72 2nd Spot," *Washington Star*, August 20, 1971, n.p., Washingtonia Collection, Martin Luther King Library, Washington, D.C.

10 Petition to the Honorable Henry W. Maier, Mayor of Milwaukee, from John H. Givens, Chairman of CORE, and Elner McCraty, Vice Chairman of CORE, September 9, 1963, http://www.uwm.edu/Library/arch/curguide/Lins-1.

11 TV/radio editorial by Bob Heiss of WTMJ, November 11, 1963—CORE Demonstration at the county courthouse, http://www.uwm.edu/Library/arch/curguide/Lins-2.html.

12 Jones, "The Selma of the North," 220–57.

13 For the somewhat analogous role of Gloria Clark in New Bedford, see Lazerow, "The Black Panthers at the Water's Edge: Oakland, Boston, and the New Bedford 'Riots' of 1970" in this volume.

14 Jones, "The Selma of the North," 220–57.

15 "NAACP Commandos Called to Rights Battle, *Marion* (Ohio) *Star*, July 6, 1962, 12.

16 Ibid.

17 Jones, "The Selma of the North," 293–95.

18 The Hill Parents Association in New Haven, Connecticut is an example. See Williams, *Black Politics/White Power*.

19 Jones, "The Selma of the North," 365–90.

20 Proclamation by Mayor Henry Maier, August 30, 1967, banning night demonstrations and marches; telegram from Roy Wilkins, executive director of the NAACP, to Henry Maier, the mayor of Milwaukee, September 1, 1967—Arrests at the Freedom House Rally, http://www.uwm.edu/Library/arch/curguide/MMR -2.html.

21 Drew Pearson, "Bills to Protect Housewives," *Daily Times* (Burlington, N.C.), September 16, 1967, 4A; "Negroes Clean Up City," *Syracuse Herald-Journal,* August 8, 1967, 2; "Who's in Touch with the Poor Negroes?," *News Journal* (Mansfield, Ohio), August 7, 1967, 5.

22 "Negroes Rebuff Father Groppi after Mayfield Confrontation, *Washington Star,* September 29, 1967, n.p.; "Groppi Delays Departure after Mayfield Clash," ibid., September 30, 1967; "Groppi Denies Any Difference with Mayfield," ibid., October 1, 1967.

23 "Fr. Groppi Leaves Negro Unit," *Washington Star,* November 17, 1968, n.p.

24 "Groppi to Start Parish in Slum House," *Washington Post,* August 16, 1969, n.p., Washingtonia Collection.

25 Peniel E. Joseph quoted in "Black Power's Powerful Legacy," *Chronicle Review,* July 21, 2006. For a full accounting, see Peniel Joseph, *Waiting 'Til the Midnight Hour.*

26 Telephone interview, Hubert Canfield, May 19, 2004, Dover, Delaware.

27 Telephone interview, Kenny Williamson, May 20, 2004, Dover, Delaware.

28 Quoted in Miriam White, "The Black Panthers' Free Breakfast for Children Program" (master's thesis, University of Wisconsin, 1988), 90.

29 *The Black Panther,* July 5, 1969, 5; White, "Black Panthers' Free Breakfast for Children Program," 91.

30 J. Edgar Hoover quoted in *Book III: Final Report of the Select Committee to Study Government Operations with Respect to Intelligence Activities,* S.R. no. 94–755, 99th Congress, 2nd sess. (Washington, D.C.: U.S. Government Printing Office, 1976), 188; see also Reginald Major, *A Panther Is a Black Cat* (New York: William Morrow and Co., 1971), 300; Huey P. Newton, "War Against the Panthers: A Study of Repression in America" (Ph.D. diss., University of California, Santa Cruz, 1980), 14. For an expanded discussion of the FBI's program against the Panthers, see Ward Churchill and Jim Vander Wall, *Agents of Repression: The FBI's Secret Wars Against the Black Panther Party and the American Indian Movement* (Boston: South End Press, 1990), 37–99.

31 U.S. House of Representatives, Committee on Internal Security, *Black Panther Party, Part 4, National Office Operations in Des Moines, Iowa, and Omaha, Nebraska,* 91st Congress, 2nd sess. (Washington, D.C.: U.S. Government Printing Office, 1971), 4718.

32 J. Edgar Hoover quoted in Peter Zimroth, *Perversions of Justice: The Prosecution and Acquittal of the Panther 21* (New York: Viking, 1974), 43.

33 "The Persecution and Assassination of the Black Panthers," *Ramparts*, January 7, 1969, 120–26.

34 Gene Marine, *The Black Panthers: The Compelling Study of the Angry Young Revolutionaries Who Have Shaken a Black Fist at White America* (New York: Signet Books, 1969).

35 Interview, Williamson.

36 Ibid.

37 "Pig Harassment—7 Panthers Busted," *The Black Panther*, July 5, 1969, 10.

38 On the New Haven case, see Williams, *Black Politics/White Power*; Donald Freed, *Agony in New Haven: The Trial of Bobby Seale, Ericka Huggins and the Black Panther Party* (New York: Simon and Shuster, 1973); Kai Erikson, ed., *In Search of Common Ground* (New York: Norton, 1973).

39 "Harassment of Illinois Panthers," *The Black Panther*, June 21, 1969, 7; "Fascist Action against the People of Sacramento," ibid., June 21, 1969, 12.

40 E.g., Ward Churchill and Jim Vander Wall, *The CONINTELPRO Papers* (Boston: South End Press, 1988). For harassment of Panthers selling Panther papers, see Rahman, "Marching Blind: The Rise and Fall of the Black Panther Party in Detroit," in this volume.

41 On the Evans affair, see Louis Masotti and Jerome Corsi, "Shoot-out in Cleveland: Black Militants and the Police," in *To Establish Justice, To Insure Domestic Tranquility: The Final Report of the National Commission on the Causes and Prevention of Violence* (New York: Praeger, 1969). For a detailed discussion of the case, see also Leonard Moore, *Carl B. Stokes and the Rise of Black Political Power* (Urbana: University of Illinois Press, 2003).

42 Ibid.

43 James Rodabaugh, "The Negro in Ohio," *Journal of Negro History* (January 1946): 9–29.

44 "Cleveland: Most Democratic City in U.S.," *Ebony*, September 1950, 43.

45 Louis Masotti and Jerome Corsi, "Shoot-out in Cleveland," viii–xi.

46 Peniel Joseph, "Black Liberation without Apology: Reconceptualizing the Black Power Movement," *Black Scholar* (fall/winter 2001): 2–17; Robert O. Self, "To Plan Our Liberation: Black Politics and the Politics of Place in Oakland, California, 1965–1977," *Journal of Urban History* 26, no. 6 (September 2000): 759–92. Komozi Woodard, *A Nation within a Nation: Amiri Baraka and Black Power Politics* (Chapel Hill: University of North Carolina Press, 1998); Charles E. Jones, ed., *The Black Panther Party [Reconsidered]* (Baltimore: Black Classic Press, 1998); Joseph, "Waiting Till the Midnight Hour: Reconceptualizing the Heroic Period of the Civil Rights Movement, 1954–1965," *Souls* 2, no. 2 (spring 2000): 6–17; Rod Bush, *We Are Not What We Seem: Black Nationalism and the American Century* (New York: New York University Press, 1999); Michael Newton, *Bitter Grain: Huey Newton and the Black Panther Party* (1981; repr., Los Angeles: Holloway House, 1991).

47 "Three Charged with Murder in Milwaukee," *Sheboygan Press*, September 23, 1969, 12; also, *State of Wisconsin v. Jesse Lee White, et al.*, January 6, 1972, 53 Wisconsin, 2d 549, 193 N.W. 2d 36.

48 *State of Wisconson v. Jesse Lee White, et al.*

49 "Protestors Occupy Wisconsin Capitol," *Facts on File World News Digest*, October 22, 1969.

50 *The Black Panther*, November 15, 1969, quoted in U.S. House of Representatives Committee on Internal Security, *The Black Panther Party: Its Origins and Development as Reflected in its Official Weekly Newspaper, The Black Panther Community News Service*, 91st Congress, 2nd sess. (Washington, D.C.: U.S. Government Printing Office, 1970), 89.

51 For Judge Seraphim's comments, see *State of Wisconsin v. Jesse Lee White, et al.*, January 6, 1972, 53 Wis, 2d 549, 193 N.W. 2d 36.

52 "Two Panthers Are Convicted," *Edwardsville Intelligencer*, September 23, 1970, 1. The paltry one-year sentences were insignificant compared to the lengthy prison terms for the attempted murder of Patrolman Schroeder imposed on the defendants by the state the following year. White and Collins both got thirty years, while Leverette received ten. With less faith in the appeals process, Leverette skipped town a week before sentencing while he was out on bond. In 1971, he was captured in Cincinnati, where he was working in a chemical plant. "Gunman Wanted in Wounding of Cop Seized," *Sheboygan Press*, October 20, 1971, 20.

53 Huey Newton quoted in "Power," *Eyes on the Prize* (video recording, PBS Home Video, 1995).

54 Telephone interview, Williamson, May 20, 2004, Dover, Delaware. On the Chicago BPP, see Jon Frank, "Black Radicalism on Chicago's West Side: A History of the Illinois Black Panther Party" (Ph.D. diss., Northern Illinois University, 1998).

55 "Why I Killed 11 Men," *Ebony*, January 1950, 51–52.

56 For a reference to the MNCCF, see U.S. House of Representatives, Committee on Internal Security, *Gun-Barrel Politics: The Black Panther Party, 1966–1971*, 92nd Congress, 1st sess. (Washington, D.C.: U.S. Government Printing Office, 1971), 89.

57 Telephone interview, Canfield, May 19, 2004, Dover Delaware.

58 Interviews, Canfield, Williamson; White, "Black Panthers' Free Breakfast for Children Program," 90–104.

59 Interviews, Canfield, Williamson.

60 Ibid.

61 Ibid.

62 Ibid.

63 Telephone interview, Williamson, May 20, 2004, Dover, Delaware.

64 Geneva McGee, *The Black Panther*, June 16, 1975, 2.

65 White, "Black Panthers' Free Breakfast for Children Program," 97–98.

66 Ibid., 83–84.

67 Interview, Williamson.

68 Ibid.

69 McGee quoted in Andrew Witt, "'Picking Up the Hammer': A Re-evaluation of the Black Panther Party, with Emphasis on the Milwaukee branch, 1969–1976" (paper presented at the Black Panther Party in Historical Perspective conference, Wheelock College, Boston, June 13–15, 2003, unpublished paper in author's possession).

Devin Fergus

EPILOGUE

The Black Panther Party in

the Disunited States of America

CONSTITUTIONALISM, WATERGATE, AND

THE CLOSING OF THE AMERICANISTS' MINDS

All such teachers of openness [that is, those educating young people at America's best universities, who will have the greatest moral and intellectual effect on the nation] had either no interest in or were actively hostile to the Declaration of Independence and the Constitution.

The civil rights movement provides a good example of this change in thought. . . . The blacks were the true Americans in demanding the equality that belongs to them as human beings by natural and political right. This stance implied a firm conviction of the truth of the principles of natural right and of their fundamental efficacy within the Constitutional tradition, which, although tarnished, tends in the long run toward fulfilling those principles. They therefore worked through Congress, the Presidency, and, above all, the Judiciary. By contrast, the Black Power movement that supplanted the older civil rights movement—leaving aside both its excesses and its very under-standable emphasis on self-respect and refusal to beg for acceptance—had at its core the view that the Constitutional tradition was always corrupt and was constructed as a defense of slavery.

So begins Allan Bloom's *The Closing of the American Mind*, whose critique of higher education in general, and the teaching of American history in particular, made it a national bestseller.[1] Within a generation, his depiction of black power had found its way into mainstream historiography. Its migration is best, if unwittingly, captured in Gary Gerstle's *American Crucible* and the peer reviews his prize-winning synthesis has spawned.[2] Embracing his thesis—that black nationalists' radical political views, which "insist[ed] on the bankruptcy of the civic nationalist tradition," ultimately "broke a liberal nation apart"—reviewers have effectively canonized its author, recommending Gerstle's enshrinement into history's hall of fame alongside some of modern America's greatest historians, such as Richard Hofstadter, C. Vann Woodward, and Warren Susman. "With this book, he enters their league," wrote one historian. It is "the most probing and thought-provoking history of American nationalism ever written," remarked another.[3] But, the Bloom-Gerstle depiction of black power does not hold when it is extended into the 1970s. Precisely when cynicism defined American politics, the most notorious black radicals of the 1960s, the Black Panthers, seized the moment—not to issue jeremiads against an incorrigible system beyond reform—but to exhibit unprecedented adherence to the legal and political system. Teachers and scholars, whether classicists or post-nationalists, must thus reassess their views of black power.[4]

Toward that end, this essay seeks to historicize the Black Panther Party (BPP) during the mid-1970s, in the period after the Panther heyday plumbed in this volume.[5] After a short review of the roots of the Panthers' constitutionalism, I examine a series of civil court cases the BPP brought forward during its later years. Next, I locate these cases and other public transcripts, which document the Panthers' engagement with agencies of government, in the context of political life in the 1970s. Finally, I conclude with a brief consideration of the Panther chapter in North Carolina, whose significance lay in its ability to operationalize the constitutional agenda of the BPP's central office in Oakland, California, an agenda that simply does not conform to now standard views of either the Panthers or the black power movement. The evidence, like the evidence in New Bedford, Birmingham, Detroit, and Milwaukee, demonstrates that a close examination of what the Panthers did in particular places at specific moments—that is, placing them in historical context—renders untenable much of what we think we know.

"Armed Negroes Protest Gun Bill"
Panther Constitutionalism in the Early Years, 1966–71

The Panthers' use of constitutionalism dates to the party's founding in 1966. Its Ten-Point Platform and Program (especially points seven, nine, and ten) announced a commitment to the Second and Fourteenth Amendments to the Constitution, as well as the Declaration of Independence. Similar signs, if in inconsistent fashion, were evident in Eldridge Cleaver's symbolic presidential run with the Peace and Freedom Party in 1968 and the Panthers' call for a Revolutionary People's Constitutional Convention in 1970. And, at the local level, too, in the late 1960s, Panthers in Detroit consistently championed the right to bear arms, while would-be Panthers in Birmingham, Alabama, used the courthouse lawn to advocate legal protection of the rights of the accused. All represented fealty to the mechanisms of American governance, but they add up to, at best, a halting trend toward constitutionalism.

What defined the Panthers, from 1966 to early 1971, was confrontation not constitutionalism. Even good faith efforts to foreground constitutional matters often got lost amid their penchant for confrontation. Thus, in May 1967, "an armed delegation of Panther 'lobbyists,'" "invaded" the Sacramento State House to protest a new gun bill aimed at disrupting the Panthers' "patrolling of the police."[6] The show of weapons inside the State House—indeed, by accident, on the floor of the Assembly itself—upstaged the Panthers' stated intent of going to Sacramento in the first place: to inform *America* of the Panthers' constitutional claims to their Second Amendment rights.

Ultimately, the action in Sacramento proved as much a political boon for Governor Ronald Reagan as for the BPP. Since Barry Goldwater's rout in the previous presidential election, Reagan and his PR handlers had worked assiduously to recast the actor-turned-presidential aspirant from "the darling of the extremists" to "a sensible, reasonable guy."[7] Reagan, whose Goldwateresque rhetoric included describing John Kennedy as a "tousled[,] boyish" incarnation of Adolph Hitler and Karl Marx, was particularly vulnerable to charges of extremism.[8] Yet, the showdown at the State House, spurring interest among *hundreds* of urban black youths, gave *millions* of newspaper readers, radio listeners, and television viewers the chance to reconsider a made-over Reagan as the new, more compassionate face of modern conservatism.

Working with an amenable media, Reagan seized the opportunity. As UPI reported, no sooner had the "anti-white Black Panthers," with loaded rifles and shotguns in hand and bedecked in military attire, poured out of the legislature, than a doting Reagan emerged, shepherding a group of schoolchildren to a nearby picnic. "This is a ridiculous way to solve problems," he told the wire reporter. "There's no reason why a citizen should be carrying loaded weapons on the street today."[9] The wire service promptly disseminated Reagan's words to the *New York Times* and other media outlets across America. It was a masterful moment of juxtaposition by a master of political demonology: placing the right's newfangled politics of respectability side-by-side with the Panthers' putative politics of rage.

The Panthers had unwittingly helped to distance the governor in the public's mind from the "dangerous extremism" of the Far Right.[10] The BPP's cult of the gun overshadowed its constitutional concerns, and, in the event, undermined its relations with the black community. Elsewhere, from Milwaukee to New Bedford and beyond, politicians and police fixated on the Panthers' angry rhetoric, often providing the occasion for repression and distraction from the BPP's larger goals. As one North Carolina Panther put it later, "We wanted to [work with the community] earlier, but hell we were standing in court all the time."[11]

By the 1970s, however, Panther confrontations with the government more often gave way to Panther engagement with it. Three interrelated dynamics help account for this sea change, which undoubtedly reflected a combination of strategy, tactics, and ultimately philosophy. First, in part because of challenges launched by the American Civil Liberties Union, law enforcement backed off its extralegal harassment of the party. Second, under Minister of Defense Huey Newton, who was freed from prison in August 1970, Panthers increasingly recognized that their own volatile public actions isolated them—socially, politically, and culturally—from core black constituencies. Third, concomitant with its sense of community alienation, the BPP realized diminishing returns on its martial image and thus began downplaying the cult of the gun. As a result, by the spring of 1971, the Panthers had reframed their relations to the black community and the state after a bloody split with those members, mainly followers of Minister of Information Eldridge Cleaver, who sought to ratchet up the armed struggle.

If laws reflect the codified values of western society, as Emile Durkheim and others have suggested, then the repositioning of the Panthers represented an evolving perception that refashioning their values might hew them to the broader society's social and legal order.[12] Their altered public position on the church in early 1971, for example, indicated the shift.[13] "On the Relevance of the Church" reevaluated the party's theretofore hostility toward institutional religion in the black community. Affixed next to this editorial in the Panther newspaper was a Depression-era photograph of a woman carrying a placard that read: "Father Divine Is the Supplier and the Satisfier of Every Good Desire." The selection of a photo of the black charismatic who was active in the 1930s by Panther editors provided powerful symbolism, capturing in image what might have been missed in words: personal or social reality could be changed through hard work, self-pride, and model citizenship (that is, Max Weber's Protestant work ethic). In exhuming Father Divine, the editors appropriated the iconic figure to help make the case for the Panthers' new relationship with the black church, the black community, and even the state.[14]

Programmatically, the shift away from Marxian dialectical materialism, which the Panthers had openly embraced in the late 1960s, to the Protestant spirit of capitalism manifested itself in the Panthers' army of social service projects. Such bureaucratic layering did not go unnoticed by the Marxists the Panthers left behind. As one Communist Party member chafed later, "The problem with the Panther's [new] approach to politics . . . [was that they] were substituting themselves for the welfare department."[15] In the genealogy of Panther thought on religion and capitalism—and with it a commitment to the legal order—Max not Marx proved closer kin by the early 1970s.

What may have started as a strategic shift—given the changed conditions as the 1960s gave way to the 1970s—eventually wrought a philosophical revisiting. The "epistemological closure"—defined by Michael Ignatieff as "a conviction that . . . history locks [one] into a situation that can only be understood from the inside, never from the outside; that all outsiders . . . can never be true or reliable friends"—so common among ethnic, not civic, nationalists, never materialized among Panthers. Suggestive of epistemological openness, they changed over time; openly courted media, perpetually hoping to understand and be understood by outsiders; shifted alliances, both inside and outside the black community, to collaborate with putative enemies; and ultimately interrogated Marxist doctrine itself. But this epistemological malleability is rarely, if ever, taken as a sign of civic nationalism, as scholars such as Ignatieff have done in studies of minority nationalist movements in liberal democratic Western Europe. Instead, the Panthers' openness fueled charges, then and now, of rank opportunism.[16]

Viewed in tandem, the earlier and later Panther plays to constitutional and social order are noteworthy in their own right. When placed in the context of an America putatively unraveling in the 1970s, though, when citizens' cynicism about the state reached a post–Civil War crescendo, the larger meaning of the Panthers' policy of engagement becomes much clearer. Contrary to the prevailing Americanist view, the Panthers, in their own, unique way, were part of America's civic nationalist tradition.

"Above All, the Judiciary"
Panther Constitutionalism and the Courts in the 1970s

It may be true that the worst that can happen to an American is to become a defendant in a trial—but not if Panthers are the plaintiffs.[17] The ubiquitous image of Black Panthers in criminal court, gagged and shackled as defendants, has been immortalized in media lore since the days of Bobby Seale and the Chicago conspiracy trial. But the popular and scholarly image of an anti-statist outfit established during the late 1960s obscures an important fact: by 1972, the Panthers were in civil court, not criminal, and they were there as plaintiffs, not defendants—they were doing the suing. Between 1972 and 1978, when the BPP effectively ceased most of its operations, for example, Oakland's central office averaged nearly one suit per year against state and private parties.[18]

Moreover, Panther plaintiffs beseeching civil courts for injunctive relief were not limited to Oakland. Across the bridge, the Panthers joined forces with San Francisco senior citizens in suing California's consumer affairs department.[19] Beyond the Bay, in Seattle, Chicago, Dallas, and Houston, chapters initiated civil suits against local, state, and federal officials, in each instance genuflecting to courts as the final arbiters of law and order.[20] The largest case was filed on December 1, 1976, when the Panthers sued twenty-one current and former officials of the CIA, FBI, Treasury, IRS, U.S. Postal Service, and other agencies for "repeated and continuous violations of their Constitutional and statutory rights."[21] Among the defendants named in the class-action suit were the attorneys general John Mitchell and Edward Levi, and the CIA directors Richard Helms and George Bush. Elaine Brown, the chairwoman of the Panthers, told reporters that seeking civil damages against the so-called Federal 21, in excess of $100 million, was a way of "exposing [how] the most extreme and violent actions were employed by high government officials against the citizens of this nation."[22] Asserting their rights as citizens, then, the Panthers sued rather than opting out of the system.[23] They actively located themselves within the bounds of existing law, contrary to the wont of true revolutionaries, who reform constitutions or shed them entirely as shibboleths.

The significance of the Panthers' engagement with the federal court system is not the number of cases won or lost—often, the latter proved more instructive. Take Chicago in the mid-1970s, when the Panthers protested the infamous killings in 1969 of Fred Hampton and Mark Clark by filing federal civil damages against Edward Hanrahan, the former attorney general of Cook County. The case was dismissed in June 1977 after an eighteen-month trial, before the deadlocked jury reached its verdict. The Panthers responded by appealing and having the case reinstated, once more working patiently through the temperate maze of judicial review.[24] Contrary to their subversive image, their actions suggest that they viewed America as a nation of laws, not of men.

In Chicago and elsewhere, the legal weapon brandished was often the Fourteenth Amendment, which defines citizenship. The Panthers' rationale was that, as American citizens, Panthers had a right to equal protection under the law and to a jury trial of their peers, and, as citizens of the nation-state, they could not be deprived of life, liberty, or property without due process of law. Whether one agrees with the Panthers' invocations or reading of constitutional text, it is clear they appropriated, and likely believed themselves heirs to, civic nationalism.

The Panthers also sued without any grand constitutional issue, as Ike and Tina Turner discovered when they headlined in the Panthers' legal act in August 1973. Just four days after the Turners reportedly walked out of a Panther benefit concert some fifteen minutes into a one-hour show, before a thousand or so paying customers, the party sued the entertainers for breach of contract. The public salvo came across the bow to those crossing the Panthers: sword in sheath but tort in hand.[25]

Unsurprisingly, conservatives at the time roundly condemned the judiciary for its activism. Liberals and racial minorities turned to activist courts because of their chronic failure to get favorable laws through legislatures, opined William Kristol, then a doctoral student at Harvard who was finishing his dissertation in political science.[26] Perhaps he was correct. The judiciary did appear receptive, and, significantly, the Panthers offered few apologies for pursuing the path of least resistance by working within the system. Recent history had been replete with models of extra-constitutional defiance of the government's legitimacy, when interposing officials disapproved of court rulings. Following *Brown v. Board of Education*, for example, contempt for the law was certainly the precedent set by Virginia and Georgia, where massive resistance campaigns were supported by state legislators as well as governors such as Arkansas's Orval Faubus, who unilaterally "declared [decisions] unconstitutional and pledged to disobey" them.[27] And, here in the 1970s were the armed, revolutionary Black Panthers repeatedly seeking redress not in the streets, but in the courts.

Power to the System
Black Panthers in the Age of Watergate, 1972–80

Beyond the courts, what explained the party's continued turn to other, more hostile branches of government and processes of governance? And why did this occur during a period in our national history when so few Americans exhibited any faith in public institutions whatsoever? My intent is not to exaggerate the number of interlegal exchanges initiated by the BPP during the 1970s, but rather to exhume the abundant records of a party toeing the line of American constitutionalism in a general climate of public skepticism about the government.

Coming out of the 1960s, America was, to borrow one historian's winsome title, a nation "coming apart."[28] The series of government abuses directed toward its citizens during this tumultuous period, 1965–76, has been well documented—in the Pentagon Papers, in the exposures of COINTELPRO and the Tuskegee syphilis experiment, in the Watergate hearings and trials, in the revelations of the post-Watergate Church Committee. By the mid-1970s, these self-inflicted crises had so damaged the credibility of state institutions that every phase of government was called into question.

Of course, nothing quite crystallized the breach of public trust like Watergate. Gripping the media and then the public consciousness soon after the start of Nixon's second term in January 1972, the revelations of the break-in at the Democratic headquarters and the subsequent cover-up plunged the nation into a constitutional crisis unprecedented since the end days of Reconstruction. As Watergate morphed into a metaphor for a decade's worth of public deceit and duplicity, the Panthers nationally shared with their reading audience, on August 4, 1973, the common ground they held with the U.S. Senate, in particular, with Senator Sam

Ervin of North Carolina, the chairman of the Select Watergate Committee. Ervin had an indefensible civil rights record. His congressional "rap sheet" of civil rights cloture and filibustering in the areas of housing, jobs, voting rights, and ERA legislation made him arguably the Senate's best-known bigot. But for the Panthers, Ervin's record on the Bill of Rights trumped his civil rights shortcomings. Civil liberties had defined Ervin's career since the early 1950s, when as a freshman senator he took a leading role in bringing down his colleague Joseph McCarthy. More recently, Ervin had called the new District of Columbia Crime Control Bill into question. This "smells of a police state," he said of the D.C. bill, which promised to toughen bail requirements and add a no-knock search provision to police procedure.[29] It was this latter image, of Ervin as a pro–civil libertarian, the Panthers touted. To them, the simple country lawyer from North Carolina was America's "most outspoken, determined and principled defender of the U.S. Constitution."[30]

However, critics of Ervin, such as the leftist journalist Bob White, found the Black Panthers' fealty to Congress, particularly to the judiciary chairman, absurd. Flummoxed, White told readers of the British-based *Workers' Power*, "The Panther who sold me this paper was completely serious even after a long conversation with me." In White's perspective, the Panthers had grown indistinguishable from American liberals. Both believed in the "sham of constitutional democracy." And both glorified Ervin—portrayed by the editors of *Workers' Power* as an unreconstructed "Southern racist" who still believed that the "Bill of Rights [was for] Whites Only." Beyond this, because of their repeated constitutional appeals, the Panthers had turned into racial apologists for a founding generation of propertied white men who "openly recognized slavery in America," wrote White. And "what about the 'constitutional foundation upon which the nation was built' (to quote another gem from the Panther article)?"[31]

The Panthers countered, explaining to their readers the larger concern at stake: "If constitutional democracy is to exist in America, every citizen of this land has a duty to actively and resolutely support Senator Ervin in this historic confrontation."[32] With college-age students placing lack of trust and confidence in the nation's leaders consistently near the top of the list of America's problems, the future of democracy was in jeopardy.[33] The party reasoned that by entering into government service, young people could avoid compounding "the tragedy of Watergate for this country" and help restore the nation's self-confidence. In thus calling for national service, the

Panthers registered their views alongside those of two-thirds of Americans over thirty.[34] In most instances, however, the Panthers' attitudes and behavior toward government offered *relief* from the stark disaffection of the general public from public institutions.

By early 1974, Nixon faced mounting disapproval from a most unlikely quarter: manual workers, whites, and people with average educations, those he had long identified as the silent majority of middle America.[35] Plummeting forty-four points in the polls from January to July 1974, Nixon's approval rating was unheard of in the history of Gallup.[36] Though an obvious target for the public's disaffection, Nixon appeared merely the worst among equals. The Democrat-led Congress garnered only 30 percent approval before Nixon's resignation in August that year; six months later it flat-lined at 32 percent.[37] The courts, meanwhile, completed the race to the bottom. According to Gallup, they inspired less trust than Gerald Ford, the unelected president whose pardoning of Nixon in September sunk his credibility rating among Americans faster than any previous president's.[38] Breached trust between the government and the people seemed the defining feature of the mid-1970s.[39]

It was precisely amid this era of collapsed confidence that the BPP sought to deepen its bond with government. While it backed Ervin, the party recognized that changes in the government's accountability structure were necessary—so long as they could be justified constitutionally. A strengthened Congress would help. Thus, the Panthers lobbied Congress (unsuccessfully) with the evocatively titled petition "Eliminate the Presidency," published originally on February 2, 1974 and reprinted in the fall of that year.

Betraying its eyebrow-raising headline, "Eliminate the Presidency" admitted that abolishing the executive office was not simply impractical but, more important, unconstitutional. What the article actually addressed was the failure of the system of checks and balances in recent years. Too much power had been consolidated in the executive branch, shrinking the Congress's constitutional prerogatives and rendering the presidency captive to special interests. "Eliminate the Presidency" thus petitioned the Senate to restore the balance of power between Congress and the president by challenging the doctrine of executive privilege.[40] Moreover, this was a familiar refrain. Both liberals and conservatives at the time expressed qualms over an imperial presidency.[41]

Further, the Panthers made sure to comfort legal purists. Executive restructuring was constitutional, they explained. It would be "change that neither defies tradition nor violates the law," being "consistent with the intent of the Preamble to the U.S. Constitution and its Bill of Rights." The petition made no mention of or case for any new constitutional amendment because no changes to the Constitution would be required. It was the Panthers' intent to work within the existing framework as their preferred text of civic instruction.

In fact, the Panthers insisted that both the framers and Western tradition were on their side in the matter. Steeling remaining skeptics, Newton proclaimed, "Let us be unafraid to meet the challenge laid before us by our founders, so long ago."[42] The Panthers' position was closer to the original intent of the Constitution as, "in constructing a republican form of government, the framers intended the president to be a prime ministerial figure, tending to but not dominating the workings of the federal government." The framers had implemented what Newton praised as the "unique and revolutionary concept" of "checks and balances of power" to safeguard against the rise of an imperial president. Their insertion into the Constitution of Article I, Section 8 and Article II, Section 2, which checked presidential authority, was "a stroke of genius."

Eager to tap the founders' legacy, the Panthers claimed the Western tradition, rather than rejecting it: "[The] Founding Fathers drew on some two thousand years of recorded Western history . . . of the Greco-Roman, Judeo-Christian, Anglo-Saxon traditions." This naturally meant that the party's vision was located firmly within the bounds of liberal universalism: "The ideas of individual dignity, governmental accountability to the governed, equal justice under the law—were time honored." Therefore, working within the system was the "only path to realizing the American Dream."[43] Government might be corrupt, but it was not incorrigible.

The public, however, showed little interest in protracted debates over defying original intent or "meet[ing] the challenge laid before us by our founders, so long ago." Most Americans called for constitutional overhaul. By an almost two-to-one margin, they believed that nothing short of "revamp[ing] the whole electoral process, from the selection of candidates to [abolishing] the Electoral College," would restore the public's confidence in whomever was leading the country.[44]

Americans in fact were disillusioned with the entire party system. With nearly half (49 percent) of college students in early 1974 calling themselves "independent," most assumed that disenchantment with and political alienation from the parties would only get worse. By January-February 1974, the number of independents reached an all-time high, with some 34 percent of Americans surveyed.[45] "Has the time come to have a new political party arrangement in the United States?" Gallup felt compelled to query voters.[46] And, the end of the Watergate crisis brought no improvement. As expected, Republican affiliation declined to its lowest point in 35 years. But, with Democratic affiliation also declining to 44 percent from 47 percent just a year before, establishment politics had no victors. Only independent affiliation rose.[47] While such opinion takers as Gallup were suggesting that the death of the party system was imminent, social critics and policy experts across the political continuum were already penning its epitaph. The conservative standard-bearer, *National Review*, ran a feature article titled "The Two-Party System, RIP?" The Brookings Institution, meanwhile, could revel in its seeming clairvoyance. Writing for the liberal think tank, senior fellow James Sundquist had already pronounced the party system dead, buried, and, to borrow his necrophilic phrasing, "decomposing," nearly one year before Nixon's nadir.[48]

But the Panthers' political engagement with the two-party system continued, despite wavering from pundits, policy experts, and the general public. After flirting briefly with the third-party concept in 1973, the Panther Party soon entered into a fledgling if unequal relationship with the Democratic Party. By that fall, Bobby Seale and Elaine Brown were running their respective campaigns for mayor and a seat on the city council of Oakland under the slogan "Elect Two Democrats."[49] They lost.[50] Still, Panthers not only continued to support candidates and run for elective office themselves, but opted to do so within the existing two-party structure. Perhaps the most blatant example of their obliging the two-party establishment came in the following presidential election. Before the 1976 Democratic convention, the Panthers showed their willingness to appease a leading party contributor by removing the Panther Erica Huggins as a delegate to the convention. Despite this accommodation, the Panthers' preferred candidate, Jerry Brown, did not win the nomination.[51] The Panthers achieved victory a year later, however, when they canvassed for Judge Lionel Wilson of the Oakland Superior Court in his campaign for mayor.[52] Wilson welcomed the Panthers who were getting out the vote on his behalf. "Dissident groups who show desire to work within the system . . . should be encouraged," he told ABC News. The Panthers "are a different group now than when formed," ABC's Harry Reasoner reported.[53]

Meanwhile in January 1975, Congress had razed the notorious red-baiting House Committee on Internal Security and then promptly announced the creation of the Select Senate Committee to Study Governmental Operations with Respect to Intelligence Activities, popularly known as the Church Committee. Congress hoped that the newly established committee, named for Frank Church, the senator from Idaho who was chairing it, would allay rising public skepticism about governmental abuses toward American citizens, as well as foreign figures and governments.[54] Among those hankering to aid the Senate toward this constructive end was the BPP. "My clients," Charles Garry, the attorney for the Panthers, wrote obsequiously to Chairman Frank Church, "are tremendously interested in the investigation that your new committee is undertaking" and are willing "to participate in whatever way that your committee, counsel, or yourself deems advisable."[55] How Church and other members of the eleven-person, bipartisan team, whose ranking member was the archconservative Barry Goldwater of Arizona, saw fit to use the Panthers was completely the panel's choice, Garry assured them. Rebuffing the Panthers, the Church Committee would fall well short of its stated objective when it expired a year later.[56]

Instead of tamping cynicism, the committee's findings heightened it. The list of abuses exposed by the committee—from CIA assassination plots and government overthrows to FBI campaigns against the Panthers and other Americans, including Robert Kennedy, Martin Luther King Jr., and the actress Eartha Kitt—had inadvertently converted "healthy skepticism" into "corrosive cynicism." "The impact of these revelations," poisoning attitudes toward government, "is hard to overestimate," lamented Max Holland, a contributing editor to the nonpartisan, policy-oriented *Wilson Quarterly.* "Now the burden of proof shifted decisively and unfairly from critics to defenders of the official [CIA and FBI] story."[57]

While government appeared to have abused the last remnants of the public's goodwill, the BPP further ensconced itself in the system by continuing to petition the courts, participating—by either backing candidates or running themselves—in elections, and by lobbying Congress. In Milwaukee, for example, Barry Bazzell, the head of the BPP's chapter there, pressed the issue of the potentially deleterious impact of Senate Bill 1, the Criminal Justice Reform Act, with his U.S. senators, William Proxmire and Gaylord Nelson, and others in Congress. "As presently constituted," Bazzell cautioned, the pending bill strayed too far from the Supreme Court's decision in *Furman vs. Georgia*, a ruling that effectively outlawed capital punishment, and original recommendations of the National Commission on Reform of Federal Criminal Laws. Nelson responded, assuring Milwaukee Panthers that he had already introduced measures reflecting their common objective of strengthening existing civil liberties. The pen was mightier, or at least more baleful, than the sword. So Bazzell thought, as he urged fellow Americans to flood their local legislators with letters and calls.[58] In one of its final lobbying efforts, the party turned to Congress in mid-1978 to vindicate the life and death of Malcolm X. The Panthers, who had always styled themselves as his ideological successors, apparently believed only Congress possessed the resources and legitimacy to expose the truth behind the assassination of the avatar of black power.[59]

Meanwhile, the party's changing gender composition, within both its ranks and its brass, paralleled its more aggressive petitioning of the courts and Congress. The precise relationship between these two developments awaits further research, but the correlation is striking. In any case, from October 1972 until May 1973, the female percentage rose to nearly half the total membership. By the fall of 1974, the party had its first female chair, who told the media, "Members aren't ris[ing] to overthrow [the] establishment" anymore.[60]

Between 1974 and 1977, five of the ten central committee members were women. During the same period, internal policies reflected changing sensibilities as issues of reproduction, motherhood, and family came to the fore within the party. Abortion rights had produced some of the most critical early publications among all black nationalist groups. The Panthers, for example, initially viewed skeptically all forms of contraception—whether voluntary or not—by women of color. As Jennifer Nelson notes, they had argued that "any birth control rhetoric that suggested [that] population reduction would help alleviate poverty was not in the interest of people of color and termed these 'population control' efforts genocidal." That position slowly changed by the 1970s, once women inside the party pushed and persuaded the rest of the membership "to distinguish between reproductive abuses such as coerced or forced sterilization and the choice to limit fertility voluntarily" by birth control and abortion.[61] Externally, community programs such as shoe drives, sickle cell anemia testing, pest prevention, senior citizen watches, and voter registration drives—though rooted in the Panthers' early years—rose in profile and expressed programmatically the Panthers' newfound introspection.

These programs emerged as incarceration, exile, and killings were eviscerating the male membership. Despite (or perhaps because of) this feminization of the party and the changes it wrought, the Panthers' revised agenda remained invisible to most Americans. Panther-sponsored projects such as blood pressure screenings accrued little media attention and capital. Arguments that these measures were revolutionary are untenable; what Panther women did was facilitate reform. However, most Americans were blind to both Panther women and reform.

Under Elaine Brown's leadership in the mid-1970s, the Panthers severed their storied relations with Angela Davis, the generation's best-known black Communist. For much of the party's brief existence, she had come to personify its courtship with Communism. But by the summer of 1975, the Panthers were pressing supporters and sympathizers to join them in repudiating the Communist Party and Davis especially. "I don't feel they have anything to offer Black people except deceit," David Du Bois, the editor-in-chief of *The Black Panther*, admonished readers. Du Bois, whose adoptive father, W. E. B. Du Bois, was among the Communist Party's most celebrated cold war recruits, stood tall as a fitting and visible mast for once-rudderless black radicalism's return from the Rubicon. In cutting ties with Davis publicly, the Panthers followed the pattern set a quarter century earlier by the NAACP and key Jewish groups, who were eager to prove their civic nationalist bona fides. Caught up in the currents of the cold war, all explicitly derogated the Communist Party and singled out for particular rebuke those individual Communists who "shared their ethnic or racial background."[62]

The very openness celebrated by Bloom marked the party in this period, giving it the operational space and flexibility both to be self-critical and to engage with others. The earlier impact of Jean Genet, the noted French playwright, underscores the point. At the party's invitation, Genet traveled across America for two months in early 1970. While he lectured at fifteen universities nationwide on the Panthers' behalf, Genet nevertheless voiced strong objections to the Panthers' repeated verbal denunciations of their white male enemies. Swayed by Genet to rethink their views, party officials stopped the party's propagation of such dehumanizing references. By the mid-1970s, the BPP's publications ceased blanket ascriptions to all police officers as pigs and derogations of Nixon as "faggot" and "punk." This move away from the language of demonization was a conscious attempt to acknowledge the full humanity of those the Panthers despised most. It also augured a collective psychological retreat from the rhetorical precipice of race war, which Cleaver and others had warned about from the early days of the party, and an embrace of liberal universalism. As Samantha Power has written in *A Problem from Hell: America and the Age of Genocide*, ultimately the motif and process of dehumanizing the Other is quite often the most common step nihilists take in their descent toward ethnic cleansing, racial war, and genocide. For the Panthers, openness undermined the psychological inurement to political violence, serving instead as a catalyst toward civic nationalism and reform.[63]

For black America especially, COINTELPRO and particularly Tuskegee reified constitutional abstractions into corporeal tragedies of life and death, as blacks, in the view of the Tuskegee lawyer Fred Gray, seemed singled out for extermination by their government. News of the syphilis experiment and ensuing lawsuits had spread throughout the black community by 1975. "No scientific experiment inflicted more damage on the collective psyche of black Americans than the Tuskegee study," wrote James H. Jones, the author of *Bad Blood*. The abrupt withdrawal of trust was traceable to decades of government lies stemming from the Tuskegee study, which, for the southern historian C. Vann Woodward, laid bare the deceit and betrayal of the national government.[64] But not even these colorized versions of state betrayal (which fostered blacks' distrust of authority well into the 1990s, according to Jones) drove Panthers from the ranks of constitutional loyalists. What could have easily proved a death knell for the Panthers' deep-seated commitment to constitutionalism actually cued America to it.

Indeed, the Panthers' quest for ideological consistency in this realm led them, if ever so briefly in the fall of 1977, to the unlikeliest of constitutional bedfellows: Allan Bakke. In siding with Bakke against the University of California, Davis, in *Regents of the University of California v. Bakke*, the Panthers wrote to William Coblentz, the chairman of the board of regents, urging him to change the university's admissions policy and drop its appeal against the spurned thirty-two-year-old applicant to the university's medical school. The letter called the special admissions program "bitterly divisive" and unconstitutional because it did not accept any whites. Once more, the Panthers, draping themselves in the rhetoric of civic virtue, had spurned factionalism for the greater good, though community pressure caused the party to reverse its position a week later.[65] That the Black Panther Party would even attempt to take such a position reveals dramatically what a difference a decade made.

Civic Nationalism up Close
The North Carolina Chapter of the Black Panther Party

Nowhere was the agenda of the central office better instituted than in North Carolina. Winston-Salem's transition from revolutionary confrontation to mainstream electoral politics was, according to Huey Newton, an example for the party generally.[66] David Hilliard would later claim that the branch was exemplary in seeking to "enforce [the Constitution] regardless of race or socioeconomic background."[67] It was among the very first to initiate lawsuits, and the last-standing official branch on the East Coast to close its doors, in 1978. As such, it offers a window onto what the party was as well as what the party aspired to be.[68]

The chapter here is especially useful in understanding the Panthers' commitment to civic nationalism, for the American Civil Liberties Union of North Carolina (NCCLU) provided it legal sponsorship while offering only "legal assistance in cases involving constitutional rights and civil liberties violations." (Private disputants were told to take their cases to the Equal Economic Opportunity Commission, Prisoner Legal Services, or the state attorney general's office.) Like Panther affiliates nationally, North Carolina's point of contention was not the value of the U.S. Constitution and its amendments as much as contested interpretations of it.[69] In closing, then, we briefly turn our attention to this local Panther chapter, which was founded in 1969 and was based in the urban Piedmont town of Winston-Salem.

In North Carolina, attempts at establishing BPP branches in Greensboro and Charlotte failed. The shroud of criminality, much of it self-inflicted, undid prospective branches in both cities. While plagued by this image initially, Winston-Salem succeeded, thanks in no small part to the legal patronage of liberal groups such as the NCCLU. This space helped free the Winston-Salem branch to establish an array of social service programs, including sickle cell anemia testing, a free shoe program, and free ambulance and legal advice services. Ultimately, its head, Larry Little, enrolled in law school at Wake Forest University and joined the state's legal fraternity. For an entire generation, Panthers dominated local and ward politics in Winston-Salem, entrenching party members such as Little and Nelson Malloy in what North Ward residents would come to refer to as the "permanent Panther seat."

While the Winston-Salem Panthers began aggressively pushing for constitutional protection after 1972, their reform spirit could be glimpsed prior to that. Indeed, in a series of court cases beginning in 1969, the NCCLU was enlisted to protect the party's constitutional rights. The issues concerned a court contempt charge, police brutality, and finally electoral politics.

The relationship between the Panthers and the NCCLU was cemented by a police raid on the Panthers' headquarters in January 1971, leading to the indictment of three Panthers, which in turn spawned several criminal cases, including one for larceny. Because the larceny charge generated a criminal proceeding, the NCCLU was not the official legal sponsor for the three indicted Panthers; nevertheless, their counsels, James E. Keenan and James Ferguson of Charlotte, both worked, at one time, under the auspices of the NCCLU. Ferguson, the successful co-counsel in the landmark case *Swann v. Mecklenburg County*, and Keenan, told reporters that their defense of local party members was "without fee" and at the behest of the New York BPP. Invited by the defense, supporters of the Panthers filled the entire courtroom by 9:30 a.m.; the bailiff allowed only witnesses, lawyers, reporters, and others not identified with the defendants to remain.[70]

Holding a press conference shortly after their bonds were reduced and posted, the Panthers sharply contradicted the police account, insisting that they were "victims of a frame-up" and that the state's leading witness, fifteen-year-old Willie Coe, had been sequestered and pressured. Though the NCCLU could not officially get involved, it echoed the Panthers' mantra. "The Civil Liberties Union sent a lawyer here to represent the Panther," commented an investigative reporter in the first of a series of exposés on the Winston-Salem branch of the party, "and the lawyer said the charge against him was a 'frame-up.'" Confident in their case, the Panthers' attorneys requested that the defendants be consolidated for trial. Defense attorneys continued with seven pretrial motions. Filed with each of these motions was a demand "to inspect and copy all records, memoranda, and other writings, recordings or things pertaining to telephonic or other electronic surveillance." In response, County Solicitor Frank Yeager pressed for trial postponement. Over the objections of the Panthers' attorneys, the trial was postponed until September. That did not deter the Panthers from "mobiliz[ing] . . . defenses," as one Panther defendant promised outside the courthouse.[71]

On March 8, 1971, Larry Little stood trial for carrying a concealed weapon, pleading innocent.[72] Acting as his own lawyer, rather than accepting a court-appointed public defender when the state district court denied his attorney a second continuance, proved an abysmal miscue for the twenty-one-year-old defendant. First, he was convicted on the weapon's charge. Then, after bluntly telling the presiding judge, among other things, that the "court was biased and had prejudged the case and that [he] was a political prisoner,"[73] Little was slapped with a thirty-day sentence for contempt and physically removed from the courtroom.[74] That brought in the NCCLU and national scrutiny of the state's criminal justice system.

On March 16, the NCCLU petitioned the state superior court to overturn the contempt charge. Attorney Norman B. Smith argued that Judge A. Lincoln Sherk of the state district court had abused his summary contempt powers in judging and criminally punishing Little for his accusation of bias and, thus, abridged the due process clause of the Fourteenth Amendment.[75] The state superior and appellate courts disagreed, however.[76] After the state supreme court refused to hear the case in June 1971, the NCCLU successfully carried the appeal to the U.S. Supreme Court in late January 1972.[77] Between the contempt charge and the Supreme Court's ruling in January 1972, the NCCLU had established that it would not only protect the Panthers' legal standing, but, when the opportunity presented itself, aggressively contest police action against them.

The second case, also in 1971, contested local police. Following its legal sponsorship and victory in the Supreme Court, the NCCLU, on behalf of Panthers Deloris Wright, Larry Little, and Hazel Mack, took the civil offensive against the local police department and the city of Winston-Salem itself. Arguing constitutional abridgments by police under the First, Fourth, Ninth, and Fourteenth Amendments in their illegal seizure and removal of property owned by the Panthers in a fire in November 1970 and a raid in January 1971, the NCCLU pressed the Panthers' claims of legitimacy.[78] That summer, attorneys for the city fought with equal vigor to prevent the case from going to the federal courts.

In their effort to have the fire and raid case dismissed, or at least remanded to a friendlier judiciary, the city's attorneys argued that the Panthers had no "legal standing to bring the suit and, moreover, that the U.S. Middle District Court lacked jurisdiction to hear it." The judge disagreed. "More than mere infringement of property rights is involved," Judge Eugene Gordon admonished the city's attorneys in refusing to kill the suit, for "the plaintiffs . . . have alleged violation of freedom of speech and freedom of illegal search and seizure."[79] Three years elapsed between the initial request in July 1971 and the case's resolution in the party's favor on September 18, 1974. By then, however, the commitment of Winston-Salem's Panthers to judicial mechanisms and faith in constitutional law was coupled with its considerable strides toward mainstream politics, which, in turn, led to yet a third Panther case in which the NCCLU was involved.

Only a few short years before, hardly any Winstonian fathomed a local Panther running and winning electoral office—at any level of government. But by late 1972 and 1973, the Panthers' criminal image had diminished with news stories of community-centered survival programs, revelations about covert law enforcement activity, press clippings of constitutional challenges stewarded by the ACLU, and rumors of Panthers running for elective office. The immediate beneficiary, most assumed, would be Larry Little, the local Panther spokesperson and coordinator. After all, voter registration drives and numerous community rallies were a boon in marshalling an electoral base for the chapter's most visible figure. In addition, the party boasted about one hundred volunteers who were well familiar with parochial issues and solicitation. Such infrastructural backing made the twenty-four-year-old Little a formidable opponent for the Democratic incumbent, Richard N. Davis. By March 1974, having been swayed also by the dictates of national headquarters and party members running for office in other cities, Little announced plans to seek the alderman's seat in North Winston. Significantly, rather than campaign as a third party or independent candidate, Little, like Panthers nationally, opted for the old-guard apparatus of the Democratic Party.

Little's campaign for alderman, however, came to a curt and controversial end on May 7, 1974, in the primary election. Davis, also African American, narrowly edged Little by the slimmest of margins—a mere eight votes. The defeat only heightened the controversy that had simmered in previous weeks over a purge, on March 11, of three hundred voters, which followed a cursory investigation of procedural irregularities of three registrars.[80] Once again, the local Panther leader sought legal recourse through the NCCLU.[81]

The NCCLU challenged the purge of North Ward voters by the Republican-controlled board of elections. While the NCCLU did not contest the point that alleged procedural infractions might have occurred, it did challenge the drastic action of striking registrants without due process of law. The board never met or heard the challenges of the three hundred voters, the NCCLU explained later to the State Supreme Court. The wholesale elimination of registered voters was done and upheld "without proper notice, without hearing, and despite [the county board of election's] own concession that these voters had acted properly and in good faith."[82] Moreover, nullification occurred despite registrants' and embattled registrars' sworn testimony denying wrongdoing.

Perhaps more troubling was the arbitrary manner in which the democratic process had been subverted. Rather than remove voters who were registered by the three embattled registrars, Thomas J. Keith, the chairman of the county board of elections, picked and eventually disfranchised "only those voters who had the misfortune of having their registration cards sitting in a particular stack on [the] Chairman['s] . . . desk on March 11, 1974." As a result, from the testimony of only 10 percent of the registrants, three hundred lost suffrage. The NCCLU's general council made plain the collective concern of Little, his organization, and three hundred aggrieved citizens to the state board of elections, and then later to an appellate court. "Voters may fall prey to the whims of county board of elections and may suffer disenfranchisement without even a modicum of the due process of law."[83] Even the chairman of the board of elections admitted that these voters had been prevented from going to the polls "because of an error not [of] their own making."[84]

The state board of elections was unwilling to remedy this fraudulent election, however—even as it agreed with the NCCLU that "voters held valid registrations and that the methods used by the Forsyth County board of elections to void those valid registrations violated" the due process of law.[85]

By the time the case reached the court of appeals, on April 2, 1975, five months after the general citywide election in November, the court deemed the Panthers' claim "academic" and moot. "That general election has been held, and it is not now possible to give the petitioner the relief which he sought."[86] Victory would be delayed until the next election in November 1977, when Little won with more than 80 percent of the black vote.

Salient in each of the above three cases was the Panthers' Fourteenth Amendment claim. In having the ACLU pursue their rights under this amendment, the Winston-Salem members averred that they, as American citizens, had a right to due process and equal protection of the law. Here we see the Panthers making explicit legal challenges to the constitutional amendment that speaks directly to American citizenship. The courts often sided with Little and other local Panthers in recognizing that their constitutional rights had been breached. And when judges made contrary rulings, the Winston-Salem members appealed to the state and federal courts. But how cases were ultimately resolved is far less significant than the fact that the Panthers voluntarily invested themselves in the legal and political system.[87]

Also notable is the "openness" of the ACLU here. In attacking constitutional violations encroaching on freedom of speech and assembly and on freedom from search and seizure, the NCCLU aggressively protected local Panthers from legal repression. In attacking the excessive actions of law enforcement, which were chiefly responsible for limiting the group's operational space and good name, the North Carolina Civil Liberties Union forced the police to abate. In so doing, the legal stewardship of the NCCLU itself challenges myths about the party's willingness to work within the existing boundaries of the U.S. Constitution and other codified norms.

Conclusion Opening the American Historians' Minds

The best-known black radicals of the post–civil rights generation, the Black Panther Party, imagined themselves as heirs to America's civic nationalist tradition. They did so by investing in the mechanisms of American jurisprudence, legislative governance, and social policy, as well as electoral politics—during a time when state credibility and political legitimacy were being destabilized among the public at large. Viewed within the spatial, legal, and historical bounds in which they operated—in a civic nation in the throes of crisis—the Panthers appear radically different from the nihilists of Allan Bloom's and Gary Gerstle's imaginations. The notion that the modern origin of anti-Americanism has its roots in black power and the movement's "contempt for rules governing civic order" simply cannot stand historical scrutiny regarding the Black Panther Party. The dissident culture of black power, including those believed to be most deviant in it, actually was bound up with the country's ethos of civic nationalism.

Notes

Thanks to Gary Gerstle and this book's editors for their criticism and commentary.

1 Allan Bloom, *The Closing of the American Mind* (New York: Simon and Schuster, 1987), 33.

2 Gary Gerstle, *American Crucible: Race and Nation in the Twentieth Century* (Princeton, N.J.: Princeton University Press, 2001).

3 Nelson Lichtenstein review, http://www.pup.princeton.edu/quotes/q7020 .html. Gerstle's thesis is the default interpretation of a farrago of recent books on America after 1945. E.g., Allen Matusow, *The Unraveling of America: A History of Liberalism in the 1960s* (New York: Harper and Row, 1984); Richard Polenberg, *One Nation Divisible: Class, Race and Ethnicity in the United States Since 1938* (Magnolia: Peter Smith, 1993); David Farber, *The Age of Great Dreams: America in the 1960s* (New York: Hill and Wang, 1994); Maurice Isserman and Michael Kazin, *America Divided: The Civil War of the 1960s* (New York: Oxford University Press, 2000); Michael J. Heale, *The Sixties in America: History, Politics and Protest* (London: Fitzroy Dearborn, 2001).

4 "By the spring of 1969, black nationalist organizations were on the defensive and in decline" (Gerstle, *American Crucible*, 310), but the Panthers, whose membership had yet to peak, accelerated their attack after 1970—on the legal front. Charles Pinderhughes, "Periodizing the Black Panther Party" (paper presented at the Black Panther Party in Historical Perspective conference, Wheelock College, Boston, June 11–13, 2003). Beyond the Panthers, the scholarly literature offers a far different picture than Gerstle paints. The most ambitious attempt to unite black power leadership—the conference in Gary, Indiana, that organized cultural nationalists, radical black Marxists, and integrationists such as Coretta Scott King, all operating under the rhetorical call of "Nation Time"—was still three years away. Moreover, the gathering launched an entire decade of black political conventions. Similarly, some of the era's most durable institutions, such as the Institute for the Black World, the Black Economic Research Center, and the Soul City (N.C.) project, had barely entered gestation.

5 In using the BPP, my intention is not to reduce the entire black power movement to the BPP; rather, it is to test the hypothesis—that black power adherents were constitutional heretics, functioning beyond the constitutional borders of America—by applying it to the most well-known group of the black power period.

6 Chris Booker, "Lumpenization: A Critical Error of the Black Panther Party," in *The Black Panther Party [Reconsidered]*, ed. Charles E. Jones, 343 (Baltimore: Black Classic Press, 1998).

7 Lisa McGirr, *Suburban Warriors: The Origins of the New American Right* (Princeton, N.J.: Princeton University Press, 2001), 196.

8 Kiron K. Skinner et al., eds., *Reagan: A Life in Letters* (New York: Simon and Schuster, 2003), 704–5.

9 "Armed Negroes Protest Gun Bill: 30 Black Panthers Invade Sacramento Legislature," *New York Times*, May 3, 1967, 23; Michael Rogin, *Ronald Reagan, the Movie: And Other Episodes in Political Demonology* (Berkeley: University of California Press, 1987).

10 McGirr, *Suburban Warriors*, 195–97.

11 Quoted in my "The Ordeal of Liberalism and Black Nationalism in an American Southern State, 1965–1980" (Ph.D. diss., Columbia University, 2002), 160.

12 Emile Durkheim, *Division of Labor of Society*, trans. George Simpson (New York: Macmillan, 1933), esp. chap. 2; Anthony Giddens, *Emile Durkheim: Selected Writings* (London: Cambridge University Press, 1972); also, Paul Rabinow, ed., *Foucault Reader* (New York: Pantheon, 1984); Alan Hunt and Gary Wickham, *Foucault and the Law* (London: Pluto, 1994).

13 Huey P. Newton, "On the Relevance of the Church: May 19, 1971," in *To Die for the People: The Writings of Huey P. Newton*, 60–78 (New York: Vintage, 1972). For other shifts, see Newton's, "Black Capitalism Re-analyzed I: June 5, 1971" and "Black Capitalism Re-analyzed II (Practical Application): August 9, 1971," both in *To Die for the People*, 101–8 and 109–11 respectively. All were originally published in *The Black Panther* and periodically reprinted.

14 Such dramatic reversals of previous party positions were, of course, enmeshed with the Newton-Cleaver "split" of February 1971. Newton's pronouncement on that matter, predating by weeks the new positions on the church and capitalism, is "On the Defection of Eldridge Cleaver from the Black Panther Party and the Defection of the Black Panther Party from the Black Community: April 17, 1971," in *To Die for the People*, 44–53.

15 Quoted in Judson L. Jeffries, *Huey P. Newton: The Radical Theorist* (Jackson: University Press of Mississippi, 2002), 132.

16 Michael Ignatieff, "Nationalism and Toleration," in *Europe's New Nationalism: States and Minorities in Conflict*, ed. Richard Caplan and John Feffer, 220 (New York: Oxford University Press, 1996).

17 To my knowledge, Supreme Court Justice Learned Hand (1872–1961) is the original source for the quip.

18 Robyn Ceanne Spencer, "Repression Breeds Resistance: The Rise and Fall of the Black Panther Party in Oakland, CA, 1966–1982" (Ph.D. diss., Columbia University, 2001). While organized criminal and violent behavior is certainly part of the historical record, what remains curious is how the Panthers handled such allegations.

19 "BPP Wins Consumer Fight," *The Black Panther*, June 29, 1974; "BPP Wins Consumer Fight for 2nd Time," ibid., November 9, 1974.

20 E.g., "Dallas BPP Wins Suit on Citizens' Review of Police," *The Black Panther*, February 28, 1976, 5; "People's Victory in Dallas: BPP Chapter Wins Rent-Free Office Space," ibid., August 11, 1975, 6.

21 "BPP Files Amended Complaint Against FBI, CIA, IRS," *The Black Panther*, April 16, 1977.

22 Attorneys for the Panthers alleged that the government attempted to (1) destroy the Panthers' press and distribution; (2) deprive the organization of funds by setting high bails; (3) eliminate financial support by threatening the finances of supporters; (4) discredit the group in the eyes of the general public; and, particularly, (5) discredit Huey Newton with slanderously false charges. Nancy Cole, "Black Panthers Sue Government," *The Militant*, December 17, 1976; "21 Past, Present U.S. Officials Named as Defendants in $100 Million BPP Lawsuit," *The Black Panther*, December 11, 1976; T. Grendel, "Black Panther Party Files Suits Against FBI, CIA for Murder," *Workers World*, December 24, 1976; "Chief Counsel in BPP Lawsuit," *The Black Panther*, December 25, 1976; "BPP Files Amended Complaint Against FBI, CIA, IRS," *The Black Panther*, April 16, 1977; "BPP Seeks Funds to Continue Lawsuit Against FBI, CIA," *The Black Panther*, February 3–16, 1979.

23 Rather than "offing pigs" accused of murdering two black youths, the Dallas BPP took the police and city council to court—for violating Chapter 16, Section 15 of the Dallas City Charter, which stipulates the right to conduct public and open trials for municipal and civil service employees—when word spread that the killings would be looked into in closed hearings. The national office praised Fred Bell, the local Panther coordinator, for holding public employees accountable. "Dallas BPP Wins Public Hearing," *The Black Panther*, June 9, 1975; "Dallas BPP Wins Office Space," ibid., November 11, 1975.

24 CBS Evening News, June 20, 1977; Jeff Sorel, "Dismissal of Panther Lawsuit Reversed," *Workers World*, May 4, 1979.

25 "Black Panther Party Files Suit," *The Black Panther*, August 11, 1973.

26 Nina J. Easton, *Gang of Five: Leaders at the Center of the Conservative Crusade* (New York: Simon and Schuster, 2000), 46–47.

27 Morton J. Horowitz, *The Warren Court and the Pursuit of Justice* (New York: Hill and Wang, 1968), 15.

28 William O'Neill contends that America had crossed some kind of political Rubicon in the late 1960s, encapsulated by the intractability of white apathy and backlash, on the one hand, and black rage, on the other: "There was no going back where Negroes were concerned. There seemed no way to go ahead, either. It did not take a Jeremiah to see in this a recipe for fresh disasters." O'Neill, *Coming Apart: An Informal History of America in the 1960s* (New York: Quadrangle, 1971), 194.

29 Melvin Small, *The Presidency of Richard Nixon* (Lincoln: University Press of Kansas, 1999), 157.

30 Bob White, "Panthers Laud Racist Watergate Hero," *Workers' Power*, September 1–13, 1973, 13.

31 Ibid. *Workers' Power* was the organ of an international socialist group of the same name.

32 "Sam Ervin—Defender of the Constitution," *The Black Panther*, August 4, 1973.

33 *The Gallup Poll: Public Opinion* (Wilmington, Dela.: Scholarly Resources, 1972–77), 1:257.

34 Ibid., 212.

35 Ibid., 197.

36 Ibid., 325.

37 Ibid., 256.

38 Ibid., 528–29, 364.

39 Ibid., 257.

40 Indeed, the entire petition was predicated on the constitutionality of abolishing executive privilege and strengthening Congress, and it argued the case in that vein. BPP Position Paper, "Eliminate the Presidency," in *The Coevolution Quarterly* (fall 1974): 61–68; "Establishment Media Ignores BPP Proposal to Eliminate Presidency," *The Black Panther*, February 16, 1974; Jeffries, *Huey P. Newton*, chap 3.

41 For a sampling of how liberals and conservatives took issue with the rise of the imperial presidency, see Arthur Schlesinger, *The Imperial Presidency* (Boston: Houghton Mifflin, 1973); William A. Rusher, "An End to the Imperial Presidency," *Human Events* 34 (August 31, 1974). Perhaps the most significant contemporary treatise regarding executive privilege is Raoul Berger's *Executive Privilege: A Constitutional Myth* (Cambridge, Mass.: Harvard University Press, 1974). See also, "'Executive Privilege'—What Uproar Is All About," *U.S. News and World Report* 70 (March 15, 1971): 94; Evans M. Stanton, "When Liberals Backed Executive Privilege," *Human Events* 33 (August 18, 1973): 12; Clark Mollenhoff, "The Dangers of the Abuse of Executive Privilege," *Human Events* 32 (August 5, 1972): 21; "Constitutional Law-Executive Privilege: Tilting the Scales in the Favor of Secrecy," *North Carolina Law Review* 53 (December 1974): 419;

Abraham D. Sofaer, "Executive Privilege: A Historical Note," *Columbia Law Review* 75 (November 1975): 1318.

42 "Eliminate the Presidency," *Coevolution Quarterly* (fall 1974): 65.

43 "Stunned Reaction," *The Black Panther*, February 9, 1974.

44 *The Gallup Poll*, 391.

45 Ibid., 233.

46 Ibid., 257–58.

47 Ibid., 561–62.

48 The political scientist then turned to pontificating on the long-term possibility of the future rebirth of the two-party system. "The Two Party System, RIP?" *National Review* (November 29, 1974): 177; James L. Saudquist, "Whither the American Party System?" *Political Science Quarterly* (December 1973): 559. See also, *Brookings Bulletin* (summer 1973): 4; Edmund Ions, "The End of the Two Party System," *Listener* (March 7, 1974): 305; Kevin P. Phillips, "The Two-Party System Isn't Dead Yet," *Human Events* (October 23, 1971): 11; Everett Carll Ladd Jr., "'Reform' Is Wrecking the U.S. Party System," *Fortune* (November 1977): 177; Everett Carll Ladd Jr., with Charles D. Hadley, *Transformations of the American Political System: Political Coalitions from the New Deal to the 1970s* (New York: Norton, 1975).

49 White, "Panthers Laud Racist Watergate Hero"; Donald Freed, "Kennedy/Wallace in '76—A Threat to America," *The Black Panther*, July 21, 1973, 3.

50 The defeat did not deter the Panther Ericka Huggins from running and winning a seat on the Alameda County Board of Education.

51 Brown, the thirty-eight-year-old populist governor of California, lost to Jimmy Carter, despite promising early primary showings in Maryland and his home state.

52 "Endorsements for April 19 Election," *The Black Panther*, April 16, 1977; Kenneth Morris, *Jimmy Carter: American Moralist* (Athens: University of Georgia Press, 1996), 231–34.

53 "Headline: Black Panthers/Newton," ABC Evening News, July 19, 1977, TV News Archives.

54 Recommendations would be offered to Congress based on the findings of the Church Committee.

55 "BPP Offers to Aid Senate Probe of CIA," *The Black Panther*, February 8, 1975, 5.

56 According to Kenneth O'Reilly, "The Church Committee members and staff did the most thorough job of all congressional investigating committees." O'Reilly, *"Racial Matters": The FBI's Secret File on Black America, 1960–1972* (New York: Free Press, 1989), 352. Given what it unearthed, and the impact that it had on public attitudes, perhaps it was too successful. See U.S. Senate, 94th Congress, 2nd sess., *Supplementary Detailed Staff Reports of Intelligence Ac-*

tivities and the Rights of Americans, Book III: Final Reports of the Select Committee to Study Governmental Operations with Respect to Intelligence Activities (Washington, D.C.: U.S. Government Printing Office, 1976).

57 Max Holland, "After Thirty Years: Making Sense of the Assassination," *Reviews in American History* 22 (1994): 191–209.

58 According to *The Black Panther*, Congressman Reuss replied, "Like you I was very concerned . . . about . . . the threat that measure would pose for constitutional rights and liberties." Nelson: "I'm sure we must agree that we must remain militantly aware of legislation which may have the unwitting effect of nibbling away at the rights which we value most," continuing, "please be assured that my votes in the Senate will reflect this belief. . . ." Proxmire: "I will keep your views in mind should S. 1 reach the floor [of] the Senate during the 94th Congress." "Wisconsin BPP Writes Legislators on Senate Bill No. 1," *The Black Panther*, April 12, 1975, 5.

59 "1978: A Year of Victories for the BPP," *The Black Panther*, January 12, 1979.

60 "Headline: Black Panthers/Newton," ABC Evening News, July 19, 1977, TV News Archives.

61 *Women of Color and the Reproductive Rights Movement* (New York: New York University Press, 2003), 106.

62 Gerstle, *American Crucible*, 262.

63 Edmund White, *Genet: A Biography* (New York: Alfred A. Knopf, 1993), 520–46; Samantha Power, *A Problem from Hell: America and the Age of Genocide* (New York: Basic Books, 2002).

64 Woodward's view is on the book jacket of Jones's *Bad Blood: The Tuskegee Syphilis Experiment* (1981; repr., New York: Free Press, 1993), 220–21; see also Susan M. Reverby, *Tuskegee's Truths: Rethinking the Tuskegee Syphilis Study* (Chapel Hill: University of North Carolina, 2000).

65 Morris Wright, "Panthers on Bakke: Call Quotas Divisive," *Guardian*, October 12, 1977, 6.

66 Devin Fergus, "The Ordeal of Liberalism and Black Nationalism in an American Southern State" (Ph.D. diss., Columbia University, 2002), 120–21.

67 Ibid., 183n160.

68 The aim here is not to privilege North Carolina because it was exceptional. Indeed, in its history of postwar civil rights activism, ranging from the armed confrontational politics of Robert F. Williams, the branch leader of the NAACP, in the 1950s to the Greensboro student sit-in movement of the 1960s, the state was more emblematic than exceptional when compared to others. Fergus, "Ordeal of Liberalism," chap. 3.

69 NCCLU Records of the General Counsel, 1971–74, Box 1; 1975–80, Box 55; Special Collections, Duke University.

70 *Winston-Salem Journal,* January 23, 1971.

71 Ibid., January 15, 1971; May 4, 9, 11, 1971.

72 Joseph H. Tieger to James Yates, Solicitor, District Court of Forsyth County, March 2, 1971, Folder 1, Box B-55, NCCLU Records; *Winston-Salem Journal,* March 9, 1971.

73 Admittedly, not yet completely schooled in courtroom etiquette, Little called "the presiding judge a M—F—." The expletive-laden utterance, which followed his questioning of the court's impartiality, however, was "not relied upon by either the District Court or the Superior Court for the conviction and sentence and the State defend[ed] the conviction in [the U.S. Supreme] Court without any reference to it. . . . Therefore [the Supreme Court] also lay [sic] it aside for . . . [its] decision." See "In the Matter of Larry Little," Supreme Court of the United States, No. 71–244, January 24, 1972.

74 "In the Matter of Larry Little, Petitioner," U.S. Supreme Court Reports— U.S. 30 L Ed 2d 708, 92 S Ct- [No. 71–244], January 24, 1972, Larry D. Little (In the Matter of the Imprisonment of), Folder 1, Box B-55, NCCLU Records, Closed Cases 1975–80.

75 Relying in large part on a decision in January by the Supreme Court, which interpreted a similar matter in Pennsylvania, Smith added that his client had been entitled to "a public trial before a judge other than the one reviled by the [defendant]." *Winston-Salem Journal,* March 19, 1971.

76 In upholding the original decision, the courts ruled, "Little's claim of being a political prisoner and his charge . . . [of] bias . . . constituted direct criminal contempt within the meaning of North Carolina law." Ibid.

77 Ibid., June 17, 1971.

78 Ibid., March 20, 1971.

79 While the ACLU's motion for preliminary injunction prohibiting the police from interfering with Panther activity was also denied, far more damaging was the denial to the defense by Judge Eugene Gordon of the U.S. District Court. Citing *First Citizen v. Camp,* Gordon stated that it was standard procedure not to issue a preliminary injunction if parties could comply—as the police had recently done—without court interference. *Winston-Salem Journal,* July 6, 1971; "Brief in Support of the Defense of the Lack of Jurisdiction Over the Subject Matter," in NCCLU Papers, 1973–83; "Brief in Opposition of the Defense of the Lack of Jurisdiction of the Subject Matter," in NCCLU Papers, 1973–83.

80 One or more of the following infractions were alleged to have occurred: (1) oaths may not have been administered; (2) third persons, rather than the official registrar, may have actually done the registering; (3) "proper identification may not have been procured from the registrants." *Little v. North Carolina State Board of Elections et al.,* Folder 3, Box B-55, NCCLU Records, Cases Closed, 1975–80.

81 The party had transported more than 150 disfranchised voters to appeal the decision by the board of elections. Sworn affidavits from 9 were submitted to the courts verifying their intent to vote for Little. *Larry D. Little v. North Carolina State Board of Elections*, Supreme Court of North Carolina (1975), in *Larry D. Little v. North Carolina Board of Elections et al.*, Folder 3, Box B-55, NCCLU Records, Cases Closed, 1975–80.

82 Ibid.

83 At a later meeting of the county board, when registrants were questioned about their registration, many who had previously testified that their registrar had not followed proper procedure now voiced uncertainty about the process they had followed to become registered. Ibid.

84 Ibid.; *Little v. North Carolina State Board*, in the General Court of Justice, Superior Court Division (1974).

85 *Little v. North Carolina State Board*, Supreme Court of North Carolina (1975).

86 Ibid.

87 This space helped the Panthers of Winston-Salem to pursue, largely free from extra-legal harassment, a social agenda for community betterment, with moderates and liberals in support. Memorandum of Bishop L. Moultrie Moore to Rectors and Senior Wardens, April 27, 1973, Episcopal Diocese of North Carolina, Raleigh.

CONTRIBUTORS

Devin Fergus is a professor of history at Vanderbilt University.
He is finishing a book on the relationship between liberalism and black
nationalism in cold war America.

Jama Lazerow is a professor of history at Wheelock College.
He is the author of *Religion and the Working Class in Antebellum America*
(Washington, D.C.: Smithsonian Institution Press, 1995); the co-editor (with
Yohuru Williams) of *In Search of the Black Panther Party: New Perspectives
on a Revolutionary Movement* (Durham, N.C.: Duke University Press, 2006);
and the author of the forthcoming *The Awakening of a Sleeping Giant: New
Bedford, the Black Panthers, and the 1960s.*

Ahmad A. Rahman is an assistant professor of history at the University of
Michigan, Dearborn. He is the author of *The Regime Change of Kwame
Nkrumah: Epic Heroism in Africa and the Diaspora* (New York: Palgrave
Macmillan, 2007).

Robert W. Widell Jr. received his Ph.D. in American history from Emory
University. He is the author of a forthcoming study of black activism in
Birmingham, Alabama, during the late 1960s and early 1970s.

Yohuru Williams is an associate professor of history at Fairfield University.
He is the author of *Black Politics/White Power: Civil Rights, Black Power,
and the Black Panthers in New Haven* (St. James, N.Y.: Brandywine Press,
2000); the co-editor (with Jama Lazerow) of *In Search of the Black Panther
Party: New Perspectives on a Revolutionary Movement* (Durham, N.C.: Duke
University Press, 2006); and the editor of *A Constant Struggle: African-
American History Since 1865; Documents and Essays* (2003).

INDEX

Little, Larry, 282–86, 293n73
Los Angeles Black Panther Party, 46

Magnett, James ("Jimmy"), 96, 110, 118n6
Maier, Henry W., 235, 238
Malcolm X, 9, 12, 41, 51, 147, 194, 197–98, 200, 240, 242, 278
Mao Tse-tung, 17, 39, 98, 103, 154, 156, 186, 197, 204
March on Washington, 107, 140, 236
Marighella, Carlos, 206–7, 215–16
Marine, Gene, 44, 47, 71n57, 245
Marshall, Thurgood, 146
Marshall, Tony, 115–16
Marxism, 185, 269
masculinity, 190
Matthews, Dukie, 111–12, 116
Matula, Floyd, 12–13
Matusow, Allen, 38–40
Mayfield, Rufus ("Catfish"), 239, 247
McClure, Malik, 192–97, 204–5
McGee, Michael, 52, 232–33, 251, 253–56
Michigan Chronicle, 195, 213
migration, 9, 182
militarism, 1, 23, 38, 50, 52, 249, 252
military, U.S., 152–53, 175n108, 228n118, 248; National Guard, 13–14, 36, 184
Milwaukee Black Panther Party, 232–58
Minard, Larry, 4–5, 8, 20–22
Minneapolis Black Panther Party, 30n63
Miranda, Doug, 100–102
Mississippi Freedom Summer, 90
Morrison, Frank B., 11–13, 22

National Association for the Advancement of Colored People, 9, 13–14, 42, 53, 143, 279; in Massachusetts, 90–92, 106; in Milwaukee, 233–34, 236–38, 252
National Committee to Combat Fascism, 5, 94, 102, 253; in Detroit, 192–93, 196, 204–5, 209, 215; in New Bedford, Mass., 92, 104, 113, 118n6; in Omaha, 8, 19, 20–22
National Guard, 13–14, 36, 184
nationalism, 1, 19, 66n25, 95, 185, 190, 266, 287n4
National Urban League, 10, 13–14
Nation of Islam, 13, 16, 57, 99, 108, 185, 254
Neblett, Chico, 102, 148
New Bedford, Mass., 7, 21, 85–117, 126n52, 133n113
New Bedford (Mass.) Black Panther Party, 85–117
New Bedford Standard Times, 86, 95–96, 98
New Black Panther Party, 259n3
New Haven, Conn., 7, 24, 40
New Left, 41
Newton, Huey P., 2–3, 5, 8, 18–19, 23, 193, 212; death of, 52–53; law enforcement and, 36, 48–49, 77n119, 87, 196, 246; as Panthers' leader, 44–45, 51, 64n17, 111, 139, 163, 240; Peace and Freedom Party and, 221n31, 251, 268, 275, 281; *Revolutionary Suicide*, 46, 201; on self-defense philosophy, 35, 203; split between Eldridge Cleaver and, 59, 114, 214; violence of, 39–40, 58, 186–87
New York Black Panther Party, 46, 54
New York Times, 1, 5, 41, 55, 268
Nixon, Richard M., 179n164, 272–74, 276, 280
Norman, Tony, 195, 208, 215
North Carolina Black Panther Party, 24, 159, 281–86, 292n68

Yohuru Williams is an associate professor of history at Fairfield University. He is the author of *Black Politics/White Power: Civil Rights, Black Power, and Black Panthers* (2000). He is a co-editor (with Jama Lazerow) of *In Search of the Black Panther Party: New Perspectives on a Revolutionary Movement* (Duke, 2006) and editor of *A Constant Struggle: African-American History Since 1865, Documents and Essays* (2003).

Jama Lazerow is a professor of history at Wheelock College. He is the author of *Religion and the Working Class in Antebellum America* (1995). He is the co-editor (with Yohuru Williams) of *In Search of the Black Panther Party: New Perspectives on a Revolutionary Movement* (Duke, 2006).

Library of Congress Cataloging-in-Publication Data
Liberated territory : untold local perspectives on the Black Panther Party / edited by Yohuru Williams and Jama Lazerow.
p. cm.
Includes bibliographical references and index.
ISBN 978-0-8223-4343-1 (cloth : alk. paper)
ISBN 978-0-8223-4326-4 (pbk. : alk. paper)
1. Black Panther Party—History. 2. Community life—United States—History—20th century. 3. United States—History, Local. 4. African Americans—Politics and government—20th century. 5. Black power—United States—History—20th century. 6. Radicalism—United States—History—20th century. 7. African Americans—Civil rights—History—20th century. 8. Civil rights movements—United States—History—20th century. 9. United States—Race relations—History—20th century. 10. United States—Race relations—Political aspects—History—20th century. I. Williams, Yohuru R. II. Lazerow, Jama.
E185.615.L4776 2008
322.4'20973—dc22   2008023970

Liberated Territory

DATE DUE

JUL 0 5 2012	